DATE DUE

GAYLORD			PRINTED IN U.S.A.

IN SEARCH OF
SACCO & VANZETTI

IN SEARCH OF

SUSAN TEJADA

SACCO & VANZETTI

DOUBLE LIVES, TROUBLED TIMES,
& THE MASSACHUSETTS MURDER CASE
THAT SHOOK THE WORLD

NORTHEASTERN UNIVERSITY PRESS
BOSTON

NORTHEASTERN UNIVERSITY PRESS
An imprint of University Press of New England
www.upne.com
© 2012 Susan Tejada
All rights reserved
Manufactured in the United States of America
Designed by Eric M. Brooks
Typeset in Arno Pro and Concurso Italian by Passumpsic Publishing

University Press of New England is a member of the Green Press
Initiative. The paper used in this book meets their minimum requirement
for recycled paper.

Library of Congress Cataloging-in-Publication Data
Tejada, Susan Mondshein, 1945–
In search of Sacco and Vanzetti: double lives, troubled times, and the
Massachusetts murder case that shook the world / Susan Tejada.
    p. cm.
Includes bibliographical references and index.
ISBN 978-1-55553-730-2 (cloth : alk. paper) —
ISBN 978-1-55553-778-4 (ebook)
1. Sacco, Nicola, 1891–1927. 2. Vanzetti, Bartolomeo, 1888–1927.
3. Anarchists — United States — Biography. 4. Murderers — United States —
Biography. 5. Murder investigation — Massachusetts — Case studies.
6. Sacco-Vanzetti Trial, Dedham, Mass., 1921. I. Title.
HX843.7.S23T45   2012
364.152'30922744—dc23   [B]   2011048670

5 4 3 2

In loving memory of
JACK & GITTIE MONDSHEIN

CONTENTS

INTRODUCTION

When young Nicola Sacco and Bartolomeo Vanzetti arrived in the United States, they were indistinguishable from the nearly two million other Italians who sailed to American shores in the first decade of the twentieth century. Nicola docked in Boston in 1908; Bartolomeo landed in New York the same year. They were strangers to each other at the time, but nineteen years later, convicted of murder and on the brink of execution, they stood together at the center of a legal vortex. When they died in the Massachusetts electric chair in 1927, hundreds of thousands of supporters around the world, people who believed in their innocence, marched in protest. In a parallel universe across a wide political divide, detractors were at best indifferent, at worst poised for violence. Small wonder that reasonable people on both sides of the divide hoped that the conflict and emotion swirling around the case would finally fade.

But that was not to be.

⁓ My goal in writing this book has been to decouple Sacco from Vanzetti and to write a double biography. The many photographs of the men that show them side by side, manacled at the wrist, literally conjoined, are misleading. Sacco and Vanzetti met for the first time in 1917, were arrested three years later, then spent most of the next seven years incarcerated in prisons miles apart.

To learn about each man's separate life, I pored over their own words in trial testimony and in published and unpublished letters, as well as the memoirs and oral histories of Aldino Felicani and other defense committee associates. I discovered often overlooked material from supporting players in the drama. The papers of Mary Donovan and of Elizabeth Glendower Evans shed light on the ups and downs of the committee and on the inner lives of Nick and Bartolo. The letters of Alice Stone Blackwell, and interviews with descendants of Cerise Carman Jack, Virginia MacMechan, and Mary Donovan illuminate the defendants' thoughts and feelings. Reports of prison psychiatrists outline Sacco's descent into madness and subsequent recovery. Letters that Vanzetti wrote to his family in Italian portray the sad child he was and the angry man he became, angrier than his published letters in English might indicate. When the pieces of the puzzle are assembled, a portrait of two complex individuals emerges, with Vanzetti appearing more intolerant, and Sacco more reflective and realistic, than they have often been pictured.

My other goal has been to look at Sacco and Vanzetti in situ, in the turbulence of the early twentieth century. For help in deciding which aspects of the era to focus on, I turned to the men themselves. They consistently said that four factors influenced their fate — not only their often-cited anarchism and ethnicity, but also their labor activism and draft status during World War I. Were they right to think so? Rather than conflate the four issues, I decided to look at each one separately. Thus, in Part One, chapters on the criminal case crosscut with chapters that interweave biography and the stories of Italian-American immigration, labor organizing, wartime patriotism, and radical politics, particularly the violent radical politics advocated by anarchist Luigi Galleani. The anarchist threat of violence was limited, but in 1919 and 1920 it seemed as perilous as global terrorism today.

In an effort to sidestep preconceptions when writing about a case that has been as extensively studied as this one, I have included opposing viewpoints, and have relied heavily on first-person primary sources to let participants speak for themselves.

Many lawyers and statisticians and forensics experts have considered the question of the defendants' guilt or innocence from every angle. To this particular discussion I believed little could be added, and to do so was not my goal. But unexpectedly, as I came across neglected sources and followed the research trail, I began to form an alternative theory of how the crime at the heart of the case might have been planned. This theory is presented in the final chapter.

The book is not a Sacco-Vanzetti encyclopedia. I touch only in passing on some important subjects that I considered secondary to the book's main goals. I know that the book could, as Barbara Tuchman said of *The Proud Tower*, "be written all over again under the same title with entirely other subject matter."

— In 1999, in the company of a police escort and with the permission of the Norfolk County Sheriff's Office, I toured Dedham Jail, where Sacco was confined for seven years. The jail had long since been decommissioned and shuttered, and that day the only signs of life — or death — were flying pigeons, the mewing of an unseen stray cat, the carcasses of squirrels and sparrows, discarded office furniture, and an empty bag of Doritos.

To prepare for the visit, I had spoken to a historian who told me I would find Sacco's cell on the bottom floor of the east wing. My escort, a former guard at the jail, took me to what he said was Sacco's cell; it was on the bottom floor of a different wing. I later read testimony from a 1923 hearing in which an officer of the jail placed Sacco's cell on another floor altogether.

The seeming contradictions symbolize an essential truth about this case: every aspect was, and remains, open to dispute.

Note on the Text

Nicola Sacco and Bartolomeo Vanzetti grew up speaking Italian, their native language. During their nineteen years in America, they learned to read, write, and speak English — Vanzetti with some fluency and Sacco with less — but neither mastered the language. Their broken English is quoted here as they wrote it, uncorrected. Remarks by Vanzetti that do appear in correct English were, in most cases, edited long ago by Virginia MacMechan, his tutor in prison.

Different court stenographers used different spellings for some witness names. Where one spelling has become more accepted over time, it is used here. Where the spelling in the court record seems questionable but has not been corrected over time (usually because the witness was not involved in post-trial proceedings), the questionable spelling is still the only "official" one, and is retained here.

Part One

Forecast at 8 a.m. for Boston and
its vicinity — Unsettled
— U.S. Weather Report, April 15, 1920

1 | SUDDEN DEATH

Looking back, it would seem that suspicious-looking characters had been skulking around all over South Braintree that day.

Five men driving a car through the square looked like a tough bunch, Harry Dolbeare said. Two nervous men were acting "kind of funny," sitting "beside the gent's toilet" at the train station, according to William Heron. Two "light complexioned boys" sitting on a fence attracted Hans Behrsin's attention. William Tracy was annoyed to see two strangers in dark hats slouching against a building that he owned. A dark man and an emaciated man were hanging around a car, Lola Andrews recalled. Shelley Neal spotted a man with sunken eyes and hollow cheeks who was standing in a doorway.[1]

It was Thursday, April 15, 1920.

Less than fifteen miles away, at Fenway Park in Boston, it was opening day for the Red Sox. A few months earlier, the Sox had sold Babe Ruth to the Yankees in a "good deal," the Boston papers claimed, since the Sox "probably never would win a pennant with the slugger in the lineup."[2] On April 15, as the Sox won their season opener a day after Ruth and the Yankees lost theirs, it seemed that the prognosticators were right, and getting rid of the Babe really had been a brilliant move.

Bostonians blasé about baseball had other amusements on that April 15. "Thousands of fishermen" cast their lines into nearby streams and brooks on the first day of trout season. Music lovers shopped at the Jordan Marsh Company, buying tables for their Victrolas and some "very high class vocal and instrumental records" by Gluck, Caruso, and Heifetz. Thrill-seekers went to the moving pictures, no less racy for being black-and-white and silent. In *Terror Island*, spellbound Bostonians watched Harry Houdini rescue a damsel in distress from a locked safe sunken in the South Seas, and in the boldly named *Sex*, they watched screen siren Louise Glaum steal other women's husbands.[3]

Enticing as the diversions of the city were, it's unlikely that workers at the Slater & Morrill Shoe Company in South Braintree took the day off to enjoy them. Thursday, April 15, was their payday. They used to get paid on Wednesdays, but the factory had recently altered the schedule,[4] and the shoemakers — the skivers, vampers, cutters, and stitchers; the trimmers, turn lasters, cementers, and assemblers — were looking forward to having more money in their pockets at the end of the day.

Horses still shared the roads with cars and trucks in 1920, and computers and automated payrolls were still a dream undreamt. Thus, on paydays, people in South Braintree relied on Shelley Neal. It was the American Express agent's job to drive his horses and wagon to the town railroad station, pick up the iron safe arriving by train from Boston, and deliver the thousands of dollars in payroll money it contained to factories with payrolls to meet that day. On April 15, Neal hoisted the safe onto the wagon and "started for the office." There, he said, he backed the team of horses "up in front of the door, took out the safe, took it into my office, broke the seal on it, took the key that we have that comes in a sealed package, opened the safe and took Slater & Morrill's payroll out. [Then I] locked the safe up, leaving the other [factory's] payroll in there."[5] Around nine-thirty in the morning, Neal delivered $15,776.51 in bills and coins to Margaret Mahoney, a paymaster at Slater & Morrill.

Mahoney spent the next few hours carefully dividing all that cash into the exact amounts due each worker for the week. She put the wages into some five hundred envelopes, the envelopes into wooden boxes, and the wooden boxes inside two heavy steel boxes. A few minutes before three o'clock, she locked the boxes and gave them to assistant paymaster Frederick Parmenter and security guard Alessandro Berardelli to deliver to another Slater & Morrill factory down the street. She did not go with them on their route, as she often did.[6]

Parmenter had been with the company for twenty years.[7] Berardelli was a new hire. A former barber and private detective, he had started working for Slater & Morrill in the fall of 1919.[8] A third man, Harold Lewis, usually accompanied them on their delivery route, but Lewis had recently quit Slater & Morrill. A fourth man, James Reynolds, paymaster for a neighboring factory, also usually accompanied them on a portion of their route, but on April 15 Reynolds was delayed.[9]

Berardelli pocketed his own pay, $27.60. Then he and Parmenter set off on foot, walking down Pearl Street, carrying the steel boxes. "Many times" they had driven the short distance in the boss's car, but on April 15 Mr. Slater "would not let them take an automobile." They passed James Bostock, a mechanic, walking up the street. "Bostock," said Parmenter, "when you go . . . into the other factory [building,] . . . fix the pulley on the motor."[10]

Then, said a witness, "all of a sudden, bang bang bang."[11]

Two gunmen charged into the street, firing wildly. Parmenter fell, shot in the back. Berardelli fell, and when he did one of the gunmen stood over his crouched body, pumping more bullets into it, then swung around and fired two shots wide at Bostock. The gunmen seized the money boxes, threw them into an approaching getaway car that had three accomplices inside, jumped into the car themselves, and tore off, still shooting.

From first shot to getaway, the crime took less than a minute.[12]

Berardelli, 44, died on the spot, there in the street. "I wiped his mouth out, and he lay in my arm," James Bostock recalled, "and as he lay in my arm I thought he died in my arm."[13] Berardelli was survived by his wife and two young children, Jacob and Ida.

Parmenter, still breathing, was carried in a horse blanket to a nearby home, then rushed to Quincy Hospital. Doctors removed a bullet from his body, but it was too late to save him. Parmenter, 45, died early in the morning of the following day. He, too, left behind a wife and a young son and daughter, Richard and Jeannette.[14]

— The bandits in the getaway car sped off, taking "the corner on two wheels, they were going so fast." The driver wanted to dash across the railroad tracks in South Braintree, but a train was coming and the crossing gate was down. "[T]he first thing I knew, there was a revolver pointed . . . at my head," the gate tender, Michael Levangie, recalled. Levangie quickly raised the gate, and the car zipped across ahead of the train. Later the car encountered a similar obstacle at another railroad crossing, this time in Matfield, where a more determined guard planted himself by the tracks and held up a stop sign to block the car from the path of another oncoming train. "[T]hey did not seem to want to stop . . .," the guard said. "[O]ne of them in the automobile asked me, 'What to hell I was holding him up for?'"[15] The train passed, the car sped across the tracks and disappeared, only to reappear minutes later, retracing its path.

From the open windows of the speeding getaway car, the bandits tossed tacks into the road. They had modified the tacks to fall upright to puncture the tires of pursuing vehicles. They needn't have bothered. Only one driver attempted to pursue them, and he quickly lost their trail.[16] Not all law enforcement officials had cars in 1920, or even knew how to drive. Sometimes they relied on loaners, or on trains or hired horse-and-carriage teams. Eleven more years would pass before the Braintree Police Department acquired its first car, in 1931.[17]

It was a scandal, really. "Without the automobile," said one judge, "most of the great and small of the more daring robberies would never be attempted." Criminals were leaving police in their dust. The *Boston Evening Transcript* demanded that officials study this serious new problem of the "bandit on wheels."[18] On April 15, the only witnesses to the escape from South Braintree, beyond those at the immediate crime scene, were a few scattered bystanders along the route.

— One day after the crime, on Friday, April 16, in a short article buried on an inside page, the *Transcript* reported that police were searching in several states for the "yeggs."[19]

Two days after the crime, on Saturday, April 17, a couple of friends from Brockton went horseback riding. Charles Fuller and Max Wind were trotting along a bridle path in the woods when, to their surprise, they came upon an abandoned, damp and dusty seven-passenger Buick. "The path was so narrow that we had to get off our horses and lead our horses by," Fuller said. The license plates had been removed from the Buick. The rear window had also been removed and was lying on the floor. Two sets of tire tracks marked the ground — those made by the Buick, and another set of tracks made by a different car. Fuller and Wind galloped to a nearby house and called the Brockton police.[20]

Officer William Hill responded. He drove the Buick to the police station. Neither Fuller, Wind, Hill, nor the city marshal who accompanied Hill noticed any bullet holes in the car, but when Hill reported for work the next day, several officers pointed out to him a bullet hole they said they had found in the car's right rear door the night before. The Buick, it turned out, had been stolen. It was blue, the owner said later; green, said Wind; and black, according to Hill.[21]

— An inquest into the South Braintree murders was held at District Court in Quincy on April 17, the day that the Buick materialized in the woods. At this point the crime was only forty-eight hours old. Recollections of witnesses were fresh but contradictory.

James McGlone described how he and his brother had carried the wounded Parmenter to a nearby house, the home of a Maurice Colbert. Several doctors had rushed to the scene. Colbert testified that Parmenter had managed to give a brief description of the bandits to a doctor. One gunman was stocky, Parmenter had said; another was slim, and both were short. Three witnesses at the inquest were certain that the getaway car was a Buick; another, that it was possibly a Buick; another, simply that it was "not a Ford."[22]

Annie Nichols, a nearby resident, thought that the man she saw shoot Berardelli had spoken to him before killing him. Lewis Wade, a shoe worker at

Slater & Morrill, also believed Berardelli knew his assassin. "I think so and will always think so," Wade testified at the inquest. "It looks as though this fellow wanted him out of the way. . . . Berardelli was on the ground and why should this fellow want to turn around and want to kill him when the money box was [already] on the ground? I think they knew each other." James Bostock would later say that he, too, thought Berardelli had spoken to the bandits: "He acted to them as though he knew the men and spoke to them."[23]

Thomas Fraher, a superintendent at Slater & Morrill, said that Parmenter and Berardelli usually carried weapons on the job, but he didn't know if they had been armed on April 15.[24]

Many witnesses at the inquest described a pale, sickly-looking man as one of the bandits in the getaway car. Some said this ghostly fellow was the driver, but others thought the driver was dark.[25]

Some said only one car was involved in the crime, but others, including Shelley Neal, said they had seen two cars.[26] A year later at trial, Neal would testify that he saw only one car; his inquest statement was unavailable, and the discrepancy would go unchallenged.

Two workers from Slater & Morrill said the windows at their factory were too dirty to permit anyone to get a good look at either the car or the bandits. Except for witness Lewis Wade, who was so close to the car he "could have stepped out and touched" it, and who also remained calm enough to describe what he had seen in detail, the witnesses at the inquest said they had been badly shaken. "It all happened in two seconds . . . and I am very sorry to think I [saw it]," Annie Nichols said. According to Maurice Colbert, "It was all done so quickly, I didn't have a chance to see anything." Edgar Langlois, a shoe company foreman, was thoroughly confused. "[W]hen I think about it," he said, "I never have the same thought twice. . . . [A]t one time I thought there were four [bandits] and then only two. . . . I don't think anybody could identify them, it was all so quick." Langlois discussed the crime with a co-worker "[t]wo minutes after [it happened] . . . and he says one thing and I another."[27]

— The vicious murders in South Braintree shocked one Massachusetts lawmaker into action. Five days after the crime, State Senator David McIntosh of Quincy proposed authorizing a reward of up to twenty-five thousand dollars for the arrest and conviction of the killers. That was almost ten thousand dollars more than the stolen payroll. The large amount was necessary, McIntosh argued, because of the "deep feeling which has been stirred up by this brutal, cowardly shooting. Every resource of the State . . . should be utilized to apprehend the murderers."

A crime wave was terrorizing his district. In addition to the South Braintree crime, the senator cited a bank robbery in Randolph and an attempted robbery in Bridgewater. Citizens were "wrought up" and "tormented by the failure of the authorities to run these men down." Outlaws were taking over. They had to be stopped. "Talk about the Wild West!" cried McIntosh. "Conditions would seem to be wilder and more dangerous" right here in the suburbs of Boston.[28]

[O]ur immigrants now largely represent . . . social discards.
— Madison Grant,
The Passing of the Great Race

2 | "THIS HUMAN FLOTSAM"

Life was good for young Bartolomeo Vanzetti. To be the eldest son, to grow up with an adoring mother and a successful father in a land of beauty and bounty—a boy with blessings like these could be happy and carefree. Small wonder that Bartolo, looking back on his childhood, would sigh, "I love my valley."[1]

Vanzetti was born on June 11, 1888, in Villafalletto, a small town ringed by farms in the Piemonte region of northern Italy.[2] His father, Giovanni, "as sturdy and upright as the mountains that surround him,"[3] was "an intelligent agriculturer"[4] who worked his own land and planted the area's first peach trees.[5] His mother, Giovanna, already wed and widowed at an early age, married Giovanni, her second husband, when she was twenty-five. Bartolomeo arrived a year later, baby sister Luigia three years after that.[6]

Situated on the banks of the Magra River "in the shadows of a beautiful chain of hills,"[7] Villafalletto seemed like paradise on earth to little Bartolo. In summer he swam in the river.[8] Wildflowers bloomed, "the wonder of the garden's wonders."[9] "[U]nmatchable nightingales" and other songbirds filled the air with music.[10] In winter snow-chased highlanders came down to the valley for shelter on the farms. Bartolo always remembered the "very clean and decent" family of tenants who wintered in his father's house.[11]

The land was fertile; the harvests, abundant. Vanzetti later recalled that so many varieties of fruit flourished there, so many "apples, pears, cherries, grapes, plums, figs, peaches, berries, etc. etc., [that the] nearby hills are all a fruit-garden, wine yards and woods of chestnut and of hazelnuts. Blackberries, strawberries and mushroom grow wonderfully up there." Women raised silkworms, so "every field is planted of lines of mulberry trees."[12]

Here in Bartolo's childhood utopia, even going to school was a joy. He "loved study with a real passion,"[13] he said later, and some of his earliest memories were "of prizes won in school examinations, including a second prize in the religious catechism."[14] His faithful Catholic father surely approved of that award.

Religious though he may have been, Giovanni Vanzetti was also practical, and it was his practicality that brought Bartolo's sunlit youth "in the bosom of my family" to a crashing halt. As Bartolo turned thirteen, he found to his dismay that his father was "undecided whether to let me [continue my] studies or to apprentice me to some artisan."[15]

Here were the facts as Mr. Vanzetti no doubt saw them: he had opened a café in town, and could use his son's help there, especially if the boy learned how to make pastry. On the other hand, what good would more schooling do? Hadn't the newspaper just reported that in Turin an oversupply of lawyers was competing for a single low-paying job? The father's choice seemed clear: no more useless schooling. Bartolo had no say in the matter. "[M]y father determined that I should learn a trade and become a shop-keeper. And so in the year 1901 he conducted me to Signor Conino, who ran a pastry shop in the [provincial capital] city of Cuneo, and left me there to taste, for the first time, the flavor of hard, relentless labor."[16]

Life as he knew it changed then, abruptly and completely. For the next six years, his entire adolescence, Bartolo lived and worked on his own, far from his valley, far from his family, boarding in different cities and toiling long hours, often fifteen hours a day, seven days a week, with a few hours off every other Sunday. He worked nearly two years in the pastry shop, then three years in a bakery, and finally, after several months of unemployment, he did a stint as a caramel maker in Turin. He didn't like the path he was on, he said, "but I stuck to it to please my father and because I did not know what else to choose."[17]

The teenager was lonely and homesick. Christmas should be family time, he wrote his parents in December 1902, when he was fourteen, "and I would give so much to spend it among people as affectionate and sacred as you are to me. However, I can't."[18]

He was "tired of this miserable life," he wrote on the day before his fifteenth birthday.[19] "I hope to come visit you this spring," he told his parents the following Christmas,[20] and again, when he was seventeen, "I hope to make a trip home this summer."[21]

If Bartolo had visited his family during those years, he would have found it had grown. After he left Villafalletto, his parents had two more children. Little sister Vincenzina and brother Ettore were virtually a generation younger than Bartolomeo and Luigia.[22] But there is no evidence that Bartolo did return home. Instead, he coped on his own with short funds,[23] incompetent employment agents,[24] and, worst of all, ill health. He complained of goiter when he was thirteen, of burning sensations in his feet when he was fourteen, of chilblains when he was seventeen. He had two operations. He didn't say what kind of operations, but wrote home that the second was more painful than the first.[25]

The grind caught up with him when he was a few months shy of his nineteenth birthday. In February 1907, Bartolomeo came down with pleurisy in Turin.

This time he did not write home. Maybe he was too ill, or maybe he was afraid of disappointing his father. It was his boss who took "care of me and . . . wrote my father to come to see me because I was sick."[26] Mr. Vanzetti arrived to fetch the invalid home. There "I would be cared for by my mother, my good, my best-beloved mother. And so I returned, after six years spent in the fetid atmosphere of bakeries and restaurant kitchens. . . . Six years," he added with regret, "that might have been beautiful to a boy avid of learning."[27]

Home at last, the lonesome young wanderer received the attention he had missed for so long. "My mother received me tenderly. . . . She put me in bed — I had almost forgotten that hands could caress so tenderly. There I remained for a month, and for two months more I went about with the aid of a heavy walking stick. At last I recovered my health. From then until the day I parted for America I remained in the house of my father. That was one of the happiest periods of my life."[28]

It was a brief interlude. After Vanzetti recovered, his adored and adoring mother, Giovanna, became sick herself, a victim of cancer at age forty-five.[29] Her "sufferings became so agonizing," Bartolo recalled, "that neither my father, nor her relatives, nor her dearest friends had the courage to approach her." It was her eldest son who kept a lonely bedside vigil, trying to comfort his mother. "Day and night I remained with her, tortured by the sight of her suffering. . . . After three months of brutal illness she breathed her last in my arms."[30]

Bartolomeo made the funeral arrangements. "It was I who laid her in her coffin; I who accompanied her to the final resting place; I who threw the first handful of earth over her bier. And it was right that I should do so, for I was burying part of myself."[31]

Giovanna Vanzetti had been several years younger than her husband. He must have been shocked that she predeceased him, and worried about the future of the youngest children who were, after all, still toddlers. He could turn to his religious faith for spiritual comfort. He could turn to his two older children for help with more practical matters.

Or so he must have thought, but if he did, he would have been wrong. Bartolomeo was too overwhelmed by his own grief to help anyone else.

The memory of his mother was, he said, the most sacred thing in the world to him.[32] Once a self-described "fervent Catholic,"[33] Bartolo had felt his faith weaken during his lonely adolescence. Now, in the shadow of his mother's loss, "the most painful misfortune that can strike a man,"[34] depression descended. Bartolo wandered in sorrow and silence through nearby woods, thinking "many times" about killing himself.[35]

"[T]here was nothing for me to do but come away," he concluded. "I had to put the seas between me and my grief."[36] In his "desperate state of mind," he resolved to leave his homeland and travel to America.[37]

His father did not approve. Mr. Vanzetti wanted his son at home now, and was "speechless in his profound sorrow." Luigia, 16, also surely wanted her brother to stay. The responsibility to keep house and watch the young ones was now on her slender shoulders, and she needed his support. Bartolo loved his sister, but he wouldn't change his mind. He would no longer abide by his father's wishes. He wanted to escape the past even more than he wanted to embrace the future. And so, he said, on "June 9, 1908, I left my dear ones."[38]

He traveled by himself across the sea, alone in a crowd of fellow passengers. He landed in New York alone. He had already lived an eventful life, and he had just turned twenty.

— Unlike Vanzetti, Nicola Sacco hailed from the south, from the small town of Torremaggiore in the Puglia region, between Naples and the Adriatic Sea. Three years younger than Vanzetti, he was born on April 23, 1891.[39]

Nicola's father, Michele Sacco, a man of strong voice and animated expression,[40] managed a family olive oil business. He also owned land: a fruit and vegetable garden, and a large vineyard, source of grapes for the wine he made and marketed.[41] Nick's mother, Angelina, had her hands full taking care of children. As Nick, the third son, once put it, his family was "big very big,"[42] and Angelina and Michele may have had as many as seventeen children. (Nick mentioned that number in 1921, but in 1927 he gave the names of only five siblings on a prison form.)[43]

Called Nando as a child — a nickname for Ferdinando, his given name — Nick left school at age fourteen, possibly earlier, to help his father manage the land.[44] Sometimes, driving a cart around the countryside, he would buy supplies or pay workers.[45] And "[e]very year in autumn," he later recalled, ". . . I usd take care my father vineyard and sometime I usd keep watch," shooing wandering animals away and sleeping all night in the open air. "The place where I used to sleep it was a big large hayrick that my good father and my brothers and I build . . . near the well in the middle of our vineyard!"[46]

Before sunrise Nick watered the garden. "While I was finishing my work the sun shining was just coming up and I used always jump upon well wall . . . and I do not know how long I usd remane there look at that enchanted scene of beautiful."[47]

His house in town was a twenty-minute walk from the vineyard. "I used go back and forth . . . and I usd bring to my dear an poor mother two big basket full of vegetables and fruits and big bounch flowers. . . . And in the middle . . . I used always put one of lovely red rose and I used walk one mile [out of my way to find it]."[48] As long as he lived, the glimpse of a flower or whiff of a fragrance familiar from his childhood would rekindle in Nick a sense of joy.

In 1904 Sabino Sacco, Nick's older brother, was drafted into the Italian army. When he came back to Torremaggiore three years later, he was ready for adventure. Thousands of Europeans were trying their luck in America. Why not join them? Nick, now sixteen, wanted to come along. He was fascinated by machines. Maybe he could become a mechanic in America, that "free country, the country that was always in my dreams."[49]

Michele Sacco wasn't crazy about the idea, but did what he could to launch his sons on their journey. He contacted an Italian friend who had settled in Milford, Massachusetts. Writing back, the friend was encouraging, perhaps promising to help the brothers find work and a place to stay.[50] So Nick and Sabino piled their bundles onto a cart[51] and set out from Torremaggiore, two more Italians leaving the homeland. Together they sailed to America (though only Nick was seasick on the journey).[52] Together they landed in Boston. It was April 12, 1908.[53] Nick was not quite seventeen.

— Nicola Sacco and Bartolomeo Vanzetti were two individuals in the jostling crowd of 129,000 Italians who came to America in 1908, their heads filled with hopes for a better future. More than that number of Italians had come in each of the preceding seven years, and more than that number would follow in each of the following six years.[54] Italy, it was said at the time, was "a splendid place for the poor man to leave."[55] Neither Sacco nor Vanzetti was fleeing poverty, but many of their countrymen were. In fact, a reporter was told, in some parts of Italy there were only two industries: agriculture, and going to America.[56]

Immigration from countries of eastern and southern Europe, including Italy, had been increasing dramatically for years. A backlash against these new immigrants was well under way in 1908, when Vanzetti docked in New York and Sacco landed in Boston.

The shift in immigrants' countries of origin had been profound. Between 1880 and 1889, almost seventy percent of all immigrants to the United States

Inspectors look for signs of contagious eye disease in immigrants arriving at Ellis Island around 1913. Vanzetti, who immigrated in 1908, wrote that officials treated new arrivals "like so many animals." Library of Congress, Prints & Photographs Divison.

had come from Ireland, Germany, Great Britain, and Scandinavia. Less than fifteen percent had come from Italy, Russia, and Austria-Hungary.[57]

Twenty years later, the pattern had been reversed. Almost seventy percent of immigrants who came to the United States between 1900 and 1909 came from Italy, Russia, and Austria-Hungary.[58]

Americans, especially American businessmen, encouraged immigration in good economic times. Cheap labor was needed to build the railroads, work the mines, and run the factory equipment. In a weak economy, however, Americans worried, then as now, that immigration would keep wages down or drive unemployment up.

Economic worries alone did not explain opposition to immigration. Nativism had intensified with the shift in immigrants' countries of origin. Nativists were zealous to safeguard American values from outside influences. When they looked at the new immigrants, they saw worthless riffraff: "the lowest stratum of the Mediterranean basin and the Balkans"; "human flotsam"; "the backward, unassimilatable, undesirable"; "the weak, the broken and the mentally crippled."[59]

In some large cities, the new immigrants outnumbered the native-born by as much as two to one.[60]

— As early as 1751, before there *was* a United States of America, founding-father-to-be Benjamin Franklin worried about immigrants—in his case, German immigrants. He complained that they were arriving in droves and, he wondered, "Why should Pennsylvania, founded by the English, become a Colony of *Aliens*, who will shortly be so numerous as to Germanize us instead of our Anglifying them, and will never adopt our Language or Customs, any more than they can acquire our Complexion."[61]

A century and a half later, immigrants really were coming to America in droves, more than one million in the peak year of 1907.[62]

The America of poet Emma Lazarus may have welcomed the tired and the poor, the "huddled masses yearning to breathe free," but the America of the nativists did not. Confronting the inrush of new immigrants, nativist intellectuals penned pseudoscientific but influential justifications for racism. In 1916 Madison Grant pulled together and popularized such justifications in his book *The Passing of the Great Race*. Grant worried because "the higher races . . . when mixed with generalized or primitive characters, tend to disappear."[63]

Grant sounded the alarm about what he described as race suicide — the tendency of "the most valuable classes" to have fewer children when times are good while "the birth rate of the lower classes remains unaffected."[64] Immigrants, he feared, may "literally [breed] out their former masters. . . . This is occurring today in many parts of America, especially in New England." In America, Grant lamented, natives — by which he meant descendants of colonial settlers — "will not bring children into the world to compete in the labor market with the Slovak, the Italian, the Syrian, and the Jew," with the result that survival of the fittest is "better described as the 'survival of the unfit.'"[65]

Acknowledging a debt of gratitude to Grant, reporter Kenneth Roberts traveled to Europe, where he observed immigration at its source. In his 1922 book *Why Europe Leaves Home*, Roberts described streams of "peculiar, alien people" who were "oozing slowly but ceaselessly out of Central Europe to America," and southern Italians, who were "incapable of self-government and totally devoid of initiative or creative ability."[66]

"It is not particularly pleasant," Roberts lamented, "to continue to harp on the necessity of keeping the United States a nation of Nordics; for there are always a large number of sentimentally inclined readers, whose belief in the whimsical fairy tale of the melting pot is stronger than their common sense." He urged ever more restrictive immigration laws to "[swing] the tide of immigration back toward the Nordic stock," to prevent America from becoming "thoroughly mongrelized."[67]

Today, at the beginning of the twenty-first century, when most European immigrants and their descendants have fully assimilated into American society, and the focus of the immigration debate in the United States has shifted to non-Europeans, the arguments of a Madison Grant or a Kenneth Roberts against immigration from southern and eastern Europe sound anachronistic and paranoid. In their day, however, Grant, the chairman of the New York Zoological Society, and Roberts, a writer for the *Saturday Evening Post*, were mainstream, their words widely read and accepted.

— Of all the new undesirables in America, the Italian was thought to be among the worst.[68] Vanzetti himself proved susceptible to such sentiment. Although he later recognized that he had "suffered because I was an Italian" in America,[69] in 1911 he wrote his sister that he usually stayed by himself, "because the Italians [here] are in general too ignorant."[70]

The worst of the worst were said to be the peasants from southern Italy. They were, said Roberts, "as different from the north Italians of Nordic descent as an alligator pear is different from an alligator."[71]

"Steerage passengers from a Naples boat show a distressing frequency of low foreheads, open mouths, weak chins, poor features, skew faces, small or knobby crania, and backless heads. Such people lack the power to take rational care of themselves."[72] Thus opined Edward Alsworth Ross in the popular magazine *Century*. Like Grant and Roberts, Ross was not an uncredentialed maverick; he was president of the American Sociological Society and a professor at the University of Wisconsin when the *Century* article was published.

In the opinion of many, including Ross, northern Italians were far superior to their compatriots from the south. Unfortunately, Ross pointed out, in the United States "only a fifth of our Italians are from the North. It is the backward and benighted provinces from Naples to Sicily that send us the flood of 'gross little aliens,'"[73] a fact that would eventually spell doom for Anglo-Saxon America.

Ross was correct on at least one point. Most Italian immigrants to the United States did come from the south of Italy. Of some four and a half million Italians who immigrated between 1880 and 1921, more than eighty percent came from the south.[74]

Ross criticized Italian immigrants for their clannishness, for drifting "round and round in a 'Little Italy' eddy," living a life "*under* America, not *of* it."[75] Clergyman Enrico Sartorio looked at the same phenomenon and viewed it more sympathetically. The immigrants "are isolated from the rest of the American world by . . . the instinct of self-preservation; they know that as soon as they step outside of the Italian colony they are almost as helpless as babies, owing to their lack of knowledge of the language, customs and laws of this country."[76]

In time most of the immigrants would overcome the obstacles they encountered. As early as 1904 Italians in New York were reported to have collective savings of more than $15 million, real estate holdings of $20 million, and businesses worth some $7 million. They patronized sixteen Italian-language papers in the city, supported a hospital and several churches, and counted among their number more than a hundred physicians and a handful of other professionals.[77] Long before the days of Joe DiMaggio and Frank Sinatra, a few talented Italians even became superstars. Tenor Enrico Caruso made his Metropolitan Opera debut in New York in 1903. Actor Rudolph Valentino made his feature film debut in Hollywood in 1921. They transcended their southern Italian origins to become widely popular celebrities.

— Notwithstanding the success of some and the hard work of many, Italian immigrants, especially those from southern Italy, were the subject of criticism in the majority of articles published about them in American magazines between 1880 and 1920.[78]

Americans worried about what they saw as the southern Italian's propensity for violence. "Frequent stabbing affrays . . . have led many to think of the Italian and the stiletto as inseparable," reported a writer in *Charities* magazine.[79] (In private, Vanzetti would have agreed. Many of the young men who hailed from the south belonged to criminal gangs and "live off the fruits of their crimes," he wrote his sister.)[80]

The United States Immigration Commission, a congressional committee, reported in 1911 that "certain kinds of criminality are inherent in the Italian race."[81]

Day in, day out, Moustache Pete dealt with the stereotyping. Pete, a fictional character, recalled being arrested when he took out a knife to peel an apple on the street. "I ask why Mista Policeman hit me, and he say some-a-thing like, all you dagoes carry knives and make trouble. . . . Anyway I get out of jail after a few days."[82]

Behind the caustic humor lies the phenomenon of ethnic profiling, and the consequences could involve more than a few days in jail. Forty-seven Italians were lynched in the United States between 1890 and 1915.[83] They were lynched in Arkansas, Colorado, Florida, Illinois, Louisiana, Mississippi, West Virginia, and other states.[84] The largest mass lynching in American history took place in New Orleans in 1891, when eleven jailed Italians were killed in a single night. Five of them were awaiting trial for murder; of the other six, three had experienced a mistrial in the same case and three had already been acquitted.[85]

— Action, no matter how drastic, against individual immigrants was not the ultimate goal of nativists. In the latter part of the nineteenth century, they began working toward a broader goal — to toughen immigration laws and restrict immigration from southern and eastern Europe at its source. In time they would succeed, but for years the battle over immigration reform waxed and waned, depending in part on politics, in part on the fluid state of the economy and the corresponding over- or undersupply of workers.

Immigration had been chiefly a state concern before 1882. That year Congress passed a law requiring each immigrant to pay on arrival "a duty of fifty cents"[86] into a national immigrant welfare fund. The law also barred entry to certain people deemed undesirable, including any "lunatic, idiot, or any person unable to take care of himself or herself" and "all foreign convicts except those convicted of political offenses."[87]

The 1882 law split the responsibility for handling immigration issues between federal and state governments. In 1891 Congress placed the responsibility wholly on the federal government, establishing a federal office of immigration. (It consisted in its entirety of a staff of four.)[88] The 1891 law also added more categories of banned undesirables, including polygamists and "persons suffering from a loathsome or dangerous contagious disease."[89]

To restrictionists, these regulations were just a start. In 1894 three Bostonians — Charles Warren, Robert DeCourcy Ward, and Prescott Farnsworth Hall — launched what would become the Immigration Restriction League of Boston. This trio of young Harvard grads, class of '89, believed that solving "the one great problem of foreign immigration" would go a long way toward solving all social problems.[90]

League members were alarmed by what they saw in their own backyard. In Massachusetts in 1885 immigrants and their children outnumbered the native-born. Sixty-three percent of Boston's population was either foreign-born or of foreign parentage. The percentage was even higher in mill towns such as Fall River, Lowell, and Lawrence. Irish immigrants "had taken over the police and fire departments of Boston and the mill towns,"[91] and in 1884 had helped elect Boston's first Irish Catholic mayor. These developments dismayed the descendants of the Puritans, the so-called Boston Brahmins.

The Immigration Restriction League spawned affiliates throughout the United States and settled on a primary goal: to require immigrants to prove they could read in order to be allowed to enter the country. This requirement would, they believed, keep out the many immigrants from southern and eastern Europe who were illiterate. A league-drafted literacy bill passed both houses of Congress, but President Grover Cleveland vetoed it in 1897.

Until 1917 all other attempts to pass a literacy law likewise failed. Interest groups blocking passage of a literacy law included business owners in need of immigrant workers, politicians in need of immigrant votes, and organizations of immigrants themselves. President Woodrow Wilson pointed out the irony inherent in any literacy law: "Those who come seeking opportunity are not to be admitted unless they have already had one of the chief of the opportunities they seek, the opportunity of education."[92]

Although restrictionists kept encountering defeat on the road to a literacy law, they were succeeding in their push for laws to control immigration more tightly and to exclude more categories of undesirables. The immigration law of 1903 barred entry to epileptics, beggars, prostitutes and procurers, and people who were either insane, had been insane in the past five years, or had ever had two "attacks of insanity."[93] The 1903 law, coming two years after anarchist Leon Czolgosz assassinated President William McKinley, also banned "anarchists, or persons who believe in or advocate the overthrow by force or violence of the Government of the United States."[94]

In 1907 more categories of undesirables were banned, including "idiots, imbeciles, feeble-minded persons," tuberculars, and children under age sixteen unaccompanied by a parent.[95] Amendments in 1910 banned not only polygamists but also "persons who admit their belief in the practice of polygamy."[96]

Finally in 1917 members of Congress made literacy tests for new immigrants the law of the land. They overrode President Wilson's veto to do so. In addition to banning ever vaguer categories of undesirables — "persons of constitutional psychopathic inferiority [and] persons with chronic alcoholism" — the immigration act of 1917 stipulated that, within three months of the act's passage, "All aliens over sixteen years of age, physically capable of reading, who can not read the English language, or some other language or dialect," would be prohibited from entering the United States.[97]

It was assumed that this would amount to a de facto quota system, because "there was a higher rate of illiteracy in southern and eastern Europe."[98]

Between the time the law passed in February 1917 and the time the literacy provision took effect three months later, the United States entered World War I. Immigration rates fell, but they began to rise again after the war ended in 1918. The literacy test wasn't accomplishing what its backers had hoped for. "The postwar inrush of immigrants who could pass the test showed every sign of soon equaling the size of the indiscriminate, prewar movement," writes historian John Higham. "[T]he jam at Ellis Island had become so great that immigration authorities were hastily diverting New York–bound ships to Boston."[99]

In such a climate the debate over immigration reform revived. Senator William Dillingham of Vermont, who had chaired the U.S. Immigration Commission, revisited its recommendations, and in 1920 drafted a bill to limit immigration based on a national quota system. Dillingham proposed to restrict immigration from European countries to five percent of the number of immigrants from those countries who had been in the United States in 1910. The House reduced the quota to three percent.[100]

European immigration would be reduced to a yearly maximum of about 350,000. Most of that number would be assigned to countries of northwestern Europe.

President Wilson did not sign the bill. But his term in office was almost at an end, and Warren Harding, his successor, did sign it.

The 1921 immigration restriction law marked what was at the time "the most important turning-point in American immigration policy," writes Higham. "It imposed the first sharp and absolute numerical limits on European immigration. It established a nationality quota system based on the pre-existing composition of the American population."[101] Before 1921, an "illegal immigrant" was someone who lacked specified desirable qualities, someone from a banned category of people such as convicts, polygamists, or anarchists. After 1921, an illegal immigrant was anyone who exceeded the quota of his country of origin. A system that had aimed for quality control gave way to a system based on nationality and numbers. The Immigration Act of 1924 lowered quotas further.[102] The great wave of immigration from southern and eastern Europe was over.

— Three days after the 1921 quota law took effect, a brief item appeared on the front page of the June 6 *Boston Evening Transcript*: "White Star liner *Canopic* arrives from Italy with 1564 passengers; many immigrants inadmissible under emergency immigration law."[103]

Here was a new and knotty and apparently unforeseen problem. The quota law had stipulated monthly as well as annual quotas for "the number of aliens of any nationality who may be admitted."[104] When the law took effect, some immigrants, including those on board the *Canopic*, were already at sea. Their arrival would exceed the first month's quota. Should they be shipped back to their native lands even after they had, in many cases, sold everything they owned to pay for the trip? Or should Congress pass a law to permit their entry?

Legislators generally agreed that such passengers were innocent victims who should be admitted, but *how*? A humanitarian solution would require discussion. Meanwhile, back in Boston, White Star wanted its ship back. So government officials decided to transfer the boatload of Italians to temporary housing in an unlocked prison on Deer Island in Boston harbor. The steamboat *Mayflower* out of Nantasket Beach was engaged to ferry the stranded passengers from their ship to the island.

To the unlucky Italians of the *Canopic*, this twentieth-century *Mayflower* seemed bound for misery, not freedom. "Aliens in Wild Riot," the *Boston Globe* proclaimed on June 12; "Fifty Boston Police Compel Immigrants to Land at Deer Island—Women, at Sight of the Cells, Flee Back, Shrieking, to the *Mayflower*."[105]

The women, first to disembark with the youngest children, had thought they were all being thrown into prison and locked up. Panic-stricken, they "broke away and ran screaming [back] toward the *Mayflower*, where the men were still being held. . . . [T]he women swarmed over the side of the *Mayflower* like flies, passing their screaming children to willing hands and then clambering back on board themselves. In doing this they tore down the starboard railing of the promenade deck."[106]

A day later, the "wild excitement and the hysteria"[107] of the "swarm" of immigrants subsided. The *Canopic* passengers would be admitted, the *Globe* reported.

∼ As the story of the *Canopic* passengers and their "wild riot" played out on the front pages, two other Italian immigrants were also making headlines in Boston. They stood accused of a vicious crime, murder in the shoot-up at South Braintree. Their names: Nicola Sacco and Bartolomeo Vanzetti.

3 | CRIME WAVE

Murder and mayhem in Massachusetts. The cold-blooded killings in South Braintree were part of a reign of terror sweeping through the Boston area, said State Senator David McIntosh, and it had to be stopped.

The crime wave included a four-month-old attempted robbery, still unsolved, in the town of Bridgewater.

There, early in the morning of a cold, damp, and foggy day, December 24, 1919, armed robbers had tried to hold up a "treasure truck" delivering $33,113.31 in payroll cash to the L. Q. White Shoe Company. A driver, a guard, and a paymaster were in the truck. The would-be robbers and the guard fired at each other. No one was hit. Nothing was stolen. The driver of the truck "calmly kept his [vehicle] on the move with bullets hurtling past his head," and sped away.[1] The "baffled ruffians," as one newspaper described the failed bandits, escaped in a getaway car.[2]

Authorities had mounted a rapid response. Michael Stewart arrived at the scene of the attempted crime within minutes. Son of an immigrant shoe worker from Ireland, Stewart was chief of the Bridgewater police department, which consisted of himself and two officers. Factory owner Loring Q. White immediately offered a reward "for the capture of the men in question," and his insurance company quickly hired the Pinkerton detective agency. Pinkerton investigator J. J. Hayes was on the ground and interviewing witnesses that afternoon.[3]

The accounts of truck driver John Graves, guard Benjamin Bowles, and paymaster Alfred Cox differed. Cox had seen two robbers; Graves, three; and Bowles, four. They all had seen a bandit who was armed with a shotgun, but they didn't agree about what he'd been wearing. As to ethnicity, Graves thought the shotgun bandit was Greek; Bowles thought he was Italian or Portuguese; and Cox said he must have been Russian, Polish, or Austrian. They did agree that the shotgun bandit had a mustache—a "closely cropped" mustache, according to both Cox and Bowles.[4]

Two witnesses who knew something about cars—Graves, the driver, and Frank Harding, a Bridgewater mechanic—identified the getaway car as a Hudson or "like a Hudson."[5]

In Boston, Pinkerton superintendent H. J. Murray heard that "foreigners, possibly Italians" might have been involved, so he let his Italian informants know about the reward.[6]

Investigator Hayes worked through the evening—Christmas Eve. He interviewed Chief Stewart, who told him that "he believed that the holdup was the work of an out-of-town band of Russians" with a possible accomplice inside the factory. Bridgewater, Stewart said, had a large foreign population, including "a lot of Reds and Bolshevists" at the White company. Stewart also reported that the license plates on the getaway car had been stolen a week earlier from a garage in Needham.[7]

The Pinkerton investigation got under way in earnest on the day after Christmas. Detectives learned that a black, seven-passenger Buick had also been stolen from Needham. "[T]his car may have been used by the men [in Bridgewater]," a Pinkerton man reported. Two new witnesses came forward to identify the Bridgewater getaway car as a Buick.[8] From then on, its identity as a Hudson began to evaporate.

Detectives fanned out to several towns to question police chiefs about local criminals. Chief Stewart reported that he now had a description of the driver of the getaway car: stocky, thirty-five years old, Italian, with black hair and a black mustache, and dressed in a black fur coat. Stewart recommended that the detectives ask the other chiefs about "Italians in their districts."[9]

Superintendent Murray heard reports of an Italian man in Boston who had said either that he knew the Bridgewater bandits or that he had driven the getaway car himself. The superintendent assigned detectives to tail the man, whose description in many particulars matched Stewart's description of the getaway driver. He was a dashing "Spaniard or an Italian," a dapper dresser who seemed to enjoy toying with his Pinkerton shadows, leading them through Boston on a wild-goose chase in and out of stores, saloons, and factories, ending up at a house with a "Scarlet Fever" quarantine sign on the front door, from which he emerged two days later to lead his followers on another merry pursuit, ending up back at the same house.[10]

On December 30, 1919, Superintendent Murray learned that this man had been overheard saying that the would-be bandits were Italian anarchists, that they kept their car in a shack near Bridgewater, and that after the botched robbery they had abandoned the car and taken a trolley to Quincy.[11] A Pinkerton detective passed this information on to Chief Stewart.

Stewart, along with a detective and a state police officer, finally caught up with the man on January 3. His name, he said, was C. A. Barr (originally Barasso). He was Italian. He claimed that he had invented a machine "with which he could detect who had committed a crime no matter where it was committed. He stated that one Mrs. Vetilia . . . had looked into the machine and saw the [attempted Bridgewater] holdup happening and saw the men plainly but did not know who they were."[12]

Barr's claim was "a rambling statement," a detective noted.[13] There is no evidence that investigators tried to examine Barr's miraculous invention or to question the gifted Mrs. Vetilia. The inquiry into the Bridgewater crime petered out a few days later.

— On April 16, 1920—four months after Bridgewater, one day after South Braintree—Chief Stewart was asked to assist in an immigration investigation of Feruccio Coacci, an Italian who until recently had worked at the Slater & Morrill factory. Coacci was an anarchist deportable under the Anarchist Exclusion Act of 1918. He had been arrested two years earlier, but had posted bond and been released. Now the bond had expired and he was requesting an extension in order, he said, to care for his sick wife.[14]

Coacci lived with his family and with a friend, Mario Buda, also known as Mike Boda, in a small house that Buda rented in West Bridgewater. Buda also owned a car, a 1914 hand-cranked, right-hand-drive Overland automobile, which he garaged in a shed out back.[15]

Stewart sent one of his officers to assist the immigration inspector in questioning Coacci. Against expectations, they found Mrs. Coacci healthy enough, and Coacci himself packing to leave. He declined the inspector's offer of a temporary delay of deportation. He was taken into custody, and within two days was aboard a ship bound for Italy.[16]

When Stewart learned what happened at the house, he had a eureka moment. "Something hit me," he later recalled, "the dates involved, the bond, and the phony illness."[17] Former suspect C. A. Barr had said that Italian anarchists were responsible for the attempted Bridgewater crime, anarchists who kept a car in a shack. Coacci's strange behavior followed the South Braintree murders by one day. Stewart put these pieces together and decided that both crimes must have been committed by the same gang, a gang of which Coacci must have been a member. The theory was reinforced a day later, when the abandoned Buick was discovered in woods less than two miles from Coacci's house.

Stewart now resolved to see the house for himself. He went there three times in three days. On April 20, he gained entry by falsely identifying himself to Mario Buda as an immigration inspector seeking a picture of Coacci.[18] Buda willingly showed the house and shed to Stewart and the officer with him, explaining that the shed was empty because his car was at a West Bridgewater garage for repairs. Stewart took note of a "recently raked" dirt floor in the shed, and of an empty drawer where, Buda told him, Coacci had kept a gun.[19]

The next day Stewart returned to question Buda again, but Buda saw him coming and slipped out the back door.[20] On Stewart's third and final trip to the house the following day, Buda was gone and so was the furniture.

Recalling that two sets of tire tracks had been found near the abandoned Buick, Stewart speculated that the bandits had transferred in the woods to a second car, which must have been Buda's Overland. He paid a visit to Simon Johnson, manager of the garage where the Overland had been left for repairs. Call me, he told Johnson, when somebody comes for that car.

— Bartolomeo Vanzetti was going on a trip. He and his anarchist comrades in the Boston area were concerned about two Italians in federal custody in New York. Roberto Elia and Andrea Salsedo, printers by trade, were being interrogated by agents of the Bureau of Investigation about suspected anarchist bombings. The detainees had already been held for nearly two months.[21] Reportedly they were cooperating with investigators.[22]

Salsedo had smuggled letters to Vanzetti, telling him of the prisoners' predicament and asking for money for better legal aid. "We wanted to help [them]," Vanzetti's friend, Aldino Felicani, later recalled. "Vanzetti and I were much worried about this." Since Vanzetti, single and between jobs, had few commitments, a group of friends "sent [him] down to New York to see what was happening. If they needed defense lawyers, we would be willing to pay for them."[23]

Vanzetti embarked for New York by train on April 25, a few days after Stewart's last visit to the Buda-Coacci house.[24] Once in New York, he learned what he could about the Elia-Salsedo situation by meeting with anarchist journalist Carlo Tresca and Luigi Quintiliano, representative of a committee to defend "all Italian political prisoners."[25] Vanzetti also tried to visit the Statue of Liberty, but missed the boat.[26]

The people Vanzetti met gave him some advice: Go home and tell your friends to hide all their radical pamphlets and newspapers. May Day — May 1 — an important date in the radical labor movement, was just around the corner. The Justice Department was anticipating violence on May Day 1920, and wanted to prevent it, possibly by raiding homes of suspected radicals. "I learned," Vanzetti later testified, "that most probably for the May 1st there will be many arrest of radical and I was set wise if I have literature and correspondence, something, papers in the home, to bring away, and to tell to my friends to clean them up the house, [so] the literature will not be found if the police-men go to the house."[27]

On April 30, Vanzetti returned home to Massachusetts.

Boston police girded for trouble on May Day. There was none. All was quiet. In Plymouth, Vanzetti went to the seashore and dug for clams to sell.

— The quiet shattered soon enough. Early in the morning of May 3, Andrea Salsedo jumped or fell or was pushed out of a fourteenth-story window of the Manhattan building where federal agents had been questioning him.

When Salsedo's body hit the pavement, the thud reverberated. To protect the secrecy of its investigation, the Department of Justice tried at first to conceal the dead man's identity, saying he was a Communist named Tony Tazio. Quickly the ruse had to be dropped. Narciso Donato, a lawyer in the same building, said he represented both Salsedo and Elia. Those two men "were held for alleged connection with the bomb plots [of 1919]," Donato said, "when, as a matter of fact, they knew about as much concerning them as I knew about the World War. . . . I am confident that Salsedo was driven to a state of insanity by his confinement."[28]

The sensational story was front-page news. "Red's Death Plunge, 14 Stories, Bares Long Bomb Trail," the New York Times reported on May 4. Salsedo had been "high in the councils of the Galliani [sic] group of destructionists," according to the paper, and had told his interrogators that the group was responsible for the bombings under investigation. The same day, the Boston Globe and the Boston Herald also reported Salsedo's death.[29]

Nick Sacco read the Globe every morning.[30] He and his confederates were part of the group that Salsedo was said to have fingered. They had not yet acted on Vanzetti's advice to gather and hide their anarchist tracts. Now they must have felt an urgent need to do so. They would need a car for the task. Mario Buda would have to get his Overland out of the garage in West Bridgewater.

On May 5, 1920, as Elia, Salsedo's fellow prisoner, was whisked to Ellis Island to await a deportation hearing, four friends assembled at Sacco's house in Stoughton: Ricardo Orciani, Mario Buda, Bartolomeo Vanzetti, and Sacco himself. Only two were needed for the task at hand: Vanzetti, because he had accepted responsibility for rounding up the documents, and Buda, because he had the car. If they alone had gone to the garage, there would have been no Sacco-Vanzetti case.

But all four went. Orciani gave Buda a ride to the garage in the sidecar of his motorcycle. Vanzetti took a streetcar. Sacco went with him to keep him company.

It is tempting to speculate whether Rosina Sacco, Nick's wife, wanted her husband to stay home that evening. Surely she could have used his help. Nick's mother had died in Italy two months earlier, prompting him to plan a visit to his family in Torremaggiore for the first time since he'd left there in 1908. Rosina, Nick, and their young son, Dante, were planning to leave for Italy in a few days. In preparation, Rosina, who was pregnant, had been working hard, "cleaning up the house and packing up the things, my stuff that I wanted to take across to the old country."[31] She was also tending to her son and cooking supper for her husband and his friends. Rosina must have been bone-tired that night. Maybe she did ask her husband to stay home. Fate had other plans for him.

— Nick and Bartolomeo reconnoitered with Mario Buda and Ricardo Orciani in West Bridgewater.

The garage was closed. And so it was that around nine o'clock on the night of Wednesday, May 5, 1920, Buda knocked on the front door of the nearby yellow and white house of garage manager Simon Johnson.[32]

Ruth Johnson opened the door. "I saw a man standing by the pole, and he walked towards me," she later recalled. "I wondered if there was anybody with him and I looked and saw two more." She told the man approaching her that her husband "would be right out," then she walked to the next-door neighbor's house to call the police, as prearranged with Chief Stewart. "These two men seemed to come right along with me," she said, "only on the other side of the street." She also saw "a fourth man standing beside a motorcycle.[33]

Inside the neighbor's house Mrs. Johnson called the West Bridgewater police, then walked back home. "[T]wo men walked alongside of me ... [t]he same [men] that followed me up. . . . I could see them plain. . . . I walked right along up to my front door, and my husband was talking to a man ... [t]he man that was standing by the pole."[34]

That man was Buda. Johnson told him the repairs were done, but advised him not to take the car yet because it didn't have 1920 license plates. Buda said he would take it anyway, then changed his mind and said he would send someone for it the following day.[35]

Buda and Orciani left as they had arrived, by motorcycle. As for Sacco and Vanzetti, they boarded a streetcar to Brockton. By the time Chief Stewart arrived at the Johnson house, Buda, the man he sought, was gone, and so were his unknown companions.

Stewart alerted Brockton police.

Shortly after ten o'clock the streetcar driver made a stop in front of Keith's Theater on Main Street in Brockton. Police officers Michael Connolly and Earl

Vaughn boarded the car. "I looked the length of the car to see if I could see two foreigners, which the telephone had said had tried to steal or take an automobile in Bridgewater," Connolly recalled. He saw them. " 'Well,' I said, 'I want you, you are under arrest.' . . . They wanted to know what they were arrested for. I says, 'Suspicious characters.' " [36]

The suspicious character in a dark suit and derby hat was Nicola Sacco. The suspicious character in a light coat and black slouch hat was Bartolomeo Vanzetti.[37] Sacco had just turned twenty-nine. Vanzetti was one month shy of his thirty-second birthday. Neither man would sleep under his own roof again.

— Officers Connolly and Vaughn did a weapons search on the spot. They found a loaded .38 caliber Harrington & Richardson revolver in Vanzetti's right hip pocket. Connolly, who for some reason "just gave Sacco a slight going over," missed the gun tucked into Sacco's waistband. He missed it again, a few moments later in the police car when, he said, "I puts my hand under [Sacco's] coat." It wasn't until they arrived at the Brockton police station that another officer found Sacco's loaded .32 caliber Colt automatic. In addition to the weapons, Sacco was carrying twenty-three cartridges, and Vanzetti, four shells.[38]

A year later, at trial, Vanzetti would claim that Connolly had pointed a revolver at him on the streetcar and said, "You don't move, you dirty thing," and Connolly would claim that, when arrested, both men had made moves as if to draw their weapons.[39] But Vaughn, who was with Connolly, never made such a claim, nor did Connolly himself make the claim at pretrial inquiries.

— Sacco and Vanzetti were put in separate cells at the Brockton police station. Chief Stewart quickly arrived. Perhaps he was disappointed to find these two unknowns instead of his intended quarry, Mario Buda.

The chief interrogated Vanzetti first. "I said," Stewart later testified, " 'I am going to ask you some questions, and as you are under arrest for crime, you are not obliged to answer them unless you see fit. But if you do, what you say may be later used against you.' " [40]

Vanzetti, who, in those pre-*Miranda* days, did not know that he had the right to have an attorney present, and probably did not fully grasp that he also had the right to remain silent, replied, "Well, I will tell you what you want to know."[41] He then proceeded to lie. He told Stewart that he had gone to West Bridgewater that night to see a friend named Pappi, that he had not seen a motorcycle while there, and that he did not know Mario Buda. Stewart asked Vanzetti if he belonged to any clubs or societies, if he was an anarchist, if he liked the government, if he believed in changing government by force, if he subscribed to anarchist newspapers, if he received anarchist papers by mail, if he was a U.S. citizen, and if he had a permit to carry a gun.

Stewart's questions did not touch on robbery or murder. They concerned a different, and deportable, offense: belief in anarchism.

Stewart then questioned Sacco along similar lines, and Nick replied in a similar way: he also lied.[42] He said that he had not seen a motorcycle that night and that he did not know Mario Buda. Stewart asked Sacco if he belonged to any clubs or societies, if he was a communist, if he was an anarchist, and if he believed in the American system of government. Stewart questioned Vanzetti a second time, then left the police station sometime after midnight on May 6.

Sacco and Vanzetti had been caught in a trap set for someone else, but they helped ensnare themselves with the lies they told that night.

— Stewart didn't ask his prisoners about their whereabouts on the dates of the Bridgewater or South Braintree crimes. Neither the chief nor the officers with him that night informed the men of any charges against them although, according to Vanzetti, "I asked them many times. They say, 'Oh, you know, you know why.'"[43]

Sacco and Vanzetti thought they did know why.

They assumed they had been arrested for their radical beliefs and associations. "I never think anything else than Radical," Sacco said. "[I]n that time there," Vanzetti explained, "there was the deportation, and the reaction was more vivid . . . and more mad."[44]

Vanzetti claimed that policemen harassed the men in their cells at the station that first night. One, he said, waved a fist at him. Another spat and pointed a loaded gun at him. Still another declined to bring the prisoners blankets, saying they would be lined up and shot in the morning anyway. Stewart denied that anyone had threatened to punch or shoot the prisoners. He also said he did not remember Vanzetti asking him about the charges.[45]

In the early morning hours, after Stewart left, Sacco and Vanzetti, separated by one cell, talked, but only briefly, because "we were scared."[46]

— On Thursday, May 6, 1920, the story that would later dominate headlines around the world made its first appearance in the Boston press. The *Herald* buried news of the arrest of Sacco and Vanzetti in sixteen lines on page 10, but the arrest was already front-page news in the *Globe*. Both papers reported what Nick and Bartolomeo did not yet know themselves, that police were hoping "Bert Vanzetti" and "Mike Saco" would be able to "throw some light on the Braintree shooting."[47]

Mug shots of Nicola Sacco, top, and Bartolomeo Vanzetti. Courtesy of Historical and Special Collections, Harvard Law School Library.

Ricardo Orciani was taken into custody that afternoon.[48] Police brought several witnesses to the Brockton jail to identify the suspects. They informed Rosina that her husband was in jail, and searched the Sacco home, finding a rifle and "Socialistic, Radical newspapers and books."[49] In Vanzetti's rented room they found "alleged Bolshevik literature."[50]

Police also began monitoring visitors to the jail. Michael Kelley, Sacco's boss and landlord, visited his friend immediately.[51] A few days later, Aldino Felicani

recalled, "[w]hen I approached the line to go through to the station . . ., I was subjected to all kinds of questions — why I wanted to see the men, and so on." The atmosphere around the jail seemed dangerous to Felicani, as if, he said, "lynching was in the air."[52]

— Frederick G. Katzmann, district attorney for Norfolk and Plymouth counties, was a native son of Massachusetts — born in Roxbury; educated at Boston Latin, Harvard College, and Boston University Law School; and a legislator in the Massachusetts House of Representatives in 1908, when Sacco and Vanzetti came to America. Katzmann's ancestry was Scottish and German, but if his German surname occasioned any awkward moments in the patriotic fervor of World War I, it hadn't held him back. In 1916, he was elected district attorney, a position he still held in 1920. Katzmann played tennis, voted Republican,[53] and dominated a courtroom. He was smart, intense, and relentless.

Katzmann encountered Sacco and Vanzetti for the first time on May 6, the morning after their arrest, in the Brockton police station. It is intriguing to imagine the initial meeting. The prisoners had spent a restless night in their cells. "We were sick, disgusted, offended and outraged," Vanzetti said later. "Our clothes were soiled and wrinkled, and our hair ruffled."[54]

The two Italians normally took pride in their appearance. When Sacco had attended night school to learn English, he always put on a clean shirt.[55] He didn't wear his factory overalls on the street; he always donned a derby when he went to town; and he seemed insulted when asked at trial if a certain cap was his. "That cap looks too dirty to me," he said, "because I never wear dirty cap. I think I always have fifty cents to buy a cap."[56] Even the shabbier Vanzetti took offense at trial when asked to identify a shirt as his: "[Y]ou think I have only one shirt? I am a poor man but I like to go clean."[57]

On May 6 they could not "go clean." They had slept in their clothes. In some of their mug shots, they appear disheveled. (Vanzetti claimed the police released to the press the worst pictures of the men, retouched to appear even more menacing.[58]) No amount of good grooming would have helped anyway. They were without counsel, and no match for Katzmann.

The record of Katzmann's initial interrogation reports the prisoners' responses, but not the district attorney's questions. Based on the responses, it appears that Katzmann did not tell the suspects why they had been arrested, nor did he inform them of their right to an attorney, but he did treat them with a show of courtesy.[59] "Oh, [that day] you treat me as a gentleman ought," Vanzetti conceded.

Vanzetti recalled that Katzmann told him that "if I don't want to speak, you don't compel me to speak." Nevertheless Bartolo agreed to speak because, he later explained, "I was there like a piece of paper. . . . I do not know the rule of the jail. I do not know very well the language. . . . I never was arrested before."[60]

Vanzetti answered Katzmann's questions about his politics: "I am not an anarchist. I don't know what I am exactly."[61] Vanzetti answered questions about his acquaintances, his gun, his mustache, and his whereabouts on the day before and the day of his arrest. He denied several times ever having been in Bridgewater. He also said he had never been to "Braintree." He thought, he said later, that "they arrested me for a political matter."[62]

Katzmann interviewed Sacco next. Nick said he understood that he had the right to refuse to answer questions. He understood that anything he said could be used against him.

Then Sacco did something that apparently to this day has remained unreported. He asked for an attorney.[63]

It appears that he made the request spontaneously, that Katzmann had not informed him of his right to counsel. One can only speculate how the case might have turned out if questioning had stopped when Sacco said, as he did, "I would like to have a lawyer." But Katzmann ignored the request, and Sacco did not insist on it. He replied to the district attorney's queries.

Sacco answered questions about his friends, his gun, and his whereabouts, particularly in April. He said he had been in Bridgewater "a long time ago" to look for work, but was not there "the day before Christmas." He said he had passed through Braintree "many times" while traveling to Boston. He said he took off "a whole day in April" and "quite a few half days in April" to get a passport for his trip back to Italy. He said he read about the South Braintree "bandits" in the newspaper, did not remember if he had worked the day before reading of the crime, and did not know "this Berardelli."[64]

In their responses to Katzmann and Stewart, Sacco and Vanzetti mixed truths with lies. The lies showed they were guilty of *something*. Was it murder? Chief Stewart was sure that Sacco and Vanzetti were the killers he sought, but Katzmann was more cautious. "The case isn't any too strong yet," he was reported as saying. "We need a lot more evidence."[65]

— May 6 was a "nice warm day. Undoubtedly the warmest of the season," one Bostonian wrote in his diary. Gentlemen were beginning to shed their heavy winter coats and hats, and to don their "hay derbies," or straw boaters.[66] It would have been a perfect day for Nick, Rosina, and Dante to begin their planned trip to Italy. Instead, for Sacco as well as for Vanzetti, May 6 became the first of a long procession of days behind bars.

There is pow'r, there is pow'r, in a band
of workingmen.
— Joe Hill, "There Is Power in a Union"

4 | "Organize! O Toilers"

Nicola Sacco's seventeenth birthday was unlike any he had celebrated before. For the first sixteen years of his life he had lived in Torremaggiore, his hometown in Italy's Foggia province. But as he turned seventeen on April 23, 1908, he was living in a kind of Little Foggia — Milford, Massachusetts, some forty miles outside Boston. Along with brother Sabino, Nick had been in the United States for less than two weeks.

Most immigrants arriving at the port of Boston disembarked and immediately encountered "hopeless confusion." Bewildered and gullible, they were easy marks for hustlers hawking the services of banks, hotels, and railroads. Later, when they went to find work, they were often victimized by employment agency scams. But Nick and Sabino were luckier than most. Their father's friend, Antonio Calzone, took the brothers under his wing. He brought them home to live with his family in Milford, where most of the neighbors also hailed from Foggia.[1]

The brothers arrived in the midst of a recession in America, but they found work quickly, in Nick's case with Calzone's help.

Nick, in fact, worked three jobs during his first year in America. He started out in the spring as water boy on a construction project in Milford. By summer he moved up to pick-and-shovel man, and his earnings rose to $1.75 a day. When winter blew in, he took the third job, cleaning castings for the Draper Company, a textile machinery manufacturer in nearby Hopedale. Calzone himself worked here, as did many of Milford's Italians.[2]

Sabino also worked a variety of jobs during that first year. The brothers reacted differently to their similar experiences. America, Sabino decided, was not for him. He returned to Torremaggiore in 1909 and remained there for the rest of his life. He hoped his younger brother would return with him, but Nick wanted to stay. "The last thing I told [him before I left]," Sabino said, "was to learn a trade at any cost."[3]

Nick liked his new home. In a photograph taken about this time, he appears self-assured and comfortable in a well-cut suit (borrowed, perhaps?), a handkerchief poking jauntily out of his jacket pocket. He faces the camera head-on

and strikes a casual pose. With his handsome features, thick mop of dark hair, and forthright gaze, he is the image of a young man content with the present and confident about the future.

Nick followed Sabino's advice about getting ahead. Through Milford's Italian grapevine he heard about a shoe manufacturing training program for immigrants. Michael Kelley, then superintendent of the Milford Shoe Company, was offering the three-month course for a fee of fifty dollars. That wasn't cheap. Nick would have to withdraw the money from his small savings, and forgo earning more money while studying. His future, he decided, was worth the investment, and he signed up.[4] When he finished, early in 1910—an eighteen-year-old brimming with ambition and enthusiasm—he left the world of heavy labor behind and became a skilled worker in the shoe industry, one of the oldest industries in Massachusetts.

⁓ Legend has it that shoemakers were so prized by the earliest English settlers in Massachusetts that when, in 1622, an able-bodied cobbler was sentenced to hang for stealing corn, a "bed-ridden weaver" was assigned to take his place on the gallows. The next year, a leather tanner with the confidence-inspiring name of Experience Miller sailed to Plymouth to ply his trade, and in 1635 two English shoemakers in Lynn began teaching their craft to anyone who wanted to learn. By 1700 the Massachusetts Bay Colony was exporting leather shoes and saddles to the rest of the colonies. By 1930 Massachusetts boasted seventy shoemaking towns, including Boston, which, with its thousand-plus factories, was touted as "the world's greatest shoe and leather city."[5]

Early cordwainers, or cobblers, had worked together at home, fashioning shoes by hand. Mechanization transformed the craft, and by 1910, when Nicola Sacco became a part of the Massachusetts shoe industry, it would not have been unusual for the production of a single pair of shoes to require the labor of more than a hundred different workers, each doing a single task and together using anywhere from fifty to a hundred different machines.[6]

Nick trained to become an edge trimmer. It was the edge trimmers who, near the end of the manufacturing process, cut leather soles with small round mechanical knives spinning at speeds of up to eleven thousand revolutions per minute. They made sure that the sole of each shoe exactly matched the sole of its mate. The job required good eyes and steady hands. Sacco became a master at it. He "was a genius at his work . . . that machine running so fast, sharp like a razor," a friend recalled. Precision was essential and mistakes were costly; if "you miss a thousandth of an inch . . . you ruin the shoe." A former employer who had seen many edge trimmers come and go remembered Sacco as the fastest of all. Sacco himself recalled being able to finish forty to fifty dozen pairs of shoes a day, many more than the normal output of twenty-five to thirty dozen.[7]

Like most edge trimmers, Sacco probably sat on a stool near the factory window. He wore overalls and probably worked in a cloud of fine dust spewing from beneath the spinning knives.

When he finished training with Michael Kelley, Nick found a job at a shoe factory in Webster, Massachusetts. But he missed Milford, and after some months returned there. And there he remained, working at the Milford Shoe Company for the next seven years.[8]

~ Unlike Sacco, who journeyed across the seas with a relative and was met by a friend, Bartolomeo Vanzetti was on his own, unaccompanied as he crossed the Atlantic in steerage, unaccompanied as his ship docked in New York in June 1908. Only twenty years old, he was a man who, by his own admission, was "ignorant of life and something of a dreamer."[9]

As soon as he got off the boat, Vanzetti had his "first great surprise. I saw the steerage passengers handled by the officials like so many animals." After clearing inspection, Bartolo made his way to the Lower East Side of Manhattan. There he stood, "alone, with a few poor belongings in the way of clothes, and very little money. . . . Where was I to go? What was I to do?"[10]

Vanzetti would spend the next five years much as he had spent his adolescent years: as a wanderer, searching for work. He did odd jobs along a route that took him back and forth between New York, Connecticut, and Massachusetts. Unlike Sacco, he would never earn a steady paycheck.

In that first year in New York, a stranger in a strange land, "a land where my language meant little more . . . than the pitiful noises of a dumb animal," Bartolo washed dishes. He painted a rosy picture of life on the job when he wrote home. "I had the good luck to find work right away in hotels," he brightly informed sister Luigia, "and for ten months I knew no misfortune." Of one filthy kitchen where he toiled, he told her only that he worked in "a French restaurant, where I learned a little bit of the language."[11]

He may have downplayed his problems to pacify his father, but later he viewed them through a darker lens. He bunked in a garret so "suffocatingly hot" that he preferred to sleep outside in a park at night. The food he received on one job, in a restaurant, was "hardly fit for dogs." He earned up to six dollars a week there for washing dishes twelve to fourteen hours a day, seven days a week, in a room where the ceiling dripped grease, the floor was covered in standing water, and the garbage stank. He was given five hours off every other Sunday. "After eight months I left the place for fear of contracting consumption."[12] He was out of work for the next few months.

Vanzetti probably spent his twenty-first birthday, June 11, 1909, job hunting. In an employment agency he befriended a *paesano*, "a young man more forlorn and unfortunate than I." He bought the hungry fellow a meal, then, on a whim, spent what was nearly his last dime to buy them both passage on a steamboat to Hartford, Connecticut. "[T]here was more chance of work [there], without counting the pure air and the sun which [cost] nothing."

From Hartford the two vagabonds "tramped along the road, and finally got up enough courage to knock at a cottage door" and ask for work. Vanzetti would always remember the kindness of the "American farmer" who fed the men, tried to help them find work, then "out of pity . . . , took us on his farm, although he had no need of our assistance. He kept us there two weeks."[13]

Then Vanzetti and his companion tramped on, hungry and homeless. "From town to town, village to village, farm to farm, [factory to factory,] we went . . . and were sent away." Finally the two drifters got work tending the furnaces at a brick factory in Springfield, Massachusetts. His friend soon moved on, but Vanzetti stayed for the better part of a year, finding at last "quite a colony" of fellow northern Italians who "became almost a family." Still, he felt like an outsider. When, at the end of a day of hard labor, "[s]omeone would strike up a tune" and dancing would lift everyone's spirits for a while, Bartolo "sat aside watching. I have always watched and enjoyed in other folks' happiness."[14] After Springfield came two years of hard work in the stone pits of Meriden, Connecticut.

By now Vanzetti had been in America for a few years, and all his work experiences had been negative. "I remember a time," he later wrote a friend, "in which the bosses used to spit upon the feet of the work-seekers."[15] In the brick factory and the stone pits, Vanzetti began to question what he saw as inequalities all around him: "I learned that class-consciousness was not a phrase invented by propagandists, but was a real, vital force."

Bartolo had one valuable skill he had not yet tried to use in the American job market. In his years of apprenticeship in Italy, he had learned how to make pastry. Friends urged him to put this skill to use. So Vanzetti returned to New York. There he found it was easier to get a job as a pastry chef's assistant than to keep it. Within a year he had been hired and fired by two restaurants. It was a scam, he learned. Chefs took kickbacks from employment agencies. "The more often they sacked men, the more often they could get new ones and their commission."[16]

Italian friends "begged me not to despair," Vanzetti recalled. Still, after several months of unemployment and mounting debts, he decided to go back to construction work. "[T]ogether with a herd of other ragged men," he was sent off to Springfield, Massachusetts, to work on railroad construction. He paid off his debts, then moved to Worcester, worked "in several of the factories" there for about a year, and hit the road again, heading east across the state to Plymouth.[17]

In Plymouth the rootless itinerant finally began to put down roots.

— Plymouth, *Mayflower*'s landfall, Pilgrims' harbor, sits on the western shore of Cape Cod Bay on the Massachusetts coast. In 1913, when Vanzetti arrived there, the Pilgrims were long gone. A visitor to Plymouth Rock in the summer

of 1913 would have heard the hum and clatter of machines echoing through the open windows of the town's mills and factories—Puritan Mill, Standish Worsted Company, American Woolen Company, and especially the Plymouth Cordage Company, world's largest producer of rope[18] and bedrock of the town's economy.

Bourne Spooner, "descendant of several Pilgrim Fathers," had incorporated the Cordage in 1824 to capture a share of the huge maritime demand for ropes. By 1860, the company employed 140 workers. "For the most part," according to historian Samuel Eliot Morison, "these were still of old Yankee stock, from Plymouth County or other parts of New England. Very few members of the 'Irish invasion' of New England . . . came to Plymouth."[19]

When maritime demand for rope began to wane after the Civil War, the Cordage diversified into new markets: binder twine, fishing nets, corset twine, and rope cables for oil drilling and power transmission. The factory quadrupled its workforce between 1874 and 1924. "The first sharp change in the composition of labor came . . . with an inflow of Northern Italians [around 1880].

... Naturally these newcomers entered at the bottom." By 1910, a few years before Bartolomeo Vanzetti came to town, nearly one-third of the population of Plymouth consisted of foreign-born residents.[20]

Bartolo continued to job-hop after settling in Plymouth. He worked as caretaker on a private estate, loaded rope onto freight cars at the Cordage, and did heavy labor on construction projects around town. At the Cordage, he worked outdoors, and wrote his aunt that he liked the job and the climate. But when in 1915 he was transferred to indoor work, he quit.[21]

During his years as an itinerant, Vanzetti had one constant: books. It's unclear how he managed to come by his volumes, but he later recalled studying everything from the Bible to Darwin. His eclectic reading list took in world history, poetry, anarchist theory, socialist and religious journals, and the novels of Hugo, Zola, and Tolstoy. He realized that his formal education, which had ended when he was thirteen, was inadequate for taking in "all this vast material" and that his concentration suffered because he was tired, reading at night after a hard day's work. Undaunted, he read on, and the texts, together with his life experiences, taught him, he said, to champion the oppressed and to grasp "the concept of fraternity, of universal love."[22]

— In Plymouth Vanzetti found another welcome constant: a surrogate family.

He missed his mother. He had left home grieving her death, only to discover that physical distance didn't matter; he still thought about her every day.[23]

He missed his sister Luigia, too. Ever since he left her behind with a heavy burden of family responsibilities, he had been sending her advice. He often reminded her to do something that he himself had been unable to do: "Be loving and patient with Papa. Think how much he must be suffering from losing Mama and from my departure. . . . Try to lighten his sorrows any way you can, fulfilling well your household and filial duties."[24]

At the same time that Bartolo was counseling Luigia to be affectionate with their father and to "try to win him over with sweetness" instead of bitterness,[25] the emotional distance between father and son was growing.

Mr. Vanzetti was conservative, authoritarian, and a believing Catholic. His son was becoming the exact opposite: radical, rebellious, and an atheist. (He had neglected his church membership since "circa 1909," he later stated on his prison record.)[26]

The son's politics and religious heresy mystified the father, as did his choice to live like a common laborer in America instead of returning to a comfortable and dutiful family life in Italy. But "what would I do in Villafalletto?" Bartolo wrote his sister from Plymouth. "How would things go with Papa? How would

I express my own way of doing things . . . ?" He was curbing any desire to go home, he wrote his aunt, because, with his ideas, he felt so different from his relatives and countrymen.[27]

So when this solitary drifter tossed up in a happy home in Plymouth, he must have felt as if he had reached safe harbor at long last. On an unpaved street called Suosso Lane, in a house across the street from the Amerigo Vespucci Hall, Vanzetti rented a room from the Brini family—father Vincenzo, mother Alfonsina, son Beltrando, then 6, and daughters Lefevre, 7, and Zora, 3.[28] Over the four years that he roomed with them, Vanzetti became more than a tenant; he was a beloved member of the family.

He was especially close to Beltrando, taking the boy's talents and ambitions seriously and giving him the fatherly advice he surely wished he had received from his own father. Select your reading material carefully, Vanzetti counseled him; concentrate on history and science, read critically, be of good courage, and "[l]earn to swim."[29] "Vanzetti made me feel useful by sending me on little errands," Beltrando later recalled; he "made me feel very proud of my ability to do anything."[30]

∽ When Nicola Sacco and Bartolomeo Vanzetti joined the ranks of American workers in 1908, there was no federal minimum wage. There were no comprehensive child labor laws and no workplace health and safety laws. Workers had no unemployment compensation or workmen's compensation or Social Security. Non-unionized workers in manufacturing industries worked about sixty hours a week to earn on average ten dollars and change.[31]

In this vacuum of protection, some workers began to organize into labor unions to improve their conditions. Employers not surprisingly took a dim view of such activity, seeing labor as a commodity to be bought and sold at a business owner's discretion, like any other raw material, and unionization as the result of outside intervention, not poor working conditions. Even when the United States entered World War I in 1917, and the federal government granted workers the right to organize into trade unions, "many of the largest [employers] were never reconciled to it."[32]

Early attempts to organize labor unions in the United States had begun after the Civil War. The first to succeed was the Knights of Labor, a "curious movement" that originated in 1869 as a secret society and evolved into a leading, if short-lived, union.[33] The Knights preached solidarity and practiced it, too. They made the first real effort to organize unskilled as well as skilled workers, and to recruit black workers.

Membership in the Knights of Labor peaked in 1886, the same year that a former cigar maker named Samuel Gompers and a group of associates founded the American Federation of Labor (AFL) as an organization for skilled craft workers. Gompers would go on to lead the AFL for almost forty years.

The lifespan of the Knights was shorter than the tenure of Gompers, but the motto of the Knights — "An injury to one is the concern of all"[34] — would inspire labor activists in years to come, including, indirectly, Sacco and Vanzetti.

— In a crowded Chicago auditorium in June 1905, Big Bill Haywood, a one-eyed former hard-rock miner who was now a national official of the Western Federation of Miners, called to order what he referred to as the Continental Congress of the working class. "We are here," Haywood proclaimed to more than two hundred delegates, "to confederate the workers of this country into a working class movement that shall have for its purpose the emancipation of the working class from the slave bondage of capitalism. . . . The American Federation of Labor . . . does not represent the working class. . . . [Our new] organization will be formed, based and founded on the class struggle, having in view no compromise and no surrender, and but one object and one purpose and that is to bring the workers of this country into the possession of the full value of the product of their toil."[35]

The choice of Industrial Workers of the World as a name for the new group was unanimous. Members soon became known as Wobblies, a sobriquet supposedly based on a Chinese restaurateur's mispronunciation of IWW, the organization's acronym, as "Eye-Wobble-Wobble."[36]

The IWW used provocative language guaranteed to put business owners and public officials in a state of red alert. "The working class and the employing class have nothing in common," stated the preamble to the IWW constitution. "Between these two classes a struggle must go on until the workers of the world organize as a class, take possession of the earth and the machinery of production, and abolish the wage system."[37]

Given the incendiary rhetoric, it wasn't surprising that eventually almost everyone in America hated the Wobblies: liberals, conservatives, bureaucrats, clergymen, newspaper reporters, businessmen, even members of other unions. (Gompers instructed AFL members not to support IWW strikes.)[38] Wobblies, according to one study, were perceived as the root of all evil, "a gang of irrational saboteurs, vile agents of corruption and free love, destroyers of the church and the family, unconscionable traitors and, during the World War, [enemy] agents."[39]

Seasonal IWW workers — farmhands and loggers, for example — sometimes engaged in free-speech fights, a kind of off-season urban street theater. Soapbox orators would repeatedly violate speaking bans in order to get arrested and clog jails and court dockets. It was a way for the IWW to organize itinerants, but it drove city residents crazy. "Hanging is none too good for [Wobblies], and they would be much better dead," proclaimed the *San Diego Evening Tribune* during a free-speech fight in that city in 1912. Wobblies "are the waste material of creation and should be drained off into the sewer of oblivion there to rot in cold obstruction like any other excrement."[40]

Such dehumanizing language was "the psychologically necessary prelude to violent repression," writes John Clendenin Townsend.[41] The repression was real. In the more notorious cases, vigilantes shot at a boatload of Wobblies on the docks in Everett, Washington, in November 1916; shipped more than twelve hundred suspected Wobblies in cattle cars to the desert outside Bisbee, Arizona, in July 1917; and four months later tarred, feathered, and whipped seventeen Wobblies and supporters in Tulsa, Oklahoma.[42] In cases more gruesome still, masked men lynched IWW organizer Frank Little in Butte, Montana, in August 1917; and a mob dragged, castrated, and lynched United States Army war veteran and IWW demonstrator Wesley Everest in Centralia, Washington, in November 1919.[43]

Why were the ragtag Wobblies so feared and reviled? How was it possible that, as an observer at the 1913 IWW convention wondered, "this bunch of porkchop philosophers, agitators who have no real, great organizing ability or creative brain power, are able to frighten the capitalistic class more than any other labor movement organized in America?"[44]

Wobblies were viewed literally as foreign invaders. Threatening property and mocking middle-class values, they evoked a kind of siege mentality. Perhaps because many were seasonal workers with regular downtime, Wobblies were also perceived as lazy, shiftless idlers immune to the American work ethic. ("I Won't Work" was one popular take on the IWW initials.)[45]

IWW leaders never minced words in declaring their intention to do away with capitalism and to organize workers to seize "the machinery of production." The struggle against business and government would be unceasing, Vincent St. John proclaimed in a 1913 pamphlet, and the organization would "use any and all tactics": strikes and sabotage against industry, and "open violation of the government's orders, going to jail en masse." The organization believed in militant direct action and, said St. John, "The question of 'right' and 'wrong' does not concern us."[46]

Compared to such an organization, the AFL appeared positively benign. Where the AFL emphasized collective bargaining, the IWW stressed strikes and propaganda. Where the AFL directed its efforts to skilled craft workers,

Child laborers from the textile mills of Lawrence, Massachusetts. In January 1912, four months after this picture was taken, thousands of workers spontaneously went on strike against the mills to protest a pay cut. Repercussions of the strike probably helped radicalize Sacco and Vanzetti. Library of Congress, Prints & Photographs Div., Lewis Hine photograph.

the IWW reached out to migrants, miners, factory hands, and drifters. Both groups sought improvements in wages and working conditions. Only the IWW also sought revolution.

— On Thursday, January 11, 1912, in the mill city of Lawrence on the banks of the Merrimack River in northern Massachusetts, all hell broke loose. On that cold day, the first payday of the new year, textile workers opened their pay envelopes and discovered that their week's pay had been cut, in most cases by thirty-two cents.

The Massachusetts legislature had passed a law restricting the amount of time that women and children could work to fifty-four hours a week, beginning in 1912.[47] (The previous limit had been fifty-six hours.) The new law was supposed to protect the weakest workers. Resentful employers decided to reduce hours for all workers, and to reduce pay correspondingly. News of the impending cuts was not widely disseminated.

A loss of thirty-two cents a week would scarcely be noticed by a worker today. But to an experienced textile worker in Lawrence in 1912, who earned about $8.75 a week (inexperienced workers earned less),[48] thirty-two cents could mean ten loaves of bread, or four quarts of milk, or three bags of coal. Families needed those thirty-two cents, and workers believed they had earned them. Furious, they stormed out of the textile mills.

The great Lawrence strike was on.

The next day, Friday, snow began falling at seven thirty in the morning. In the "whirling whiteness," a crowd of strikers grew.[49] Within a few hours more than twelve thousand workers had walked out of four mills. The strikers "were practically all Italians and Syrians," according to the *Boston Globe*, which reported that they shut off power in the mills, tore belts from pulleys, threw bobbins, and overturned tables "to hasten the operatives in leaving their work."[50] In response, William Wood, president of the American Woolen Company, which owned most of the Lawrence mills, issued a statement absolving manufacturers of responsibility for the situation. He condemned "mistaken labor interests" for pushing the fifty-four-hour law.[51] He insisted it was ridiculous to assume that manufacturers would pay people for two hours more than they actually worked — although in 1910, when the legislature had reduced the weekly limit on hours from fifty-eight to fifty-six, employers had not changed workers' pay. Wood expressed confidence that, "when the employees find that justice is not on their side, the strike cannot possibly be long-lived."

Striking laborers believed justice *was* on their side. Here they were, shivering through the frosty winters of northern Massachusetts, working in the worsted wool capital of the world,[52] yet few could afford the price of a new wool coat. Immigrants and their children made up eighty-six percent of the population of Lawrence. Typically, the city's immigrant children left school at age fourteen to work in the mills;[53] half the population of Lawrence between the ages of fourteen and eighteen went off each day to a factory, not to a classroom. Workers paid high rents for dingy tenements in slum areas where, the city building inspector warned, congestion was "drawing close to the danger line." Lawrence had a high infant mortality rate, a high tuberculosis rate, and a low adult life expectancy.[54]

The IWW sent organizers to Lawrence immediately. Joseph Ettor arrived from New York on Saturday, January 13, and rallied more than a thousand workers at a mass meeting at City Hall the same afternoon. "Smiling Joe," the Brooklyn-born child of Italian immigrants, was only twenty-six, but he knew how to deliver a stem-winder. Now, he told the Lawrence strikers, there was only one way to prevail: "You cannot win by fighting with your fists against men armed or the militia, but you have a weapon that they have not got. You have the weapon of labor, and with that you can beat them down if you stick together."[55]

For help in Lawrence, Ettor called on Arturo Giovannitti, secretary of the Italian Socialist Federation, director of *Il Proletario* newspaper, and an IWW supporter.

Success seemed unlikely for the Lawrence strikers, who had never organized before. Ettor needed to find a way to give common cause to immigrants who came from different countries and spoke different languages.

The local militia unwittingly helped him achieve his goals. On Monday morning, January 15, at the start of the first full week of the strike, local militiamen blasted marching strikers with water from fire hoses. "The shock of the icy water in subzero temperatures united the workers . . . and probably saved the strike from ignominious collapse." By Monday night "Lawrence was an armed camp."[56] Militiamen and police officers were brought in from other cities to guard the mills and patrol the slum areas.

By the end of the first week, some twenty-two thousand workers had walked off the job. They were demanding a fifteen percent wage increase, abolition of the premium pay system, and rehiring of all strikers.[57]

— There was no obvious reason for Nick Sacco to become involved in the Lawrence strike.

His decision to learn a trade had paid off. He had become a skilled worker and valued employee at the Milford Shoe Company, earning forty to fifty dollars a week, more than most shoe workers and enough to send money home to his family in Italy occasionally. He boarded with an Italian family in Milford whose dining room was a friendly neighborhood gathering place. He was popular — not surprisingly, since he was handsome, clean-cut, good-natured, and polite. He didn't drink. He didn't swear. He took evening classes to improve his English.[58]

And he was in love.

Sacco met Rosina Zambelli in 1911, at a benefit dance for a disabled musician. Rosina had attended a convent school in northern Italy, and now was living with her family in Milford.[59] Petite, slim, fair-skinned and auburn-haired Rosina, 16, and compact, energetic Nicola, 20, must have made a strikingly attractive young couple.[60]

They were courting when the strike erupted in Lawrence. Sacco's life was already full, yet he felt compelled to do something. Perhaps he thought that, if not for the help he had been lucky enough to receive when he first arrived, he might have ended up in circumstances like those of the strikers. Whatever his motivation, the "fight of the textile workers in Lawrence became Sacco's fight."[61] He collected money for the strikers and donated funds himself. One Sunday he may even have traveled to Lawrence to join a parade and listen to stirring speeches. If so, he would not have been disappointed, for some of the Wobblies' most charismatic leaders had come to Lawrence.

~ Young Elizabeth Gurley Flynn was among them. Still in her early twenties, the spitfire speaker had been in demand at demonstrations and on picket lines around the country since she was a teenager.[62] The "Rebel Girl" stood out in the nearly all-male world of IWW leaders. Bill Haywood, no slouch in the rousing oratory department, also arrived in Lawrence.

Curious Bostonians journeyed the thirty miles to Lawrence to see for themselves what was transpiring. "All my part of the world seemed to be there," said well-connected Brahmin activist Elizabeth Glendower Evans, then 56. Evans went to Lawrence, most likely in early March. She and Haywood stayed at the same hotel, and one day the two talked for hours. "He is a natural leader," she concluded, "a dynamo of human power, and whatever may be his sins, and his impossibilist program, he is doing a deed in welding this heterogeneous mass of foreign people into . . . a pursuit of common ends; that is a service of simply incalculable value."[63]

Haywood, Flynn, Ettor, Giovannitti, and other IWW organizers used tactics in Lawrence that would influence labor strategy for years. A large general strike committee represented workers from all the striking mills, all the largest ethnic groups, and all phases of the manufacturing process. Picketing took place on a scale never seen before. Thousands of singing strikers marched in parades every few days. Fifteen relief stations and five soup kitchens handed out food, clothing, and medicine. And the children left town.[64]

Relying on a strategy "long familiar to labor organizers in Italy," the strike committee decided to evacuate the children of some of the strikers in order to have them fed and cared for out of harm's way. With their parents' consent, a group of 119 children left Lawrence by train on February 10 for temporary safety with friends and well-wishers in New York. A week later, 91 more children followed, and 35 others went to families in Barre, Vermont.[65]

On Saturday, February 24, when more children went to the train station despite a new police ban against further departures, police roughed up and actually arrested several mothers and children. "A wave of indignation rose from all over the country. Not only was the brutality, but the unconstitutionality, of the whole proceeding, vigorously denounced."[66]

It was the beginning of the end of the strike in Lawrence. The last serious confrontation between strikers and police took place a couple of days later, on February 26. On March 1 the American Woolen Company offered all its workers a wage increase. Negotiations began, and on March 14 strikers accepted a settlement and ended the walkout. The "strikers of Lawrence have won the most signal victory of any organized body of workers in the world," Haywood crowed.[67]

The results of the Lawrence strike reverberated. Manufacturers throughout New England raised wages for textile workers to prevent strikes at their own mills.[68] Immigrant workers realized they could overcome their differences to organize for a common cause. Wobblies realized their tactics, developed in the western United States, could work in the east. Wobbly critics realized the same thing, and it troubled them. Lawrence "stirred the country with the alarming slogans of a new kind of revolution" and a new kind of solidarity. "We will sing one song," proclaimed a Wobbly anthem: "Organize! O, toilers, come organize your might."[69]

~ For some laborers, May Day—May 1—was a day of celebration and commemoration. On May Day 1912, less than two months after the Lawrence strike ended, Nicola Sacco put on a new blue suit. He asked permission to take "my dear Rosina" shopping. He bought her a blue suit, too, a white slip, and brown accessories—shoes, stockings, and hat. "I wish you could [have seen] Rosina," he later wrote a friend, "how nise she was look. . . ." A few months later, beautiful seventeen-year-old Rosina Zambelli married Nicola Sacco, her twenty-one-year-old beau, an ardent man with a seemingly bright future.[70] They moved into an apartment in Milford and set up housekeeping.

~ When the strike ended in Lawrence, another battle remained. Joseph Ettor and Arturo Giovannitti were in prison. The IWW shifted gears to legal defense.

Police and workers had often confronted each other during the strike. Ettor had preached passive resistance, yet violence had occurred. It peaked at the end of January. Before dawn on January 29, strikers (or agents provocateurs, according to the IWW) had attacked streetcars with rocks and chunks of ice, smashing windows and harassing non-strikers trying to enter the mills. That evening strikers marching in one of their frequent parades found a police barricade in their way. There was pushing, shoving, stabbing, shooting. In the chaos Annie LoPezzi, a young striker, was shot dead; Oscar Benoit, a police officer, was stabbed, but survived. The next morning, when strikers tried to hold another parade, an eighteen-year-old protester named John Remi was bayoneted in the back and died.[71]

Remi had undoubtedly been killed by a soldier; strikers didn't carry bayonets. It was not clear who had killed LoPezzi. Strikers accused policeman Benoit, while policemen accused a striker, Joseph Caruso. They arrested Caruso—*and* Ettor and Giovannitti—and locked them up in Lawrence Jail. The two strike leaders had not been present at the parade, but they were accused of inciting the riot that led to LoPezzi's death, making them accessories to murder.

Freeing Ettor and Giovannitti became an immediate goal of the IWW. Caruso was included in the defense, but did not figure as prominently as his better-known co-prisoners. IWW leaders hired local attorneys to represent the defendants. Assisting them was the organization's general counsel, Fred Moore, an "able attorney who was prone to nervous attacks which kept him out of court."[72]

Support for Ettor, Giovannitti, and Caruso spread around the world, said IWW spokesman Justus Ebert, "to Europe, Australia, Canada, Hawaii, Cuba, Panama and even Argentine." Ebert believed that the international support "exerted considerable economic and political influence in behalf of the three prisoners."[73]

From his jail cell, Giovannitti recommended that his friend and fellow journalist Carlo Tresca be called to Lawrence to help lead demonstrations. Tresca had also been in prison that year, serving a nine-month sentence for libeling a priest.[74] Now he was free, publishing *L'Avvenire*, an Italian-language anarchist newspaper in Pennsylvania, and eager to join the action. "I went to Lawrence . . . with burning faith in my heart," Tresca recalled. "When the conductor called 'Lawrence' at the station my heart began to palpitate like the engine of a great electric generator."[75]

A born rebel, Tresca had left Italy eight years earlier to avoid doing time for libel there. In the United States he used his talents as an agitator and journalist to lead striking Italian workers against their bosses, and to rail against the influence of Italian diplomats, wealthy businessmen, and priests. "Tresca never makes trouble," journalist Max Eastman said of his friend. "He merely goes where it is, cultivates it, . . . nurtures and nurses it along, so that from being a little, mean, and measly trouble, it becomes a fine, big tumultuous catastrophe, approaching the proportions of a national crisis."[76]

Tresca began organizing demonstrations for the Lawrence strikers in September. Controversy broke out on Sunday, September 29, 1912, when he defied police and led a parade that became, in the words of a local historian, one of "the most disgraceful scenes ever witnessed in Lawrence."[77] An American flag was trampled, and thousands of out-of-town supporters marched with red flags and a banner proclaiming "No God, No Master."[78] In the enraged backlash that followed, citizens of Lawrence staged a counterdemonstration. Elizabeth Gurley Flynn later rued the "unfortunate" impact of the banner.[79]

The trial of Ettor, Giovannitti, and Caruso got under way a few days after the infamous march, in the courthouse in Salem, Massachusetts. Reporters from around the country converged on the town. It seemed as if the IWW itself were on trial.

The courtroom drama lasted two months. Defense lawyers reportedly lacked "depth, grasp and courage";[80] their work was a "clumsy handling" of the case. But lawyers for the prosecution lacked something more important: evidence. Ettor and Giovannitti, both eloquent speakers, testified on their own behalf. Against the advice of their lawyers they made closing statements, too. Ettor was passionate, but it was Arturo Giovannitti who "carried away the hearers." Making his first public speech in English, he said that if he and Ettor were to be executed for trying to improve workers' lives, "then I say that tomorrow we shall pass into a greater judgment . . . where history shall give its last word to us."[81] His speech was said to have been so moving that it made veteran reporters cry.

IWW MEN FREE, read the page 1 headline of the *Boston Evening Transcript* on Tuesday, November 26, 1912. After six hours of deliberation, the Salem jury acquitted all three defendants. Supporters in the Salem courthouse were ecstatic. Moore quickly telegraphed Haywood to tell him of the verdict.

— Sacco and Vanzetti would feel the repercussions of the 1912 Lawrence strike for years to come.

It was in Lawrence that Elizabeth Glendower Evans committed herself to helping the labor movement. "It [was] as if a new 'world' were opened," she said.[82] Evans would become the staunchest American supporter and patron of Sacco and Vanzetti.

In Lawrence, Elizabeth Gurley Flynn met Carlo Tresca.[83] Their attraction was mutual and immediate. Tresca left his wife and daughter and moved to New York to be with Flynn; they lived and worked together for years. Both were well acquainted with Fred Moore, the lawyer whom Flynn referred to as "brilliant" and who was one of her "close friends." In 1920, after Sacco and Vanzetti were arrested, Tresca and Flynn would recommend Fred Moore as defense counsel.[84]

In Lawrence, Moore, the veteran labor lawyer, was part of the winning team. This represented his first legal victory in the east and the biggest legal victory of his career. But success in Lawrence would perhaps give Moore a false sense of security nine years later, when he represented Sacco and Vanzetti.

In Lawrence, Judge Webster Thayer, then a practicing attorney in Worcester, may have found validation for an abiding prejudice against Italians. Such was the belief of the Reverend Roland Sawyer, a minister, state legislator, and supporter of Ettor and Giovannitti, who said that the prominent role Italians played in the strike frightened "men like Thayer."[85]

And the Lawrence strike, erupting just four years after Sacco and Vanzetti arrived in America, was surely a decisive force in propelling them toward increasingly radical sympathies. Sacco knew of, and supported, what was going on in Lawrence. Given the extensive news coverage, it is highly likely that Vanzetti knew of it, too. Both men may have read strike literature and thus been exposed to the IWW's goal of ending capitalism through militant action. In Lawrence both men may also have first become aware of Luigi Galleani, an influential Italian anarchist who supported the strike.[86] Vanzetti took out his first subscription to Galleani's newspaper, *Cronaca sovversiva* (Subversive chronicle), on November 30, 1912, a mere four days after the end of the Ettor-Giovannitti trial.[87] Within a year of the trial, Sacco would also begin subscribing to *Cronaca* and attending meetings of an anarchist group in Milford.[88]

The sequence of events strongly suggests that, for Sacco and Vanzetti, the seed of anarchism sprouted in Lawrence, under the radical wing of the American labor movement. The two men had not yet crossed paths. But after Lawrence each of them, separately, would become increasingly activist.

— Success turned out to be the exception, not the rule, for the IWW. In 1913, just a year after winning advances for Lawrence strikers, the organization led and lost strikes of hotel workers in New York, silk workers in New Jersey, rubber workers in Ohio, auto workers in Michigan,[89] and machinery workers in Hopedale, Massachusetts.

Hopedale in 1913 was a five-cent streetcar ride away from neighboring Milford, adopted hometown of Nicola Sacco. The Draper Company of Hopedale manufactured machines for textile production. Of the more than two thousand workers at Draper, most commuted from Milford.[90] Nick probably knew many of them; he himself had briefly worked at Draper during his first year in America.

On April 1, 1913, Draper employees walked off the job. It must have seemed as if half of the workers in Massachusetts were on strike that year, including machinists in Hyde Park, hosiery workers in Ipswich, and shipbuilders, barbers, and bootblacks in Boston.[91] Joseph Coldwell, an IWW organizer from Worcester, hurried to Hopedale to organize the strike there. Workers wanted a nine-hour day, a minimum wage of two dollars a day (about twenty-two cents an hour), an end to the piecework system, and rehiring of all strikers.

No less a luminary than a recent governor of Massachusetts was principal owner and director of the Draper Company. Former governor Eben Draper refused the strikers' demands, refused an offer by the State Board of Conciliation and Arbitration to help settle the strike, refused a similar offer by the Milford Merchants Association,[92] and refused to meet with Coldwell, whom he saw as an outside agitator and advocate of anarchy representing an organization so reprehensible that he could barely bring himself to speak its name, referring to it repeatedly as "the IWW, so-called."

Noting that strike funds in Hopedale were skimpy, the *Boston Globe* predicted early on that "something like normal conditions are not at all unlikely in a few days."[93]

The following day workers voted to continue the strike indefinitely.

Nick Sacco rallied to the cause of the Hopedale strikers. He continued to work at the shoe company during the day, but before and after work, in early morning and in the evening, he took off for Hopedale to march on the picket line. He "always took an active part" at nighttime committee meetings to plan strike relief.[94] Rosina was pregnant, expecting the couple's first child; Nick's commitment to the strike must have been passionate for him to spend this time away from home. "Now that is Nicola," Sabino once said of his brother's enthusiasms. "He puts his whole heart into whatever he does, whether it is learning a trade or arranging a meeting."[95]

In the absence of IWW media magnets in Hopedale such as Haywood and Flynn, Joseph Coldwell continued to lead the strike. It was "pure idealism that impelled Nick to take an interest in this strike," Coldwell said. "The [shoe] industry in which he worked was not affected. . . . He was not an orator, or even a fluent speaker, but he was a mighty good worker in detail matters and never hesitated to do his share." Sacco avoided the limelight. "He was one of the silent, active, sincere workers, giving of his time and money," Coldwell recalled. "I looked upon Nick as one of my personal aides [in Hopedale]."[96]

Perhaps Sacco was in Hopedale to witness one of the stranger scenes of the strike. On April 15, 1913, as picketers passed the offices of the Draper Company, "Coldwell noticed Ex-Gov. Draper and his son at one of the large windows. [Coldwell] at once halted the parade, beseeching Mr. Draper to meet some of the strikers and ascertain their real motives for leaving work, predicting that if he would do so the strike would immediately be concluded."

Behind the closed window, Draper made no response. His mind was as closed as his window.[97]

— The strike against Draper collapsed some three months after it started. By then Nick's life had changed. He and Rosina had become the joyful parents of a healthy son, Dante, born during the Hopedale strike on May 10, 1913, and named for the poet, "a great man in my country."[98] The father doted on the boy. He was "always my dear and lovely boy," Sacco wrote later, from prison. He remembered evenings when he, Rosina, and little Dante used to walk to a friend's house. Dante was so full of questions "that some time it was impesseble for me to explain." On the walk back home, Dante "was always sleeping, so I youst bring him always in my arm . . . [and] some time Rosina she youst halp me to carry him and . . . both us we youst give him a warm kisses on is rosy face. Those day . . . they was a some happy day."[99]

"I never saw a man that was more attentive to his family," one of Sacco's bosses said of him later.[100]

— Cape Cod Bay shelters the town of Plymouth, but in 1916 there was no shelter, even in Plymouth, from labor unrest. The Plymouth Cordage Company provided workers and their families with an array of quality-of-life benefits: cafeterias, a nutrition clinic, free kindergarten, vocational classes, athletic fields and a beach, a limited amount of housing, and a library that, Vanzetti reported, subscribed to several Italian newspapers. According to Samuel Eliot Morison, "It would be hard to exaggerate the pride that the directors and officers of the Company showed in these welfare activities."[101]

So it came as a complete surprise—the *Boston Globe* called it a "mystery strike"—when workers at the Cordage walked off the job on January 17, 1916. Most men then working at the Cordage earned between nine and ten dollars a week; women, about six dollars. Wages had not kept up with the cost of living, especially since, as Vanzetti explained to his aunt, the war then raging through Europe was driving up the prices of basic necessities in the United States.[102] The problem at the Cordage was neatly summed up on a protester's banner: WE CAN'T EAT BEANS 21 TIMES A WEEK. The solution seemed obvious to one striker: "Have the company give up its social welfare work . . . and put the money into our pay envelopes."[103]

Management was under the "illusion that Plymouth Cordage was one big happy family," Morison said. "But the Company had not taken cognizance of the fact that it was paying insufficient wages for people to live on decently."[104]

Vincenzo Brini, Vanzetti's friend and landlord, worked at the Cordage. Vanzetti himself had once worked there, but had left a year before the strike and returned to construction work. Now he actively supported the strike, "making speeches . . . doing his turn on the picket-line . . . [and] gathering . . . money for the strike fund."[105] The import of his role is unclear. According to Morison, Vanzetti's name did not appear in any of the various detailed accounts and reports on the strike. According to Vanzetti, however, he was a strike leader. Of all the local men who played a prominent role in the strike, he recalled years later, "I was the only one who did not yield or betray the workers . . . [and] the only one who, instead of being compensated, was blacklisted."[106] (The company would have had no reason to compensate him, since he was not then in its employ.)

Luigi Galleani went to Plymouth to urge the strikers to hold firm.[107] But two weeks after his visit, employees accepted a compromise pay increase, and the walkout at the Cordage ended.[108] The strike probably would have vanished from the annals of labor history if not for the connection to Vanzetti. Cordage was the only strike in which he is known to have participated. It was enough, in his view, to condemn him to police surveillance and frame-up. If Vanzetti exaggerated the repercussions of his role in the Cordage strike, he wasn't the only one. Immediately after his arrest in 1920, the press reported that he was "well known as a leader" of that strike.[109]

~ Still unknown to each other, Nick and Bartolo were traveling on parallel paths in 1916. While Vanzetti was helping Cordage strikers in Plymouth, Sacco in Milford was becoming involved in one more labor strike. He went back to the barricades in 1916, when his son, Dante, was a toddler. This time the strikers he supported were not neighbors in Massachusetts, but miners in faraway Minnesota.

The miners, many of them immigrants, worked the underground and open-pit iron ore mines in the hills of the Mesabi Range, north of Duluth. On June 3, 1916, workers at one mine spontaneously struck for a minimum wage of three dollars a day and for a pay system based on hours worked, not ore extracted. The strike spread quickly to other mines. By the end of June, ten thousand miners on the Mesabi Range and another fifteen thousand on the Vermilion Range northeast of the Mesabi had walked off their jobs.

As in Lawrence four years earlier, IWW organizers quickly arrived on the scene. When two men were killed in a confrontation with company guards in Biwabik, Minnesota, police arrested several strike sympathizers, including Carlo Tresca and other IWW organizers who had been miles from Biwabik at the time. "It was," writes historian Melvyn Dubofsky, "the Ettor-Giovannitti affair all over again."[110]

In response to events in Minnesota, and perhaps spurred by Tresca's arrest, Sacco and other Italian anarchists in Milford began meeting to raise money for the Mesabi miners. (All three of the strikes that Sacco supported—Lawrence, Hopedale, and Mesabi—were ıww-organized.) Even after the Mesabi strike ended in defeat for the miners in September, the Milford group continued to meet and raise money for the prisoners' legal defense.

Police in Milford objected to the meetings; the chief banned them; the activists ignored the ban and met again. When they did, on December 3, 1916, police arrested three men, including Nicola Sacco, on charges of speaking without a permit.[111]

A judge eventually dismissed the charges. And a large defense fund turned out to be unnecessary. On December 8, 1916, less than a week after Sacco's arrest, the Mesabi prisoners settled with the state's attorney. Three pleaded guilty to manslaughter; the others, including Tresca, were released.[112]

The episode left scars. After Mesabi and a falling-out with Haywood, Tresca distanced himself from the ıww. Sacco moved away from public participation in the labor movement. He and Rosina were by then carrying a sad burden, grieving the loss of a newborn daughter. Baby Alba died in December 1916, having lived less than a month, "as if," *Cronaca sovversiva* reported, "she did not value this wretched world of ours."[113]

— Bostonians had a lot to think about on September 8, 1919.

There was good news. Babe Ruth, then still playing for the Red Sox, hit his twenty-sixth home run of the season, shattering the existing record that had "endured the onslaughts of Father Time for a fifth of a century."[114]

There was bad news. A rare tornado-like storm swept through sections of Boston, causing death and destruction.

And there was shocking news. After Boston policemen decided to affiliate with the AFL in violation of a police department order, and after the police commissioner suspended nineteen men for the violation, policemen took a vote and overwhelmingly decided to go on strike.[115]

Of the more than thirty-six hundred work stoppages that rattled the United States in the postwar year of 1919, the Boston police strike had to have been the most unsettling.[116] It wasn't that the concept of unionized public employees was new; the AFL had created its first national union of government workers, the National Federation of Post Office Clerks, in 1906, and by 1918 teachers, letter carriers, and firefighters had also formed national unions. It wasn't even that the concept of unionized policemen was new. In June 1919, reversing its previous stance, the AFL decided to charter police locals and, to the chagrin of public officials, granted thirty-seven such charters in three months.[117] But the possible consequences of a unionized police force—divided loyalties, walkouts, and sympathy strikes — greatly alarmed citizens. If policemen were to leave their jobs en masse, who would defend the public safety?

Reaction to the Boston police strike was chaotic and immediate. Rioting and looting sent shock waves through the city. Eight people died and more than seventy were injured. Property worth hundreds of thousands of dollars was stolen or destroyed. Firemen and park police considered the possibility of going out on sympathy strikes.[118]

Three days after the strike began, Samuel Gompers, AFL chief, asked the policemen to go back to work. They agreed to do so, but Massachusetts governor Calvin Coolidge had news for them. They were deserters, not strikers, and would not be reinstated. As Coolidge famously telegraphed Gompers, "There is no right to strike against the public safety by anybody, anywhere, anytime."[119] Coolidge's stand "finished the Policemen's Union once and for all, and at the same time made [him] a national hero."[120]

— Ironically, while the policemen were on strike, former strike supporters Sacco and Vanzetti were at work.

By 1919 Nick, Rosina, and six-year-old Dante had moved closer to Boston. They lived in Stoughton, Massachusetts, where Nick, now 28, trimmed shoe soles for Michael Kelley, the same man who had taught him the craft some ten years earlier. Kelley now owned his own company, Three K. Sacco was a "good workman," Kelley's son George recalled. "The [edge-trimming] position he held was . . . a 'one-man job.' If he was out, the work blocked. . . . He worked very steady from seven in the morning until quitting time at night and was on the job every day that you could expect any healthy man to work."[121] Sometimes Dante came to the factory and stood beside his father's workbench, making a pile of the finished soles. "That boy was my comrade, my friend," Sacco remembered. "He would say, 'Let me help, Papa, I like to help.'"[122] After work, father and son raced each other home.

As he had once guarded his father's vineyards during childhood nights in Torremaggiore, so Nick now guarded property in Stoughton, doing double duty as the night watchman at Three K. Michael Kelley wanted his watchmen to be armed, and Nick carried a gun. He "had the keys to our factory, and the whole thing was in his hands there in the evening after everybody had gone home," Kelley said.[123]

Sacco had also once helped look after his father's gardens. In Stoughton his inner gardener reemerged. The Saccos rented a cottage from Michael Kelley, less than a hundred feet from the boss's own home. Nick planted a garden by the cottage, and tended his vegetables as he had once tended to strike duties in Hopedale — before and after work. He was "in his garden at four o'clock in the morning, and at the factory at seven o'clock, and in his garden again after supper and until nine and ten at night, carrying water and raising vegetables beyond his own needs, which he would bring to me to give to the poor," Michael Kelley recalled.[124]

As for Bartolomeo Vanzetti, he had made a home for himself in Plymouth. "I learned to look upon the place with a real affection," he recalled later, "because as time went on it held more and more of the people dear to my heart." He worked on construction jobs all over the city, to the point where he believed he must have had a hand in building "all the principal public works in Plymouth," including a breakwater near Plymouth Rock.[125]

Feeling that years of backbreaking work and periods of unemployment had sapped his strength, Bartolo looked about for a healthier way to earn a living and, around the time of the police strike, he thought he had found it. A fish peddler he knew was moving back to Italy. Vanzetti bought the man's pushcart, knives, and scales. "[A]nd so [I] became a fish-vender, largely out of love for independence."

The winter of 1919 was "bitter-cold" in Plymouth. Realizing belatedly that "pushing a cart along is not warming work," Vanzetti did odd jobs, cutting ice (which could not have been any warmer than pushing a cart!), shoveling coal, digging ditches, clearing snow, laying a water main. When a railroad strike cut off shipments of construction supplies, Vanzetti went "back to my fish-selling." Sometimes he walked to the shore and dug up clams to sell.[126]

Sacco in Stoughton and Vanzetti in Plymouth must have been as surprised as anyone by the police strike unfolding in nearby Boston. Neither one of them had ever actually joined a union, or gone on strike against a current employer. But both had supported striking workers. Both had witnessed police opposition. They would do so again within a year. This time the issue would not be labor unrest, but murder in cold blood.

I see that I have to be careful and to
remember well if I want to save my life.
— Bartolomeo Vanzetti

5 | CONSTRUCTING A CASE

It was early spring in Massachusetts, but Nicola Sacco, Bartolomeo Vanzetti, and Ricardo Orciani could not enjoy it. On May 6, 1920, they were being held without bail, initially on minor charges: carrying concealed weapons for Sacco and Vanzetti and, for the motorcycle-driving Orciani, speeding and operating a vehicle without a taillight.

Chief Michael Stewart of Bridgewater suspected they were guilty of far worse, and by the evening of May 6 police were reported to have linked the men to three criminal endeavors — not only to those in Bridgewater and South Braintree, but also to a *future* holdup, supposedly planned for that very day.[1]

Prime suspect Mario Buda remained at large, but Chief Stewart was convinced that he had captured at least some of the bandits. He was not in charge of the investigation, however. For now, that responsibility rested with the Massachusetts State Police under the command of veteran investigator Captain William Proctor. (Within two months Stewart would replace Proctor.)[2]

Inspector George Chase, a Brockton police officer, had taken prints of "finger marks" on the Buick that had been found in the woods on April 17.[3] A few days later, state police investigators also made "records of the fingerprint tracings and photographs taken from the bandit auto."[4]

Now, Sacco and Vanzetti were fingerprinted. On May 6 Chase compared their prints to those from the car. The following day, after Chase finished the comparisons, senior police officials met with representatives of the district attorney's office. And there the fingerprint trail stopped. "Nothing is stated about the result" of the meeting, the *Brockton Times* reported. "It is kept a close secret."[5]

Two days later the prints from the car were "thrown away because it soon developed that the car had been handled by several persons before the arrival of the police."[6]

In a capital case, the fingerprint evidence was destroyed. This made it impossible to prove that the prints from the car were flawed, and it left a lingering question: if they were defective, why did investigators try to use them in the first place, looking for a match to the suspects' prints?

"Dactyloscopy," or fingerprint identification, was a relatively new technology; the first murder conviction in the United States based on such evidence had been obtained only ten years earlier, in Chicago in 1910.[7] Massachusetts police in 1920 may not have had the expertise to interpret fingerprint evidence. Or the car prints may have been sound, but not a match. Only this can be stated with assurance: If there had been a match, the prints would have surfaced as evidence at trial, and they did not.

— Without confessions and without fingerprint evidence, investigators would have to make a case using eyewitness identifications or physical evidence.

If Mario Buda and Feruccio Coacci had been part of the South Braintree gang, as Stewart believed, each could now have a cut of the loot. Buda was nowhere to be found, but everyone knew where Coacci was: on his way to Italy under order of deportation, "carrying with him," police believed, "his share of the spoils." But when Coacci landed in Naples and Italian police searched his luggage, they found no trace of the missing money. Nor did investigators find any of the money in Massachusetts — not in Coacci's old room in West Bridgewater and not in a trunk he'd stored in a friend's garage before leaving. Federal agents also checked Carlo Tresca's bank accounts for the money but came up dry.[8] None of the stolen money would ever be found in the possession of any of the suspects or their associates.

Police searched for incriminating physical evidence in the suspects' homes, but came up dry again, finding only a rifle unconnected to the crime, shells, and anarchist books and newspapers in Sacco's house; "a radical newspaper printed in Italian" in Vanzetti's rented room; and "nothing" helpful in Orciani's home.[9]

It appeared that it would be up to eyewitnesses to make or break the case. Dozens of potential witnesses, some in large groups, many escorted by Stewart, came to check out the suspects at the Brockton police station. There police dispensed with customary multi-man lineups, instead presenting each suspect alone.[10] Each was made to strike poses or wear clothes similar to those that witnesses remembered from the crime scenes. "They make me just [pretend] to shoot, wait for somebody to hold up money, with a dirty cap on my head," Sacco recalled. "The second time [a policeman arranged my] hair like that with the hands, and I turned around. . . . [T]hey put . . . the old cap on again."[11] Orciani was made to help stage a crime scene reenactment at South Braintree, so "that people who witnessed the original might be better able to identify [him]."[12]

Results were mixed. One witness from South Braintree and one witness from Bridgewater identified both Sacco and Vanzetti which, if the identifications were correct, meant that both suspects had been involved in both crimes. But several witnesses could not make a positive identification of either man. As for Orciani, one witness positively identified him as one of the Braintree bandits, swearing that the only possibility of a mistake would be if he had seen Orciani's twin.[13]

Arguments continue to this day over how much, if at all, the men's ethnicity and radical political beliefs influenced the case. What is certain is that their nationality and political leanings at once became the subject of local press coverage, in a way that stigmatized the men. Vanzetti had been a "leader" of the Cordage strike, the *Herald* noted.[14] In World War I, he had been "in the last draft and left town, failing to show up for examination," the *Globe* added.[15] Sacco had been "prominent in 1913 in the Draper Corporation mill strike at Hopedale . . . and his sympathies were decidedly radical," according to the *Globe*. "He took part in the Socialist parades and meetings . . . but when draft time arrived for service in the recent war he left Milford."[16] The *Globe* also reported that Sacco had been "one of the agitators" for the Mesabi miners. "He was arrested and paid a fine. It is also said that [he] was included in the draft and disappeared before he was called. The Federal authorities will prosecute him on the charge of being a draft dodger if the other charges fall through."[17] Vanzetti kept "alleged Red literature" in his room.[18] Furthermore, "[b]oth men are Italians," the *Herald* pointed out, and the deported Coacci was one of "the alleged Reds gathered in during the recent raids."[19]

"The American public . . . was doped against us," Vanzetti contended.[20] Rosina Sacco was alarmed; she burned whatever radical books and papers police had left behind in the house.

— After being questioned, and after being displayed to witnesses without legal representation, Nick and Bartolo were surely worried. "I don't know anything about trials, jails," Vanzetti said later. "I was disturbed." Sacco lost ten pounds in the first eight days.[21] Aside from Sacco's arrest for speaking without a permit in 1916, charges later dismissed, neither man had previously been in trouble with the law. But they desperately needed help now.

On Sunday, May 9, 1920, a few friends of Sacco and Vanzetti huddled together. "What to do? We had to form a committee," Aldino Felicani recalled. "[N]obody wanted to have their name associated with it. I said, 'All right, I'll do it. . . .' We had to let people know about this. We had to have other people send contributions."[22]

Felicani and Vanzetti had been friends for a year, since beginning work on a

clandestine anarchist newspaper, *Cara Compagna*. "I trusted Vanzetti the same way I trusted myself. . . . I knew he didn't do [this crime]." Felicani knew Sacco, too, "a fighter well respected everywhere . . . a marvelous human being." It was Vanzetti, though, whom he considered "my real friend."[23]

With the permission of his boss at *La Notizia*, the newspaper where he worked as a printer, Felicani formed the Sacco-Vanzetti Defense Committee. Its earliest members "were all Italians, and were mostly anarchists." In this serious situation, "[w]e really didn't know what to do," Felicani said. "We had no experience actually. I didn't have any connection with any lawyers at all."[24]

The committee hired Brockton lawyer William Callahan. Then, Vanzetti recalled, "I was visited late at night by several of my Plymouth friends, who had come with [attorney John] Vahey in his own automobile. A Mr. Doviglio Govoni was with them."[25] The group convinced Vanzetti to fire Callahan and hire Vahey, with Govoni as his "agent," apparently because Vahey's brother James was a "great lawyer" whom they believed could help if needed. (James Vahey had represented Boston's ill-fated police union.) Vanzetti agreed to the plan. Attorney James Graham was also retained "on the suggestion of a friend."[26] Vanzetti would later regret firing Callahan, and come to think of Govoni, Vahey, and Graham as "betrayers and unfit lawyers."[27]

Govoni may have been a runner, or agent, designated to drum up business for John Vahey. A 1923 study of encounters between immigrants and the

American court system found that runners solicited foreign-born clients for lawyers in return for kickbacks; some runners were court interpreters, as Govoni had once been.[28] More than twenty runners swarmed daily in the corridors of Boston's Municipal Criminal Court in 1918, "[p]retending to have great influence . . ., ready to guarantee the discharge of accused persons, whether innocent or guilty, on payment of a fee." Laws to regulate runners were not enforced, so that by 1923 the Boston courts were "still infested with runners." "[L]awyers who depend for their business upon runners," the study noted, "are only too frequently found engaged in practices of exploitation" such as overcharging, failing to mount an adequate defense, or, worst of all, collaborating with the prosecution[29] — all charges that Vanzetti would eventually level against John Vahey.

∼ Sacco, Vanzetti, Orciani: three suspects for two crimes — until the alibis were checked.

Orciani was released about a week after his arrest. Despite the certitude of the witness who swore he had seen either Orciani or his twin, factory time records showed that Orciani had been at work when both the Bridgewater and South Braintree crimes had been committed.[30] Time records showed that Sacco, too, had been at work during the attempted holdup in Bridgewater, so he could not be charged with that crime, although he remained a suspect for South Braintree.

Only the self-employed Vanzetti had no time records, and Katzmann decided to try him alone, and quickly, for the lesser crime, the attempted robbery at Bridgewater. "If you are charging a man with a crime punishable with death, and at the same time charging him with . . . lesser crimes, the custom is to try him for the bigger crime with which he is charged, and not hamper his defense by bringing in the other cases," a defense attorney would later say in criticism of the district attorney's move.[31]

Katzmann would attribute his decision to the vagaries of court calendars, to defense-requested postponements, and to insufficient early evidence linking Vanzetti to the South Braintree murders. Whatever his reasons, it was a calculated risk, and a canny move. If Katzmann could secure a guilty verdict in the Bridgewater case, then Vanzetti would go on to his next trial as a convicted criminal.

Oh, Johnny! Oh, Johnny! Why do you lag, . . .
You're a big husky chap, Uncle Sam's in a scrap.
You must Go! Johnny, go! Johnny, go!
~ *Songs for Army Men*

6 | "CONSCRIPTION WAS UPON THEM"

Did Bartolomeo Vanzetti join the cheering crowd along the route of the Patriots' Day parade in Plymouth on April 19, 1917? Did he see the marchers proudly sally forth — soldiers and policemen, Boy Scouts and Camp Fire Girls, members of the Bavarian Benefit Society and the Franco-Prussian Veteran Society? Did he agree with the *Old Colony Memorial* newspaper that the parade was "the greatest . . . showing of sentiment that the old town has ever seen"?[1]

Or was he oblivious to the festivities, preoccupied with a plan to leave his beloved Plymouth, to leave the United States, for who knew how long?

Seventeen days earlier, on a cool, damp evening in Washington, D.C., President Woodrow Wilson had asked Congress to declare war against Germany. Wilson had won reelection in 1916 running on the slogan "He kept us out of war" — specifically, the war that had been raging in Europe since 1914.[2] But Wilson had become convinced that American neutrality was no longer an option. Germany's proposed alliance with Mexico, with its secretly promised payoff of "the lost territory" of Texas, Arizona, and New Mexico, and Germany's resumption of sink-at-sight submarine warfare against any ship suspected of trading with the Allies, constituted "nothing less than war against the Government and people of the United States."

"American ships have been sunk, American lives taken . . .," Wilson told a somber assembly of senators and representatives on April 2. "With a profound sense of the solemn and even tragical character of the step I am taking . . . I advise that the Congress . . . formally accept the status of belligerent which has thus been thrust upon it. . . . The world must be made safe for democracy."[3]

Four days later the United States was at war.

The president urged every American — including every farmer, merchant, miner, manufacturer, publisher, clergyman, and thrifty housewife — to do his or her part to support the war effort. "[N]o one," he said, "can now expect ever to be excused or forgiven for ignoring" the dictates of patriotism.[4]

— Fighters were needed to fight the fight. Congress passed the Selective Service Act of May 18, 1917, authorizing a compulsory military draft for the first time since the Civil War. It empowered the president to draft members of the National Guard and National Guard Reserves; to draft half a million former Army and Coast Guard men and graduates of military schools; and to draft an additional half a million men from among "all male citizens, or male persons not alien enemies who have declared their intention to become citizens" between the ages of twenty-one and thirty.[5]

"[I]t shall be the duty of all persons of the designated ages," except those already on active duty, to register for the draft, the law specified. Failure to register could result in a prison term of up to one year.[6]

Registration did not mean that the registrant would automatically be inducted. Only twelve percent of men who registered actually served.[7] Certain categories of registrants were eligible for exemptions, including workers in essential industries, men with dependents, and men who were "physically or morally deficient." Conscientious objectors — defined as people belonging to "any well-recognized religious sect or organization . . . whose existing creed or principles forbid its members to participate in war" — could also be exempted, but were subject to serve in non-combatant status.

Officials designated June 5, 1917, as draft registration day.

— The decision to go to war had not been unanimous. Six senators and fifty representatives had voted against it, and many citizens agreed with them. Some were isolationist; some, unwilling to accept the inevitable mass casualties. Others were angered by what they believed was a conspiracy by the capitalist class to enrich itself; neutrality had already been hugely profitable for American business.[8]

The labor movement was split on the subject of the war. The American Federation of Labor supported the war, and AFL chief Samuel Gompers served on an advisory defense commission. But the Industrial Workers of the World maintained that the only war worth fighting was the class war. "It is better to be a traitor to your country than to your class," Bill Haywood said in 1914.[9]

After the United States joined the battle, however, the IWW became more cautious. "I am at a loss as to definite steps to be taken against the war," Haywood confided in a letter to a fellow Wobbly.[10] The IWW neither took an official position on conscription nor organized resistance against it.[11] Eventually almost all Wobblies who were required to register for the draft did so.

Unlike Bill Haywood, Luigi Galleani had no ambivalence about the war.

In 1917 Galleani was "the most important figure in the Italian anarchist movement in America, winning more converts and inspiring greater devotion than any other single individual . . . [and he] opposed the First World War with all the strength and eloquence at his command," recounts historian Paul Avrich.[12]

An outspoken anarchist with a middle-class upbringing, Galleani arrived in the United States in 1901, at the age of forty, an eloquent zealot with a "hatred of capitalism and government [that] would burn with undiminished intensity for the rest of his life." Constantly in trouble with authorities because of his radical propagandizing, he had lived in prison or in exile for years.[13]

Once in the United States, Galleani settled in New Jersey, then Vermont, and in 1912, the year of the Lawrence strike, he moved to Massachusetts. Wherever he went, he hurled his most effective weapon — words — into the fight for workers' rights and against capitalism. He was said to be a powerful and precise speaker, his voice "full of warmth, his glance alive and penetrating, his gestures of exceptional vigor and flawless distinction." Or, as one listener put it more explicitly, when you heard him speak, "you were ready to shoot the first policeman you saw."[14]

It was as a writer, however, that Galleani exerted his greatest influence. In 1903 he began publishing the weekly anarchist journal, *Cronaca sovversiva*.

Galleani opposed World War I from the beginning as a war in which workers were being forced to fight to benefit capitalists. His slogan in speeches and in the pages of *Cronaca* was direct: "Against war, against peace, for social revolution!"[15] ("Contro la guerra, contro la pace, per la rivoluzione sociale!") Galleani did not soften his position after America entered the fight. On May 26, 1917, ten days before the June 5 registration deadline, he advised his readers that it would be dangerous for them to register. In the future, he argued, non-citizens might become eligible for the draft or for non-combatant service, and if they had registered, their draft boards would know where to find them. On the other hand, if they didn't register, they were unlikely to be found and, even if found, unlikely to be drafted for fear they would make trouble in the Army.[16]

~ To register and comply with the law, or not to register and break the law? Every man had to decide for himself. "Conscription was upon them . . . [and nearly] each man had a different solution," observed IWW chronicler Charles Ashleigh.[17]

On June 5, nearly ten million men showed up to register at four thousand sites across America. To the surprise of officials, there were no serious protests.

When America went to war, artists "rallied to the colors," said George Creel. This iconic 1917 recruitment poster is by James Montgomery Flagg. Dover Publications, Inc.

Enthusiasm ran especially high on college campuses. At Princeton University, President Wilson's former domain, students had to be dissuaded from enlisting en masse even before war was declared. At the University of Wisconsin, students formerly devoted to "the football god gave themselves wholeheartedly to the new master. They marched in new regiments [on campus]. ... They sang new songs." At Pulpit Hill, Thomas Wolfe's fictional stand-in for the University of North Carolina, "[b]efore the month was out, all the young men ... who were eligible ... were going into service. ... The fraternity men joined first."[18]

Nicola Sacco and Bartolomeo Vanzetti were not fraternity men. But in June 1917, Nick, 26, and Bartolo, a month shy of 29, were well within the draft-eligible age range of 21 to 30.

Non-citizens in the United States could be drafted if they had "declared their intention to become [American] citizens." Vanzetti had indeed recently applied to become a citizen.[19] Sacco had not.[20] Under the law, both men were required to register, but only Vanzetti was actually eligible for the draft. Sacco, even if he had qualified for the draft, would have been eligible for exemption as the sole support of a dependent family.

For five years, ever since the Lawrence strike in 1912, Vanzetti had been subscribing to Luigi Galleani's newspaper. Sacco had been subscribing almost as long. Galleani was essentially advising his readers not to register, and many of them decided to take his advice. Quickly, in the days leading up to June 5, the Galleanisti, as his followers were known, went underground. They changed their names. They moved to other towns. They fled to Canada. Or, like Sacco and Vanzetti, they escaped to Mexico.

Sources disagree about the precise moment when Nick Sacco and Bartolomeo Vanzetti first met, but it was at some point during this frantic period in late May 1917, probably when they gathered with other Galleanisti to plan their departures.

~ Nick, Bartolomeo, and a group of fellow Italian anarchists traveled from New York to San Antonio by train, continued on to Laredo, then crossed the Rio Grande and kept going south, to Monterrey.[21] The flight would have serious consequences later, but at the outset it might have seemed like an adventure. More Galleanisti arrived, until between thirty and a hundred draft-evading men (including Mario Buda) formed a kind of commune on the outskirts of Monterrey.[22] They lived in adobe houses, took what jobs they could find, and shared what little they had. One member of the group—possibly Vanzetti, considering his experience as a pastry maker—worked for a while in a bakery.

Bartolo described his first two months south of the border as a period of "projects, hopes, uncertainties, and fears." In a letter to his family in Italy, he said it was impossible to earn a living in Mexico. He intended to remain a little while longer to observe in safety how the draft laws were being enforced, then he would return to the United States. "[T]he threat of conscription and deportation, made by the United States, may be a bluff," he wrote, "and if that's true, so much the better for me." He was in good health. He had read more than a hundred books in Mexico. The family shouldn't worry about him "because life, in this lost Mexico, is as safe as in other places."[23]

For Nick, life in Mexico was strange. He didn't understand the language, he didn't like the food, he couldn't find work as a skilled shoe worker, and "I don't think I did sacrifice to learn a job [just] to go to [hard labor with] pick and shovel in Mexico." The men with whom he shared his voluntary exile formed tight bonds. Still, Sacco said, "I leave my wife [at home] and my boy. I could not stay no more far away from them."[24]

The Mexican interlude was short. The Galleanisti had begun arriving in late May. By early September, just as the first contingent of soldiers from Plymouth was preparing to go overseas to fight the Germans, Sacco had returned to the United States. Vanzetti followed a few weeks later.[25] By November all the Italians who had traveled to Mexico were gone, lured back across the border, perhaps by tales of high wartime wages and low probability of capture and punishment, or perhaps by a desire for revenge against the wartime American government that in June had arrested the man they looked up to, Luigi Galleani.

Why did Sacco and Vanzetti go to Mexico, a flight that was unnecessary for at least one of them? That depends on who is doing the explaining.

Elizabeth Glendower Evans said Nick and Bartolo went to Mexico because they possessed "a certain romantic strain" and because they were ineligible for the draft but didn't know it. John Dos Passos said they went because they were among the few "who were morally opposed to any war or to capitalist war [and] had the nerve to protest." An agent for the Department of Justice, which had the group of anarchists under surveillance, said they went to Mexico because they were learning how to make bombs.[26]

Sacco said he was opposed to World War I because it was a "war for business," not freedom, and because he didn't want to kill people who had not harmed him personally: "I don't believe in no war. I want to destroy those guns." Vanzetti also said he believed war was unjustified, and described himself as a pacifist.[27]

Joseph Moro, an anarchist comrade of Sacco and Vanzetti, may have come closest to the truth when he said that the Italians went to Mexico to be free to fight in the revolution that Luigi Galleani "was certain . . . would break out in Italy any day."[28] Members of the group "were alarmed by the idea that, remaining in the United States, they would be forcibly restrained from leaving for Europe, where the revolution that had burst out in Russia that February promised to spread all over the continent."[29]

When revolution did not spread, and "the reason for remaining together [had] failed," the group broke up.[30]

~ Back in the United States by the fall of 1917, Sacco and Vanzetti found that little had changed. The country was still at war, the draft law was still in effect, and the two slackers, or draft evaders, still needed to avoid arrest. They kept a low profile. They moved around a lot, and used aliases.

Sacco, going by his mother's maiden name, Mosmacotelli, returned to Rosina and Dante in Massachusetts, but not to Milford, where people knew him.[31] He worked in different factories in different towns in the Boston area, doing construction work between factory jobs. Things settled down for him around the time of the Armistice, November 11, 1918, when he went to work for Michael Kelley.

Vanzetti at first stayed away from Massachusetts altogether. Going by the name Negrini, he did factory and construction work in the Midwest. In May 1918 he wrote to "Dearest Papa" from Youngstown, Ohio, where he was working in a steel mill. Wartime production had attracted so many workers to Youngstown, he told his father, that the city resembled "a huge human ant swarm. Everyone speculates off the sweat of the laborers in the most impudent manner."[32] Vanzetti returned to Plymouth the following year. He stopped using an alias and let a year pass before he informed his family in Italy of his whereabouts.

— Life on the lam lasted eighteen months for Nick and Bartolo — the same eighteen months that the United States was at war, the eighteen-month life span of the Committee on Public Information (CPI), and the eighteen-month period when, thanks in no small part to the CPI and its director, George Creel, hyperpatriotism exploded in America.

Creel, an experienced journalist with a genius for hype, took the helm of the newly created committee a mere eight days after the country went to war. He set out to win hearts and minds at home and overseas, and to do it fast. In the process he virtually invented the modern global media campaign.

As Creel saw it, the committee's job was a "fight for the minds of men . . . and the battle-line ran through every home in every country." The war differed from all previous wars "in [the] recognition of Public Opinion as a major force." This "vast enterprise in salesmanship" had one goal: to "weld the people of the United States into one white-hot mass instinct with fraternity, devotion, courage, and deathless determination."[33]

The reach of the CPI would be the envy of any modern publicist. The committee distributed more than seventy-five million pamphlets in the United States, "each one a printed bullet that found its mark." It established a nationwide speakers' bureau of seventy-five thousand "Four Minute Men," volunteers who, Creel claimed, addressed audiences totaling more than 130 million people. Creel arranged for foreign journalists to go on press tours in the United States, and for American reporters to go on inspection tours of the front lines in Europe. The CPI Division of News poured "a steady stream of American information into international channels of communication." And the "best work of the best artists" delivered patriotic messages from CPI-commissioned posters.[34]

With the CPI harnessing public opinion, the country at war, and American troops at risk, tolerance waned. School districts banned the teaching of German. Public libraries removed German-language books from their shelves.

Symphony orchestras eliminated German composers from their repertoires. In a phenomenon that would recur at a time of anti-French sentiment in 2003, when French fries were temporarily renamed "Freedom fries" in the cafeteria of the United States House of Representatives, so in 1917 sauerkraut morphed into liberty cabbage; hamburgers into liberty sandwiches; and dachshunds into liberty pups.

In such an atmosphere, a new, government-sanctioned organization, the American Protective League (APL), attracted hundreds of thousands of volunteers, men eager for military service but too old to be drafted, or otherwise exempt. They "embarked on unwarranted searches and seizures, detained and arrested draft-age men without charges, intimidated allegedly disloyal Americans, and broke up strikes."[35] By 1918 league members had focused on draft dodgers. They staged so-called slacker raids in several cities, rounding up thousands of alleged draft evaders, almost all of whom were quickly released.

The patriotism of the APL and its ilk was, said George Creel, "a thing of . . . extremes; they outjingoed the worst of the jingoes." Creel believed that "the overwhelming majority of aliens [had] an almost passionate desire to serve America that was impeded at every turn by the meannesses of chauvinism and the brutalities of prejudice."[36] He regretted that he was unable to convince other Americans of this.

At the other end of the spectrum, former president Theodore Roosevelt declared that "[i]f a man is not an American, and nothing else, he should be sent out of this country. . . . And, incidentally, I wish to say that is my view of the conscientious objector, too."[37]

~ Twenty-one thousand American men who were inducted into the Army during the First World War claimed conscientious objector status — twenty-one thousand out of nearly three million inductees and an overall total of twenty-four million registrants.[38] The Army eventually recognized about four thousand men as conscientious objectors. Most of them accepted non-combatant service, but some five hundred who did not were imprisoned.[39]

The federal government set up a board of inquiry during the war to determine the sincerity of conscientious objectors. Major Walter Kellogg of the Judge Advocate General's Office chaired the board. "Numerically, the problem [of conscientious objectors] indeed is of small importance," Kellogg conceded, but "as a matter of principle it is of great importance."[40]

Objectors fell into three categories, according to Kellogg: those with objections based on religion, idealism, or socialism. Kellogg, who personally interviewed many of them, viewed them all with an equally jaundiced eye, seeing the religious objector as "a moron"; the idealist objector as impractical and "half-baked"; and the socialist objector as intelligent but fanatical, "egotistical and self-centered . . . simply 'nuts.'"[41]

Kellogg's harsh assessments were, comparatively speaking, generous. Other observers decried conscientious objectors as cowards and enemy sympathizers. Even objectors who performed alternative service on farm furloughs sparked resentment. "For many Americans, 'conscientious objector' was just a fancy term for 'slacker,'" writes historian Christopher Capozzola.[42]

On Army bases or inside prisons, this emotion found expression. Conscientious objector Ernest Meyer recalled hearing of others who experienced beatings, restraints, solitary confinement, and bread-and-water diets. Meyer himself was taunted on base as a traitor and a yellowback, and threatened with lynching and running the gauntlet.[43]

⏤ The Selective Service Act of 1917 granted exemptions not only to conscientious objectors but also to men with dependents.

Boxer Jack Dempsey registered for the draft, but claimed exemption as the main support of his wife, mother, father, widowed sister, and her three children. While the country was mobilizing in 1917, Dempsey was winning nine straight fights, staking his claim to a championship match. His manager told reporters that between bouts Dempsey was helping his country by working in a shipyard.[44]

Two events persuaded people that the boxer was a slacker. A photograph of Dempsey at the shipyard turned out to have been staged, and Dempsey's now former wife accused him of not having supported her. After a sensational trial in 1920, a jury acquitted Dempsey of draft dodging.

Neither the acquittal nor the world heavyweight title, which Dempsey won in 1919, prevented boxing fans and sportswriters from taunting him as "Slacker Jack." He was denounced on the floor of the United States House of Representatives as a slacker and a "big bum." The insults never stopped. "I'm walking down a street in New York," Dempsey recalled years later. "Or I'm on some street out in Hollywood and here comes someone yelling out a car window 'slacker.' . . . I heard them all the time."[45]

Dempsey lived a long, productive life. But when he died in 1983 at the age of eighty-seven, the *New York Times* noted that, in addition to his many accomplishments, he had been "reviled as a slacker during World War I, and . . . the odium clung to him."[46]

— In the court of public opinion, legal exemptions didn't matter very much. Men who qualified as conscientious objectors and men who supported dependents were all legally draft-exempt, but scorned as slackers nonetheless.

Stealth draft dodgers, those without legal exemptions, could fare even worse. More than three hundred thousand men who registered for the draft went into hiding to avoid service, and as many as three million eligible men didn't register at all.[47] They simply went underground. Rarely were they arrested or prosecuted. Their crime went with them to the grave unless, like Nicola Sacco and Bartolomeo Vanzetti, they ran up against the law again. Then their secret emerged in the harsh glare of a courtroom.

Perhaps no one symbolized the hated stealth draft dodger better than a wealthy young Philadelphian of German descent with the improbable name of Grover Cleveland Bergdoll. He registered for the draft in June 1917 but then went into hiding, reportedly because he didn't want to fight against Germany, the land of his ancestors.[48] When Bergdoll ran away he kicked off a twenty-year saga of capture, court-martial, imprisonment, escape, manhunts, and life as a fugitive in Germany.[49] His very public success at avoiding kidnapping attempts and extradition made him a hero to Germans,[50] but such a thorn in the side of Americans that Congress repeatedly investigated him and his family, with one congressman actually pulling a gun on Bergdoll's brother on the House floor.[51] In 1939, twenty-two years after registering for the draft, Bergdoll returned to the United States voluntarily and served a prison sentence for desertion.[52]

— Contempt for draft dodgers did not end when the war ended.

In 1924, six years after the Armistice and three years after the trial of Sacco and Vanzetti, a Boston newspaper opined that it was "as difficult today as in the most harrowing periods of the war, at least to the average, full-blooded patriotic American citizen, to look upon the conscientious objector or the draft evader with calmness. . . . It did not seem possible that in time of such extreme danger to all that was dear in American life, large groups of young men could refuse to help at all their country."[53]

Personal choices made in wartime linger. Jack Dempsey was the Manassa Mauler, but he remained Slacker Jack — as Jane Fonda, decades later, was both Barbarella and Hanoi Jane.

Nicola Sacco and Bartolomeo Vanzetti made their personal choices in wartime. When their adopted country went to war, their boots were not on the ground.

Their decision had nothing to do with their Italian ancestry. An estimated three hundred thousand Italians served in the U.S. Army during World War I.[54]

Remember Your First Thrill of
AMERICAN LIBERTY

YOUR DUTY-*Buy*
United States Government *Bonds*
2nd Liberty Loan of 1917

A 1917 poster by an unknown artist urges immigrants to support their adopted country. During the war, posters were used to influence public opinion in what George Creel called the "battle of the fences." Dover Publications, Inc.

One hundred seventy-nine Italian-born residents of Massachusetts died while serving. Although non-citizens who had not applied for American citizenship were not eligible for the draft, many volunteered and served anyway. The official record of Massachusetts war dead noted "the large number of voluntary enlistments of foreign-born in our forces, especially of men who might have claimed exemption from the draft."[55]

Hundreds of thousands of Italians also worked on the "inner lines" in American defense industries. There was "no shipyard, ammunition-factory, airplane-factory, steel mill, mine, lumber-camp, or docks in which the Italians did not play a large part, and often the most prominent part, in actual and efficient work . . . with full and affectionate loyalty toward the government of the United States," said George Creel.[56] When bonds were sold, Italians "poured out their means in Liberty Loans."[57]

Sacco and Vanzetti were not part of this community. By 1917 they belonged to a much smaller and very different group of Italian-Americans, anarchists unequivocally opposed to the war. Sacco actually lost one job because he refused to buy a Liberty bond.[58]

Motives for draft evasion were irrelevant as far as public opinion was concerned. No one cared why Sacco and Vanzetti fled, only that they did flee. They would never be able to shake their image as unpatriotic, draft-dodging immigrants, and they knew it. Sacco assumed he was arrested "because I was active in the movement of labor work and because I was a slacker."[59] Vanzetti believed "we were really tried not for murder, but for being Radicals, draft evaders, and pacifists."[60] The two men must have come to regret their flight to Mexico and their life in hiding, if only for the way it later colored people's perceptions of them. In his autobiography, *The Story of a Proletarian Life*, Vanzetti makes no mention of his life as a fugitive, as if it had never happened.

When Sacco and Vanzetti went on trial in 1921, World War I had been over for three years, but doughboys and draft dodgers were still in the news.

In the midst of the trial, Jack Dempsey defended his heavyweight championship against Georges Carpentier of France. It was the "Battle of the Century," the first million-dollar gate in boxing history, and it was punctuated by catcalls of "Slacker" ringing out in the huge stadium built for the event.[61]

Also in the midst of the trial, Americans read about a Pennsylvanian named Russell Gross, identified as the soldier "whom destiny called to fill the place in the firing line which should have been [Grover Cleveland] Bergdoll's." Bergdoll was alive, but Gross was dead. "In the War Department records the blackest lines which can be written next the name of a man are beside that of Bergdoll."[62]

When Vanzetti, then Sacco, took the stand at trial, each was cross-examined about his motives for dodging the draft. The questioning was prejudicial and irrelevant to the crimes with which they were charged, but it ensured that if jurors had missed early press coverage, they would still know that the men before them were non-registrants and slackers — at best, lawbreakers; at worst, traitors.

Suassos Lane is just an alley
Up here in old north Plymouth
You saw my fish cart
Roll here in Suassos Lane
— Woody Guthrie, "Suassos Lane"

7 | Dry Run at Plymouth

The Italians of Plymouth were concerned. In the rented rooms and company housing, at the Amerigo Vespucci and Cristoforo Colombo clubs, at Broccoli's Market and the Plymouth Theater, on Suosso Lane, Court Street, Cherry Street, and South Cherry Street, people were talking. The housewives, the barbers and bakers, the fishermen and boat builders, the textile workers and rope makers and sardine packers, the *paesani* who measured their days by clockwork blasts of factory whistles — they were talking about Bartolomeo Vanzetti.

The fish peddler was about to go where they hoped never to have to go themselves, into an American courtroom. The two charges against him: assault with intent to rob and assault with intent to murder in the attempted robbery of the L. Q. White Shoe Company in Bridgewater on December 24, 1919.

Vanzetti's neighbors tended to disapprove of his politics. The majority of them "were not anarchists but ordinary Italians and mostly devout Catholics. They had no sympathy for Vanzetti's views. But they had bought eels from him [that day] and knew that he was innocent" of the crime at Bridgewater.[1]

His customers might be poor and uneducated and unskilled in the English language. They might fear the American legal system. But Vanzetti needed them. They possessed something more precious to him than gold: an alibi.

— *Commonwealth vs. Bartolomeo Vanzetti* opened on June 22, 1920, at Superior Court in Plymouth. (Bridgewater, scene of the attempted crime, is part of Plymouth County.) District attorney Fred Katzmann headed up the prosecution, aided by William Kane. Representing Vanzetti were attorneys John Vahey and James Graham.

Police chief Michael Stewart drove "Bertie" Vanzetti from Plymouth Jail to the courthouse each morning during the trial. Vanzetti must have been confident of victory at first because, according to Stewart, "he used to sing songs for us in Italian on the way over, and he had quite a voice." After Stewart testified, however, he said that Vanzetti "never spoke to me again."[2]

Overseeing the proceedings was Judge Webster Thayer, 64, of Worcester.

Thayer, despite his wizened appearance in later years, had once been an outstanding athlete, captain of both the baseball and football teams at Dartmouth College in the 1870s. After graduation he returned to Worcester and read law for two years in the office of a local attorney. Admitted to the state bar in 1882, Thayer practiced law in Worcester and dabbled in local politics for the next thirty-five years. He deeply regretted that he had been too old to enlist in the Army in 1917,[3] but was cheered when, that same year, Governor Samuel McCall, a Dartmouth classmate, appointed him to a judgeship on the Superior Court.

Thayer's tenure on the bench had been unremarkable until an incident in April 1920 put him on page 1. Sergis Zakoff, a man on trial for the crime of advocating anarchy, was found not guilty. Jurors interpreted Judge Thayer's instructions as meaning that the defendant had to have actually used violence, not merely spoken about it, in order to be found guilty.[4]

Thayer took the unusual step of rebuking the jury for its decision.

If Bartolomeo Vanzetti had known about this, perhaps he wouldn't have been singing on his way to the courthouse.

~ Opening for the prosecution in Plymouth, assistant district attorney William Kane said the state would show that Vanzetti was part of a gang that had tried to rob a truck in Bridgewater on December 24, 1919, and, specifically, that he was the bandit who held and fired a shotgun and who escaped in a getaway car — the stolen Buick found in the woods on April 17.

Two witnesses who had been inside the truck during the attempted robbery identified Vanzetti as the shotgun-toting bandit. Guard Benjamin Bowles was "positive" and paymaster Alfred Cox was "sure," although, he said, "I can't say that I am positive." Their identifications had been more tentative at the preliminary hearing on May 18, when Bowles had been "pretty positive" and Cox had expressed "a doubt. . . . I think [Vanzetti] looks enough like the man to be the man."[5] (The third person who had been inside the truck, driver John Graves, died before Vanzetti was arrested.)

Two other witnesses also identified Vanzetti as the shotgun bandit. Passerby Frank Harding said he had seen Vanzetti at the crime scene, "running, . . . a gun in his right hand." Harding had first made this identification after Vanzetti's arrest, and had reiterated it at the preliminary hearing.[6] And paperboy Maynard Shaw, 14, said that as he started his route on the day of the crime, he got a "fleeting glance" of a man with a gun, and the man was Vanzetti. Young Shaw insisted he knew the shotgun bandit was a foreigner, either an Italian or a Russian, "by the way he ran."[7] Shaw had not testified at the preliminary hearing.

Georgina Brooks identified Vanzetti, not as the gunman but as the man she had seen at the wheel of a parked car as she walked to the Bridgewater railroad station moments before the attempted robbery. He "was a foreigner" and gave her a "severe" look from the car, where he sat with three other men. Brooks had given similar testimony at the preliminary hearing.[8]

Vanzetti was the sole defendant, but sometimes it seemed as if he had a co-defendant — his extravagant big, bushy walrus mustache, the most noticeable and prominent feature on his face. The mustache took on a life of its own at the trial in Plymouth.

The previous December, just hours after the attempted holdup, Bowles and Cox, when questioned by Pinkerton detectives, had described the gunman's mustache as "closely cropped," while Harding said he "did not get much of a look at [the shotgun bandit's] face."[9] (The defense did not see these Pinkerton reports until 1927.)

Five months later, at the preliminary hearing on May 18, Bowles and Cox still described the shotgun bandit's mustache as "short [and] croppy," while Harding, the man who "did not get much of a look at [the bandit's] face," nevertheless now described the bandit's mustache as one that "seemed to be croppy. Not little and small, but one trimmed up."

By the time of the trial in June, the mustache had morphed into one miraculously resembling the very specimen blooming on the upper lip of the defendant. Bowles said he had been wrong to call the bandit's mustache cropped. "I meant trimmed instead of cropped." Cox, too, rejected his previous description of "croppy," now insisting that the mustache in question had been simply "short and well-trimmed." And Harding now described the mustache as heavy, dark, and trimmed, denying that anything had happened to make him drop the word "croppy" from his earlier description. Despite the fact that Harding had said he did not get a good look at the bandit's face, he also now described the bandit's high forehead, high cheekbones, broad face, bullet-shaped head, and ruddy complexion.[10]

Vanzetti had his own explanation for the evolution of testimony by the eyewitnesses: the bandit they saw and described at the preliminary hearing was "a very different man than I. . . . So when they testified at the trial, they did their best to modify as much as possible their former testimony about the physical appearance of the bandit who should have been me."[11]

Several defense witnesses, including a policeman, testified that Vanzetti's mustache in Plymouth "always looked the same," had never been cropped, and had "always [been] long."[12]

— The defense called no eyewitnesses to the attempted robbery, choosing instead to build a case that rested almost entirely on Vanzetti's alibi. Fourteen witnesses testified that the fish peddler had been selling eels from his pushcart in Plymouth when the bandits struck in Bridgewater, as well as later that same day.

"To eat eels and fish on Christmas Eve is with the Italian people an ancient tradition," Vanzetti later explained. (Elizabeth Glendower Evans called the custom the "equivalent of turkeys on Thanksgiving Day among Yankees.") On December 24 the fish peddler was selling eels that his customers had already ordered. Advance ordering was a novelty; its "newness and the solemnity of the day . . . made the thing memorable to my customers," Vanzetti said.[13]

As the fourteen alibi witnesses — all Italian, most requiring an interpreter — described Vanzetti's transactions, they established a chronology that ran from the evening of December 23 through the afternoon of December 25.

Mary Fortini, Vanzetti's landlady in 1919, said that a barrel of eels had been delivered to her house on December 22 or 23. Vanzetti ate supper at the house at 6:00 in the evening of December 23, she said, then went out for a short while. He spent that time visiting his friends and former landlords, the Brinis, according to thirteen-year-old Beltrando Brini and his mother, Alfonsina Brini, who both also said that Vanzetti asked the boy to help out with deliveries the next day.[14]

Vanzetti returned home about 8:00 in the evening on December 23, according to Mrs. Fortini, and he worked in her kitchen until midnight packaging the eels for his customers. On December 24, at 6:15 in the morning, she called upstairs to wake him. A customer was waiting, Carlo Balboni, on his way home after working the night shift as a fireman at the Cordage. Vanzetti dressed quickly, came downstairs in his stocking feet, gave Balboni his order, had a cup of warm milk for breakfast, put on a pair of shoes, and went out to start the deliveries.[15]

At about 7:05 a.m. on December 24, Vanzetti delivered eels to the house of factory worker Vincent Longhi on Cherry Street; Longhi said he remembered the time because he was putting on his coat to go catch the 7:10 streetcar to work. Housewife Rosa Balboni said she saw Vanzetti making a delivery in the street at around the same time, while she was walking to a bakery oven on Cherry Street.[16]

Between 7:00 and 7:40, Vanzetti delivered eels to shoemaker John Di-Carli, who said he remembered the time because he was cleaning the shop after opening at 7:00. Between 7:00 and 8:00, Vanzetti delivered eels to the home of housewife Terese Malauci; she said she established the time because she knew the delivery had taken place between the 7:00 and 8:00 factory whistles.[17]

Baker Enrico Bastoni said Vanzetti came to see him just before 8:00 a.m.; he fixed the time by the Cordage whistle, which blew "just a few minutes" later. Vanzetti wanted to borrow Bastoni's horse for his deliveries, but the baker needed the animal himself.[18]

At about 7:30 young Beltrando Brini said he spoke to Vanzetti on Court Street. The boy then spoke to his father, Vincenzo Brini, who had come home from the night shift at the Cordage and was taking bread dough to a bakery oven on Court Street. His father told him to go home and put on a pair of boots before going out to help Vanzetti. Beltrando said he did so, then went to Vanzetti's lodgings, arriving at about 8:00.[19] Mrs. Fortini said she saw Vanzetti with Beltrando in the front yard.[20]

Between 9:00 and 10:00 in the morning, Vanzetti delivered eels to housewife Margaretta Fiochi. During the same time frame, Fiochi's neighbor, Adeladi Bonjionanni, received her order of eels from the Brini boy, but she saw Vanzetti, too, when she went outside to get change from him.[21]

Between 10:30 and 10:45, Vanzetti delivered an order to another neighbor, Emma Borsari. Just after 11:00, Beltrando delivered eels to the Christophori home, said daughter Esther Esteno Christophori. Around noon, Vanzetti went back to his lodgings for lunch, according to Mrs. Fortini, then left again around 12:30 to finish his deliveries.[22]

Sometime between 5:00 and 5:30, Vanzetti returned home, ate supper, and went out. He visited the Brinis. Beltrando and Vincenzo Brini both testified that Vanzetti spent that Christmas Eve with their family at home. Rose Forni, who boarded with the family, also said she saw Vanzetti at the Brini house that evening, slipping some money into the children's Christmas stockings. In his stocking the next day, Beltrando said, he found two half-dollars, a two-dollar bill, and other small gifts. After lunch on Christmas Day, Vanzetti visited the family again according to the testimony of Beltrando and Vincenzo Brini.[23]

The Bridgewater bandits had struck at about 7:30 in the morning of December 24. Eight witnesses had now put Vanzetti on the streets of Plymouth between 7:00 and 8:00 on that day. If they were correct, Vanzetti's alibi was ironclad.

Eight witnesses also put Vanzetti in Plymouth later in the day on December 24 (including two who had seen him that morning as well) and on December 25. If they were correct, Vanzetti's actions were precisely those to be expected of a working fish peddler, not of a thwarted gunman.[24]

— Vanzetti's alibi witnesses came from North Plymouth, the heavily Italian part of town. Most were unassimilated but hardworking immigrants. The district attorney would have had a hard time impeaching their credibility by challenging their reputations. Instead he attacked their recall ability and implied that they were lying to protect a friend and countryman. (According to Vanzetti, Katzmann warned jurors that "the dagoes stand together," but this remark does not appear in the incomplete trial transcript that survives.)[25]

Katzmann was a skilled and effective cross-examiner. In *Commonwealth vs. Bartolomeo Vanzetti* Katzmann could deploy his tactics easily, since one of the defense witnesses was a child and most of the others had a poor grasp of English.

Katzmann disparaged the cues—the factory whistles, streetcar schedules, and holiday preparations—that defense witnesses used to reconstruct the events of December 24, suggesting that since most of these cues occurred on a regular basis they didn't differentiate one day from another. He also contended that witnesses had concocted and rehearsed false alibis. Beltrando Brini bore the brunt of this line of questioning, accused by Katzmann of memorizing the story of how he had helped Vanzetti on December 24, "just like a piece at school."

"I did not learn [my story] by heart," the boy insisted.[26]

"I was only thirteen then and I was scared. I'd never been in a court before," Brini later recalled. "I *was* there with [Vanzetti] all that morning long, and I couldn't make them believe me."[27]

— The issue of consciousness of guilt became a factor in Vanzetti's trial when Austin Cole testified.

Chief Stewart had read his interrogation of Vanzetti into the record, including Vanzetti's denial that he had been in Bridgewater or West Bridgewater prior to the night of his arrest. If the prosecution could prove otherwise, Judge Thayer said, then that would be consciousness of guilt, because "the Court says that . . . an innocent man tells the truth."[28]

Cole, a streetcar conductor, testified for the prosecution that Vanzetti had twice been a passenger on his Bridgewater–Brockton route, once in April 1920 and once in May, and that each time Vanzetti boarded the car in West Bridgewater. If Cole was correct, then Vanzetti was lying.[29]

— Katzmann wanted to prove that the Buick stolen in Needham in November 1919, the getaway car used in Bridgewater in December 1919, and the Buick found in the woods near Brockton in April 1920 were one and the same car.

Francis Murphy, owner of the stolen car, identified the Buick now in police custody as his. (Judge Thayer was nonplussed to discover that Murphy's car had not been returned to him, but that the state police were using it.[30])

Connecting the car to Bridgewater was problematic. College student Richard Casey testified that he had seen a dark Buick in Bridgewater at 7:20 a.m. on December 24, 1919, and John King said that he had also seen a dark Buick pass by that day at around 7:30.[31]

However, the now-deceased John Graves had told a detective on the day of the crime that the car was a Hudson. Frank Harding, who testified at trial that the car was a Buick, told a detective on the day of the crime that it was "a black Hudson #6 auto." Benjamin Bowles said at trial that the car was a dark Buick, but admitted on cross-examination that he hadn't paid any attention to the car's make. Alfred Cox said only that the bandits' vehicle was "a heavy touring car."[32]

Linking the car to Vanzetti proved impossible. Napoleon Ensher of West Bridgewater testified that he had once seen Mario Buda drive a Buick but, said the judge, that "of itself is of no significance." And Rose Forni and Enrico Bastoni both testified that they had never seen Vanzetti drive a car at all. Indeed, Vanzetti did not know how to drive, a fact the defense failed to use to rebut

Georgina Brooks's identification of him as the man she had seen behind the wheel.[33]

~ Ballistics testimony in the Plymouth courtroom was confusing and marked by loose-to-nonexistent chain of custody procedures — a foreshadowing of the upcoming trial at Dedham.

John Murphy, a doctor with an office near the Bridgewater crime scene, testified that he heard shots fired on December 24, ran into the street to see if anyone was hurt, and picked up a spent 12-gauge Winchester shell, which he identified as the one shown him in court. Police officer Michael Connolly then testified that Vanzetti had four shells in his pocket when arrested on May 5, including a 12-gauge Winchester. Four shells were admitted in evidence as Vanzetti's, but they were not marked to differentiate them from each other, and Connolly did not identify them positively as Vanzetti's shells.[34]

It would be "stretching the story to absolute limit," John Vahey argued, to attempt to connect one shell found on a Bridgewater street in December to another shell found in someone's pocket in Brockton four months later. "[U]ntil the Commonwealth has more firmly established the connection . . . this evidence ought to be excluded," Vahey continued. "It seems to me you might just as well say that if [Vanzetti] is guilty of one crime — and we are trying him for one crime — he is guilty of another. . . . [I]t would be doing this defendant a gross injustice."[35]

The only additional ballistics testimony came from Captain Proctor of the state police. He identified two of the four shells said to have been taken from Vanzetti as Winchesters, contradicting Connolly, who had said only one was a Winchester.[36] Vahey tried to establish that the Winchester shell picked up on the street in Bridgewater contained birdshot, but neither Murphy nor Proctor was definitive on this point.

~ The most important witness in the Plymouth trial never took the stand.

Bartolomeo Vanzetti did plan to testify at first. "[H]e will give you the names [and] numbers of persons he saw" on December 24, co-counsel James Graham told jurors in the opening statement for the defense.[37]

"I was willing to take the stand," Vanzetti later wrote, "but [as time went by] Mr. Vahey opposed and resisted it until I accepted his will. . . . He asked me how I would explain from the stand the meaning of Socialism, or Communism, or Bolshevism. . . . At such a query, I would begin an explanation on these subjects, and Mr. Vahey would cut it off. . . . 'Hush, if you will tell such things to the ignorant, conservative jurors, they will send you to the state prison right away.' I contend that was . . . an excuse to hinder me from testifying, because Mr. Vahey . . . knew that he could have impeded the district attorney in putting such political questions."[38]

Nearly forty years later, James Graham disputed Vanzetti's assertion. Graham said that he and Vahey spent considerable time with Vanzetti at the Plymouth Jail. "Mr. Vahey said . . . 'I can advise you . . . but you are the one who has got to make the decision as to whether you will testify or not,' and it was after that that Vanzetti wanted me to go up to Dedham [Jail] and talk to Sacco. After I [did so] . . . and the case was further discussed, he said, in substance, 'I don't think I can improve upon the alibi which has been established. I had better not take the stand.'" There was no fear that Vanzetti's radical politics might become an issue, Graham continued, "because his connection with 'Bolshevism,' as it was called in those days, did not ever enter into the trial."[39]

This was not accurate. Katzmann cross-examined witnesses about Vanzetti's politics. "Have you not discussed governmental theories . . . between you? . . . Have you discussed the question of the poor man and the rich man . . . ?" Katzmann asked shoemaker John DiCarli. "Do you belong to any organization that Vanzetti belongs to? . . . Do you know anything of his political beliefs? . . . Have you ever heard him make any speeches to fellow workers at the Cordage?" Katzmann asked Matthew Sassi. "Did you hear [Vanzetti and your father] talk about our government? . . . Did your papa and Vanzetti and the baker belong to any society or organization? . . . Did you ever hear Mr. Vanzetti making any speeches to the Italians?" Katzmann asked Beltrando Brini.[40]

Vanzetti thought that Vahey had betrayed him, but Herbert Ehrmann, who represented the defense in the late stages of the case, believed the decision to keep Vanzetti off the stand was justifiable. His alibi was solid, and the defense had a strong case without his testimony.

~ On July 1, 1920, a thousand Congregationalist church members visited Plymouth Rock. Town planners continued preparations for the upcoming tercentenary of the Pilgrims' landing. And *Commonwealth vs. Bartolomeo Vanzetti* went to the jury.

Inside the jury room, curious members of the panel decided to open one or two of the four shotgun shells said to have been in Vanzetti's pocket when he was arrested.[41]

Testimony had not established whether the shells contained birdshot or buckshot. The jury wanted to know, and decided to find out. If they contained birdshot, then intent to murder would be unlikely, but if they contained the larger pellets of buckshot, murderous intent might be inferred. The jury opened the shells and found buckshot.

At 4:20 p.m., less than five and a half hours after beginning deliberations, jurors announced the verdict: guilty of assault with intent to murder on three counts, and guilty of assault with intent to rob on one count. "If I had not seen the contents of the shell, my verdict would [have been] not guilty . . . of . . . intent to murder," one juror said later.[42]

Judge Thayer thanked jurors for dealing with the case "in accordance with the law. . . . You may go to your homes with the feeling that you did respond as the soldier responded to his service when he went across the seas to the call of the Commonwealth. I thank you, gentlemen."[43]

"We were just in despair," Vanzetti's friend, Aldino Felicani, recalled.[44]

Policemen cuffed Vanzetti to take him back to jail. "[H]e turned to his fellow-countrymen in the courtroom, who had been in attendance every day of the trial," the *Globe* reported, "and in Italian shouted, 'Courage!' "[45]

Independence Day was three days off, but there would be no independence in Vanzetti's future.

After the trial, in a store in Brockton, one of the jurors ran into Judge Thayer and showed him a pellet of buckshot he had kept as a souvenir from the jury room. Thus the judge learned what the jury had done in secret during its deliberations. When Katzmann was informed, he retrieved the souvenir pellets, and cautioned the jurors to keep quiet about what they had done.[46]

Defendants have the right to be tried on evidence in open court. For Vanzetti, this right had been violated, but so far only the judge, the jury, and the prosecutor knew what had happened. "Some judges would have ordered a mistrial or a new trial," Herbert Ehrmann observed. Thayer did not, nor did he make a note for the record about what he had learned.[47]

Thayer scheduled sentencing for August 16. On that cloudy summer day, the courthouse was heavily guarded, with officers "at every entrance and exit to be ready for any trouble." The police car bringing the prisoner to court was followed by another car, carrying officers "armed with riot guns."[48] Authorities were said to fear that sympathizers might try to grab Vanzetti and escape.[49]

Katzmann asked for a stiff sentence for the convicted man, while Vahey argued for leniency since no one had been hurt in Bridgewater, nothing had been stolen, and it was the defendant's first offense. Then Thayer spoke at length. Aldino Felicani recalled the judge linking "Vanzetti's political ideas to crimes," and Vanzetti recalled the judge saying that "the defendant's ideals are cognate with the crime,"[50] but these statements do not appear in the incomplete record of Thayer's remarks that survives. Thayer sentenced Vanzetti to twelve to fifteen years in Charlestown State Prison on one of the two charges against him: assault with intent to rob.

"[T]he Plymouth people [were] flabbergasted" by the sentence, said Felicani.[51]

Lawyer Robert Montgomery, in his book in support of the prosecution's case, argues that the evidence tampering that took place in the jury room, while improper, was harmless, "because Judge Thayer imposed [Vanzetti's] sentence on one count only, assault with intent to *rob*." But, Herbert Ehrmann points out, the "effect . . . was to cut the ground from under any [future] moves by the defense based on the jury's wrongful act, and still give due weight to the buckshot evidence by imposing a heavy sentence."[52]

Vanzetti had been confined in local jails in Brockton and Plymouth. That was about to change. "A few hours after the sentence I heard the iron door of [Charlestown State Prison] closing itself at my shoulder," he recalled; "a few minutes after that I was in a dark cell."[53]

⁓ Just as the 1916 strike at the Plymouth Cordage Company might have vanished from the annals of labor history if not for the connection to Vanzetti, so the trial for attempted robbery in Bridgewater might be unknown today if not for the impact it had on the joint trial of Sacco and Vanzetti.

The two men "would never have been found guilty of murder and executed if Vanzetti had not been framed in the earlier case," said defense supporter Art Shields. "The conviction . . . destroyed the presumption of innocence." Other supporters agreed. "[A]t Dedham, the fact that Vanzetti was already serving time . . . went far toward condemning him . . . and it served to drag down Sacco too," said Elizabeth Glendower Evans. Vanzetti himself said that his "Plymouth conviction was a stepping stone toward the electric chair, for both of us."[54] Indeed, later research has found that defendants with prior criminal records who are subsequently convicted of first-degree murder are more likely to receive the death penalty than defendants with a similar conviction but no prior record.[55]

Katzmann owed his victory at Plymouth as much to defense failures as to his own skills. He discredited the defense's strong alibi evidence by asking witnesses impossible questions about random events on random dates, but defense attorneys did not explain the technique to jurors.

Ehrmann believed that Vahey and Graham were competent but fallible. A bitter Vanzetti put a less benign spin on things. He charged that Vahey deliberately sabotaged the defense, selling him out "as a rabbit is sold at a market." Vahey "asked me very little concerning my defense," Vanzetti said. "On the contrary, he began to promise me the electric chair," while crudely miming the effects of electrocution.[56]

Members of the small defense committee felt duped. Aldino Felicani said that Vahey and Graham "didn't put up the fight I expected them to put up. . . . [They] performed just in a perfunctory way."[57]

— After the trial, Carlo Tresca went to Boston to meet with Felicani. Tresca had been the target of a long smear campaign by anarchist Luigi Galleani, but Galleani was now in Italy, having been deported a year earlier, and "Tresca, by 1920, was indisputably the most important Italian radical in the United States," according to historian Nunzio Pernicone. Tresca was "very critical of us for not having hired a radical lawyer in the very beginning," Felicani recalled. "We didn't ask Tresca for help. He came to see us and offered help."[58]

Back in New York, Tresca asked Elizabeth Gurley Flynn to meet with Felicani on an upcoming trip to Boston. "[T]wo Italian comrades [are] in big trouble in Massachusetts," he told her. "[G]et the Americans to help." Defense committee members pleaded with Flynn and a Boston colleague, Marion Emerson, "to do two things — arrange some protest meetings with English speakers . . ., and help them get a labor lawyer."

Flynn found that "Fred Moore, the IWW lawyer, was in [New York]. . . . Carlo and I asked him to go to Boston, to meet with the . . . committee and investigate the case. We urged him favorably to consider undertaking their defense. He spent a few weeks there and finally decided to do so."[59]

On August 19, 1920, three days after Vanzetti was sentenced, Felicani gave Moore five hundred dollars to retain his services for the upcoming trial of Sacco and Vanzetti.

Fred Moore was on the case. His imprint would prove indelible.

— The story of Fred Moore parallels the story of the American labor movement "at its fighting front."[60]

Born in 1882 to a family as peripatetic as he himself would become, Moore, often described as hailing from Los Angeles or Spokane, was actually a native of Detroit, with a mother from Vermont and a father from New York.[61] He was, said a friend, a "brilliant lawyer . . . handicapped by a genius for nonconformity."[62] Divorced, Moore was always getting "himself into some private emotional scrape."[63] He also had a strange habit of going missing from time to time. "He'd hole up in a hotel room, nobody would know where he was, and he'd stay there till he'd quieted down," said a colleague.[64] Although he could sometimes be disturbingly intense, Moore had a captivating smile, knew how to charm, and "was always the best of good fellows."[65]

For more than a decade, from 1909 to 1920, Fred Moore had traveled the country as counsel to the Industrial Workers of the World, defending the miners, migrant workers, timber beasts, and other roustabouts and itinerants who made up the union's core.

Moore's first high-profile involvement on behalf of the IWW came not long after the organization was formed. In the Spokane free-speech fight of 1909 and 1910, he represented hundreds of Wobblies who had been arrested for disorderly conduct when they defied a city council ban and took to the streets to declaim against exploitative employment agencies.[66] (One of those he represented was then twenty-year-old Elizabeth Gurley Flynn.) Ultimately, because the cost of trying so many people was prohibitive, Spokane reached an agreement with the IWW in March 1910 that permitted the Wobblies to hold peaceful outdoor meetings. The settlement was seen as an "impressive triumph," and Moore "gained the acclaim of the Wobblies."[67]

Moore's next big IWW case came two years later, when he was part of the legal team that scored a major victory in the Lawrence strike trial. Friends of Moore maintained that he was in charge of the Lawrence defense, and that his work there was "brilliant and daring." Others carped that Moore was only a "leg lawyer" in Lawrence, running errands for local attorneys, and that the defendants were acquitted due to their own effective testimony, no thanks to the lawyers' efforts. Either way, Moore shared credit for success in Lawrence.[68]

Moore again took up the Wobbly banner in 1916. On November 5, armed and deputized vigilantes on the docks in Everett, Washington, attacked Wobblies, many of them also armed, who were arriving by boat from Seattle to stage a pro-union free-speech rally. By the time the steamer headed back across Puget Sound, Wobblies lay dead on the deck of the ship and in the water, deputies lay dead or dying on the docks, and wounded men from both sides lay everywhere.[69]

Who had shot whom in the mayhem of what became known as the Everett Massacre was impossible to determine, but back in Seattle police met the returning boat and arrested all the passengers. Seventy-four of them were charged with murder in the death of one deputy. Moore took on the task of defending them, with assistance from Seattle lawyer George Vanderveer.

The trial of the first Everett defendant, Tom Tracy, lasted almost nine weeks. On May 5, 1917, a jury found Tracy not guilty. The state released the remaining seventy-three defendants. It was another triumph for Moore. But in his victory lay hidden warning signs for future defendants Sacco and Vanzetti.

Moore did not pinch pennies. The budget-busting cost of the Everett case was thirty-eight thousand dollars.[70]

Also, Moore appeared more interested in politicizing the case than in winning it, according to George Vanderveer. All that Moore and the other Wobblies "seem to be interested in . . . is getting the prosecution to introduce their pamphlets as evidence so they can argue the points in open court," Vanderveer told his wife; "God only knows where it will wind up!"[71]

Moore believed the significance of the Everett case transcended the defendants. Accordingly, he played to an audience far beyond the courtroom. "We are here as the mouthpiece of the workers of America," he said in his closing statement, addressing reporters as much as jurors.[72]

The IWW called Moore's summation in the Everett case "one of the greatest speeches ever delivered in a courtroom."[73] But the lawyer's track record of success on behalf of the IWW was about to come to a crashing halt.

— In the spring of 1917, while the Everett Massacre case was unfolding in a Seattle courtroom, the United States went to war. Suddenly, striking workers imperiled more than corporate profit margins; they imperiled the provisioning of American troops. IWW strikes were hurting wartime production of lumber and copper. Wobblies began to hear accusations that they were aiding the German enemy, and now the initials IWW were sometimes said to stand for "Imperial Wilhelm's Warriors."[74]

On September 5, 1917, federal agents and local police raided IWW offices in Chicago and other cities. They seized more than five tons of Wobbly papers and equipment. Within weeks, more than a hundred IWW leaders, including Bill Haywood, were indicted in Chicago.[75] They went on trial on April Fool's Day, April 1, 1918, on charges related to hindering America's war effort. The large defense team included Moore protégés George Vanderveer and Caroline Lowe, but Moore himself played a small role, if any. He seems to have had a breakdown of some sort, and was missing, according to various reports, anywhere from a week to a year.[76]

On August 17, 1918, a jury found the Chicago defendants guilty. It was the beginning of the end of the IWW as a viable union. Yet its problems were far from over, and for a while Moore remained at the center of the action.

On October 29, 1917, dynamite had destroyed part of the home of an oil company official in Tulsa, Oklahoma. Police arrested eleven men in the Oil Workers Industrial Union hall and charged them with vagrancy. They were found guilty three days later and, along with six supporters in the courtroom, were herded by city police into waiting cars, driven to the railroad tracks, tied up, stripped to the waist, horsewhipped, tarred, feathered, and chased away in a fusillade of shotgun blasts by a group of men in masks calling themselves the Knights of Liberty.[77]

Unrest had spread quickly to Kansas, where on November 20 and 21 federal and local authorities raided union halls, seized documents, and initially held forty-two men on vagrancy charges. More than half of them would eventually be tried in a Wichita courtroom.[78]

The repercussions of these events in Oklahoma and Kansas kept Moore on the move in 1919. Adding to his headaches was the emergence of a dispute within the IWW about legal methods. Some Wobblies now contended that radical attorneys were more of a hindrance than a help. Worse, some questioned the need for lawyers at all, and a hostile internal debate played out in the pages of the organization's newspaper.[79]

The dispute must have infuriated Moore, who had devoted most of his career to helping the IWW in the courtroom. But in the fall of 1919, with trial dates for the Tulsa and Wichita cases approaching, he gave the pre-trial work for Wichita to Kansas City attorney John Atwood, and headed to Tulsa to defend Wobbly Charles Krieger, accused of conspiracy in the house bombing.[80]

That trial began on October 6. Moore focused on proving that Krieger was not in Tulsa when the conspiracy was planned. The case went to the jury on November 8. After forty-one hours of deliberation, jurors, hopelessly deadlocked, were dismissed.[81]

It was victory of a sort, but there was no time to savor it. John Atwood had resigned.[82] Moore and co-counsel Caroline Lowe, both surely exhausted and disheartened, hastened to Wichita to prepare for trial there on December 1.

Twenty-eight of the Kansas Wobblies had been charged with seditious conspiracy. Each faced four counts related to impeding the war effort. Moore was off his game in Wichita. He botched cross-examinations, actually bringing to light information that damaged his own case. More surprisingly, after the prosecution rested, Moore decided not to offer a defense. On December 18, 1919, a jury found the Wichita defendants guilty.[83]

The IWW had hoped the trial would be a turning point in its misfortunes. As bad as the defeat was, however, it was the aftermath that doomed Moore.

The organization wanted to appeal the Wichita verdicts. Moore requested and was granted ninety days to pursue an appeal. The time came and went. He failed to file the appeal.[84] Bill Haywood accused him of criminal negligence.

In April 1920 Moore was summoned to IWW headquarters in Chicago. The Wobblies would have no more work for him.[85] He was thirty-seven years old, and unemployed.

— Moore lost his job with the IWW one month before Sacco and Vanzetti were arrested. When he jumped into a car in New York at the urging of Carlo Tresca and Elizabeth Gurley Flynn and drove north to Boston to meet with Aldino Felicani and the rest of the Sacco-Vanzetti Defense Committee, Moore was damaged goods. But no one bothered to tell that to the committee.

In her autobiography Elizabeth Gurley Flynn notes only that Moore had been "in town" in New York after having "successfully defended" Krieger in Tulsa, and that "[a]t the moment he was not involved in any big case elsewhere."[86] Surely she and Tresca knew about the Wichita fiasco. Surely they understood that Moore's professional reputation had been tarnished. But they did not pass on the information. They told Felicani, as he later recalled, that Moore "was the best man to hire. . . . We had no misgivings about it. . . . He had so much experience." Felicani knew of Moore's connection with the defense at Lawrence eight years earlier, but his knowledge did not extend to Moore's recent cases.

The honeymoon period would be brief. "If I knew what I learned from [the papers Moore left behind] at the beginning," Felicani explained, ". . . I would have said, 'Nothing doing.'"[87]

— Fred Moore had spent the better part of his professional life defending a labor union that saw the world through the prism of class warfare. He saw his new case through the same prism.

Moore also was accustomed to working with the legal, financial, and public relations resources of an organization behind him. He wanted to prepare for his new case as if he still had these resources. But the Sacco-Vanzetti Defense Committee in 1920 was a small and flimsy affair.

Vanzetti's lawyers in Plymouth had looked upon that trial as a routine criminal case, and the upcoming trial of both defendants was shaping up in the same way. "There's no story in it," a reporter told Tresca, "just a couple of wops in a jam."[88]

Moore's arrival changed such thinking. "No one could have handled the case better [than Moore did] from a publicity standpoint," Felicani admitted. "[T]he first thing he did was to circularize the . . . case among the Americans. . . . He viewed it from the beginning as a political case."[89] Winning hearts and minds was still as important to the lawyer as winning cases.

Moore encouraged sympathetic pieces about Sacco and Vanzetti by a trio of left-leaning journalists: John Nicholas Beffel, Art Shields, and Eugene Lyons. In December 1920, four months after Moore took on the Sacco-Vanzetti case, *The New Republic* published "Eels and the Electric Chair" by Beffel, the first article about the case to appear in English in a national magazine. In early 1921 the Workers Defense Union published "Are They Doomed?," a pamphlet by Shields. Lyons traveled to Italy and sent back press releases and articles about the defendants' families and hometowns. Sacco-Vanzetti hagiography began with Moore, Beffel, Shields, and Lyons.

— Sacco and Vanzetti are conjoined in history. In reality, they were separated shortly after their arrest.

Nick went to Dedham Jail to await trial for the South Braintree murders. After his conviction at Plymouth, Bartolomeo went to Charlestown State Prison. Their respective lockups were twenty-five miles apart. For the next seven years the two men would see each other only during times of active legal proceedings.

On October 1, 1920, three months after his conviction, Vanzetti confronted a personal problem he could no longer avoid. He picked up a pen and told his father what had befallen him.

Father and son had been in a strained relationship for years, and each surely had a long list of grievances against the other. Yet as recently as 1919, his father had asked him to return to Italy, and Bartolo had considered going, "to see once more my dear ones at home."[90] But he had not gone. And now he sat behind bars in America, convicted of one crime and charged with another more terrible than the first.

Bartolo tried to put a good face on things. Day after day, he wrote, he'd been resisting the desire to communicate because he hoped, at any moment, to be able to send good news. But things were continuing to go badly. "I know how painful this occurrence in my life must be for all of you, it is this thought that makes me suffer the most. I beg you to be as strong as I am, and to forgive me for the pain that I am causing you involuntarily and guiltlessly." He had an important message for his father and other relatives and friends: "Don't hide my arrest. Don't keep silent, I am innocent and you should not be ashamed. . . . No, don't keep silent, silence would mean shame."

Then, as he had done so often in his youthful letters home, Bartolo put a positive spin on his negative circumstances. Prison was very comfortable, and people admired and helped him: "If you knew how much they have done, are doing, and will do for me, you would feel proud." Vanzetti closed by reassuring his father that a new trial for the Bridgewater crime was "almost certain."[91]

Meanwhile, sitting in Dedham Jail, Sacco must have experienced intense but conflicting emotions: gloom due to his dire situation, and joy because he had become a father once again. Wife Rosina, pregnant at the time of his arrest in May, gave birth to a healthy girl in October. Baby Ines looked like her father. Donations from well-wishers helped keep the family afloat. When someone sent a fur coat and silverware to Rosina, Moore wrote the donor that the fur would be raffled off because "Mrs. Sacco has a coat and . . . she is in serious need of other things."[92]

Around this time Nick and Rosina began having second thoughts about their new lawyer. "[P]oor Mrs. Sacco . . . didn't want Moore," Herbert Ehrmann told an interviewer in 1968, "[a]nd Sacco had never wanted Moore."[93]

⁓ With Sacco and Vanzetti behind bars, the year 1920 came to an end, but one of the strangest episodes of their case was just beginning.

On a cold Sunday afternoon, January 2, 1921, a young woman in her early twenties named Angelina DeFalco appeared in the office where Aldino Felicani was working. She was, she explained, an Italian–English interpreter in the Dedham courthouse and, according to witnesses, she said that she had a proposition for the defense committee. For the right amount of money, she could fix it so that Sacco would be acquitted in his upcoming trial. It would be harder to fix the verdict for Vanzetti, because he now had a conviction on his record, but even that might be arranged, "provided you are in a position to pay."[94]

"Of course I decided not to talk with her alone," Felicani later recalled. He consulted Felice Guadagni, another defense committee member.[95] Over the next couple of days they met DeFalco at a restaurant and spoke to her by phone. She allegedly claimed to have connections to district attorney Fred Katzmann; to his brother, attorney Percy Katzmann; and to attorney Francis Squires, clerk of Norfolk County Superior Court. A "ring" existed in Norfolk County, she said. If defendants paid off lawyers in the ring, they would be acquitted. Otherwise, they would be convicted, regardless of guilt or innocence.[96]

With Sacco and Vanzetti, it would work this way, DeFalco said: for fifty thousand dollars, with ten thousand down, Percy Katzmann would take the case. Then his brother, the district attorney, would assign an assistant to prosecute. The jury foreman would be paid to fix the jury. And Sacco would be acquitted. DeFalco even offered a professional reference, one Carimina Fucci, a woman who supposedly paid ten thousand dollars to have murder charges against her reduced to manslaughter.[97]

DeFalco invited Felicani to dinner at her house in Dedham on Friday evening, January 7, to talk the deal over with Squires and others.

Fred Moore got wind of what was happening, and insisted that Felicani stay away from the dinner. "I think [he and Guadagni] feared a trap," Felicani said. DeFalco was upset: "She almost cried because I was spoiling the whole business."[98]

Though Felicani avoided the dinner, he went to Dedham around ten in the evening anyway to scope things out. "Sure enough, there [was] a line of cars in front of [DeFalco's] house and I took down the license numbers. . . . In the morning we checked. There was Katzmann's car, Katzmann's brother's car, Squires' car."[99]

Felicani had asked DeFalco to come to the defense committee office the following day. Committee members bought an early-model Dictaphone to record surreptitiously what took place. "[W]e placed [the device] in such a way that the girl who handled it had to go down to the coal bin and take the dictation there."

When DeFalco showed up, she told the group that the price of acquittal had been lowered. It was now forty thousand dollars, with five thousand down, and it covered both men. One thing had not changed, however: no money would still mean no acquittals.

Moore decided to have DeFalco arrested.

Felicani disagreed, but gave in. "I went to swear the warrant. . . . This woman was arrested immediately. A few days later [on January 27] we went to court."[100]

The explosive allegations of corruption in high places guaranteed front-page headlines.

Since no money had yet changed hands, DeFalco was charged with soliciting law business while not an attorney. Witnesses testified that they had heard her offer to get Sacco and Vanzetti off for a price, and had seen her at the defense committee office.

DeFalco admitted talking on some occasions with members of the defense committee, but said that they were the ones who had approached her.[101] Francis Squires and Percy Katzmann said they had occasionally employed DeFalco as an interpreter; Fred Katzmann denied knowing her at all.[102]

Testimony went on for six days. When it ended, the judge dismissed the charges. Angelina DeFalco's actions, he said, were "unwise, but not criminal." Furthermore, the "use made of [district attorney Katzmann's] name . . . was wholly unwarranted and unjust, and . . . all attempt to thus cast discredit upon him or upon his great office was reprehensible to the last degree."[103]

— Was DeFalco's offer for real?

Court interpreters of the day did sometimes act as runners, procuring immigrant clients for lawyers. Runners did sometimes promise freedom for a fee, and the number of runners was significant. DeFalco herself was convicted of grand larceny in 1931 and sentenced to six months in jail for accepting money to buy a prisoner's release,[104] and Joe Rossi, also known as Joseph Ross, who served as court interpreter during the Dedham trial, was convicted of larceny in 1926 and served time for attempting to bribe a judge.[105]

Even the allegations of a courthouse ring were not that shocking. It was an era "when the district attorneys around us [in Boston] were falling like pins in a bowling alley, with proof on every side of their frame-ups and corruption."[106] The "pins" included Nathan Tufts, Middlesex County DA, removed from office in 1921, and Joseph Pelletier, Suffolk County DA, removed in 1922, both on charges of extortion; and state attorney general Arthur Reading, impeached for extortion in 1928.[107]

If DeFalco's offer was the real deal, Moore had several choices, none good, all risky. He could have paid the bribe, ignored it, taken it public, or tried to use it as a springboard to negotiate a plea bargain and get the charges against Sacco and Vanzetti reduced.

He chose the worst option. He went public, denigrating none other than the district attorney who would soon be prosecuting his clients, and openly attacking the system that would be deciding their fate. It was as if the former defender of Wobblies were still strategizing for the IWW, as if he thought he were back in Spokane or Lawrence or Everett, as if he believed that the best defense was always a good offense, and that making the system look bad would make his clients look good.

The decision backfired. There would be no plea bargaining, only a renewed search by the prosecution for evidence. "We . . . actually . . . put the Massachusetts court on trial in a Massachusetts court," Felicani summed up later. "That's the thing that Judge Thayer never forgave us for. We sealed, at [Mrs. DeFalco's] trial, the fate of Sacco and Vanzetti."[108]

[W]e are, above all, against government. . . .
We intend to use force against government,
because it is by force that we are kept in
subjection by government.
— Errico Malatesta

8 | "Terrorist Plot Is Seen"

Terror struck New York on a clear September day. Bloodied workers fled panic-stricken through the eye of the storm—the financial district, symbol of American capitalism.

A reporter who was on the scene at the moment of the attack described "a crash out of blue sky—an unexpected, death-dealing bolt." He felt a concussion of air, then "a sharp resounding crash which shook to their foundations the monster buildings facing either side of Wall Street." Horrible noises blasted forth, the cacophony of shattered glass raining down from a thousand broken windows, the screams of the injured. Smoke rose up everywhere, clouds of dust, white vapor, and a "mushroom-shaped cloud of yellowish green." Bodies, said the reporter, "most of them silent in death, lay nearby. As I gazed horror-stricken at the sight, one of these forms, half naked and seared with burns, started to rise. It struggled, then toppled and fell lifeless into the gutter."[1]

The president of the New York Stock Exchange listened for "a second to cries and groans and excited shouting and running feet," and immediately suspended all trading. Within five minutes, a mass of ten thousand people was swarming through the narrow streets. Moving away from a burning car, the mass turned into a "flying wedge and thousands . . . [were] lifted off their feet."[2]

Incoming calls from alarmed citizens overwhelmed phone services. Telephones went dead.

Doctors, nurses, fire trucks, and ambulances rushed to the scene. Rescuers commandeered vehicles to speed the wounded off to hospitals. Hundreds of anxious people streamed through the city morgue late into the night, searching for the bodies of relatives and friends.

Fear gripped the nation. Police protection went up quickly around financial districts in other American cities.

As long as they lived, Wall Street financiers and clerks would remember where they had been on the day that terrorism struck New York. That day was

Terrorism strikes Wall Street on September 16, 1920, with a deadly wagonload of dynamite. Rising above the carnage is a statue of George Washington, upper right. Library of Congress, Prints & Photographs Div., NYWT&S Collection.

September 16, 1920. The World Trade Center did not yet exist, but the affected buildings were equally symbolic: the Wall Street headquarters of J. P. Morgan & Co., the most influential private bank in the world, and the United States Subtreasury and United States Assay Office. Destruction was inflicted not by means of an airplane, but by its technological antithesis, a horse-drawn wagon laden with dynamite, the progenitor of all truck bombs. The terrorists were not a band of jihadists but, according to the most widely accepted theory, a single anarchist acting alone, a short Italian man who ran a laundry with his brother and whose best friends were fellow anarchists Nick Sacco and Barto-lomeo Vanzetti.[3]

— The periods surrounding two of the most notorious days in New York— September 11, 2001, and September 16, 1920—share many similarities. Since 9/11, Americans have felt threatened by evil and mysterious forces. In the years preceding 9/16, Americans felt the same way.

Homeland security in 1920 was tenuous. Assassinations, bombings, and paralyzing strikes had Americans on edge. The federal government enacted far-reaching new laws, conducted mass raids and secret trials, and suspended civil liberties. Most American citizens approved of these measures at first. They saw all radicals — socialists, communists, and anarchists — as malevolent perpetrators of a terror that seemed to lurk everywhere.

Leading the alarmists in 1920 was the attorney general of the United States. A. Mitchell Palmer warned that the "blaze of revolution was sweeping over every American institution of law and order, eating its way into the homes of the American workmen." Its "sharp tongues of revolutionary heat were . . . burning up the foundations of society." He was speaking of communism, but conflated it with anarchism, adding that the anarchist's creed is a fanaticism "that admits no respect of any other creed."[4] Palmer's words may sound hyperbolic today, but in 1920 anarchists provoked fear and fury as intense as any provoked by modern terrorists.

— Anarchism as a political ideology took root in Europe in the late nineteeth century and the early twentieth. It had many philosophers and definitions, but its diverse branches shared a common belief in abolishing government, indeed in abolishing "all forms of compulsion, of authority, of exploitation."[5] Italian anarchist Errico Malatesta advocated abolishing private property and national frontiers, organizing society based on voluntary free association of producers and consumers, guaranteeing the "means of life" to children and "all who are prevented from providing for themselves," waging "war on religion and all lies," and freeing the family unit "from every legal tie."[6] In a nutshell, according to Luigi Galleani, everything in an anarchist society "must belong to everybody and must present the hypothesis of a world without god, without king, without government, without masters."[7]

To achieve such a harmonious and collaborative world of equals, violence might be necessary.

Anarchism did not by definition require violence. It encompassed nonviolent tactics such as strikes, boycotts, work slowdowns, and education through lecture tours and a prolific radical press.

But for some, violence was a legitimate tactic in the anarchist toolbox, and terrorism became "an integral part of a revolutionary strategy," with assassination a strategic maneuver.[8] Between 1894 and 1900 in Europe, assassins killed the prime minister of Spain, the president of France, the empress of Austria, and the king of Italy. In each of these cases, as well as in a failed attempt to kill the prime minister of Italy, the assassin was an Italian anarchist.[9]

Italy was the birthplace of "propaganda by the deed" — reform through violent action, not words. According to Malatesta, anarchists were against violence but had to use it in self-defense against the violence of the ruling classes. Violence was an anarchist's necessity and duty, Malatesta explained, "but only for defense. And we mean not only . . . defense against direct . . . attack, but against all . . . institutions which use force to keep the people in a state of servitude."[10]

In Vanzetti's opinion, "Malatesta [was] a saint."[11]

The first organized group of Italian anarchists in America formed in New York in 1885, and within a decade similar groups had formed in several other cities. Anarchists dominated the "lost world" of Italian-American radicals at the dawn of the twentieth century. They published nearly a hundred anarchist newspapers, the largest number produced by any single immigrant group. The Italian anarchist "'movement' consisted of little more than its press" at times, writes historian Nunzio Pernicone.[12]

Anarchism attracted little mainstream attention in the United States until a few traumatic, violent events shone a spotlight on the movement and galvanized Americans against it.

The first such event was a labor rally gone bad in Haymarket Square in Chicago in May 1886. A bomb exploded, police fired into the crowd, and when the resulting panic subsided, police and protesters lay dead and wounded everywhere. Eight anarchist labor organizers were tried and convicted of conspiracy to commit murder by inciting the unknown bomb thrower with their speeches. Four of them were executed on November 11, 1887, defending to the death their anarchist beliefs.[13] Haymarket stimulated the growth of American anarchism; certainly Emma Goldman, the woman whom one government official called the "most dangerous [American anarchist] in public estimation," attributed her own radicalization to Haymarket.[14]

Six years after Haymarket, Alexander Berkman, Goldman's friend and fellow Russian immigrant, created a sensation when he attempted to assassinate industrialist Henry Clay Frick for his role in suppressing a steelworkers' strike in Homestead, Pennsylvania. Frick survived and Berkman went to prison, proud of committing what he called "the first terrorist act in America."[15]

Anarchism erupted into mainstream American consciousness once more in 1900. In Italy, a man named Gaetano Bresci shot and killed the king, Umberto I. The seemingly all-Italian affair had an American twist: Bresci was an immigrant factory worker who lived in Paterson, New Jersey, and was said to have planned the assassination with other anarchists in the United States.[16]

The fourth and most traumatic anarchist episode for Americans occurred the following year. On September 6, 1901, in Buffalo, New York, Leon Czolgosz, an American anarchist of Czech descent, shot President William McKinley.

Eight days later, the president died. Czolgosz said he felt no remorse. He repeatedly explained his motive: "I killed the President because he was the enemy of the good people—the good working people." Czolgosz had been inspired to act in part by meeting Emma Goldman and by reading about Haymarket and Bresci's assassination of the Italian king.[17]

Some anarchists justified, even praised, Czolgosz and Bresci. Malatesta defended Bresci as undeniably "inspired by altruistic intentions" and Czolgosz as someone who "gave himself in wholesale sacrifice to the cause of equality and liberty."[18] Galleani supported the "purity of . . . Bresci's sacrifice." It would inspire the downtrodden to rise up, he said, and frighten the new Italian king to be more moderate, thus illustrating that "no act of rebellion is harmful."[19]

In the view of most Americans, Czolgosz and Bresci were wretched terrorists. In the parallel universe of Malatesta and Galleani, they were courageous altruists.

Bresci's act made Americans aware of the existence of Italian anarchists on American soil. After Czolgosz murdered McKinley, all anarchists were demonized as advocates of violence. On March 3, 1903 Congress passed an immigration law that excluded—in addition to idiots, epileptics, and other undesirables—"anarchists, or persons who believe in or advocate the overthrow by force or violence of . . . government or . . . law, or the assassinations of public officials." The law further excluded anyone who was a member of an organization that backed such beliefs.[20]

~ Nick Sacco was sixteen years old when he immigrated to America in 1908. Bartolomeo Vanzetti was twenty. Whatever their reasons for leaving Italy, poverty was not one of them. Each had grown up in a comfortable, land-owning Catholic family, and neither had adopted a belief system dramatically different from his family's. But within five years of immigrating, each was on a path toward anarchism and atheism, traveling the same road as other Italian anarchists who became politicized in the United States.

As a child, Vanzetti had been a "fervent Catholic." Later he experienced hardship as an apprentice in Italy and a laborer in America. Solace came from books, and his diversified reading list included political texts—works by Malatesta, Peter Kropotkin, and Karl Marx—as well as the Bible and *The Life of Jesus*. This combination of experience and study convinced him "that in the name of God, of Law, of [Country], of Liberty . . . are perpetrated . . . the most ferocious crimes. . . . I know from experience that rights and privileges are still won and maintained by force."[21]

Vanzetti began subscribing to Galleani's *Cronaca sovversiva* in 1912. When, around the same time, he settled in Plymouth, his anarchist path was assured. Vincenzo Brini, his landlord, was himself an ardent anarchist, his home a way station for visiting speakers such as Malatesta, Galleani, and Carlo Tresca. By 1919, Bartolo had shed any remaining childhood illusions about government and religion. "I'm not the know-it-all little kid that I was when I left Italy," he told his aunt, in the last letter he would write home as a free man. As if foreshadowing the future, he continued, "I am . . . a man who fights against this present society of wolves and sheep with all his energy, ready to move forward without fear and without uncertainty, into the great battle that is about to burst out."[22]

Sacco did not experience the same hardships as Vanzetti. According to his father, Nick had been a somewhat idealistic boy, patriotic in a kind of uninformed and casual way. When he was a teenager, he encountered leftist politics through his brother Sabino, who became a socialist after a stint in the Italian army. As a skilled laborer in America, Sacco achieved what seemed to be the American dream: financial security, a beloved family, and close American and Italian friends. Still, he felt driven to raise money for striking workers, to subscribe to *Cronaca sovversiva*, and to attend meetings of a group of Italian anarchists in Milford. He found the members *simpatico*. They developed a self-contained alternative lifestyle, complete with their own social and educational activities, including picnics and lectures and "social dramas" to raise funds for radical causes. ("We left the socialists and Communists way behind when it came to plays and recitals," one Italian anarchist recalled.) Sacco found "a way of life that he embraced with all the passion of a convert," says historian Paul Avrich. Anarchism "gave his life a new purpose and direction."[23]

Returning to Massachusetts after evading the draft registration in 1917, Sacco and Vanzetti joined other Italian anarchists who were meeting in Boston. "[T]his little group of anarchists . . . were dedicated idealists, very impractical," said Gardner Jackson, who later managed press relations for the men's defense committee. "In an oversimplified way, their belief was that the perfectability of the individual is achieved best with no organization . . . [and no] government." In Jackson's opinion, "they could [never] justify their anarchism in terms of reality."[24]

But they could try. When Elizabeth Gurley Flynn visited the men in their respective jails a few months after their arrest, they told her what anarchism meant to them. Sacco, said Flynn, defined it as "[n]o government, no police, no judges, no bosses, no authority; autonomous groups of people — the people own everything — distribute by needs — equality, justice, comradeship — love each other." Vanzetti told Flynn that anarchism was "a belief in human freedom and the dignity of man."[25]

— Equality and justice. Freedom and dignity. It sounded great. It sounded positively utopian. Many supporters of Sacco and Vanzetti either gently mocked their brand of anarchism as "noble nonsense" or defended it as "philosophical" and resisted attempts to portray it otherwise. (A philosophical anarchist was "an anarchist who shaves daily, has good manners and is guaranteed not to act on his beliefs," John Dos Passos explained.) "Your proposal to picture Sacco and Vanzetti as militant anarchists calling for terrorism is most painful to me," defense attorney Herbert Ehrmann wrote novelist Upton Sinclair. Sacco "gave away the vegetables he raised to the poor of Stoughton. . . . Vanzetti . . . expressed . . . that violence is the last resort against tyranny."[26]

But violence was deemed a legitimate tactic for change in some anarchist quarters. "The question of violence [in the Italian anarchist community] was always one that troubled hell out of me," Gardner Jackson conceded. He believed that Vanzetti and his friend Aldino Felicani "did not follow the concept that you could achieve your ends by the use of violence." But, Jackson confessed, "I'm not at all sure about some of the others in [their] group."[27]

Perhaps Jackson shouldn't have been so sure about Vanzetti or Felicani, either. "I was against any type of bomb throwing," Felicani later recalled, "but I would defend those involved in it. [Also], I won't say that I'm against throwing a bomb if that bomb will bring some kind of freedom anywhere." The assassination of the Italian king had had its benefits, Felicani acknowledged. "When the new king was crowned, civil liberties were restored."[28]

Felicani said that anarchist leaders "never advocated throwing bombs," but that was not true. In 1905 Luigi Galleani published *La salute è in voi* (*Health is within you*), an instruction manual packed with tips for aspiring bomb makers. Buy pure materials from "dealers in chemical products or from pharmacists," the manual advised. Shop at different stores, to avoid arousing suspicion. If asked, pretend you need dynamite for "contraband fishing." Go to the countryside to test your explosives before using them on the ultimate targets. Bombs can come in any shape, "but spherical ones are the most effective. . . . A bomb with one-half kilogram of dynamite, with a volume of a half liter, in good conditions, can injure twenty or thirty people."[29]

It was a "wicked treatise," a New York policeman later said. Representing "the dark part of the anarchist vision," the manual urged readers to arm themselves for action with science.[30]

— In 1867 Alfred Nobel patented dynamite, an invention that made it cheaper and safer to blast through rock for large construction projects. While Nobel's name today is linked with a peace prize, this particular innovation of his quickly morphed into a weapon of violence. In 1881 a conclave of anarchists recommended a study of the revolutionary uses of recent scientific developments.[31] And in 1885, Albert Parsons, an anarchist editor and Haymarket martyr-to-be, printed a paean to Nobel's invention: "In giving dynamite to the downtrodden millions of the globe, science has done its best work."[32]

In America the story of dynamite as a weapon began with the immigration of German anarchist Johann Most in 1882, and his publication in 1885 of *The Science of Revolutionary Warfare*. Anarchist newspapers in Chicago and Cleveland reprinted chapters of Most's how-to bomb-making manual. In 1886 dynamite moved from the printed page to the street; the Haymarket bomb was the first known use of dynamite as a murder weapon in America.

— The first recorded instance of anarchists using Galleani's "wicked treatise" occurred several years later, in 1914. On the Fourth of July, in a building on Lexington Avenue in New York, anarchists were building a bomb to blow up the home of John D. Rockefeller in retaliation for brutality at a Rockefeller-owned mine in Colorado. The bomb went off prematurely, killing three men.[33] The incident helped spur the New York Police Department to create an undercover bomb squad. A few months later five more bombing incidents occurred in the city, all either targeting anarchist enemies or marking important dates on the anarchist calendar.

Galleani approved of the New York bombings of 1914. "Continue the good war ... [against] the vampires of capitalism," he counseled his readers.[34]

Detectives investigating the bombings focused on the Bresci Group, a collection of Italian anarchists in New York named after the assassin of the king of Italy. An Italian detective on the bomb squad infiltrated the group; then, with two of its members, fashioned bombs to blow up St. Patrick's Cathedral on Fifth Avenue. Moments before he could light a fuse, one of the anarchists was arrested in a police sting operation inside the cathedral; his partner was arrested at home. They claimed entrapment but were convicted. Part of the evidence against them was the document they had used and which police now took into custody: *La salute è in voi* by Luigi Galleani.

Galleani's "good war" continued, but in 1916, says Avrich, "the theater of battle shifted from New York to Boston."[35]

Between New Year's Eve and New Year's Day, 1916, someone tied one end of a rope to a knob on a basement door of the Massachusetts State House in Boston, and the other end to a small wicker suitcase concealing a powerful bomb.[36] DYNAMITE AT STATE HOUSE, the headlines screamed on January 1. The bomb was safely removed and detonated at a quarry. In February and again in December, Boston bombers were more successful in their campaign, damaging two police stations in the city.[37]

— When America went to war in 1917, an intense cycle of action and reaction, violence and repression, began for United States–based anarchists and the government.

Around the time that Nick, Bartolomeo, and other Galleanisti were fleeing to Mexico, Galleani himself was taken into custody and charged with obstructing the draft. The Bureau of Immigration recommended that he be deported, but suspended action because he had dependents here, a wife and five children. He paid a fine and was allowed to remain in the United States.

Three months later, at a patriotic pro-war rally organized by the Reverend Augusto Giuliani, an Italian cleric in Milwaukee, Galleani anarchists tore down an American flag. Two anarchists were killed and eleven arrested in the ensuing police response.[38]

The Galleanisti who had gone to Mexico were beginning to make their way back to the United States. Besides Sacco and Vanzetti, the group of thirty-plus men included Mario Buda and a good-looking carpenter named Carlo Valdinoci. On November 24, 1917, someone planted a bomb in Giuliani's church. It was discovered and removed in time, only to explode later at police headquarters, claiming eleven victims, including ten policemen. This bomb, Avrich believes, may have been the handiwork of Buda and Valdinoci, avenging the deaths and arrests from the rally.[39]

When the eleven arrested Milwaukee anarchists went on trial for assault with intent to murder, all were found guilty.

For outraged Galleanisti, it was time for another round of action and reaction.

Carlo Valdinoci, now living in Youngstown, Ohio, was in contact with Mario Buda, now in Chicago, and other comrades. These anti-organization anarchists paradoxically "were the most effectively organized group that I'd ever dealt with," Gardner Jackson later recalled. "I still believe that their means of communication with one another were the most highly effective I've ever seen."[40]

In January 1918, shortly after the guilty verdicts had been handed down in Milwaukee, Valdinoci sent a letter to a young woman in Connecticut asking her to come to Youngstown. Eighteen-year-old Gabriella Antolini — Ella — was beautiful, "like Greta Garbo."[41] She was also one of the few women anarchists prepared to carry out propaganda by the deed. She left immediately for Youngstown. There she was given a satchel containing thirty-six sticks of dynamite to carry to Chicago, where another courier apparently would take them from her and bring them to their final destination: Milwaukee. Ella traveled first with Valdinoci by train to Steubenville, then alone on an overnight train to Chicago. A suspicious porter schemed to get a look inside her satchel. Discovering the dynamite, he informed the conductor, who telegraphed authorities, and when the train pulled into Chicago, police were waiting. They seized the satchel and arrested Ella.[42]

Thus Ella's role in the plot for anarchist revenge in Milwaukee ended, but it was not the end of Ella or of the plot. Ella made headlines in Chicago as "the little Nihilist," the "Dynamite Girl"[43] with a "Death Satchel" who "fought like a tiger" against arresting officers, tried to swallow evidence, gave a false name, refused to answer questions, and defiantly proclaimed her anarchist and atheist beliefs.[44] Over months of questioning, she never informed on her comrades.

Meantime, in April, three months after her arrest, as Ella sat in jail, two powerful bombs were planted at the home of the district attorney who had successfully prosecuted the Milwaukee anarchists. Neither bomb exploded. Newspapers had speculated that Ella's mission had something to do with the trial of IWW leaders in Chicago, but the targeted district attorney was certain the bombs were "nothing more than an attempt at retaliation [against me]."[45]

Ella never knowingly violated her code of silence, but she did make a mistake. In January 1918 she wrote a letter from jail to Carlo Valdinoci in Youngstown. Although she used one of his aliases and the address of a mail drop, that was enough of a clue for agents from the Bureau of Investigation (BI), part of the U.S. Department of Justice and forerunner of the FBI. The "best anti-radical investigator" at the time was said to be agent Rayme Finch of the bureau's Cleveland office. Finch went to Youngstown and located Valdinoci's room. There he discovered a new revolver and documents, including *Faccia a faccia col nemico* (Face to face with the enemy), a collection of articles about militant anarchism by Luigi Galleani. The documents represented a possible link between the Milwaukee bombs, the missing Valdinoci, and Luigi Galleani and his followers.[46]

Finch obtained authorization for a raid on the offices of Galleani's newspaper, *Cronaca sovversiva*, in Lynn, Massachusetts. Since the Boston office of the Bureau of Investigation was understaffed, Finch himself led the raid, which took place in February 1918. Agents seized names and addresses of thousands of *Cronaca* subscribers, including those of Sacco and Vanzetti—valuable evidence about anarchists whom the government sought to detain, according to Anthony Caminetti, United States commissioner of immigration.[47]

The Bureau of Immigration issued warrants for the arrest of scores of most-wanted anarchists. Nearly fifty of the warrants were for Boston-area

Galleanisti, although Sacco and Vanzetti were not among them.[48] "The Bureau [of Immigration] considers these Italian anarchists very dangerous to this country," Caminetti said, ". . . and is therefore anxious that sufficient evidence be secured to justify their removal from the country."[49] The arrests began on May 15, 1918. Some eighty Galleanisti were taken into custody, including about thirty in and around Boston, along with hundreds of copies of anarchist publications. On May 16, Galleani himself was arrested and questioned at a second deportation hearing. To the likely consternation of BI agents and immigration officials in Washington, he again escaped deportation, his Boston immigration examiner declaring that "[t]here is no organization of [Italian] anarchists in the United States any more than there is of Italian atheists."[50] Galleani was, however, ordered to stop publishing *Cronaca sovversiva*, judged the "most dangerous newspaper . . . in this country" by the Department of Justice.[51]

Congress passed the Anarchist Exclusion Act five months later, and a month after that Caminetti recommended a warrant for Galleani's deportation. After yet another hearing, the recommendation was approved at the end of January 1919. Finally, in June, all his legal avenues exhausted, Galleani was deported to Italy.[52]

The timing of the departure would prove inopportune for government investigators. Galleani and his followers were about to become suspects in a widespread campaign of terrorist bombings.

⏤ Galleani's troubles dovetailed with American involvement in the war.

After declaring war, Congress moved quickly to enact legislation to protect the vital interests of the United States. Four new laws facilitated suppression of radicals.

The Espionage Act, passed on June 15, 1917, punished efforts to aid enemies of the United States. Title 12, "Use of Mails," specified that any printed material of any kind violating any provision of the act (Galleani's newspaper, for example) was "nonmailable."[53]

The Trading with the Enemy Act, passed on October 6, 1917, prohibited contact with enemies of the United States. Section 19 made it illegal to publish in any foreign language anything about the war or the countries in the war unless an English translation had first been filed with a local postmaster and notice of the filing appeared in the publication. Non-complying publications were also "nonmailable."[54]

The Sedition Act, passed on May 16, 1918, amended the Espionage Act by criminalizing more activities. Fines, imprisonment, or both now awaited anyone who criticized the United States in speech or writing.[55]

And the Anarchist Exclusion Act, passed on October 16, 1918, shortly before the armistice, denied admission to the United States to anyone who either was an anarchist, believed in overthrowing the government, opposed organized government, advocated assassination and property destruction, or belonged to an organization with such beliefs. There was no time limit. Aliens who adopted such beliefs after immigrating were deportable "irrespective of the time of their entry into the United States."[56]

Like the Patriot Act of 2001, the laws of the World War I era were meant to safeguard homeland security. In the process, they upended the balance between security and freedom. The laws of 1917 and 1918 criminalized not only actions, but also ideas, and the expression of the ideas in speech and writing. Beliefs became illegal, whether individuals acted on them or not.

"[I]f freedom of speech is to be meaningful," wrote William Rehnquist, longtime chief justice of the United States, then "strong criticism of government policy must be permitted even in wartime."[57] Criticism was not permitted in 1917 and 1918. Legislation that originated in a concern for national security engendered what was called, in pre-9/11 America, the "most intense repression of civil liberties the nation has ever known."[58]

The intensity of the cycle of action and reaction, violence and repression, was about to escalate.

— Sacco and Vanzetti left no record of their actual involvement, if any, with violence and bombs in the years between the time they first subscribed to Galleani's newspaper and the time of their arrest. They did leave mysterious and contradictory clues to their opinions on violence.

Nick said that he couldn't stand the sight of blood, that it made him sick, according to a report by an officer of the Massachusetts State Police. Both Nick and his friends said that he couldn't even kill a chicken. At trial, he said that he "[a]bsolutely [did] not" believe in the use of force or violence "to destroy property or individuals." He told Elizabeth Gurley Flynn that his shoemaker's hands were made for working, not killing, and he told a court psychiatrist who examined him "that he never could in his philosophy or in his character have taken a pistol and robbed a lot of workmen of their payroll." He was a loving father and husband, and "such a gentle person, you knew he wouldn't hurt a fly. He was kind beyond words," said Betty Jack Wirth, who as a teenager visited him in prison at least weekly for two years and whose mother tutored him in English.[59]

On the other hand, Flynn imagined that Sacco was an "idealistic type of kind and good Italian anarchist, who might kill a king as an act of 'social justice' — but not a mouse." Fellow anarchist Aldino Felicani said "without any hesitation" that Sacco "was capable of throwing a bomb. . . . But not Vanzetti," while Concetta Silvestri, whose husband died in 1919 while planting a bomb, believed both Sacco and Vanzetti were militants "ready to do whatever was necessary to achieve their Idea." Sacco grew to detest Fred Moore, his first lawyer. From prison he threatened Moore: "I would not be surprise if somebody will find you some morning hang on lamp-post." Later Moore reportedly told Upton Sinclair that Sacco owned a four-volume book on the chemistry of explosives and that on the night of his arrest, Sacco and his friends were hiding dynamite.[60]

As for Bartolo, he was unselfish, kind, humanitarian, described by friends as a rescuer of sick animals, an exemplar of "exquisite courtesy," and a lover of "all things good." He supportively mentored his landlord's children, and they reciprocated his affection. His dream of a more equitable distribution of wealth did "not mean robbery for a insurrection," he told Elizabeth Evans. He might be an anarchist, a friend said, but "if all the men was [nice] like him, I'd like to see all [men become] anarchists!"[61]

However, this outwardly gentle man also supported the use of violence in certain situations. "I abhor useless violence," he wrote a friend, but the "slave has the right and duty to arise against his master." Long ago, Vanzetti said, he used to feel sorry for trees if he had to cut them down, but in prison "while now thinking of my axe, a lust seizes me to [use it] on the necks and trunks of the men-eaters." In May 1927, seven years into his imprisonment, in a petition to the governor of Massachusetts to overturn the verdict in his case, Vanzetti explained his position on violence. He opposed it, he said, but "it has been the violence of tyranny that has provoked the violence of the oppressed."[62]

Human beings are complex creatures of nuance and ambiguity, capable of contradictory, dissonant behavior. Honest people cheat. Gentle people explode. Peaceful people fight. In the case of anarchists, says historian Melvyn Dubofsky, "One could be tender and loving, yet consider an existing social system so intolerable and reprehensible that one would not blink at engaging in acts of destruction in order to usher in a more perfect world."[63]

"The anarchists were brutally treated in those days," recalled a woman whose anarchist parents were deported, "and dynamite had its uses. . . . Violence is a bad thing, but sometimes it is necessary." In sum, said an anarchist of 1920s Boston, "There were a lot of people making bombs in those days just after the war."[64]

Were Sacco and Vanzetti among them? Were they the terrorists next door?

Sacco and Vanzetti led double lives, historian Paul Avrich contends, open lives of work and family, and hidden lives of insurgency. Avrich speculates that if Sacco or Vanzetti were personally involved in bombings, it would have started in Youngstown, Ohio, with other Galleanisti, en route home from Mexico in late 1917.

Nick's presence in Youngstown is unconfirmed. He may have briefly visited Rosina's brother in Ohio on his way home from Mexico, but his testimony in court implied that he had gone "straight to see my wife" in Massachusetts.[65] As for Bartolomeo, however, his temporary presence in Youngstown is certain. He wrote letters to his family from the city, and testified in court that he had spent time there.[66] Avrich believes that Vanzetti, while in Youngstown, "more than likely" was involved in the 1918 Milwaukee bomb plot, although there is no evidence to prove it.[67]

If Sacco or Vanzetti did participate in bomb plots or other acts of violence, in Youngstown or elsewhere, no proof has been found. If it ever existed, it went with them to the grave.

— With the signing of the armistice on November 11, 1918, there was good news and bad news for the United States: the fighting overseas was over, but the fighting at home between labor and management was heating up after wartime détente. War industries were shrinking. Job opportunities were vanishing just as demobilized soldiers were returning home and flooding the job market. Burgeoning inflation was driving up the cost of living.

More than thirty-six hundred strikes erupted across the country in the immediate postwar turmoil of 1919, affecting nearly every kind of organized labor. More strikes had occurred in 1916 and 1917, and almost as many in 1918.[68] But a few of the 1919 strikes were very high profile, including a general strike in Seattle and yet another textile strike in Lawrence. These two strikes differed in many particulars, but were alike in provoking near hysteria in the press, which conflated communism, socialism, anarchism, and union organizing, and viewed them all as part of a revolutionary conspiracy.

The Lawrence strike of 1919 began just a few days after approval of the deportation order for Luigi Galleani. Around the same time, a flyer entitled "Go-Head!," from a group calling itself the American Anarchists, was distributed in some New England cities. "Go-Head!" bore a chilling message of retaliation:

> The senile fossils ruling the United States . . . have decided to check the storm [that threatens them] by passing the Deportation law affecting all foreign radicals. . . . And deport us! We will dynamite you![69]

— Bombing seemed to be in the air in the spring of 1919. In March came reports of an alleged radical plot to bomb Chicago. In April similar reports came from Pittsburgh. May Day was fast approaching.[70]

The official observance of Labor Day in America had for years taken place in September, but May 1, *Primo Maggio*, remained a kind of Labor Day for radicals, an important occasion for celebrations and commemorations. May Day 1919, however, was a harbinger of fear. It marked the discovery of a nationwide terrorist bombing conspiracy.

It began with a package bomb mailed from New York to Mayor Ole Hanson in Seattle and delivered to his office on April 28, 1919.[71] The bomb failed to go off because the staff member who opened the package happened to do so from the wrong end. The next day another package bomb with similar markings was delivered to the Atlanta home of a former senator from Georgia who had chaired the Senate Committee on Immigration. He was not at home, but his wife and maid were injured when the bomb exploded.

The following day, April 30, a New York postal clerk reading a newspaper account of the package bombs realized that he had shelved sixteen identical packages for insufficient postage. It's hard to believe that bomb-building terrorists could be so inattentive to detail that they would use the wrong amount of postage, but that's what happened. The clerk notified authorities; the sixteen packages were safely intercepted. All had been mailed from New York in late April, probably for a hoped-for May Day delivery.

Post offices around the country were put on alert for more bombs, and indeed more were found—more than thirty May Day bombs in all, mailed to a virtual hit list of anarchist enemies, including cabinet officers, United States senators and representatives, governors, mayors, judges, district attorneys, a police commissioner, a newspaper editor, and three industrialists: John D. Rockefeller, J. P. Morgan, and William Wood, president of the multi-mill American Woolen Company of Lawrence.

None of the bombs hurt its intended target, but the bold plot and wide net were alarming. Angry citizens disrupted radical meetings and parades in several cities on May Day.

Then, in what seemed like the blink of an eye, bombers struck again. On June 2, 1919, explosions blasted nine new targets, spreading what the *Washington Post* called "nation-wide terror."[72] In Massachusetts, the homes of a judge in Boston and a state legislator in Newtonville were damaged. In New York City, the target was a judge's home. In Paterson, New Jersey, it was a textile executive's home, and in Cleveland, it was the home of the mayor. There were multiple targets in Pennsylvania.

Most shocking of all, a bomb rocked the Washington, D.C., home of the attorney general of the United States. Doors were blasted off, windows smashed, the front of the house shattered. Attorney general A. Mitchell Palmer, sitting near an upstairs window, was showered with glass but unhurt. This strike in the nation's capital, a mere two miles from the White House, "challenged the government," the *Post* declared; anarchists were "trying to kill the man who has an army of agents on their trail."[73]

All the June 2 bombs exploded around midnight, a time clearly chosen for maximum impact, since most of the targets were private homes likely to be occupied at that hour by sleeping residents. Each bomb contained about twenty pounds of dynamite and caused extensive damage.

Miraculously none of the people presumed to be targets of the midnight blasts was seriously injured, which isn't to say that no one died. A watchman in New York was killed, and the attorney general's would-be assassin was "blown to atoms," an early if accidental suicide bomber. Bits and pieces of his body flew up and down the street, onto doorsteps and roofs, through open windows into neighboring homes. His scalp was discovered. It had thick, dark, curly hair. That — plus a dog-eared Italian–English dictionary and a hat from an Italian haberdashery, which were also found on the scene — were the "clews [that] show terrorist was probably an Italian."

At each bomb site, investigators found identical leaflets with yet another chilling message:

[C]lass war is on. . . . [W]e have aspired to a better world, and you jailed us, you clubbed us, you deported us, you murdered us. . . . Do not expect us to sit down and pray and cry. . . . We mean to speak for [the proletariat with] the voice of dynamite, through the mouth of guns.[74]

Today a message like this would be blasted instantaneously around the world through cyberspace. In 1919 it was printed on pieces of pink paper found scattered on lawns, in streets, and in the detritus of the bombed buildings.

Entitled "Plain Words," the flyer was signed by a group calling itself the Anarchist Fighters. A group with a similar name, the American Anarchists, had signed "Go-Head!," the flyer distributed a few months earlier in New England. Neither group issued additional statements claiming responsibility for specific bombings.

The synchronicity of "Plain Words" and the June 2 bombings left little doubt that the so-called Anarchist Fighters were behind the June bombs. "Forces of law and order, shocked into activity by the bomb outrages . . . are today aligned against the anomaly of organized anarchy," the *Boston Evening*

Transcript announced on June 3, under the headline RUNNING DOWN THE TERRORISTS. The appearance of "Plain Words" at every target "was accepted as sufficient evidence of the national scope of the plot. . . . Department of Justice agents and police throughout the country are hunting the organized band of Anarchists who last night launched what they called an attempt to overthrow the government."[75]

~ Too many bombs, too many threats of violence: Americans felt encircled and endangered by unseen, unknown forces. After the 1919 May Day bombs, newspapers reported that investigators were "sleeplessly" working on the case, arrests were "imminent," and "the net tightens." After the June bombs, "newspapers were again ablaze with police reports of rapid progress. . . . [T]he bomb-throwers were hourly on the verge of capture." In fact, however, as the *Washington Post* noted, "no arrest has yet been made [in the May Day case], though a month has elapsed," and in the June case the immediate investigative results were "practically futile." As for the dead bomber, he was an anarchist, or maybe a Bolshevist, or a Wobbly. He was thought to be Italian one day, Russian another day, then Italian again and "associated with the leaders of one of the most dangerous Italian radical groups in the country," but then, after a week of "painstaking" endeavor, "not Italian." Whatever his nationality, closer examination of his scalp and skull fragments revealed, according to the *Post*, that he "must have been of a low ethnological type."[76]

The nation ratcheted up to a kind of Code Red threat alert. New terrorist attacks were predicted for the Fourth of July. Fortunately, as the *San Francisco Chronicle* succinctly put it, TERROR REIGN PREDICTED FOR FOURTH FIZZLES.[77]

Attorney general Palmer was shaken by his close call. One day after the June explosions, he began a reorganization at the Department of Justice. Ten days after the explosions, he asked Congress for more money to prevent "the wild fellows of this movement" from "ris[ing] up and destroy[ing] the Government at one fell swoop." Palmer recruited William Flynn, a former Secret Service director whom he called "the greatest anarchist expert in the United States," to head the Department's Bureau of Investigation. Within the Bureau, Palmer created a new General Intelligence Division, and promoted a young clerk to head it up. The division was tasked with surveillance of political dissent in America. The up-and-coming clerk was J. Edgar Hoover.[78]

In the immediate aftermath of the June 2 bombings, more than sixty suspects were taken in for questioning, without productive result. PUBLIC DE-

MANDS ACTION, declared the *Washington Post* on June 4. A muscular new policy was needed: ACT FIRST, THEORIZE AFTERWARD.[79]

The perpetrators continued to remain at large, however. "No arrests are in sight at this time," Flynn admitted on June 6.[80]

This was the moment when Luigi Galleani, the anarchist leader who had managed to stave off his own deportation for two years, was, along with eight followers, shipped out of the country. Precisely when it would have made sense to detain him for questioning, the big fish was released and swam through the net.

By autumn 1919, the investigation into the Palmer house bombing had hit a wall. No suspects had been charged in any of the May Day or June 2 bombings. For that matter, suspects had not been charged in the earlier bomb attacks of 1918 and 1919.[81]

The "lack of real 'leads' is remarkable," commented Louis Post, assistant secretary of labor at the time. "How was it possible for so gigantic a conspiracy of revolutionaries, if that is what it was, or so desperate an outburst of proletarian passion, if it was that, to have escaped detection when most of the detective agencies of the country . . . were pursuing the perpetrators of its crimes with tireless zeal? . . . [W]hat inference is possible, in all reason, except that the crimes were not of 'ultra-radical' origin, or else that the detectives were grossly inefficient?"[82]

— As bombs were exploding around the United States in 1919, communism had already exploded in Russia. The tsar and his family had been assassinated, and Vladimir Lenin and the Bolsheviks, now in control of the government, were calling for worldwide revolution.

The evil that most Americans saw in communism came home to roost in 1919. Communist sympathizers in the United States formed not one but two political parties: the American Communist Party and the smaller Communist Labor Party. Revolution appeared to be spreading like the plague. "In an intolerant postwar year . . . these domestic Bolsheviki seemed particularly dangerous. . . . [N]ever before had the nation been so overwhelmed with fear."[83] When coal miners, steelworkers, and Boston policemen all went on strike in the fall of 1919, many Americans thought they saw the raging menace of communism and revolution. As "faith in the loyalty of union labor finally tottered and collapsed, the last remaining barrier to hysteria disappeared."[84]

The period of the Red Scare had arrived.

Could anyone stop it? Not the president. On October 2 Wilson suffered a massive stroke and was unable to provide strong leadership for the remainder of his term. Not the attorney general either. On October 15 Palmer made a pro-immigration speech that provoked a backlash. The *New York Times* all but accused him of dereliction of duty, and an impatient United States Senate passed a unanimous resolution demanding to know if he had begun legal proceedings to arrest and deport alien anarchists yet, "and if not, why not."[85]

"I could feel it dinned into my ears — throughout the country," Palmer later said, "to do something and do it now, and do it quick."[86] On November 7, 1919 — the second anniversary of the Bolshevist revolution in Russia — the Palmer raids began in America.

— If it's an ill wind that blows no good, then an optimist might find some benefit in the Palmer raids. They did expose a need to protect American civil liberties.

The identity of the 1919 springtime bombers was still unknown in the fall. What was known was that many communists and anarchists in the United States were foreigners who opposed the government and were deportable under the Anarchist Exclusion Act of 1918 on the basis of their beliefs or organization memberships. "[T]here could be no nice distinctions drawn between the theoretical ideals of the radicals and their actual violations of our national laws," the attorney general contended.[87]

The raids began, appropriately enough, in the dark. On November 7, 1919, in several cities, including New York, agents of the Bureau of Investigation, working with local police, stormed into nighttime meetings of the Union of Russian Workers and rounded up everyone "regardless of [any] consideration except their presence there." About 450 people were arrested; most eventually were released.[88] State and local authorities staged follow-up raids, arresting hundreds more.

Palmer, who so recently had been criticized as ineffective, now began to reap praise for being strong and aggressive. On November 14 he reported to the Senate that domestic radicals seriously threatened the nation, and he lobbied to extend the Sedition Act. On November 25, agents again raided the headquarters of the Union of Russian Workers in New York; they made no arrests but announced they had discovered a secret "bomb factory."[89] The payoff of the November raids came on December 21, when a boatload of 249 deportees shipped out of New York aboard the *Buford*, a United States Army transport ship dubbed the Soviet Ark. On board and bound for Russia were 199 people arrested in the November raids, plus 43 anarchists previously slated for deportation, and 7 miscellaneous undesirables.[90]

The November raids, widespread though they were, were still "only tentative — in the nature somewhat of a laboratory experiment. The 'red' crusade began in earnest," Louis Post recalled, on January 2, 1920.[91] Undercover government agents who had infiltrated local chapters of the Communist Party and the Communist Labor Party had scheduled meetings for that day, to facilitate arrests.

By daybreak on January 3, agents had staged raids in thirty-three cities in twenty-three states. This time thousands of people — between two thousand and four thousand — were arrested. If modern polling methods had existed at the time, they would have measured Palmer's approval rating and found that it was off the charts. For the moment, the attorney general was a national hero.

But there were two fundamental problems with the Palmer raids: lawlessness and ineffectiveness. They surfaced almost immediately.

Palmer had opted for deportation as a counterterrorism strategy because it imposed fewer restrictions than criminal prosecution. Government bureaucrats, not juries, made deportation rulings, and their decisions were final; the right to due process required in criminal proceedings was not required at administrative proceedings. Inconveniently for Palmer, however, his own department, Justice, was not in charge of deportations. That was the job of the Bureau of Immigration, then part of the Department of Labor. Since "[i]n every case where any person is deported from the United States . . . the decision of the Secretary of Labor shall be final," Palmer needed the cooperation of the secretary or of his official stand-in to implement his strategy. After the raids, such cooperation began to evaporate.[92]

The justification for deporting those rounded up in the January 1920 raids was supposed to be membership in the Communist Party or the Communist Labor Party.[93] This proved to be inadequate justification.

On May 5, 1920 (the same day that Sacco and Vanzetti were arrested), Secretary of Labor William Wilson ruled that membership in the Communist Labor Party was not in itself sufficient grounds for deportation under the Anarchist Exclusion Act.[94] The Justice Department "frankly deplored the . . . decision."[95]

Three weeks later a group of prominent lawyers and legal scholars accused the attorney general and his agents — "those charged with the highest duty of enforcing the laws" — of six categories of crimes: cruel and unusual punishment of arrestees, in violation of the Eighth Amendment to the Constitution; arrests without warrants, in violation of the Fourth Amendment; unreasonable search and seizure, also in violation of the Fourth Amendment; compelling people to incriminate themselves, in violation of the Fifth Amendment;

entrapment by agents provocateurs; and misuse of office through anti-radical propaganda. The lawyers, in their *Report upon the Illegal Practices of the United States Department of Justice*, published page after page of affidavits, photographs, memoranda, letters, court transcripts, and articles—more than fifty pages of exhibits in all—to document the charges. "[B]y suppression, by ruthlessness, and by deliberate violation of the simple rules of American law and American decency," the Department of Justice had been a bigger threat to the country than the radicals, the report charged.[96]

It had now become clear that some of those rounded up in the raids were not Communists at all, but either had chanced to be near the meetings when the roundups took place, or had attended the meetings for unrelated reasons—to study Russian or algebra or geography, to form a bakers' cooperative, to attend a concert, or to discuss buying a car for mechanics' training.[97] Some detainees "did not so much as know the difference between bolshevism and rheumatism," reported Congressman George Huddleston of Alabama.[98]

Then, on June 23, 1920, Judge George Anderson of the United States Circuit Court of Appeals ruled that membership in the Communist Party was also not automatically a deportable offense under the Anarchist Exclusion Act. "There is no evidence," he wrote, "that the Communist Party is an organization advocating the overthrow of the government of the United States by force or violence. Hence all the petitioners ordered deported are entitled to be discharged from the custody of the immigration authorities."[99]

Statistics from the Palmer raids are hard to pin down with precision. Noting "the confusion of records" at the Justice Department and numbers only "purporting to be exact" from the Labor Department, Louis Post concluded that "round figures tell the story minutely enough." He estimated that of approximately six thousand arrest warrants issued, four thousand arrests were made, and less than one thousand deportations ordered.[100] The authors of the *Illegal Practices* report viewed the statistics differently. Palmer had claimed to have the names of sixty thousand radicals. By May 1920, 281 people had been deported as a result of the raids, and an additional 529 had been ordered deported. The "Attorney General has consequently got rid of 810 alien suspects, which, on his own showing, leaves him at least 59,160 [*sic*] persons (aliens and citizens) still to cope with."[101]

Palmer had warned the nation that a new terrorist plot to overthrow the government would erupt on May Day 1920. He was wrong. MAY DAY QUIET, the headlines announced.[102] Like July 4, 1919, another day of unrealized Palmer-predicted mayhem, May 1, 1920 passed without serious incident. Palmer's credibility tanked, and an anti-Palmer backlash began to pick up steam.

The man who only months earlier had been lauded as a national hero was now denounced as a national menace.

Congress had begun impeachment proceedings in April against Palmer's nemesis, Assistant Labor Secretary Louis Post, for releasing so many detainees while he had briefly served as acting secretary of labor. But after the May Day fizzle, it was Palmer who went to Capitol Hill to justify his actions. He "adamantly defended himself . . . but this time he was not convincing." Post kept his job. "The 'red' crusade began to look like a gigantic and cruel hoax," Post later recalled, "and that is what it finally proved to be."[103]

— "Alien filth": that was how Palmer in 1920 described the targets of his roundups, and by that term he meant Communists. Specifically, he said, the "nationality of most of the alien 'Reds' is Russian and German. There is almost no other nationality represented among them."[104]

Nevertheless, counterterrorism strategists at the Department of Justice had not forgotten about the Italian anarchists. William Flynn, director of the Bureau of Investigation, had come to believe that "the bomb plots of June 2 were conceived and directed by Luigi Galleani."[105]

An Italian immigrant named Eugenio Ravarini went to work for the bureau as an undercover informant in 1919.[106] His assignment: infiltrate groups of Italian anarchists to gather intelligence about the unsolved May Day and June bombings.

Posing as an ultra-militant, Ravarini gained the trust of anarchists in Boston, Providence, New York, and Paterson, New Jersey. He was a mole among them for seven months, from September 1919 to March 1920. He learned that the unidentified suicide bomber whose body had been found in bits and pieces outside Palmer's Washington home on June 2 was Carlo Valdinoci. Ravarini disappeared after Carlo Tresca began publishing suspicions about him. Though Ravarini's assignment lasted less than a year, the intelligence he gathered paved a twisty path to Sacco and Vanzetti.

Agents of the Bureau of Investigation followed Ravarini's leads to Paterson. There, on Valentine's Day 1920, they arrested members of an Italian anarchist group, seized weapons and literature, and most significantly discovered what appeared to be a smoking gun—a stash of pink paper similar to that on which the flyer "Plain Words," found at the scene of the June 2 bombings, had been printed. When agents questioned the printer in whose shop the paper was discovered, he said that the same kind of paper had been used in New York by another printer, Roberto Elia. One of the arrested Paterson anarchists also said that Elia might have printed the flyers.

Agents questioned Elia, searched his belongings, and found what they were looking for—more of the incriminating pink paper—as well as anarchist publications and an unregistered handgun. Elia admitted he was an anarchist. He was given a suspended sentence for unlawful possession of a firearm and turned over to the custody of the Bureau of Investigation for questioning about the 1919 bombings.

On March 8, 1920, Elia was taken to the bureau's New York office on Park Row in lower Manhattan. There he saw a friend, Andrea Salsedo, surrounded by four agents; later he heard Salsedo screaming and learned that he had been beaten. Elia and Salsedo had worked at the same print shop in Brooklyn, and both had also once worked for *Cronaca sovversiva*.

William Flynn came to New York to question Elia and Salsedo himself. The anarchists allegedly broke their code of silence. Elia later maintained he had revealed nothing because he knew nothing, but that Salsedo had admitted printing "Plain Words." At last, more than eight months after the June 2 bombings, investigators believed they were making progress.

Elia and Salsedo continued to be held in virtual isolation in the offices of the Bureau of Investigation for almost two more months, until the day, May 3, 1920, when Salsedo mysteriously plummeted from a fourteenth-story window to his death on a New York City sidewalk. The next day the *New York Times* reported that Salsedo had been "high in the councils of the Galliani [*sic*] group of destructionists," had admitted printing "Plain Words," and had confessed that Galleani anarchists were responsible for the bombings of June 2, 1919. Elia and Salsedo were also reported to have requested protection "against vengeance by their former confederates" for revealing information. (Elia later denied this.)[107]

Salsedo's death "materially weakened" the government's investigation, the *Times* reported. The anarchist's "death plunge" sent "the Galleanisti scurrying for cover and [exposed] the Bureau to intensive criticism for its allegedly brutal methods."[108]

Attorney general Palmer later claimed that Elia and Salsedo had "disclosed some very important information in connection with the bomb plot of June 2, 1919, and with their consent and the consent of their attorneys they remained in [custody] until the information . . . could be verified and other [conspirators] could be located." Assistant Labor Secretary Post didn't buy "this novelty of imprisonment by consent" and believed the men's detention was completely illegal, but Elia admitted that, given a choice of remaining in place or going to prison, "[we] decided we would rather stay at Park Row" to await deportation.[109]

Two days after Salsedo's death, Roberto Elia was rushed to Ellis Island to begin deportation proceedings.[110]

If Elia had really been "a bomb-plotter and important in this connection as a witness," then why, Post wondered, was the Justice Department "more anxious . . . to get him out of the country than into the dock or the witness chair of a criminal court"? Was it because he might testify not only about anarchist violence but about government violence as well? Truly, said Post, the Elia-Salsedo case was "wrapped in mystery."[111]

⁓ Agents of the Boston office of the Bureau of Investigation had known since February 1918, when they raided the offices of *Cronaca sovversiva*, that Sacco and Vanzetti subscribed to Galleani's newspaper. On May 14, 1920, nine days after Sacco and Vanzetti were arrested, agents passed this information on to the Massachusetts State Police.[112] Since Galleani supporters were by then suspected of involvement in the 1919 bombings, state authorities presumably connected the dots and realized that the two men they had in custody could be potential bombing suspects as well as potential murder suspects.

At trial the following year, Fred Katzmann questioned Sacco and Vanzetti about radicalism and draft-dodging, matters unrelated to the South Braintree murders. Two former agents in the bureau's Boston office would later swear that Katzmann had conspired with bureau agents to put this information on the record to ensure that the defendants, if acquitted of murder, could be deported for anarchism.[113]

⁓ After *Cronaca sovversiva* was shut down and Luigi Galleani deported, his supporters were in disarray. They "never went out into the streets after the Palmer raids," a sympathizer recalled.[114] Their chief concern became legal defense for their comrades, not propaganda by the deed.

With at least one possible exception: the attack on Wall Street.

When the bomb exploded in front of the Morgan bank on September 16, 1920, it killed thirty-three people immediately (more died later), and caused hundreds of injuries and millions of dollars' worth of property damage.[115] TERRORIST PLOT IS SEEN, the *New York Times* announced. Attorney general Palmer promptly ordered a "searching investigation," and went to New York to direct it.[116] His friends hoped the results would vindicate him and his anti-radical policies. On September 17, newspapers variously reported the Wall Street perpetrators to be "radicals" or "anarchist plotters" or Communists seeking revenge for the Soviet Ark deportations of the previous December.[117]

By nighttime there was another theory. William Flynn announced that five flyers had been discovered in a mailbox near the scene of the Wall Street explosion. In red ink the flyers declared: "Remember. We will not tolerate any longer. Free the political prisoners or it will be death for all of you." The threat was signed: American Anarchist Fighters.

This discovery quickly convinced investigators that "the explosion in Wall Street was caused by a bomb planted by the same group of anarchists who perpetrated the bomb outrages of June 1919"—a group previously identified in the press as followers of Luigi Galleani.[118] The "same group of Italian terrorists" responsible for the Wall Street plot was also reported to be responsible for the May Day bombings of 1919.[119]

Flynn was said to be seeking five men for questioning, including Carlo Tresca and Roberto Elia (who had already been deported). The *Chicago Tribune* reported that the five men were "disciples of Luigi Galliani [sic], himself a pupil of the notorious Malatesta of Italy. . . . To the Galliani [sic] gang was traced the bomb explosions of June 2, 1919." Flynn was reported to be confident about bringing the perpetrators to justice. " 'We'll get them,' he said. 'We solved the mystery of the June 2, 1919 bombs, but were frustrated in bringing the criminals to justice when Salsedo jumped from our offices to the street below and killed himself. That tipped our hand and the crowd [of suspects] got away. . . . [But we'll] get them.' "[120]

Flynn's optimism proved unfounded. No one was ever charged in the case of the May Day package bombs or in the case of the June 2 midnight bombs. Nor, despite hefty rewards and an exhaustive investigation, was anyone ever charged in the case of the Wall Street bomb.[121] Flynn was fired in 1921.[122] His successor, William Burns, had no better luck in the investigation. The bomb attacks became cold cases.

Historian Paul Avrich has reconstructed what he believes is a likely scenario for the Wall Street explosion. Sacco and Vanzetti were indicted for murder on September 11, 1920, at which point Mario Buda had been in hiding for months. Avrich believes it was Buda who acquired horse, wagon, and bomb, and positioned them to such deadly effect on Wall Street, in retaliation for the indictments of his friends. Buda sailed for Italy shortly thereafter and never returned to the United States.

The theory is often repeated as incontrovertible fact, but Avrich did not present it that way, noting that it "cannot be proved; documentary evidence is lacking. But it fits what we know of [Buda] and his movements. I have it, moreover, from a reliable source and believe it to be true."[123] The source most likely was Buda's friend Charles Poggi, who said that Frank Maffi, Buda's nephew, took him to Wall Street in 1933 to "see my uncle's bomb."[124] Poggi related the incident to Avrich in 1987.

As for Buda himself, he told an interviewer in 1928 that "I never saw any [bombs] and never had anything to do with any."[125]

— The Wall Street bomb caused death and destruction, and "that is all it did," the *Wall Street Journal* editorialized a day after the explosion. "The Stock Exchange . . . will resume business. . . . [H]eartbroken relatives will bury their dead. . . . The relations between capital and labor will not be changed, not even for the worse as regards labor; for no one but a fool has ever doubted Wall Street's courage."[126] After the initial shock of the attack subsided, the "nation sadly shrugged [the incident] off as the probable work of a lone fanatic, not, as Palmer continued to insist shrilly, the product of a vast subversive conspiracy."[127]

— F. Scott Fitzgerald said the Jazz Age began around the time of the May Day bombings in 1919. "It was characteristic of the Jazz Age," he observed, "that it had no interest in politics at all."[128]

Certainly Americans had had enough by the second half of 1920. Enough drama, sending young men overseas to make the world safe for democracy. Enough paranoia, trembling to the thunder of revolutionary threats and counterthreats at home. When the Republican presidential candidate, Senator Warren G. Harding, offered the philosophical equivalent of comfort food during the campaign of 1920 — "not heroism but healing, not nostrums but normalcy" — it sounded pretty good.[129] Harding's running mate was Massachusetts governor Calvin Coolidge, the stand-tough hero of the Boston police strike. They won by a landslide. On the day of their inauguration, March 4, 1921, the controversial and tumultuous tenure of Attorney general A. Mitchell Palmer came to an end.

Five months later, after Sacco and Vanzetti had been convicted of murder, the *New York Daily News* published an article charging that Boston-based followers of Luigi Galleani were behind the bombing of Wall Street. The paper illustrated the article with mug shots of Sacco and Vanzetti, implying a direct link between the men and the bomb.

Galleani anarchists had been the prime suspects in the Wall Street bombing all along, the article declared, although "[o]f course, this was not officially announced. . . . The investigators have many reasons for placing the blame . . . on the Galleani group which may never be made public. They know without a shadow of doubt that they were responsible for the [springtime 1919 bombings]. . . . Roberto Elia, an Italian anarchist . . . made a complete confession to the authorities before he was deported."[130]

The byline read "By Investigator." Fred Moore believed the anonymous author was William Burns, the man who had just replaced William Flynn as director of the Bureau of Investigation, but more likely it was the ousted Flynn himself, trying to defuse his critics.[131] Moore complained the article was "made out of whole cloth. It contains nothing that can be affirmatively denied, because it contains no affirmative allegations, except against those unnamed and unidentified persons." If investigators truly had no doubts about the identity of the Wall Street bombers, Moore asked rhetorically, then why had no one ever been charged?[132]

⁓ After the bombings and roundups and deportations had petered out, and the basis for many arrests had been overturned; after Andrea Salsedo had died and Luigi Galleani had been deported and A. Mitchell Palmer had left office; even after the Jazz Age had arrived, traces of the Red Scare remained. They continued to show up in restrictive immigration laws and anti-unionism and residual mistrust of radicals.

When they went on trial in 1921, Sacco and Vanzetti did not hide the fact that they were anarchists. By choosing to stand by their beliefs, they cast themselves in the role of ungrateful immigrants and potentially violent enemies of the state. How this influenced the jury that convicted them of murder is a never-ending conundrum.

Part
Two

Like crippled eagles fallen were the . . .
men in the cage
~ Arturo Giovannitti, "The Cage"

9 | DEDHAM: CURTAIN RISING

Boston sizzled in the summer of 1921. A record heat wave blistered the parched city. In only two of the preceding 103 years had so meager an amount of rain fallen in June. Kids sought fleeting relief in the spray of fire hydrants. When night fell, perspiring families went outside in search of a breeze and a good night's sleep, sprawling on tenement roofs and wharves, on the banks of the Charles River and the lawn of Boston Common.[1]

It was no cooler twenty miles away in Dedham, where the criminal cases of Sacco and Vanzetti were about to get under way in Norfolk County Superior Court. The players in the unfolding drama began to assemble in the nineteenth-century courthouse on High Street.

Elizabeth Glendower Evans arrived in Dedham. Now in her sixties, the socially prominent champion of progressive causes was relocating for the duration of the trial to the unoccupied Dedham home of her friend and mentor, Associate Justice Louis Brandeis of the United States Supreme Court. Years earlier when he was a practicing attorney in Boston, Brandeis had been a frequent guest of Evans and her late husband, and Evans attributed her political awakening to "Mr. Brandeis' habit of talking over his public interests at home."[2] Whenever the Sacco-Vanzetti trial was in session, Evans would be in the courtroom.

Rosina Sacco arrived in Dedham. She stayed with Evans, becoming perhaps the only wife of a defendant in a capital case ever to put up at the home of an associate justice. Rosina would also be in court every day. Son Dante, now 8, probably remained with family friends in Stoughton and continued going to school during the week, but little Ines, only seven months old, stayed in Dedham with her mother. During court recesses, Nick would be permitted to play with the daughter who had been born after his arrest.[3]

The legal teams arrived in Dedham. District attorney Frederick Katzmann would prosecute, as he had at Vanzetti's trial in Plymouth, aided by assistant district attorneys Harold Williams, William Kane, and George Adams. Brothers Thomas and Jeremiah J. (J. J.) McAnarney would defend Vanzetti, while Fred Moore and William Callahan would represent Sacco, with Moore unofficially in charge.[4]

The judge arrived in Dedham. Webster Thayer would preside. Superior Court judges were assigned to counties throughout the state on rotation. Thayer had been scheduled to sit in Fitchburg in June 1921, but he requested the change of assignment to Dedham.[5] Perhaps he wanted the chance to bring people he thought of as terrorists to justice. Perhaps he simply thought it would be a good career move. Whatever his motives, the assignment meant that Thayer would be presiding at the trial of someone he had already sentenced for another crime.

Pro-defense observers arrived in Dedham. They represented the Greater Boston Federation of Churches, the New England Civil Liberties Committee, and the Sacco-Vanzetti Defense Committee. Marquis Agostino Ferrante, the Italian consul in Boston, went to Dedham almost every day to observe the proceedings.

Undercover agents of the Boston office of the Bureau of Investigation also arrived in Dedham. Their mission was to observe the other observers.[6]

Frank Sibley arrived in Dedham. The "dean of the Boston newspapermen," Sibley would cover the trial for the *Boston Globe*.[7] The case had not yet attracted much attention in the mainstream national press, but it was front-page news in Boston.

And Bartolomeo Vanzetti arrived in Dedham, where Sacco was already incarcerated. A week earlier, Bartolomeo had written to his father from Charlestown State Prison to tell him that the trial was about to begin. He surmised that, by the time the letter reached Italy, the trial would probably be over, and "let's hope for my acquittal. . . . It could also happen that, for a second time, I am found guilty, I who am not so at all. But, by God, the error cannot last."[8]

As he was driven to Dedham Jail, Vanzetti drank in the sights along the way. At the jail, the other inmates did "their best to give me a . . . cheer up. [Then] I was brought to the Court, protected by a numerous American Cossack, as if I and Nick were a Russian Czars."[9]

The Cossacks allusion refers to the beefed-up security in place for the trial. Iron shutters and steel doors had been installed in the courtroom, to seal it off in case a bomb exploded. About two weeks into the trial, police also began patting down spectators to search for concealed weapons.[10] Four times a day—at the opening and close of proceedings, and back and forth at lunchtime—police led Sacco and Vanzetti in shackles on the short walk between jail and courthouse, tromping the peaceful streets of Dedham in a militaristic parade. It would later be argued that this unprecedented "stage scenery" was designed to prejudice a jury, but it seemed justifiable at the time as a precaution against potential violence by angry spectators or Galleani anarchists.[11]

Manacled together at the wrist and surrounded by guards, Sacco and Vanzetti walk the leafy streets of Dedham between jail and courthouse. Courtesy of the Trustees of the Boston Public Library/Rare Books.

Bartolomeo and Nick would be reunited for the duration of the trial. Nick had recently turned thirty. Bartolo turned thirty-three while the trial was in progress, but he looked much older, people said. The men had high hopes. Nick was sure he would be set free after he had a chance to tell his story.[12]

The *Boston Globe* noted that Vanzetti was already serving time for another crime, yet neither defendant "looks a desperate criminal. Both have the heavy jaws that are typical of so many Italian immigrants; both have round heads."[13]

~ On Tuesday, May 31, 1921, the players who had been converging on Dedham took their seats in the spacious paneled courtroom on the second floor.

Sacco and Vanzetti did not sit next to their attorneys at the defense table. Instead, as was the custom in capital cases in Massachusetts at the time, the defendants sat penned in a metal enclosure in front of the judge. The cage restricted easy courtroom communication between defense attorneys and their clients. Opponents believed it also had a harmful subliminal effect on a jury and made a mockery of the concept of presumed innocence.

Five hundred citizens of Norfolk County made up the initial jury pool for the trial—at the time reportedly the largest panel ever called in the state.[14] All of them were men. (Women did not become eligible to serve on juries in Massachusetts until 1950.)[15] Each juror's name, profession, and hometown was published in the press as soon as he was chosen; anonymity was not an option.

Jurors would be sequestered. Thayer urged those before him to make any sacrifice necessary to serve. "[R]emember the American soldier had other duties and he would rather have performed [them] than those that resulted in his giving up his life upon the battlefields of France," Thayer began. "I call upon you to render this service here . . . with the same spirit of patriotism, courage and devotion to duty as was exhibited by our soldier boys across the seas."[16]

Lawyers did not question jury candidates directly; the judge approved and asked all questions. Thayer declined Moore's request to ask jurors about their attitudes toward Italians and labor unions. Instead he settled on five questions to determine if potential jurors should be disqualified, either because they had already made up their minds about the case or because they were so opposed to capital punishment that they could not render a guilty verdict since, as he made clear, "The penalty upon conviction of this alleged crime is death."[17]

Thayer wanted jury selection to move quickly. For the first few days, he kept court in session until late at night, leaving just enough time for folks to catch the last train out of Dedham back to their homes. Most jurors who were excused from duty got off for opposition to the death penalty, but not before undergoing "a scorching and scornful inquiry" from Thayer. "Do you set your opinions above the law?" he asked one. To another: Do you lack courage? And to another: Did you ever do anything to get the law changed?[18]

Jury candidates paraded in and out, too old, too sick, too unwilling, or in many cases too hard-of-hearing to serve. Some brought levity to the serious business at hand. Spectators, including Nick and Bartolomeo, laughed so hard they cried at the spectacle of one potential juror trying without success to pretend that he was deaf.[19]

Despite the extended hours and the judge's exhortations, it was, the *Globe* noted, "hard work to fill jury box."[20] By the end of day 3, only seven jurors had been chosen. Worse, the supersized pool of five hundred was exhausted. Thayer ordered the sheriff of Norfolk County to round up two hundred more candidates overnight, wherever he could find them "from the bystanders or from the county at large." They "will jump [and run away] when they see me coming," Sheriff Samuel Capen dryly predicted.[21]

In towns throughout the county that night, Capen and his deputies rang doorbells in buildings wherever they saw a light still burning. They corralled

Masons from a lodge meeting, concertgoers from a band performance, even a newlywed from his wedding supper.[22] Eventually they managed to dredge up 175 new candidates. Defense lawyers unsuccessfully objected to this method of summoning a jury pool. On Friday, June 3, candidates from the new pool were questioned.

Finally, just after midnight on Saturday, June 4, the last juror was chosen. By then the other jurors were sound asleep in temporary quarters in the grand jury room. Thayer had them wakened. "[C]ollarless, their shirts open, two of them in slippers," they shuffled back into the courtroom.[23] Around one thirty in the morning, the judge swore them in, and court adjourned.

The new jurors had the rest of the weekend off, time to get acquainted and acclimate to their new quarters—a room with cots in the basement of probate court. They spent their time quietly, strolling around Dedham, going for escorted drives, listening to "canned music" on phonograph records, and "watching automobiles passing through the square."[24]

— In the first few days of the trial, before a single syllable of the opening statements had been uttered, Webster Thayer revealed such a visceral antipathy to Fred Moore that it would become the stuff of legend.

According to Aldino Felicani, Moore originally was supposed to be in charge only of pre-trial preparation, and local lawyers Jeremiah and Thomas McAnarney were supposed to handle the courtroom work. "But when the trial started," Felicani said, "the McAnarneys were pushed into [the background]."[25] They were immediately troubled by "the pronounced difficulty of Judge Thayer and Mr. Moore getting along together." It seemed, Tom McAnarney later recalled, that whenever Moore addressed the court, "it was quite similar to waving a red flag in the face of a [bull. . . . His remarks] got under Judge Thayer's skin. Judge Thayer would respond by telling him that he might be practicing law outside in the West or in California, but not in Massachusetts."

The McAnarneys consulted brother John, and asked him to take over the case. John McAnarney was not available to do that, but he asked William Thompson, a highly respected Boston attorney, to do so. Tom and Jeremiah McAnarney said they would give Thompson the fees they had already received and would continue "on with the case, having got into it, without any compensation at all if we could get Mr. Moore to retire."[26]

Thompson and John McAnarney met with Moore the following day at the courthouse. "[W]e labored for a long time in one of the anterooms to get him to withdraw from the case. He positively refused to do so."[27] The case "was his baby"; he wouldn't relinquish it, lawyer Herbert Ehrmann later explained. "He was going to make a great name for himself." Thompson gave Rosina Sacco the news. "She broke down and cried . . . ," Ehrmann said. "She didn't want Moore."[28]

Thompson stayed in court that day as a spectator, observing the Thayer-Moore interplay. He summed up his impressions for John McAnarney: "Your goose is cooked."[29]

During the trial it was the custom of reporters, lawyers, and judge to walk to the Dedham Inn when court recessed for lunch. On these midday breaks Thayer often spoke about the case to reporters. Walking back to the court-house after lunch one day during the first week of the trial, he "proceeded to discuss Attorney Moore," reporter Frank Sibley later recalled. "This subject seemed to excite him considerably and . . . he exclaimed, 'I'll show them that no long-haired anarchist from California can run this court!'"[30] Reporter (and defense supporter) John Nicholas Beffel also recalled Thayer expressing his anger during the first week—at the Italian government for sending Marquis Ferrante to observe the trial, at Moore for objecting to the method of enlarging the jury pool, and at the defense in general for claiming a fair trial was impossible. Thayer shook his fist, Beffel later recalled, and told the reporters in the restaurant, "You wait till I give my charge to the jury. I'll show 'em!"

The reporters consulted with each other about Thayer's unorthodox behavior. They agreed to keep silent about it.[31]

Why did Moore annoy the judge so much? The antipathy seems to have been based on differences in both philosophy and lifestyle.

Moore had spent years defending the IWW, an organization surely reprehensible to the conservative Thayer, and now he was on the judge's turf, defending draft dodgers affiliated with an anarchist who condoned violent terrorist acts. Moore's personal life was also controversial. "He was an unstable man," said Roger Baldwin, founder of the American Civil Liberties Union. "He had plenty of women," recalled Aldino Felicani, who also thought Moore "was using morphine, or something like that." At court Moore defied propriety, occasionally shedding his suit jacket, his vest, even his shoes because of the heat. ("For God's sake, keep that coat on in the courtroom, can't you?" Tom McAnarney chided him one day.) Moore was, in the words of Herbert Ehrmann, "singularly inept at accommodating himself to local conditions and procedures."[32]

Perhaps more than anything, however, the antipathy was based on Thayer's wounded professional pride. Moore had been working to create a pro-defense buzz before the trial in Dedham even began. Beffel's article in *The New Republic* had attacked the conduct of Vanzetti's trial at Plymouth; Art Shields's pamphlet had specifically attacked Thayer for his conduct there; and the Angelina DeFalco trial publicly challenged the integrity of the system that Thayer represented.

Thayer's supporters defended him, believing that descriptions of his behavior in the early days of the trial were false. As for Tom McAnarney, who was at the trial every day and who later became a judge himself, he came to believe that Thayer simply "couldn't conduct a trial fairly with Attorney Moore on the other side."[33]

10 | DOCKET NOS. 5545 AND 5546

On Monday, June 6, 1921, as the *Canopic* sailed into the port of Boston with its shipload of newly illegal Italian passengers, the trial of Nicola Sacco and Bartolomeo Vanzetti rolled into its second week. Taking the "dustiest ride on record in Massachusetts," jurors, lawyers, reporters, and the judge were driven in open cars over dirt roads to view sites connected to the crime.[1]

Assistant district attorney Harold Williams opened for the prosecution on Tuesday. Our "contention . . ., gentlemen," he said, "is that this crime was committed by five men."[2] The one who shot Berardelli "is described and identified as Nicola Sacco," and a bandit in the getaway car is "identified as the other defendant, Bartolomeo Vanzetti." Although no witness "saw Vanzetti fire any gun," Williams continued, if he had conspired to kill, he was as guilty as if he had pulled the trigger. The getaway car was a 1920 Buick that had been temporarily garaged in a shed "at the Coacci house"; the bandits picked Vanzetti up at a train station before the crime; they were familiar with local roads; they abandoned the Buick in the woods; a cap similar to Sacco's was found at the scene of the crime; and the bullet that killed Alessandro Berardelli came from a gun of the same make and caliber as Sacco's gun. Williams said nothing about the identity of the other three bandits, or about attempts by the defendants to draw weapons or hide guilt.

After being reminded to do so by the judge, Williams told the jury that the defendants should be presumed innocent until proven guilty beyond a reasonable doubt. Then he called the first witness.

— More than 150 people took the stand during the course of the trial.[3] Testimony spilled over into a fifth week, a sixth week, a seventh week. The opening statement for the defense came more than two weeks after the prosecution's. Day after hot day, week after long week, conflicting testimony piled up. For the sake of clarity in the account that follows, evidence is presented by category.

Lola Andrews identified Sacco as the man she had spoken to a few hours prior to the crime. She said that she took a train to South Braintree on April 15, 1920, to look for a job. As she approached the Slater & Morrill factory, she passed two men working on a car; they were still there when she left the factory a short time later. She asked them for directions to the nearby Rice & Hutchins factory. One of the men, who had been working underneath the car, stood up and directed her to her destination. That man, she said, was the man in the cage, Nicola Sacco. In the courtroom, Sacco jumped to his feet. "I am the man?" he shouted. "Do you mean me? Take a good look." "A court officer sprang at the prisoner as he stood in the cage," the *Globe* reported, "and pushed him back into his chair."[4]

Andrews was on the witness stand for three days. In the steamy courtroom, with jurors fluttering the fans they'd been given, Moore cross-examined her about discrepancies between her current and earlier statements. Andrews became confused, but Moore, astonishingly unaware of what he was doing, led her into describing an earlier promise he had made to give her a vacation and a new job,[5] apparently as a bribe.

More than two weeks after Lola Andrews took the stand, five defense witnesses refuted her testimony. *Julia Campbell*, her companion on the day of the crime, was "positively sure" that Andrews had not spoken to any man working around a car that day. *George Fay*, a policeman, said that in February Andrews had told him she had been assaulted by a man in the building where she lived; when Fay asked if the attacker was one of the bandits from South Braintree, she told him repeatedly that she had not seen their faces. *Alfred Labrecque*, a reporter who interviewed Andrews about the February attack, said she told him the same thing. *Harry Kurlansky*, a businessman and friend of Andrews, said that in February she told him that people were "bothering the life out of me. . . . [T]he Government took me down [to the jail] and want me to recognize those men [Sacco and Vanzetti] . . . and I don't know a thing about them. I have never seen them and I can't recognize them." Judge Thayer reprimanded Kurlansky for not personally investigating Andrews's allegations of government misconduct. Finally, *Lena Allen*, Andrews's landlady, testified that Andrews had a reputation as an "untruthful" person.[6]

In addition to Andrews, two other prosecution witnesses identified Sacco as someone they had seen in South Braintree prior to the crime. *William Tracy*, a real estate agent, said he noticed two men leaning against a store window a few hours before the crime and, "[w]hile I wouldn't be positive, I would say to the best of my recollection" that one of them was Sacco.[7] *William Heron*, a railroad policeman, said he observed two nervous Italians "sitting there beside the gent's toilet" in the South Braintree railroad station a few hours before the crime, and one of them, "the smallest one," was Sacco. Originally Heron had told state investigators that both men were smoking when he saw them. Sacco did not smoke, and by the time of the trial, Heron testified, "They were smoking cigarettes, one of them. The tallest one."[8]

Prosecution witness *Louis Pelser*, a shoe cutter at the Rice & Hutchins factory, identified Sacco as someone he had spotted while the crime was in progress. Pelser said he saw Sacco, or someone who was the "dead image" of him, shoot Berardelli four times and also "put a bullet over towards where Parmenter fell."[9] Pelser was the only witness who claimed to see one of the defendants fire a gun. He observed the crime, he said, from a factory window, which he opened when he heard noise outside. He also said he wrote down the license plate number of the getaway car, and on the stand he recited it. On cross-examination, Pelser admitted he had initially begged off identifying the suspects on the grounds that he hadn't gotten a good look at the bandits, and that he had told a defense investigator he didn't remember the license plate number and didn't see the shooting because he was hiding under a workbench. Now, Pelser said those were lies he told to avoid being called as a witness.

Two weeks later, the defense called three of Pelser's co-workers to refute his testimony. *Dominic Constantino* said he saw Pelser take cover under the workbench for a couple of minutes when the shooting started, then go to a window and yell for someone to "get the number." Constantino also testified he heard Pelser say, "I did not see any of the men, but I got the number of the car." *Peter McCullum* said he, not Pelser, was the one who opened and quickly closed the factory window, and that he did not see Pelser until "after the thing was all over." *William Brenner* said he was certain Pelser had not been at the window. (Katzmann addressed Brenner on the stand as "Heinie," a nickname for Heinrich and a derogatory term for Germans. Although himself of patrilineal German descent, Katzmann may have hoped the ethnic slur would discredit Brenner. "My name is William, sir," Brenner corrected him.)[10]

Prosecution witness *Lewis Wade*, a worker at Slater & Morrill, surely disappointed the attorneys who called him. Wade testified that he had just finished gassing up Mr. Slater's car when shots rang out, and he saw a man shoot Berardelli. At the Brockton police station, he had identified that man as Sacco. But now, on the stand in Dedham, he wavered. "Well, I ain't sure now," he said. "I have a little doubt. . . . [M]y best judgment is this: If I have a doubt, I don't think he is the man." Wade explained he had changed his mind because he had since seen someone else, a stranger in a barbershop, who resembled Berardelli's killer. Judge Thayer told the jury that Wade's failure to identify Sacco was "not affirmative evidence against Sacco; it only attacks the credibility of this witness."[11]

Like Wade, several other prosecution witnesses who had seen the bandits when the crime was in progress did not identify the defendants. From her kitchen window, *Annie Nichols* said she observed two bandits leaning against a fence, saw one of them speak to Berardelli, heard shots, raced outside, and saw three bandits pile into the getaway car. *James McGlone*, a laborer, said he saw "two or three" bandits leaning against a fence, heard shots, and saw two bandits pile into the car. *Edgar Langlois*, a foreman at Rice & Hutchins, said he was on the second floor of the factory when he heard noise, opened a window, saw two men firing guns, ran to a phone to call police, ran back to the window, and saw "some more shooting."[12] Neither Nichols, McGlone, nor Langlois could identify Sacco or Vanzetti as one of the bandits they had seen.[13] Likewise, *Louis DeBerardinis*, a shoemaker and witness for the prosecution, said he had seen a gunman in the getaway car, but "there is a lot of difference" between that gunman and Sacco. *Mark Carrigan*, a shoe cutter, said that, from a third-floor window at Slater & Morrill, he had seen a gunman on the front seat of the getaway car, but could not identify Sacco or Vanzetti as that man.[14] Mechanic *James Bostock* said he had seen four of the bandits, and driver *Hans Behrsin* said he had seen five of them; neither Bostock nor Behrsin could identify the men they had seen.[15]

Several defense witnesses also testified that Sacco was not among the bandits they had seen in South Braintree either prior to or during the crime. Nurse *Jennie Novelli* said the bandits' car traveled slowly "for some distance alongside of me" right before the shooting; she observed two men in the front seat, neither of whom was Sacco or Vanzetti. *Albert Frantello*, a worker at Slater & Morrill, was walking on the street right before the shooting. He said he saw two men leaning against a fence by the Rice & Hutchins factory; he was close enough to have touched them. They attracted his attention because the "first fellow was criticizing the other fellow . . . [s]peaking in the American language." Frantello was sure Sacco and Vanzetti were not the men he had seen. Three workers from a construction site across the street from the crime scene took the stand. *Henry Cerro* said he had seen one shooter, and *Sibriano Gudierres* and *Pedro Iscorla* said they had seen two shooters. Cerro, Gudierres, and Iscorla all testified that Sacco and Vanzetti were not the gunmen they had seen. And *Barbara Liscomb*, a worker on the second floor of Rice & Hutchins, said that on April 15 she had looked down from an open window to see the crime in progress. "[T]wo men [were] lying on the ground, and one man, a short dark man, [was] standing on the ground facing me, with his head up, holding a revolver." Liscomb said she would "always remember his face" and was "positively sure" that neither Sacco nor Vanzetti was that man.[16]

Had Sacco been in the getaway car after the shooting? Three prosecution witnesses said yes.

Mary Splaine, a bookkeeper at Slater & Morrill, said she had been in her office on the second floor of the factory when she heard shots, looked down onto the street from behind a closed window, saw the approaching getaway car, and saw a man standing up in the back of the car with his left hand on the front seat. She described this man—glimpsed in a moving car, from behind a second-story window—in almost photographic detail: He "was slightly taller than I am. He weighed possibly from 140 to 145 pounds. He was muscular—he was an active looking man. I noticed particularly the left hand was a good sized hand, a hand that denoted strength. . . . He had a . . . clean-cut face. . . . The forehead was high. The hair was brushed back and it was . . . two and one-half inches in length and [he] had dark eyebrows, but the complexion was a white, peculiar white that looked greenish." Splaine said she was positive she had seen this man again at the Brockton police station, and she identified him as Sacco. On cross-examination, she admitted saying at the preliminary hearing that "I don't think my opportunity afforded me the right to say he is the man." She also admitted that, when state police showed her mug shots from their rogues' gallery, she said the man in one photograph "bore a striking resemblance to the man I saw at South Braintree," but had since learned that that man had been in prison on April 15. Splaine now maintained that, having had ample time to observe Sacco in court during the hearing, "on reflection" she was sure he was the bandit she had seen.[17]

Frances Devlin, also a bookkeeper at Slater & Morrill, said she had been sitting at a second-floor window when she heard shots, saw the car approach, and saw a man in the backseat lean out with a gun in his hand and shoot into the crowd. She was sure that man was Sacco. She admitted saying at the preliminary hearing that she wasn't positive Sacco was the man, but now said she just "put it that way" because of "the immensity of the crime and everything, I hated to say right out and out."[18]

Finally, *Carlos Goodridge*, a salesman who had been in a nearby pool hall when the shooting began, said he heard shots, stepped outside, saw an approaching car, saw a man in the car point a gun at him, and ducked back inside the poolroom. He said he saw the man again in the Dedham courthouse in the fall of 1920, and that Sacco was that man. The defense tried to introduce the fact that Goodridge had been in the courthouse at that time because he himself was a defendant in a criminal case, but the judge did not allow that line of questioning.[19]

Nearly two weeks after Goodridge took the stand, four defense witnesses refuted his testimony. The manager of the pool hall, *Peter Magazu*, said Goodridge told him the bandit he had seen had "light hair, light complexion." Barber *Harry Arrogni* said Goodridge told him he had seen a man in the getaway car, "but if I have got to say who the man was, I can't say." Another barber, *Nicola Damato*, testified he heard Goodridge say that he hadn't seen anyone in the getaway car. Goodridge's employer at the time of the shooting, *Andrew Manganio*, said Goodridge told him he "could not possibly remember the faces" of any of the bandits. Manganio also said that Goodridge's reputation for telling the truth was "bad."[20]

Fourteen additional witnesses to the escape from the crime scene testified for the defense that Sacco was not one of the bandits they had seen in the getaway car. *Frank Burke*, a glassblower, said he had been walking along the street when he heard shots and saw two men jump on the running board of the slowly approaching getaway car. When the car was about ten feet away from him, a man climbed from the backseat to the front, pointed a gun at him, and yelled at him in English, "Get out of the way, you son of a B." Burke said none of the men he observed in the car was Sacco or Vanzetti. Truck driver *Elmer Chase* described two men he had seen in the front seat of the getaway car and said he was positive neither one was Sacco or Vanzetti. (Chase also testified that he heard Chief Stewart tell a police officer, "We haven't got the right men. They have got away.") Laborer *Emielio Falcone* said he heard shots and noticed "three or four persons, all in a mixup"; he described the driver and a gunman, and said neither one resembled the defendants. Truck driver *William Foley* said he saw two bandits in the car, the driver and a man in the backseat, and Sacco and Vanzetti were not those men (although, he admitted, he had not had a good view of the backseat passenger). Railroad worker *Nicolo Gatti* said he heard shots, ran toward the sound, and, from a distance of four to five feet, observed the approaching getaway car with four or five bandits inside, three of whom he saw clearly; neither Sacco nor Vanzetti was among those men.[21]

Also, seven members of a work crew who had been installing new railroad ties on the tracks in South Braintree on April 15 testified that they heard shots, then walked or ran toward the sound of the shots and observed the getaway car. *Fortinato Antonello* said he got a look at one bandit in the backseat behind the driver; *Antonio Frabizio* said he saw five bandits, and got a good look at

A *Boston Globe* image shows Vanzetti, left, and Sacco in the courtroom. They sit in a cage, as was customary for defendants in capital cases in Massachusetts at the time. Rosina Sacco, right, approaches during a break in the proceedings. Courtesy of the Trustees of the Boston Public Library/Rare Books.

the driver; *Joseph Cellucci* said he got a good look at two bandits, one in the backseat and one in the front; *Cesidio Magnerelli* said he got a look at three men in the car; *Dominic DiBona* said he saw two men in the car, one of whom he had spoken to earlier on the street; *Donato DiBona* said he observed five bandits in the car, and saw the faces of the two who were in the front seat; and *Tobia DiBona* said he saw four men in the car, and described the two in the front seat. All seven of these witnesses said that neither Sacco nor Vanzetti was among the bandits they had observed in the car.[22]

A prosecution witness was called in the trial's final week to refute the railroad crew workers. Crew foreman *Angelo Ricci* said the workers "started to go [toward the sound of the shooting], and . . . I told them not to go." He also admitted that some of them might have gone anyway, even though "I ain't seen nobody."[23]

Salesman *Walter Desmond* and laborer *Wilson Dorr* saw the getaway car on its escape route out of South Braintree. Desmond said he saw four or more men inside; he described the driver, and said neither Sacco nor Vanzetti was that man. Dorr said he "had a good look at the faces" of four men in the car, and was sure that Sacco and Vanzetti "were not the men I saw."[24]

Two witnesses for the prosecution identified Vanzetti as someone they had seen prior to the crime. *Harry Dolbeare* said he noticed "a carload of foreigners" in South Braintree several hours before the crime, and had "[n]ot a particle" of doubt that Vanzetti was among them. And *John Faulkner* testified that he traveled by train to Boston on the morning of April 15, riding at the baggage end of a smoking car. He said Vanzetti was the passenger sitting behind him on the train that day, the passenger who wanted to disembark at East Braintree but was unfamiliar with the route and so at three other stops inquired if they were at his destination yet.[25]

Two weeks after Faulkner took the stand, five railroad employees called by the defense challenged his testimony. *Edward Brooks*, a ticket agent at the East Braintree station, said the train Faulkner took that day had no combination baggage/smoking car. *Ernest Pratt*, a ticket agent in Vanzetti's hometown of Plymouth, said no Plymouth–East Braintree ticket was sold on April 15; and *Harry Cash* and *Lester Wilmarth*, ticket agents at two Plymouth-area stations, said Vanzetti was not in those stations on that day. (When he cross-examined Pratt, Katzmann pointed out that the absence of a Plymouth–East Braintree ticket sale on April 15 did not rule out the possibility that someone could have purchased a ticket to a more distant destination, then disembarked early.) Finally, conductor *Henry McNaught* said that, according to his written records, no one used a ticket to travel from any of the three Plymouth-area stations to any Braintree station on April 15. McNaught also said he didn't recall that there had ever been a combination baggage/smoking car on the train that Faulkner took.[26]

Two witnesses for the prosecution identified Vanzetti as someone they had seen subsequent to the crime, inside the getaway car. *Michael Levangie*, a railroad crossing guard in South Braintree, said that he was cleaning the window of the gatehouse at the crossing when he heard shots, saw a gunman come from behind a pile of bricks, then heard the warning sound of an approaching train, and "[p]ut down my gates." Moments later, when the bandits' getaway car reached the lowered gates, said Levangie, "the first thing I knew, there was a revolver pointed . . . at my head," and he raised the gates.[27] Levangie said he had seen only the driver, a [d]ark complected man," and was sure Vanzetti was that man. *Austin Reed*, a railroad crossing guard in Matfield, said that shortly after 4:00 the getaway car approached his crossing at the same time as an oncoming train. Reed stood in the middle of the road with a stop sign, although "they did not seem to want to stop." A man sitting next to the driver asked in English, "What to hell I was holding him up for?" After the train passed, the same man asked again in English, "What to hell did you hold us up for?"[28] The car then sped across the tracks, only to make a U-turn and backtrack. Reed said there was no doubt that the man who had spoken to him, the man sitting *next to* the driver, was Vanzetti—contradicting Levangie, who two days earlier had said Vanzetti was the driver.

Three defense witnesses refuted Levangie's testimony. *Alexander Victorson*, a railroad ticket clerk, said that about fifteen minutes after the shooting he heard Levangie say that it would be difficult to identify the bandits. *Henry McCarthy*, a railroad fireman, said that within an hour of the shooting Levangie told him that he would not recognize any of the men in the car if he saw them again: "He said all he could see was the gun and he ducked." And *Edward Carter*, a worker at Slater & Morrill, said Levangie told him the driver was a "light-complected man."[29]

When Vanzetti took the stand in his own defense, he testified that he did not drive an automobile, had never driven, and did not know how to drive.[30]

No witness identified Vanzetti as someone seen while the crime was in progress.

No witness testified to having seen both Sacco and Vanzetti in South Braintree. The only prosecution witness who said he had seen the defendants together at any time was streetcar conductor *Austin Cole*, who said they had twice boarded his Brockton-bound car in West Bridgewater, once on April 14 or 15 and once on May 5.[31]

— If Nick Sacco and Bartolomeo Vanzetti were not in South Braintree at 3:00 on April 15, 1920, where were they?

SACCO'S ALIBI

Nicola Sacco testified that he spent part of April 15 trying to get a family passport from the Italian consulate in Boston. He had received word of his mother's death a few weeks earlier, and had resolved to take his wife and son back to Italy to visit his father. Sacco said he took the 8:56 a.m. train out of Stoughton on April 15, disembarked at South Station in Boston, walked to the Little Italy section in the city's North End, bought a newspaper, took a stroll, chatted with a friend he met on the street, did some window-shopping for suits and straw hats, lunched with friends he met at Boni's restaurant, and finally arrived at the consulate at 2:00.[32]

There he presented a family photograph for use on the passport. He was informed that the seven- by nine-inch photograph was too large. He would have to return with a "small, very small" photograph. He left the consulate after about ten minutes. Then he went to a coffee shop, chatted with friends there,

On May 4, 1920, Sacco obtained this family passport for a planned trip to Italy. The next day he was arrested. The photograph of himself, son Dante, and wife Rosina was a replacement for the oversized photograph that an official of the Italian Consulate in Boston said he had rejected on April 15. Courtesy of Historical and Special Collections, Harvard Law School Library.

bought some groceries, and took the 4:12 p.m. train back to Stoughton, arriving home around 6:00. Sacco testified that he had told George Kelley, his boss, that he would try to get back to the factory early enough to put in a half-day's work, but once in Boston, had changed his mind and decided to take the whole day off: "I think better stay here. I have been working all the time." The next morning, Sacco said, he told Kelley he had been delayed because the passport office had been crowded and busy. "I did not tell him the truth . . . [because] I was ashamed."[33]

When *Rosina Sacco* took the stand, she confirmed receipt of a letter from Italy about the death of her mother-in-law. She also confirmed that her husband had gone to Boston on April 15 to get a passport.

Several defense witnesses corroborated Sacco's account of his day off, establishing a timeline of his activities from morning to late afternoon. Carpenter *Dominick Ricci* said he saw Sacco in the Stoughton railroad station between 7:15 and 7:40 a.m. on April 15. Contractor *Angelo Monello* said he bumped into

Sacco on Hanover Street in the North End about 11:00, and chatted briefly with him. Journalist *Felice Guadagni* testified that he ran into Sacco outside Boni's restaurant at 11:30, and that they had lunch there together. Editor *Albert Bosco* and newspaper ad salesman *John Williams* both testified that they were in Boni's at lunchtime, and chatted with Sacco and Guadagni. *Giuseppe Andrower*, a former passport clerk at the Italian consulate in Boston who by the time of the trial had returned to Italy, testified in a written deposition that Sacco showed him the large family photograph around 2:00 or 2:15 on April 15. "I told him that this photograph was too large," Andrower deposed. Banker *Antonio Dentamore* said he saw Sacco around 2:45 that day in Giordani's coffeehouse, and *Felice Guadagni*, Sacco's lunchtime companion, said he ran into Sacco a second time that day, around 3:00 at the coffeehouse. Grocer *Carlos Affe* said Sacco called on him between 3:00 and 4:00 on April 15, and paid a $15.50 bill for pasta, salami, cheese, olive oil, lard, and other groceries that he had bought on credit a few weeks earlier. If these witnesses were right, Sacco's alibi was solid.[34]

No one testified to seeing Sacco in Boston after 4:00 on April 15 but, from his cage in the courtroom, Sacco spotted a spectator whom, he told his lawyers, he recognized as a fellow passenger on the 4:12 train he had taken out of Boston that day. That man, *James Hayes*, a highway surveyor, took the stand and testified that he did not know Sacco but that he had indeed gone to Boston on April 15, taken the train home to Stoughton in the late afternoon, sat where Sacco described him as sitting, and arrived home between 5:00 and 6:00.[35]

A scene familiar from Vanzetti's Plymouth trial played out again in Dedham. Witnesses established April 15 as the date they had seen Sacco by connecting the encounter with other events in their lives — a doctor's appointment, a theater date, a carpentry job, a banquet. As he had done at Plymouth, Katzmann cross-examined them about other dates. The technique reached a climax of sorts with the cross-examination of carpenter Dominick Ricci. Ricci said he remembered he had worked on a porch ceiling on April 15. Katzmann asked him if he had worked April 18, April 25, May 2, May 9, and other dates all the way through to December, and Ricci said yes. Each date Katzmann had specified was a Sunday. "Long before [Ricci] got through," the *Globe* reported, "everybody in the courtroom had got the point and was laughing. And when it dawned on the witness how he had been made ridiculous, the expression on his face was worth the trip to Dedham."[36]

VANZETTI'S ALIBI

The self-employed Vanzetti testified that on April 15, 1920, he had "a few, not very many, fish" to sell, which he peddled on his regular Plymouth route.

Sometime between 11:30 a.m. and 1:00 p.m. he ran into "this man that go around with cloths," from whom he purchased a piece of suiting material, after bringing the man to meet his former landlady so she could inspect the fabric. Vanzetti said he finished selling the fish, walked to the shore and chatted for more than an hour with a fisherman who was painting his boat, then took his pushcart home, ate, and went out, "but I don't remember where I go."[37] *Joseph Rosen*, the traveling fabric salesman; *Alfonsina Brini*, the former landlady; and *Melvin Corl*, the fisherman, all confirmed Vanzetti's alibi, with Corl backed up by the testimony of his wife and Brini backed up by the testimony of her older daughter.[38] Corl testified that Vanzetti arrived "down the shore" around 2:00 in the afternoon of April 15 and remained until about 3:30. If he was correct, Vanzetti's alibi was solid.[39]

Mrs. Brini had been on sick leave from her factory job on April 15; Rosen and Corl were self-employed. Since none of them punched a time clock that day, their recollections of times could not be documented.

Vanzetti's other alibi witnesses included Boston fish dealer *Salvatore Bova*, who said he sold 425 pounds of haddock and cod to a Plymouth fish dealer on April 12, 1920; and *Antonio Carbone*, the dealer who bought Bova's fish, who said that Vanzetti, his biggest customer, took a delivery from him on April 13 or 14. Factory worker *Angelo Guidobone* said he bought codfish from Vanzetti around 12:15 on April 15, and "I still owe for it."[40]

The alibi witnesses cited events that they said jogged their memory and helped them fix April 15 as the date of their encounters with Vanzetti — a tax payment, a checkup by a visiting nurse, a spouse's birthday, an appendectomy.[41] When he cross-examined the witnesses, Katzmann, as usual, cast doubt on their recollections by asking them questions about random events on random dates, questions they could not answer.

~ Character witnesses might help jurors decide if Nick and Bartolomeo were law-abiding citizens or ruthless criminals.

Sacco's former employers spoke up for him. *John Millick*, a foreman at the Milford Shoe Company, testified that Sacco worked for him for four years, "never lost a day in that time," and had a good reputation as a peaceful and law-abiding citizen. *Michael Kelley*, who taught Nick his craft and later hired him to work at his factory, Three K, testified that Sacco's reputation for being peaceful and law-abiding was "the best." Kelley said Nick was so trustworthy and responsible that he had been given the keys to the factory to use when doing double duty as an armed night watchman. *Leon Kelley*, Michael's son and office manager, testified that Nick had a good reputation for being peaceful and law-abiding. Michael's other son, factory superintendent *George Kelley*, summoned by both prosecution and defense, said Sacco was a close friend, conscientious, and a good and steady worker who "was on the job every day that you could expect any healthy man to work."[42]

On the same day that Millick, Michael Kelley, and Leon Kelley testified to Sacco's good character, *Joseph Schilling*, a police officer from Plymouth, took the stand to do the same for Vanzetti. However, as soon as Schilling said that Vanzetti's reputation as a law-abiding, peaceful citizen was "good," his testimony was suspended.[43] The next day, July 1, Katzmann read an extraordinary statement to the jury:

> The Commonwealth assents to the request of both of the defendants that all evidence heretofore offered in the course of this trial to the effect that either or both of said defendants bore the reputation of being peaceful and law-abiding citizens be stricken from the record . . . and . . . entirely disregarded by the jury, so that as a result . . . there is no evidence before the jury that either or both of said defendants bore the reputation of being a peaceful and law-abiding citizen.[44]

Katzmann's earlier decision to try Vanzetti at Plymouth was bearing fruit. References to the prior conviction were supposed to be off-limits at Dedham—unless the defense opened the subject, which it would be doing if a defense witness were to describe Vanzetti as law-abiding.

Sacco did not have any prior criminal convictions, and testimony about his good character was already on the record. Defense lawyers must have believed that a sacrifice play by Sacco on this point was the only way to protect Vanzetti. They paid a high price for such protection, and still didn't get what they paid for. At least two Boston papers had already reported that Vanzetti was doing time for another offense, and if the jurors missed those references, they heard others at trial.[45]

⌐ Guns, ammunition, and a mystery cap made up the physical evidence in the case.

PHYSICAL EVIDENCE AGAINST SACCO

Prosecution witness *Fred Loring*, a worker at Slater & Morrill, said he found a cap on the street "about eighteen inches from Berardelli's body," picked it up, kept it for about an hour, then gave it to *Thomas Fraher*, a factory superintendent.[46]

Many people, about forty, were in the street when he found the cap, Loring said on cross-examination; he thought all of them had been wearing hats, but wasn't positive. Loring's testimony implied that the cap had been found immediately after the shooting. Later it was learned that the cap had actually been found more than twenty-four hours after the crime.[47] Fraher was not questioned about the cap.

George Kelley testified that Sacco sometimes wore a dark cap with a salt-and-pepper pattern to work, where he hung it on a nail. Assistant DA Harold Williams asked Kelley if the Loring cap resembled the one he had seen Sacco wear; Kelley replied that "it was similar in color. As far as details are concerned, I could not say it was [like Sacco's]." Williams handed Kelley the Loring cap and asked him to describe the lining; Kelley noted it was torn. Williams then asked to have the cap admitted as evidence; Moore and Jeremiah McAnarney objected. Thayer pressed Kelley for an opinion on whether the cap was like Sacco's, called him "not responsive" for repeating that the "color only" was similar, pushed him to say that the general appearance was the same, then allowed the cap to be admitted as evidence.[48]

More than two weeks later, *Nicola Sacco* took the stand in his own defense. Shown the cap, he said he "never saw it [before]," and "[n]ever in my life" had had a similar cap. Asked to put it on, Sacco tried, but it was too tight. "Could not go in," he said. "My size is 7⅛." *Rosina Sacco* was also asked to identify the Loring cap, which had fold-in earflaps and a fur lining. "My husband never wore caps with anything around for his ears, never," she testified, "because he never liked it and because . . . he don't look good in them, positively."[49]

In addition to the cap, there was physical evidence of another sort, ballistics evidence: bullets from the victims' bodies, spent shells from the crime scene, cartridges and guns from the defendants, and bullets from a test firing conducted during the trial.

Dr. Nathaniel Hunting testified that he operated on Frederick Parmenter about an hour after the shooting, removed a single bullet from his body, marked it with an identifying X, "kept it for a while, and then . . . gave it to . . . the State police, I think." *Dr. Frederick Jones*, medical examiner for Norfolk County, participated in Parmenter's autopsy, and testified that a second bullet "was found on the floor of the operating room by one of the nurses." Jones said he put that bullet in his pocket and carried it around for "[q]uite a while . . . weeks or months" before turning it over to a state police officer. More than a year later, when the trial was already a week old, Jones at last put an identifying mark, the numeral 5, on a bullet he said was the one found on the floor.[50] The fact that Drs. Hunting and Jones held on to the recovered bullets for some time, and that Jones waited so long before marking one of the bullets for identification, gives some indication of the chain of custody procedures in the case.

Dr. John Frazer, a medical examiner from Weymouth, testified that four bullets were removed from the body of Alessandro Berardelli during the autopsy, and that the fatal wound was the "one on the back of the shoulder." *Dr. George Magrath*, the medical examiner for Suffolk County who performed "the operating part" of Berardelli's autopsy, said that he marked the four bullets on the "base with the point of a needle" in the order in which they were taken from the body. "Thus, the first bullet recovered was marked 'I.' . . . [T]he second was marked with a Roman 'II' and three with a Roman 'III' and the fourth with the Roman 'IIII,' or four vertical lines."[51]

Mechanic *James Bostock* testified that he picked up "[t]hree or four" spent shells at the crime scene, put them in a desk at the Slater & Morrill factory, and later learned that "Mr. Fraher had them." Factory superintendent *Thomas Fraher* testified that Bostock gave him "four empty shells," which he turned over to the state police within a few hours.[52] At no point in the transfer of these four so-called Fraher shells from Bostock to Fraher to the state police and eventually to the sheriff and the courtroom did anyone mark them for identification.[53] People picked up more spent shells at the crime scene, Bostock testified, but they did not surface at trial.

When he was arrested, *Nick Sacco* carried, tucked in the waistband of his pants, a .32 caliber Colt automatic pistol, 1903 model, the most popular Colt pocket automatic until it was discontinued in 1946.[54] Nine cartridges were in the gun; Sacco also had twenty-three cartridges in his pocket. Six of his cartridges were Winchesters; the remainder came from various other manufacturers.

Sacco said it was a coincidence that he was armed on the night of his arrest. His wife had discovered the bullets while cleaning the house prior to their imminent departure for Italy. She "ask me . . . 'What are you going to do, Nick, with this?' . . . I said, 'Well, I go to shoot in the woods, me and Vanzetti.' . . . I took it in my pocket." After he started talking with friends Vanzetti, Orciani, and Buda, Sacco continued, "I forgot about to go in the woods shooting, so it was still left in my pocket." He said he had purchased the cartridges in Boston during the war, when they were scarce. He admitted on cross-examination that in his jailhouse interrogation he had lied about where he bought the gun and cartridges.[55] When *Rosina Sacco* testified, she confirmed that she had taken cartridges and a gun out of the bureau while cleaning, and that Nick put the cartridges in his pocket and took the gun.[56]

Brockton police officer *Merle Spear* testified that he took Sacco's gun from him at the police station. At some point while it was in his possession Spear marked it for identification with his own initials, "M.S.," but neither Spear nor anyone else at the police station recorded the gun's serial number.[57] (Captain Proctor received both of the defendants' guns the next day, and recorded both serial numbers on an undated property list.)[58] At trial Assistant DA Williams showed Spear a gun, which he identified as the Colt he had taken from Sacco. The gun was marked Exhibit 28 and admitted into evidence as Sacco's gun.

At some point very early in the trial, probably during jury selection, Fred Moore asked the district attorney if the prosecution was going to attempt to link "any particular bullet" with "any particular gun." "No, Mr. Moore," Katzmann assured him. "[A]fter he had that assurance . . . the request came [from the defense] for an opportunity to fire the Sacco gun." On June 6, Judge Thayer told the sheriff that "[c]ounsel for the defendants have made a motion . . . to have the bullets and weapons examined by their expert. I have granted that motion."[59]

Then, on June 7, before the tests took place, Williams, in his opening statement, implied a link between Bullet III and Sacco's pistol: The bullet "that caused Berardelli's death . . . was fired from a 32-Colt automatic pistol. And when Sacco was arrested three weeks afterward he had on his person . . . a . . . Colt automatic pistol of 32-calibre." Williams said that none of the other five bullets removed from the victims' bodies had been fired through a Colt. (Although Williams didn't touch on the point in his opening statement, Bullet III was a Winchester.)[60]

On Saturday, June 18, in Lowell, Massachusetts, experts for both sides test-fired several rounds through the "Colt automatic which is in evidence," then recovered the bullets and spent shells. Sacco had approved of these tests: "Why sure, let them fire the pistol if they want to," he told Moore. "Why should I care?" (Elizabeth Evans called this "consciousness of innocence.") "[If Sacco] was not [at South Braintree,] his gun was not there; no harm could result to him," Thomas McAnarney later said, although even "at that stage of the proceedings I could see that it might invite a controversy of experts."[61]

Sure enough, after the test firing, Katzmann had a change of heart. "I went to Mr. Moore," Katzmann later explained, ". . . and said, 'Mr. Moore, . . . I withdraw the statement that I made to you the other day in regard to making no claim that any particular bullet was fired from any particular gun.'"[62]

Three days after the test, two ballistics experts testified for the prosecution. *Captain William Proctor* of the Massachusetts State Police said that Bullet III, the bullet that killed Berardelli, "is consistent with being fired by that pistol" — Sacco's Colt. Proctor also identified one of the four Fraher shells recovered from the crime scene as a Winchester. Assistant DA Williams asked him to compare that Fraher shell with six shells from the test-firing, and to answer if "the marks on those seven shells are consistent with being fired from the same weapon." "I think so, the same make of weapon," Proctor replied.[63] Following Proctor on the stand, *Charles Van Amburgh* of the Remington Company ballistics department said he was "inclined to believe" that Bullet III was fired from "this Colt automatic pistol," and that the Fraher Winchester shell showed "a very strong similarity" to three of the shells from the test-firing.[64] Thus, with qualifications — "consistent with," "same make," "inclined to believe," "similarity" — both Proctor and Van Amburgh linked Bullet III to Sacco's gun, and further implied that one of the spent shells recovered from the crime scene could have come from Sacco's gun.

A week later, the defense put its experts on the stand. *James Burns*, a ballistics engineer for the United States Cartridge Company, said that Bullet III was "[n]ot in my opinion" fired from the Sacco gun. The Sacco gun had a "clean lead," Burns said, and there was "[n]o doubt in my mind" that Bullet III was fired from a gun that did not have a clean lead.[65] Burns was not cross-examined about the spent shells. *Henry Fitzgerald*, director of the testing room for the Colt Company, said that Bullet III "was not fired from the pistol given me as Exhibit 28. . . . I can see no pitting or marks on bullet No. III that would correspond with a bullet coming from this gun." On cross-examination Fitzgerald said he did not see similarities between the Fraher Winchester shell and three Winchester shells from the test-firing.[66]

Bullet III had come from a Winchester cartridge, but Burns used U.S. cartridges, not Winchesters, at Lowell. He did this, he said, "[b]ecause our [U.S.] bullet represented [Bullet III] nearer than [any] present Winchester bullet that we could buy. . . . [T]his No. III bullet . . . is not of recent manufacture." When Katzmann asked if he had contacted the Winchester factory in Connecticut to "seek to obtain any bullets of the same make, same characteristics as bullet No. 3," Burns replied that he had not; "I thought it would be the last place to find them, at the Winchester Company, because [manufacturers] do not keep old samples of ammunition." Burns said that the U.S. cartridges he tested were "the nearest thing I could get to this Winchester bullet," and there was "no perceptible difference" between the U.S. cartridges from the test and the Winchester cartridge that had housed Bullet III.[67]

PHYSICAL EVIDENCE AGAINST VANZETTI

When *Bartolomeo Vanzetti* was arrested, he had a loaded .38 caliber revolver, later identified as a Harrington & Richardson, in the hip pocket of his trousers, and four shotgun shells in his coat pocket.[68]

The six bullets from the victims' bodies and the four Fraher shells from the crime scene had all been fired by automatic pistols of .32 caliber. Vanzetti's gun was a .38 caliber revolver, not a .32 caliber pistol; and the shells in his pocket were for a shotgun, not a pistol. There appeared to be no ballistics connection at all between Vanzetti and South Braintree, and Williams implied as much in his opening statement: "The Commonwealth has no evidence of any eyewitness that saw Vanzetti fire any gun," Williams declared.[69]

Two days after saying that, Williams questioned *Margaret Mahoney*, paymaster for Slater & Morrill, about the gun of murdered guard Alessandro Berardelli. Mahoney said she knew that Berardelli had a "shiny, bright looking" revolver, and that she had seen him with it at least twice.[70] Jeremiah McAnarney and Judge Thayer were both clueless about where Williams was heading with this line of questioning; Williams assured them that later testimony would make it relevant.

Mechanic *James Bostock* then testified that he had seen Berardelli with a .38 caliber revolver "a number of times," most recently "the Saturday night before the shooting." Bostock said that Berardelli's revolver was "similar" to Vanzetti's revolver, but on cross-examination said he couldn't tell if they were one and the same gun.[71]

The guard's widow, *Sarah Berardelli*, said that when her husband was working, he carried a gun that he borrowed from his co-worker, Parmenter. She said she could describe it "if I would see it." Williams showed her Vanzetti's gun and asked her if she had seen one like it before; "I think I did," she replied. "I have seen one that my husband carried." Three weeks before the crime, Mrs. Berardelli said, she had accompanied her husband to a gun shop in Boston where he dropped off the borrowed gun for repairs because "[i]t was a spring broke." Berardelli had given the claim check for the gun to Parmenter. The widow didn't know if Parmenter had ever picked up the repaired gun, but said that he let her husband "take another one" that looked like it.[72]

Three employees of the gun shop testified about the gun Berardelli had left for repairs. Repair shop supervisor *Lincoln Wadsworth* said that on March 20, 1920, Berardelli dropped off a revolver that was of the same type and caliber as Vanzetti's revolver—that is, a .38 caliber Harrington & Richardson. Repairman *George Fitzemeyer* said that between March 19 and 22 he repaired as many as forty guns, including two Harrington & Richardson revolvers that he received "tied together, that is, two in one repair job." Fitzemeyer said at one point that he had put a "[n]ew main spring, new friction spring . . . on two [revolvers]," and, at another point, that according to his written records he had put a new *hammer* in a .32 caliber Harrington & Richardson revolver. Since Vanzetti's gun was .38 caliber, not .32, Williams questioned him further. Fitzemeyer then said he was "not sure" of the caliber of the revolver he repaired, thus at the very least impugning the accuracy of his own written record. When given Vanzetti's revolver to examine on the stand, he said that it had a new hammer. Finally gun shop salesman *James Jones* said that the gun Berardelli had dropped off was "[t]o the best of my knowledge . . . delivered [to its owner]." No record of such a delivery existed, but Jones assumed it must have taken place anyway for two reasons: the gun was no longer in the shop, and there was no record of its having been sold as unclaimed merchandise. This kind of proof, Jeremiah McAnarney argued, was "all too indefinite. . . . There is simply a blank, and from that blank we cannot predicate something affirmative."[73]

It was during Wadsworth's testimony that the intent of the prosecution became clear. Williams asked Wadsworth to compare Vanzetti's gun to the one Berardelli had left at the store. McAnarney objected. "I suppose," Judge Thayer queried Williams, "you are going to show, are you not, later . . . that [Vanzetti's] . . . revolver . . . was the same revolver that Berardelli had . . .?" "I am," Williams answered.[74]

Ten days later three defense witnesses testified to a very different trail of ownership for Vanzetti's revolver. *Eldridge Atwater* of Dexter, Maine, identified Vanzetti's gun as one that had belonged to his father-in-law, a Mr. Mogridge, one that Atwater himself had used for hunting and that he had not seen for about five years, since his father-in-law died and his mother-in-law had gone to Massachusetts. Another Mogridge son-in-law, *Rexford Slater*, identified Vanzetti's gun as one that his mother-in-law had brought with her to Norwood, Massachusetts, when she went there to visit him and his wife, her daughter. Slater said that he sold the gun to Ricardo Orciani, a "brother workman in the shop," for four dollars in the autumn of 1919. Orciani did not testify, but *Luigi Falzini*, a marble cutter who said he had known Vanzetti for five or six years, took the stand and identified Vanzetti's gun as one he had bought from Orciani in October 1919 and resold to Vanzetti a few months later.[75]

Was Berardelli even carrying a weapon when he was killed? Or was the armed guard unarmed? *Lewis Wade* said he saw Berardelli move his right hand toward his pocket just before falling. That was it. No one testified to seeing the guard with a gun that day, or to seeing a bandit grab anything from him except a money box. In fact, *Aldeah Florence* testified that before the murders Sarah Berardelli had confided that her husband "had a revolver and that he never carried it, and that it was broken, and she was going to have it taken into Boston to have it fixed." After the murders, Mrs. Berardelli boarded with Mrs. Florence for a few months. A few days after Berardelli's funeral, according to Mrs. Florence, his widow lamented, "If he had taken my advice and taken the revolver out of the shop he would not be, maybe he would not be in the same condition he is today." Katzmann cross-examined Mrs. Florence: "I am asking you if after her husband's death she said that the revolver was still in the shop . . .?" "Yes, sir," Mrs. Florence replied.[76] Katzmann did not call Mrs. Berardelli back to the stand to refute this testimony.

∼ The oppressive heat continued, unrelenting. Whirring electric fans in the courtroom made plenty of noise but provided little relief. Judge Thayer bowed to reality and gave the jurors permission to remove their suit jackets. The twelve men took to sitting "unabashed, suspenders and all, in their shirts."[77] Thayer had been holding extended sessions in an effort to speed up the trial, yet the fifth week was grinding to a close with the end still nowhere in sight.

From his jail cell, Vanzetti tried to reassure his father across the ocean: "However this trial may end, my innocence remains. . . . I will fight like a lion to save my life and obtain justice. So take courage."[78] This is the only letter Vanzetti is known to have written while the trial was in progress; it is also the last letter of substance that he addressed to his father.

Court usually met in half-day session on Saturdays. But on Saturday morning, July 2, just before Vanzetti was to begin testifying, Judge Thayer was notified that Jeremiah McAnarney had been "taken sick in the courthouse last night" and was "in a state of complete collapse." A janitor had found him lying on a table in the courthouse library, reportedly suffering from stomach problems.[79] He had tried to come to court in the morning, had been unable to make it, and was back home under a doctor's care. Monday was the Fourth of July. Court adjourned until Tuesday. The three-day break was a welcome respite. Jurors went fishing and enjoyed a lobster dinner.[80]

∼ Bartolomeo Vanzetti took the stand when the trial resumed on July 5.

A year earlier, at the defendant's trial in Plymouth, Judge Thayer explained that "if a man . . . conceals [something] because he is under suspicion, the Court says that is evidence of guilt, and they say that an innocent man tells the truth."[81]

At Dedham the challenge to the defense was to prove that the multiple lies of Sacco and Vanzetti showed the defendants were consciously guilty of harboring radical beliefs, not of committing murder, and further that the lies were a shield to protect their friends and themselves from the consequences of radical beliefs: deportation, or worse.

Politicizing the trial had its risks, but the defense saw no alternative. "By no other [means] could the actual facts be brought to the foreground," John McAnarney explained later. "I realized it was liable to prejudice the jury as citizens and men but I did not suppose it would prejudice the jury in regard to the innocence or guilt of the men."[82] Fred Moore, who once had welcomed any opportunity to politicize a case, also understood the risks now. The Sacco-Vanzetti "case cannot be used as a propaganda organization to carry on [IWW] work," he wrote early in 1921. "There are two boys in jail facing the electric chair and we cannot afford to antagonize a single element that might otherwise [help] their case."[83]

EVIDENCE OF CONSCIOUSNESS
OF GUILT AGAINST VANZETTI

Brockton police officer *Michael Connolly* testified that when he arrested the defendants on a streetcar, Vanzetti "put his hand in his hip pocket [as if to draw a weapon] and I says, 'Keep your hands out on your lap, or you will be sorry.'" (At this, Vanzetti exploded in the courtroom, crying out, "You're a liar!") Connolly's fellow officer, *Earl Vaughn*, testified that he searched Vanzetti, found the gun, and turned it over to Connolly.[84] Katzmann read aloud a record of Chief Stewart's interrogation of Vanzetti, wherein the defendant said that he had gone to West Bridgewater on May 5, 1920, to see a friend nicknamed Pappi, that he had not seen a motorcycle that night, and that he did not know Mario Buda.[85] (Stewart was in the courtroom throughout the trial as an adviser to Katzmann.)

On direct examination, speaking barely above a whisper and for the most part without an interpreter, Vanzetti described his activities in Plymouth on April 15, 1920. He had not been in South Braintree that day, he said, nor had he taken part in any shooting there. Refuting Michael Levangie's identification of him as the getaway driver, Vanzetti said he did not know how to drive a car. Refuting John Faulkner's identification of him as the confused train passenger, Vanzetti said he had never taken the train to East Braintree nor asked for directions to that station.[86]

Vanzetti testified that after April 15 he had dug clams to sell, tried without success to buy fish to peddle, sought construction work, and met with friends in Brockton and Boston.[87] At one meeting, probably on April 25, "We decided to send a man to New York that evening" to look into Salsedo's predicament, and "I was the man that they decided to go." He spent three days in New York, during which time he met with *Louis Quintiliano* to discuss "all Italian political prisoners." Quintiliano had been advised by New York attorney *Walter Nelles* to dispose of radical literature, and Quintiliano passed the advice on to Vanzetti. Both Nelles and Quintiliano were called to the stand; they confirmed this account. (The defense did not call rabble-rousing anarchist Carlo Tresca to testify, although he too had met with Vanzetti in New York.)[88]

After he left New York, Vanzetti continued, he returned to Plymouth, went to Boston on May 1, and on May 3 headed to Stoughton to visit Sacco for a few days. On the evening of May 5, Vanzetti, Sacco, Ricardo Orciani, and Mario Buda went to West Bridgewater to pick up Buda's car from Simon Johnson's garage. Nick and Bartolomeo traveled by streetcar via Brockton. Once they arrived in West Bridgewater, Vanzetti testified, he and Sacco met up with Buda, who informed them "that we cannot take the automobile . . . and we will [have to] come here some other day" to get it.[89]

"What were you going to get the automobile for?" Jeremiah McAnarney asked. And with that, the radicalism defense was triggered.

"We were going to take the automobile for to carry books and newspapers," Vanzetti replied. Friends in several different towns had "plenty of literature, and . . . we intend to take that out and put that in the proper place. . . . I mean in a place not subject to policemen go in and call for . . . as in that time they went through in the house of many men who were active in the Radical movement and Socialist and labor movement, and go there and take letters and take books and take newspapers, and put men in jail and deported many." If they had been able to get the car on the night of May 5, Vanzetti continued, they would have sought out Pappi to tell him about an upcoming meeting, and they would have driven to Plymouth to ask another friend to hide the "literature." Vanzetti said he had never been in West Bridgewater before May 5.[90]

He had purchased his revolver a few months prior to April 15, Vanzetti said; he carried cash on his fish-buying trips to Boston, and since there was a crime wave at the time, he "went to Falzini's house one day," paid five dollars, and bought the gun for self-defense. He denied that he had tried to draw the gun on the night of the arrest, and denied that Officer Connolly had warned him not to do so. He said that neither Chief Stewart nor any other policemen had specified the charges for his arrest that night, although "I asked them many times. . . . Absolutely no, they don't tell me. . . . Neither the next day." Stewart, said Vanzetti, "asked me why we were in Bridgewater, how long I know Sacco, if I am a Radical, if I am an anarchist or communist, and he asked me . . . if I believe in the use of violence against the government of the United States." In Brockton Vanzetti had not told his interrogators about collecting "literature." "I was scared to give the names and the addresses of my friends as I know that almost all of them have some books and some newspapers in their house by which the authority take a reason for arresting them and deport them." Vanzetti also testified that he left Plymouth in May 1917, "for not to be a soldier."[91]

The moment for cross-examination arrived. The courtroom was packed with spectators. The adversaries were champing at the bit.

"So," Katzmann began, "you left Plymouth, Mr. Vanzetti, in May 1917, to dodge the draft, did you? . . . Physically sound as you were, and after you had been in this country since 1908? . . . When this country was at war, you ran away so you would not have to fight as a soldier?"[92]

"It is true," Vanzetti said, but in answer to the next question, "Did you ever work in Springfield, Massachusetts?" Vanzetti burst out that he had lived "in a shanty near Springfield. . . . [Y]ou know, the little house where the Italian work and live like a beast, the Italian workingman in this country. . . . I [used the word 'shanty'] for to tell you if I refused to go to war, I don't refuse because I don't like this country or I don't like the people of this country. I will refuse even if I was in Italy, and you tell me it is a long time I am in this country and I tell you that in this country as long time I am, that I found plenty good people and some bad people, but that I was always working hard as a man can work. . . ."[93]

Katzmann then led Vanzetti through what he said was a transcript of their interview at the Brockton police station. (Vanzetti agreed that a stenographer had been present.)

In Brockton, according to the transcript, Vanzetti said he had paid eighteen or nineteen dollars for his revolver; on the stand, he said he did not remember saying that but, if he did say it, it was false, and there was "no reason" to have lied about the price. Similarly, Vanzetti admitted that, based on information in the transcript, he had lied about the exact date he had gone to Boston, about how long he had known Sacco, about when and where he had bought his revolver, about where and how he had bought his ammunition, and about firing off practice shots on the beach. At Brockton, he had said that he did not know Buda, that he had not seen a sign or a motorcycle in West Bridgewater, that he had originally left Italy in the month of July, that he did not recall his first employer in Plymouth, that his friend Pappi lived in Bridgewater proper—all details he now said were false.[94]

The litany of apparent contradictions between Vanzetti's statements at Brockton and at trial was long, and many of them had nothing to do with protecting friends or avoiding deportation. It didn't matter if the contradictions stemmed from duplicity or poor memory. Lies were lies, and the prosecution could argue that they were part of a pattern demonstrating consciousness of guilt. After Vanzetti's first day on the stand, the *Globe* summed up the damage in a front-page headline: TOLD UNTRUTHS, SAYS VANZETTI.[95]

Vanzetti attempted to explain his lies. At Brockton, he testified, he had forgotten some details of his activities, and in other cases had lied intentionally: "I have some purpose. . . . I intend to not mention the name and the house of my friends."[96] (Reflecting on this five years later, Vanzetti wrote, "Why should we turn spies?") In still other cases, Vanzetti said that, while he didn't deny the contents of the Brockton transcript Katzmann was reading, he couldn't recall making some of the statements attributed to him. In any event, while he remembered some things and not others, Vanzetti said, "[Y]ou can be sure that I can remember that I never kill a man on the 15th, because I never kill a man in my life."[97]

EVIDENCE OF CONSCIOUSNESS
OF GUILT AGAINST SACCO

When Nicola Sacco was sworn in after the noon recess on Wednesday, July 6, he looked pale, the *Globe* reported, "his blue-black beard showing through his smooth-shaven olive skin, his lips almost colorless, his nervous tension plainly high."[98]

Sacco was on the stand for four days, twice as long as Vanzetti. His testimony constituted the emotional climax of the trial. Nick was less proficient in English than his co-defendant and more easily provoked, a volatile mix. In addition, Fred Moore, not Jeremiah McAnarney, conducted the direct examination, and Moore did not bring out the best in Judge Thayer, who advised him to behave more like his co-counsel.[99]

Moore led Sacco through his early life in Italy, his immigration to the United States in 1908, and his subsequent job history. "I was crazy to come to this country," Sacco said, "because I was liked a free country, call a free country." He left the United States in June 1917, he testified, "before the registration" for the draft, and returned in August or September because "I leave my wife here and my boy." For the duration of the war, he used an alias, "Nicola Mosmacotelli, my mother's second name . . . to not get in trouble by registration." Back in Massachusetts, Sacco said he took a series of short-term jobs before going to work at the Three K factory in November 1918.[100]

Sacco testified that he was in Boston on April 15, 1920, and he described his activities and the people he met there. Refuting the eyewitnesses who had identified him, he said he had not been in South Braintree or in the South Braintree train station at any time that day. Furthermore, he said he did not shoot anyone or participate in any crime of any kind at South Braintree on that day or any other day.[101]

Sacco said that Vanzetti reported on his New York trip at a meeting in

Boston on May 2. He "told us we are . . . advised to get the books and literature to put at some place and hide not to find by the police or the state." The next day, May 3, Vanzetti visited Sacco's house, and stayed for two days. On May 5 Orciani and Buda also came to the house, and at 7:20 p.m. the four men set out "to get the automobile . . . to get the books." Sacco described his streetcar trip to Bridgewater that night, giving the same account that Vanzetti had given.[102]

Previously Brockton police officer *Michael Connolly* had testified that Sacco, like Vanzetti, tried to draw his gun on the night of the arrest. Connolly had said that, in the police car, Sacco twice made a move to put his hand under his overcoat, and that he, Connolly, twice warned him to keep his hands on his lap. Connolly had also said that Sacco told him he did not have a gun and did not want any trouble. Another Brockton officer, *Merle Spear*, who was also in the police car, had testified only that an Officer Snow told Sacco in the car "to keep hands where he could see them," and that Sacco had replied, "You need not be afraid of me." Spear said he had helped search Sacco at the police station, recovering his gun and ammunition.[103]

On the stand, Sacco refuted Connolly. Sacco said that neither he nor Vanzetti reached for their guns when arrested. Sacco also said, refuting conductor Austin Cole, that he had never taken a streetcar from West Bridgewater prior to the night of May 5.[104]

Sacco testified that at the Brockton police station Chief Stewart had asked no questions about his whereabouts on April 15. Concerning the reason for his arrest, "I never think anything else than Radical. . . . Because I was not registered [for the draft], and I was working for the movement for the working class, for the laboring class. . . . [Stewart] did ask me if I was a Socialist. I did say, 'Yes.'"[105]

Sacco conceded that he had lied to Stewart about why he was in Bridgewater "[b]ecause I was afraid . . . they arrest somebody else of the people." He hadn't been truthful with either Stewart or Katzmann because he didn't want to "name my friends to get them in trouble." Sacco said that when Katzmann interrogated him, no reference was made "to any particular crime," nor was he told that he was being charged with any particular crime. He described the way he was made to alter his appearance and assume different poses for "about one hundred" eyewitnesses who came to the police station to view him: "Any position they told me to do, I been done."[106]

Moore asked Sacco if he knew men who had been deported for their ideas. "We are going a good ways, aren't we, into this matter?" Judge Thayer asked. "I can't see why now the whole thing is not opened up. Inasmuch as it has been opened up, I do not feel disposed to cut it short. You may answer."[107] Sacco said he knew at least four men who were awaiting deportation or had already been deported.

Day 2 of Sacco's testimony, Thursday, July 7, 1921, was Judge Thayer's sixty-fourth birthday. On that day, "so hot and moist that the walls and floors [of the courthouse] were wet and the atmosphere inside was 'deadly,'" spectators crowded the courtroom, more than on any previous day of the trial. District attorney Fred Katzmann was about to begin what would later be called one of the most extraordinary cross-examinations in a capital case that has ever taken place in a modern American courtroom.[108]

As he had done with Vanzetti, Katzmann led with the issue of draft dodging.

> KATZMANN. Did you say yesterday you love a free country? . . . And in order to show your love for this United States of America when she was about to call upon you to become a soldier you ran away to Mexico?
> SACCO. I don't believe in war. . . .
> KATZMANN. . . . Why didn't you stay down in Mexico? . . .[109]

Sacco enumerated the reasons why he returned to the United States and said that they added up to love of country. "Is standing by a country when she needs a soldier evidence of love of country?" queried Katzmann. Jeremiah McAnarney objected to the question and "to this whole line of interrogation."[110] A bizarre interchange then ensued in the presence of the jury. Judge Thayer asked McAnarney if he was claiming that collecting the literature had been done "in the interest of the United States, to prevent violation of the law" by distributing it. "Absolutely we have taken no such position as that," McAnarney replied. Three times Thayer asked the question. McAnarney emphatically objected, calling it "prejudicial to the defendants." Then, for the fourth time:

> THAYER. . . . Is it your claim that . . . the collection of the literature . . . was done in the interest of the United States?
> J.J. MCANARNEY. No, I make no such broad claim as that. . . .
> KATZMANN. Then, if your Honor please, I offer the line of cross-examination I have started upon as tending to attack the credibility of this man as a witness.
> THAYER. . . . You may proceed.[111]

With his path clear, Katzmann asked Sacco to explain what he had meant when he said he loved a free country. As if uncorked, Sacco erupted in a long and fervent attempt to explain his philosophy. He had learned, he said, that life in the United States was good for "those who got money to spend, not for the working and laboring class. . . . I could see the best men . . . sent to prison." For example, Socialist leader Eugene Debs worked to help laborers, but was imprisoned. "Why?" Sacco asked rhetorically. "Because the capitalist class . . . don't want our child to go to high school or to college or Harvard College. . . . [T]hey want the working class to be a low all the times. . . . So, sometimes, you see, the Rockefellers, Morgans, they give . . . five hundred thousand dollars to Harvard College, they give a million dollars for another school. Everybody say, 'Well, D. Rockefeller is a great man. . . .' I want to ask him . . . What benefit the working class they will get by those million dollars . . .? . . . [T]he poor class, they won't have no chance to go to Harvard College."

Sacco plowed on in his broken English. "I want men to live like men. . . . So that is why my idea has been changed. . . . [World War I] is not shoots like Abraham Lincoln's and Abe Jefferson, to fight for the free country, . . . but they are war for the great millionaire. . . . They are war for business. . . . What right we have to kill each other? I been work for the Irish, I have been working with the German fellow, with the French, many other peoples. . . . Why should I go kill them men? What he done to me? He never done anything, so I don't believe in no war. I want to destroy those guns."[112]

Sacco finally stopped. He had given a coherent and passionate, if simplistic and ungrammatical, explanation of his beliefs and how he had come by them. He had also given the prosecution enough material to paint a troubling portrait of him as an ungrateful, freeloading immigrant, "a man who tells this jury that the United States of America is a disappointment to [him.]"[113] Katzmann, proud Harvard alum, grilled Sacco: Do you think the United States is a backward country? Did you think you could get a better education in Italy? "Don't you know that Harvard University educates more boys of poor people free than any other university in the United States of America? . . . Did you intend to condemn Harvard College? . . . Were you ready to say none but the rich could go there without knowing about offering scholarships? . . . Are there any schools in the town you came from in Italy that compare with the [free public] school your boy goes to?"[114]

The cross-examination had veered far off course from murder in South Braintree. The judge permitted the questioning, ostensibly as a test of the defendant's credibility, but the politically loaded questions sound more prejudicial than probative. (Dudley Ranney, an assistant district attorney who prosecuted the case in its later stages, described Katzmann's questioning as "a bitter, cruel, harsh cross-examination . . . but not beyond [legal] bounds," and even Assistant DA Williams is said to have recalled the cross-examinations, especially Sacco's, as "hard, perhaps too hard.")[115]

Katzmann moved on to reading material. Sacco testified that he used to subscribe to the anarchist newspapers *Il Martello* (The Hammer) and *Cronaca sovversiva*, that publication of both had been suspended during the war, and that he owned books about anarchism, socialism, communism—and "I got some on astronomy, too." He said that he knew a certain Fruzetti of Bridgewater who had been deported for his anarchist opinions, that he and Fruzetti had probably subscribed to the same newspapers, but that "I could not see as far as [Fruzetti] could." His intention in wanting to collect and hide books was not to destroy them, but to save them until it was safe to bring them out again, "because they are educational." "An education in anarchy, wasn't it?" asked Katzmann. "Why, certainly," Sacco replied. "Anarchistic is not criminals."[116]

Quoting what he said was a transcript of the interrogation at the Brockton police station, Katzmann led Sacco, as he had earlier led Vanzetti, through a long list of post-arrest lies. Sacco admitted he had lied about where he bought his gun and ammunition, how the ammunition was packaged, how long he had known Vanzetti, and the precise time at which he and Vanzetti left the house on May 5. He also admitted lying in Brockton when he said he had not visited Orciani's house, had not worked in South Braintree, did not know he needed a gun permit, and did not know Mario Buda.[117] Sacco was reluctant to concede that at Brockton he had told Katzmann he had worked on April 15. (His memory was correct. Although Katzmann told Sacco he said he had worked "all day long" on April 15, in fact Sacco had been less definite, saying, "I think I was working the day before I read it in the paper. I don't remember for sure if I stayed out half a day.")[118]

Sacco testified that some of his lies were inadvertent, due to confusion or poor memory, and others were deliberate, told to shield friends from prosecution for radicalism or to shield himself from prosecution for draft dodging and carrying a gun without a permit.[119] He insisted he did not remember making some of the statements at Brockton that Katzmann attributed to him.[120] Even if Katzmann had asked him some crime-related questions at Brockton—Do you know Alessandro Berardelli? Did you ever work in South Braintree? Did you hear anything about what happened in Braintree?—Sacco insisted no one told him, and he did not know, that he was being held on charges related to the South Braintree crime.[121]

Sacco's emotion-packed second day on the stand sputtered to a close. For everyone present, the debilitating heat had transformed the proceedings into an ordeal unrelieved by extra recesses. Sacco, the *Globe* reported, had done "himself an injury by his inability to express himself [in English]. It is hard to understand him at all times."[122]

The basis for a consciousness-of-guilt argument was solidifying on a foundation of admitted lies. Vanzetti was disturbed. Throughout the day he repeatedly called one of his lawyers over to the cage to whisper comments on Sacco's testimony.

— At the start of his third day of testimony on July 8, Sacco looked "paler than ever," the *Globe* noted, "and his lips were almost bloodless." He asked for an interpreter. "I have been thinking yesterday I did make some mistake. I understand wrong," he explained. Court interpreter Joseph Ross was provided, but even that proved controversial as his translations were disputed by unofficial interpreters working for the defense.[123]

On redirect by Moore, Sacco clarified that he assumed he was arrested "because I was active in the movement of labor work and because I was a slacker," that Katzmann had never told him in Brockton he was being held in connection with the South Braintree murders, and that he "absolutely" did not believe in the use of force or violence.[124] *George Kelley*, recalled to the stand a few days later, reluctantly impugned Sacco's pacifism. Kelley conceded that, when questioned earlier by police about Sacco's cap, he had said that he had an opinion about it but didn't "want to get a bomb up my ass."[125]

Before recross of Sacco could begin, the defense made an unexpected move. The McAnarney brothers requested a separate trial for Vanzetti. "I was apprehensive and fearful of what might transpire during this case were it tried in conjunction with the indictment against Nicola Sacco," Jeremiah McAnarney told the court. "It now seems to me peculiarly fitting . . . that the motion be granted for a severance of these cases. . . . [I]t would be absolutely impossible under the most careful and earnest instructions that your Honor could give this jury to eliminate from their minds what has transpired up to the present time."[126]

Court recessed for lunch.

This was not the first time the defendants had sought to separate their conjoined cases. In her memoirs Elizabeth Gurley Flynn relates that as early as October 1920, after his Plymouth conviction but well before the Dedham trial, Vanzetti told her and Moore to fight for separate trials so that his conviction wouldn't hurt Nick. "Fred assured him," said Flynn, "that they had it in mind." On May 31, 1921, the first day of the Dedham trial, Sacco submitted a motion for severance and a separate trial, citing multiple reasons why he would be harmed by "a commingling of issues and overlapping of defenses." One week later, on June 7, 1921, Vanzetti also moved for a separate trial, citing similar reasons. And now, on July 8, Vanzetti was again moving for a separate trial.[127]

Reflecting on the intertwined nature of the case, Moore later said, "I had a great temptation when I was making the closing argument. There was so little evidence against Vanzetti . . . [that] I believed that there was a good chance of an acquittal if I should push home the fact. But I felt sure, in that case, that Sacco would be found guilty. . . . I knew enough of juries to feel sure [that if they acquitted one,] they would soak the other. So I put it up to Vanzetti. 'What shall I do?' and he answered, 'Save Nick. He has the woman and child.'"[128]

What might have happened to the defendants' chances if any of the severance motions had been granted? None were, so it's impossible to know. In the end, Bartolo may have been as tarnished by Nick's testimony as Nick was by Bartolo's prior conviction.

When trial resumed after the noon recess on July 8, Vanzetti was doing "very poorly," "unable to take food," and too sick to stay in court, Jeremiah McAnarney reported.[129] Court adjourned until the next morning. Thayer told the jurors to have the sheriff take them someplace cool for the rest of the day. In the middle of the night, as if nature were in synch with the turmoil inside the courtroom, a ferocious storm struck Boston, flooding roads and igniting lightning fires.

Sacco and others delivered wrap-up testimony over the next few days. On day 35 of the trial, Tuesday, July 12, the defense rested. "Well, gentlemen," Thayer addressed the jurors, "the book of fate in these cases has been closed."[130]

11 | DEDHAM: CURTAIN FALLING

On July 13, 1921, in Plymouth, the months-long tercentenary celebration of the Pilgrims' landing reached a dramatic peak with the grand premiere of the *Pageant of the Pilgrim Spirit*, complete with orchestra, three hundred choral singers, and a thousand actors performing on a large dirt-floor plaza. Over in Dedham on that same hot summer day, the crowd was smaller but the drama more intense. The time had arrived for closing arguments in *Commonwealth vs. Sacco and Vanzetti*. Extra seats had been installed in the courtroom. All seats were taken.[1]

Renegade lawyer Fred Moore had spent most of the past year preparing for this trial. As he launched into his summation, his own fate as well as that of clients was on the line.

The legal teams had agreed to limit closing arguments to four hours per side, the defense splitting its share between Moore on behalf of Sacco, and Jeremiah McAnarney for Vanzetti. Moore began.

There were times during the trial, he confided, "when I have almost felt as though I were an alien, notwithstanding the fact that I am a citizen of one of the sister states of the forty-six, and notwithstanding, also, the fact that my mother is a Vermonter, my father a New Yorker." He mentioned this, he said, to illustrate "the status of the two men at the bar. If I, an American, have at times felt alien . . ., then how much more truly alien must the two defendants feel."[2]

No punishment, Moore said, could be too harsh for the triggermen in the "atrocious and vicious" murders at South Braintree. But had the Commonwealth proved beyond reasonable doubt who those killers were? The fact that the defendants had "opinions and ideas foreign to the opinions and ideas of the vast majority of the American citizenship" was not evidence of guilt in South Braintree.[3]

Moore challenged the credibility of prosecution witnesses. Why did Mary Splaine change her story between the preliminary hearing and the trial? How could she describe Sacco in "infinite detail" when she had only seen him from a distance in a moving car? Could the jury seriously believe Lola Andrews's allegation that Moore had tried to get her to leave town by offering an inducement as singularly unenticing as a trip to Maine in the dead of winter? Wasn't it clear that Andrews's identification of Sacco was a fabrication when so many other witnesses — even a police officer, George Fay — disputed her testimony? As for "this pool room man," Carlos Goodridge, why did he identify Sacco after telling people he had not seen the bandits? And how could anyone believe Louis Pelser when he himself admitted he had lied in an attempt to wiggle out of testifying?[4]

Moore reminded the jury that, although James Bostock, a "plain, solid, substantial type of American," and Lewis Wade, a "good, solid, substantial type of man," testified for the prosecution, they did not identify Sacco or Vanzetti, nor did several defense witnesses of "English stock and Anglo-Saxon stock."[5]

As for Sacco's lies, Moore attributed some to poor memory and most to fear — fear of prosecution for draft dodging, fear of deportation, fear of ending up dead like Salsedo. Chief Stewart's questions about radicalism only added "fuel and flame" to Sacco's suspicions, "which accounts for the false statements that he made." The fact that Rosina Sacco burned her husband's books after his arrest indicated how much the Saccos feared political persecution.[6]

As Moore neared his time limit, he touched only briefly on Sacco's alibi. It simply was not credible, he said, that so many witnesses, "some Americans and some Italians, [would] have all stooped to the commission of perjury." He moved even more quickly over the ballistics evidence, noting the nonexistent chain of custody for "these bullets and these shells," and regretting that "the time has come when a microscope must be used to determine whether a human life is going to continue to function or not and when the users of the microscope themselves can't agree."[7]

Moore carried "no brief" for the defendants' opinions, he said, but the case was not about opinions. "[Y]ou are duty bound," he exhorted jurors, "to return a verdict based solely upon the law, solely upon the facts."[8]

Moore had definitely dialed down the rhetoric since his days with the iww, but that didn't affect his delivery. "Mr. Moore was vehement," the *Globe* reported. "[H]is voice was loud, he slapped the rail at the jury box, and he perspired freely." When he finished, he "was so hoarse that he could hardly speak."[9]

~ Next up was Jeremiah McAnarney. His job was to speak about Vanzetti, but oddly he devoted his summation to both defendants, a fact that Katzmann would turn against him.

"We have drifted miles away" from South Braintree, McAnarney began. "We have drifted to the fact that these men are radicals and that they were apprehended because they were radicals, as every bit of this evidence when it is weighed absolutely proves."[10]

McAnarney sketched the conflicting physical descriptions of the bandits offered by eyewitnesses. He said some witnesses—Splaine, Goodridge, Levangie, and Andrews—had changed their stories. He reminded jurors that police had not used a lineup to display Sacco and Vanzetti for identification. He noted that two witnesses—Bostock and McGlone, "English speaking men"—had testified for the prosecution but refused to identify Sacco or Vanzetti as the bandits. He remarked that prosecutors had so disdained non-English-speaking witnesses that they hadn't bothered to cross-examine many of them.[11]

He pointed out implausibilities. Wasn't it unlikely that Vanzetti, if he really were a ruthless bandit, would rely on public transportation to get to his felonious job, and attract attention by conspicuously "bobbing up and down" on John Faulkner's train to ask directions to the scene of his next crime? Wasn't it unlikely that Lola Andrews could tap the shoulder of a man who was working *under* a car? Wasn't it unlikely that Mary Splaine, who had admitted lying on the stand about misidentifying a photograph of Sacco, could describe the *hand* of someone she had seen in a moving car from a distance of eighty feet? And wasn't it unlikely that Sacco, who had once briefly worked in South Braintree and might be recognized, would loiter around town for hours before committing a crime there? The identification of Sacco and Vanzetti "leaves the biggest, most wholesome reasonable doubt that ever was."[12]

McAnarney briefly went over the alibi evidence. For Sacco, he cited testimony of two American witnesses—James Hayes and John Williams, a "clean cut type of man"—and noted that Giuseppe Andrower, the Italian diplomat, was a person with too much dignity to perjure himself. As for Vanzetti, he had no friends of position and importance. "He has only got the poor people he traveled with and who know him," but who, like Joseph Rosen, the cloth peddler, "ring true."[13]

When he started out as a young attorney, McAnarney said, he learned a technique for cross-examination. He was advised to lead a witness "over the hurdles. Ask him about every other day but the day [in question]. . . . He won't remember a blame one of them." This was the technique Katzmann used to cross-examine alibi witnesses in the Sacco-Vanzetti case. The technique was trickery, legalistic "stock in trade," and McAnarney advised jurors not to fall for it.[14]

McAnarney poked holes in the prosecution's theory that Vanzetti's gun had once been Berardelli's. The true history of Vanzetti's revolver had been firmly established by the testimony of its previous owners, McAnarney said, and the prosecution had not refuted testimony hinting that Berardelli was unarmed when he was killed. Furthermore, the testimony of the gun shop employees was riddled with inconsistencies.[15]

Moore had barely mentioned the ballistics evidence against Sacco; McAnarney went into it in more detail. He disparaged the analysis of prosecution expert Charles Van Amburgh who, according to McAnarney, had said that "the fatal bullet that killed Berardelli came from the .32 Colt ... that was found on Sacco." Actually Van Amburgh had not been that definitive.[16] McAnarney's misstatement may have inadvertently strengthened the case against Sacco.

The fact that the defendants had been armed was unimportant, McAnarney said. Using an argument that he probably would have objected to if presented by his opponent, he contended that carrying weapons was typically Italian. "If you go out and [gather] a dozen Italians together, the chances are you will get a gun or two, anyway."[17]

The prosecution's argument that the defendants' lies revealed consciousness of guilt was a desperate ploy, McAnarney said. The prosecution has "got to get conscious guilt into this case because that identification [evidence] will not stand the test." The charge that the defendants tried to reach for their weapons, made by Officer Connolly, should be disregarded, because "no other man on that [police] car saw anything like Connolly saw." As for the defendants' lies, they had been nothing more than an attempt by fearful men to cover up political beliefs, not criminal acts, said McAnarney.[18]

It had been proven, he continued, that concern about Salsedo prompted sympathizers to send Vanzetti to New York, that in New York Vanzetti was advised to dispose of radical literature, that soon afterward Salsedo died under suspicious circumstances, and that Vanzetti "arranged to get [Buda's] car ... to ... get hold of that literature and put it out of the way. ... Wasn't it what they were arrested for? [Otherwise] why these questions, 'Are you a socialist, are you an anarchist, are you this and are you that?' How would that prove the revolver or anything else?"[19]

McAnarney did not want to burn his professional bridges. He praised the district attorney—"a perfect gentleman"—and he praised the proceedings: "[E]verything has been done as Massachusetts takes pride in doing, granting to any man, however lowly his station, the fullest rights."[20]

Now jurors would have to weigh a case against "men who you are not in sympathy with. ... Let no outside thought or prejudice be in your mind." If the jury did its job, it could reach only one conclusion: "[T]his did not transpire as they say."[21]

McAnarney's delivery was "quiet," according to the *Globe*, yet his "logical building up of the case was made at machine-gun fire rate. He went so fast that the court stenographer was finally obliged to beg for mercy."[22]

— Moore and McAnarney exceeded their time by a total of thirty minutes. After lunch Katzmann negotiated for an extra thirty minutes for himself. It had been a long morning. It would be a long afternoon.

Katzmann began the competing narrative of events with praise for all. The jurors were intelligent and free of prejudice. The judge was eminent, learned, kindly, and impartial. The defense attorneys were skillful and devoted. Outsider Fred Moore was "a credit to the West from which he comes." As for Katzmann himself, he was exhausted. "Heaven only knows," he said, "how I have been borne down by [this case] to the utter distraction of the routine work of the office for these long fourteen months" since the arrests.[23]

The prosecution's case was that Sacco killed Berardelli and took his gun, that Vanzetti aided and abetted Sacco, and that Vanzetti came into possession of the revolver "that poor Berardelli tried to draw . . . before he sunk to his knees with the blood coming out of his mouth dying on that sidewalk." Five bandits had carried out the South Braintree crime. Three remained unidentified. The prosecution "offered no evidence" about the identity of Parmenter's killer, nor about the gunman who fired the other three bullets recovered from Berardelli's body. But, Katzmann told jurors, that information was irrelevant, since the "only question [for you to consider] is, who did the shooting" of the fatal bullet, the one that caused Berardelli's death?[24]

Earlier, defense witness Peter McCullum had said that, from a factory window, he had glimpsed an unidentified bandit with a money box in his right hand and a "white gun," "revolver type," in his left hand. On the basis of this, Katzmann now postulated that the "revolver type" gun that McCullum had seen in the bandit's left hand must have been Berardelli's own revolver; that the murder weapon, a pistol, must at that moment have been concealed in the bandit's pocket; and that the bandit must have been Sacco.[25]

That argument was as dizzying as the assumption Katzmann asked jurors to make concerning the Buick found in woods near Brockton. No link had been established between the Buick and the defendants. Yet, Katzmann told the jury, the car had been found just a "mile or two" away from the place where Sacco and Vanzetti had been when arrested three weeks later. "Can you put two and two together, gentlemen?"[26]

The defense case, according to Katzmann, was that Sacco and Vanzetti were elsewhere at the time of the crime, that eyewitnesses could not identify them as the bandits, and that their lies stemmed "from consciousness of guilt of a trivial offense and not ... of this tremendous and atrocious crime of taking the lives of two innocent men ... and in cold blood to take, steal and rob ... $15,000 worth of money belonging to a capitalist, the Slater & Morrill Company."[27] Until that moment late in the trial, the prosecution had not suggested a motive for the defendants. With one word, "capitalist," Katzmann hinted not only at a motive, but also at a connection between the crime and radicalism. He did not point out that this particular capitalist money was a payroll for direct distribution to workers.

Katzmann's review of the identification testimony was the flip side of Moore's and McAnarney's: defense witnesses were unreliable; prosecution witnesses, exemplary.

Certain defense witnesses could be trusted, selectively. For example, railroad worker Joseph Cellucci had testified for the defense that Sacco and Vanzetti were not the bandits he had seen. "How much of his testimony is to be believed is doubtful in my mind," Katzmann said, "but I ask you to believe that portion of it where he says that nobody else [on the railroad work crew] save himself slipped by the boss" to get a look at the getaway car.[28]

As for prosecution witnesses who lied or made mistakes, they still deserved jurors' trust. Yes, Louis Pelser at first lied to police officers and to a defense investigator in an attempt to avoid testifying, but at least he was an equal-opportunity liar who prevaricated with both sides and was "big enough and manly enough now to tell you of his prior falsehoods." Yes, Michael Levangie had wrongly identified Vanzetti as the driver of the getaway car, but should the rest of "his testimony . . . be rejected if . . . you are satisfied he honestly meant to tell the truth?" Yes, Mary Splaine and Frances Devlin had been less certain about identifying Sacco before the trial, but "it passes the bounds of human credulity" that these women, "presumably endowed with Christian instincts," would commit perjury. And yes, Lola Andrews's testimony had been refuted by many witnesses, including a police officer, but "I cannot recall . . . that ever before I have laid eye or given ear to so convincing a witness as Lola Andrews." As for Lewis Wade, however, a star prosecution witness until he retracted his identification of Sacco, he was now someone in whom "I find little to believe."[29]

Why had both McAnarney and Moore spoken mainly of Sacco in their closing statements? Could it be, asked Katzmann, because they did not "have confidence in the alibi of the defendant Vanzetti . . .?" "I am going to do more than Vanzetti's own counsel," Katzmann said, "because I am going to discuss [his alibi,]" including that provided by "a convenient witness . . . Mrs. Brini,

[who] it is agreed in another [case] when another date was alleged, testified to the whereabouts of this same Vanzetti on that other date."[30]

The memory prompts of the alibi witnesses proved nothing about their encounters with Sacco or Vanzetti on April 15, 1920, Katzmann argued. The alibis were marked by "full absurdity and utter lack of convincing qualities."[31]

Although Katzmann didn't say so, the ballistics evidence was also absurd: confusing, weasel-worded, and based on primitive techniques that have since been discredited.[32]

Of the connection between the fatal bullet and Sacco's Colt, Katzmann repeated that it had been established by prosecution expert Van Amburgh, overlooking, like McAnarney before him, Van Amburgh's qualifying language. Oddly, Katzmann made no mention of the prosecution's other ballistics expert, Captain Proctor, but he asked jurors to disregard the opinions of the two defense experts, Burns and Fitzgerald, and to substitute their own opinions, based on their own observations of the bullets, "if you have a strong enough [magnifying] glass." He reminded jurors that, although the fatal bullet was a Winchester, Burns had test-fired "United States Bullets."[33]

Was Vanzetti's revolver actually Berardelli's? Katzmann told jurors to suspect the veracity of defense witnesses who said they had previously owned Vanzetti's gun. He reminded jurors that Vanzetti had initially lied about the gun purchase. He conceded that the paperwork from the gun repair shop was "confused," yet said he had faith in the repairman's identification of a new hammer in Vanzetti's gun.[34] (Burns and Fitzgerald had said that the hammer was not new.)

Earlier, Aldeah Florence had testified that Mrs. Berardelli said her husband did not retrieve his gun from the repair shop. The prosecution did not challenge Florence at the time, but Katzmann now claimed that her testimony had been disproved by James Bostock. According to Katzmann, Bostock said that "on the Saturday before the murder he saw Berardelli show the gun." "[J]ust one second," Moore interrupted. "Bostock did not identify this gun. He said he saw simply a bright nickel gun, he [did not] identify either as to caliber or as to make." Thayer at first told jurors to apply the evidence "according to your remembrance" but, before deliberations began, instructed them that any claim that Bostock had seen Berardelli with a gun like Vanzetti's was "not consistent with the record."[35]

Why did the defendants tell "[f]alsehood upon falsehood" after they were arrested? The defense, said Katzmann, contended that Sacco and Vanzetti felt guilt for two crimes only, "slackerdom" and distributing anarchist literature. But if this "absurd defense" were true, Katzmann asked, why was Vanzetti "loafing around" until *after* the critical date of May 1 before rounding up the literature? If Sacco was so afraid of the literature being discovered, why did he walk off and "[leave] his wife and baby with a load of books there"? If Sacco was going back to Italy anyway, why would he fear deportation, being "taken back there free of charge"?[36]

If Sacco and Vanzetti were pacifists, if they "deserted this country that has been good enough for them both" because they abhorred bloodshed, why did they have "arsenals upon them" when arrested? If they were non-violent, why did they reach for their guns? And if they feared prosecution for draft dodging and radicalism, why did they lie about unrelated matters?[37]

Further, if Sacco and Vanzetti set out on the night of May 5, 1920, only to retrieve "one poor old automobile," why did they need four men? And where was "the elusive Orciani" who had been with them that night? As a former owner of Vanzetti's revolver, he was a link in its chain of custody, and he was still in town, sometimes "out in front of this courthouse during this trial." "[W]hy didn't you permit Orciani to testify . . .? . . . The Commonwealth has a right to draw the inference that if produced he would give testimony that is not helpful to the defendants. And I . . . ask you to draw that inference."[38]

Radicalism was not on trial, Katzmann said. "This is a charge of murder and it is nothing else." Katzmann dismissed the notion that the case was a career maker for him. "Gentlemen," he said "this case means nothing whatever to me personally." He asked the jury to set sympathy aside and reach a decision based only on facts. "Gentlemen of the jury, do your duty. Do it like men. Stand together you men of Norfolk."[39]

Katzmann spoke for hours. Despite his "big frame and sturdy personality, [he] showed the strain he had been through." It was now seven o'clock in the evening at the end of a hot and exhausting July day. Everyone in the courtroom must have been dog-tired, especially the unfortunate juror who had had emergency dental extractions and "bled freely from the mouth all through the morning session."[40]

Court adjourned for the day.

~ Robert Benchley, a well-known theater critic and humorist, returned to his hometown of Worcester that July to see friends and family. On the weekend of the visit, he dropped by the Worcester Golf Club to meet a friend, Loring Coes. "When Mr. Coes came out," Benchley later recalled, "he told us what Judge Thayer, who was in the club, had just said in his presence. . . . Mr. Coes told us that Judge Thayer, whom he referred to as 'Web,' had just been telling what he . . . intended to do to Sacco and Vanzetti, whom [he] referred to as 'those bastards down there.' Mr. Coes said that Judge Thayer had referred to Sacco and Vanzetti as bolsheviki who were 'trying to intimidate him,' and had said that 'he would get them good and proper.' Mr. Coes said that Judge Thayer had told him and the other men [at the golf club] that a 'bunch of parlor radicals were trying to get those guys off and trying to bring pressure to bear on the Bench,' and that he 'would show them and would get those guys hanged,' and that he, Judge Thayer, 'would also like to hang a few dozen of the radicals.' Mr. Coes said that Judge Thayer added that 'no bolsheviki could intimidate Web Thayer.'"[41]

Later, when asked by a reporter about the conversation, Coes said that he couldn't recall what he had told Benchley.[42]

~ George Crocker, a prominent Boston attorney and former city treasurer, left his home on the shore of Buzzards Bay for a few days each week to go into the city on business. When in town during the summer of 1921, Crocker stayed at the University Club. There he was accosted by another guest, Web Thayer.

"[O]ne evening, this gentleman approached me, called me by name and I didn't recollect having met him before," Crocker later said, "but he began talking to me and told me how we must protect ourselves against reds, then he began to talk about this . . . Sacco and Vanzetti case. I finally realized he was the presiding judge in the case and he talked to me a great deal about it until I got away. He told me . . . about their being reds and anarchists and how we must . . . protect ourselves against them."[43]

Thayer subsequently spoke to Crocker "several times along the same lines. He told me about the evidence somewhat, and I got away from him as soon as I could."

On July 14, Thayer would deliver his charge to the jury. It was "likely to become a legal document of interest and importance," the *Globe* reported, noting that several libraries had already requested copies. That morning, when Thayer went to the dining room of the University Club for breakfast, he cornered Crocker. "[H]e began to talk again about this trial," Crocker recalled. "In part he talked about the counsel for the defense. . . . I didn't like to listen to it. Then he pulled out of his pocket a paper . . . and he said, 'Now Moore said so and so yesterday in his argument to the jury and I want to read you part of the charge I am going to deliver. That will hold him.' . . . It would hold him. . . . I was very uncomfortable and I got away as soon as I could. . . . I felt that he was bound to convict these men because they were reds. . . . [He said] we must stand together to protect ourselves against anarchists, reds, etc. He said they were draft dodgers and reds."[44]

— Shortly after this dining room encounter, court reconvened.

Thayer carried a "portentously thick, dark green folder," the *Globe* reported. Heartened, perhaps, by large bouquets of gladioli and pinks placed on his desk by well-wishers, the judge began his charge by thanking jurors in military metaphors. "Although you knew that [your] service would be arduous, painful and tiresome, yet you, like the true soldier, responded to that call in the spirit of supreme American loyalty. There is no better word in the English language than 'loyalty.'"[45]

Thayer's language to his peers at the Worcester Golf Club and the University Club had been imprudent, even crude, but in court the judge was grandiloquent. He urged jurors to "[l]et the star of sound judgment and profound wisdom guide your footsteps into that beautiful realm where conscience, obedience to law and to God, reigneth supreme."

Jurors should remember that while the law grants each person rights, it also grants him responsibilities, and "whoever is willing to accept the blessings of government should be perfectly willing to serve with fidelity that same government."[46] The oratory had a double edge. As it lauded the laudable — patriotism and good citizenship — it implicitly condemned the defendants for lacking those qualities.

Thayer instructed the jurors on procedures. They should consider Sacco and Vanzetti innocent until proven guilty beyond a reasonable doubt, which did not mean "beyond all imaginary or possible doubt, because everything relating to human affairs and human evidence is open to some possible or imaginary doubt." They should remember that the burden of proof rests with the prosecution: "The defendants are under no obligation to satisfy you who did commit the murders, but the Commonwealth must satisfy you beyond reasonable doubt that these defendants did."[47]

Jurors alone were responsible for evaluating witnesses and determining the "fact of identity, as well as all other facts involved in these cases." Jurors should give no consideration to the defendants' ethnic background: "They are entitled, under the law, to the same rights and consideration as though their ancestors came over in the Mayflower."[48]

It was the jury's responsibility to determine if the crime was murder in the first or second degree, and Thayer defined the terms. Motive was an important question. While motive tended to prove guilt, and lack of motive tended to prove innocence, nevertheless, the judge said, "a person may be convicted . . . without any evidence whatsoever that tends to prove motive."[49]

It might be superfluous to explain the law in this case, Thayer conceded, "because if I have followed counsel correctly the real issue that you must

Picnicking jurors and their bodyguards enjoy a break on the Fourth of July. When deliberations began ten days later, two jurors initially voted for acquittal. Robert D. Farber University Archives & Special Collections Department, Brandeis University.

determine is a very narrow one. It is one of identity," which "may be established by direct or by circumstantial evidence or by both."[50]

Jurors must determine the facts concerning the physical evidence — the fatal bullet, Vanzetti's gun, and the cap from the street. Jurors must also determine if the defendants' actions were evidence of consciousness of guilt. "But still," Thayer said, "you must remember that such consciousness of guilt, if you find such consciousness of guilt, must relate to the murders of Berardelli and Parmenter and not to the fact that [the defendants] and their friends were slackers and liable to be deported therefore."[51]

Wrapping up after almost two hours, Thayer spoke briefly of the defendants' claims that they had been elsewhere when the crime was committed. "If [you decide that] the evidence of an alibi . . . leaves reasonable doubt in your minds . . . then you will return a verdict of not guilty."[52]

From this "mass of testimony," he told the jurors, "you must determine the facts. . . . My duties are now at an end. I have tried to preside over the trial . . . in a spirit of absolute fairness and impartiality to both sides. If I have failed in any respect you must not, gentlemen, in any manner fail in yours. I therefore now commit into your sacred keeping the decision of these cases. . . . Let all the end thou aimest at be thy country's, thy God's and truth's."[53]

⁓ The twelve men who filed into the jury room at three o'clock on July 14 included two machinists, two shoe workers, two real estate agents, a grocer, a stonemason, a clothing salesman, a mill worker, a farmer, and a storekeeper.[54] Sequestered for seven weeks of summer, together in daytime, together at nighttime, living under constant guard, the jurors had bonded. "There never was a nicer crowd of men," one juror recalled years later.[55] (It also was a homogeneous crowd. The jury lists had been "remarkable," the *Globe* noted at the time, because "there were few Irish names on them and absolutely no Italian names. Foreign names generally were missing.")[56]

Inside the courtroom, jurors had listened to testimony from more than 150 people, and seen 85 exhibits.[57] If the sheer amount of evidence had not daunted them, the contradictions might have, emerging as they usually did weeks apart and out of sequence.

Walter Ripley, 69, was the oldest juror. Described in the press as a store-keeper, Ripley at the time of the trial was employed at the Quincy waterworks station. Previously he had been chief of both the police and fire departments in Quincy, as well as a former client of Assistant DA Williams. Ripley traced his ancestry back to Myles Standish, one of the founders of Plymouth Colony.[58]

Thayer had offered to excuse Ripley from jury duty because of his age, but Ripley "went ahead with it, and that was that," his son later recalled.[59] Usually in Massachusetts the judge, not the jurors, selects jury foremen, and Thayer chose Ripley to head the Sacco-Vanzetti jury.[60]

A few months after the verdict was in, details about Ripley's behavior would fuel a motion for a new trial. Consciously or unconsciously, Ripley might have been what today is called a stealth juror, someone who seeks jury duty to advance a personal agenda. If so, as foreman he would have been in a good position to achieve his goal; studies have found that, during deliberations, foremen provide about one-quarter of the total discussion.[61]

The Sacco-Vanzetti jury began its deliberations with an informal ballot: ten for conviction, two for acquittal, "with me one of the two," juror John Dever told reporter Edward Simmons in 1950. Dever recalled that after the initial ballot, "We started discussing things, reviewed the very important evidence about the bullets, and everybody had a chance to speak his piece. There never was any argument, though."[62]

Juror John Ganley found the eyewitness identifications persuasive, whereas Alfred Atwood thought "both sides made a mess of the witnesses." Ballistics evidence was the most important factor for at least five jurors. Atwood and Dever found the similarity between the out-of-date bullet in Berardelli's body and out-of-date cartridges in Sacco's possession important, although neither the judge nor any of the lawyers had linked them.[63]

While jurors deliberated, policemen, sheriffs, lawyers, and the judge sat outside on the broad courthouse steps. At six o'clock the jurors had supper. Then, just before eight, after less than five hours of deliberation, Ripley sent word that they had reached a verdict.[64]

From Dedham Jail Sacco and Vanzetti were marched back to the court-room. Jurors filed in, each staring fixedly at the floor. Ripley pronounced the

verdict: Nicola Sacco, guilty of two counts of murder in the first degree; Bartolomeo Vanzetti, guilty of two counts of murder in the first degree.

Vanzetti stood stock-still for a moment, stunned, unable to move, his right
hand frozen where he had raised it.

"I am innocent!" Sacco cried out. "They kill an innocent m[a]n! They kill
two innocent men!" Rosina Sacco screamed. She "ran to the cage and flung her
arms round Sacco's neck. Her hat fell off. '. . . What am I going to do? I've got
two children. O Nick! They kill my man!'" She clung to her husband, weeping
"more and more wildly."[65]

Police pulled her away, and marched the defendants back to the jail once
more.

Nothing remained but to give jurors final payment for their service, and to
congratulate the prosecutors. Assistant DA Williams took no pleasure in the
victory that would, if upheld, send two men to their death. On the contrary,
while Williams believed the defendants were guilty, he was reported to have
had tears in his eyes after the verdict.[66]

— Three months after the trial, in an attempt to do "what I ought to do," reporter Frank Sibley sent a confidential letter to J. Weston Allen, attorney general of Massachusetts. In it, Sibley catalogued multiple examples of what he
viewed as Judge Thayer's unfairness and objectionable behavior: belittling defense lawyers by speaking to them every day with an "intonation of contempt";
working with the prosecution to "[force] the defendants to connect up state's
evidence"; and "taking at face value the testimony of an obviously coached and
perjured policeman who said that both defendants tried to draw pistols . . . and
then making a large section of his charge on consciousness of guilt." According
to Sibley, shortly after Thayer delivered his charge, he asked reporters to print
"a statement in the newspapers that this trial has been fairly and impartially
conducted," and he boasted, "Did you see that jury when I finished making my
charge? Three of them in tears!"[67]

Nearly thirty years later, the seven surviving jurors expressed their continuing conviction that Judge Thayer had been fair to a fault, that radicalism had
played no role at the trial, and that they had reached the correct decision. It
"might have been a good idea to give them another trial," one juror conceded.
"The [guilty] verdict of two juries would [have been] more convincing."[68]

PART THREE

One-two-three-four: four paces and the wall.
One-two-three-four: four paces and the iron gate.
~ Arturo Giovannitti, "The Walker"

12 | Prison Crucible

It must have seemed like an apparition. One springtime day in 1925, Bartolomeo Vanzetti looked down from a window in Charlestown State Prison and
saw a magical sight. Below him, a circus parade was crossing a bridge over the
Charles River.[1]

One spring night a year later, asleep in his cell at Dedham Jail, Nicola Sacco
dreamed he saw a "little sweet space of the nature" while looking through
iron bars.[2]

This was the Roaring Twenties, Sacco-Vanzetti-style. Outside the prison
walls, society was changing. American women were gaining the right to vote.
Prohibition was spawning rumrunners and speakeasies. A "lost generation"
was transforming art and literature. Al Jolson was singing out loud on the sil-
ver screen; Lindbergh was soloing across the Atlantic; Clarence Darrow and
William Jennings Bryan were arguing about evolution; and around the world
supporters of Sacco and Vanzetti were organizing protests on their behalf. But
the locked-in prisoners saw none of it. For Sacco and Vanzetti, the Roaring
Twenties amounted to a glimpse of a faraway parade, a dream of nature, and
the stark reality of a jail cell.

~ In the heart of picturesque Dedham, Massachusetts, on Village Avenue
near Saint Paul's Church, stands a stone fortress erected in the 1800s to hold
the lawbreakers of Norfolk County. Built to accommodate more than a hundred prisoners, Dedham Jail housed on average less than fifty men in the 1920s,
when Sacco was confined there.[3]

Cells were arrayed on three tiers, in three wings.[4] Each cell, about six by
eight feet, functioned as a prisoner's bedroom and toilet ("a suitable bucket"
to be emptied daily, according to the 1905 *Prison Officers' Hand Book*). Cell
doors were thick wood. The only natural light to reach inside came through
small, eye-level grates in the doors.[5] Various sources have located Sacco's cell
on the bottom or middle tier of the jail. If it was on the bottom, Nick would

have been able to see a sliver of daylight if he squatted on the floor, then looked up through the grate, across the corridor, to the lower portion of a large arched window some twenty-five feet away. On restless nights, he paced back and forth in the cramped cell and squinted through the grate for a view of "the stars in the beauti blue sky." The sensory deprivation was hard to bear. In his "terrible hole," Sacco wrote, he missed not only his freedom and his family, he also longed for "all what's nice and beauty."[6]

"It is so hard for me to realize that Nicola is in prison," his brother Sabino told a reporter in Italy. "I torture my mind to picture him there, but the idea is inconceivable."[7]

Despite its drawbacks, Dedham Jail was considered to be "a well-run institution of its kind." There was a small library, a chapel that doubled as a classroom, and a reception room where visitors and prisoners could sit facing each other along opposite sides of long oak tables, separated by a low divider.[8] Outdoors, a high brick wall enclosed a sunken exercise yard.

Sacco arrived at Dedham Jail after his arrest in May 1920. One of his first English-speaking visitors was journalist Mary Heaton Vorse, who went to Dedham later that year to do a story on the case. She found Nick, then 29, "so life-loving that even six months of inaction in jail had not effaced his vividness." She wrote that he had "above all a friendly way with him almost like that of a child who had never known anything but affection. There was something about Sacco that made you think of the swift happy things — jumping fish, a bird on the wing."[9]

This impression of Sacco as a man in perpetual motion recurs in nearly all early descriptions of him: a man of action; a fighter; a "vital, radiant little bundle of energy"; passionate; "alert and expressive"; brimming with vitality. But his vitality would not stand up to the rigors of prison life for long.[10]

In the early days of his confinement, Sacco read science and history books as well as *Les Misérables*. "[F]rom my young days of adolescent," he recalled, "I was always seeking the good books."[11] But he wasn't particularly studious, and books brought cold comfort.

Religion offered no comfort. Raised as a Catholic, Sacco said he never accepted any religion. At first he carried a Sacred Heart medal in prison, but explained with some embarrassment that he did so only because he didn't want to hurt the feelings of his boss's wife who had given it to him for good luck. In fact, although he had read parts of the Bible, Sacco said he did not think there was an afterlife, he didn't care whether there was one or not, and the only life worth fighting for was the life of the living.[12]

Rosina and the children did comfort him, but it was a comfort mixed with torment at his inability to provide for them. The torment would increase with each year of confinement. Early on, in the fall of 1920 when Vorse visited him, Nick had not yet seen his newborn daughter, and was worried about his wife's health.

Sacco might have found consolation, or at least distraction, in a regular work routine. He was accustomed to working, and proud of his skills. Massachusetts prison industries in 1920 included the manufacture of brushes, clothes, umbrellas, and shoe soles and heels. But prison work was off-limits for Sacco. Convicts awaiting sentencing were not permitted to work, and Sacco would not be sentenced until he exhausted his appeals. So he struggled to endure "the one thing that is hard to bear" — idleness. Confined and unoccupied, he "droops and pines," Elizabeth Evans observed, "like some native creature of the forest cooped within a cage."[13]

Events had intensified Sacco's depression even before the trial.

In November 1920 district attorney Fred Katzmann arranged to place an informer named Domenic Carbonari, also known as Carbone, in a cell near Sacco. Carbonari's assignment was to gain Sacco's trust and pump him for information. "I am an anarchist," Carbonari is said to have told Sacco. "Have you got some anarchist books in your cell? I would like to read. Do you know where I could get some dynamite when I leave this goddam jail? I want to blow up some people."[14] Not surprisingly given such questions, Sacco grew suspicious of Carbonari. The spy left Dedham Jail after about ten days, having failed to collect incriminating information.[15]

The defense team learned about Carbonari early on, and demanded an explanation from agent William West in the Boston office of the federal Bureau of Investigation. If West replied, there is no record of his response. It wasn't until 1926 that Katzmann admitted that the spy had been placed in Dedham Jail "under an arrangement between the Boston agents of the Federal Department of Justice and [myself] ... for the purpose of obtaining information from Sacco concerning the South Braintree crime ... and other information for the benefit of the Federal Government, but ... he obtained none."[16]

Katzmann then attempted to use another informer, John Ruzzamenti. The two met face-to-face once, on December 30, 1920, in Katzmann's office. According to Ruzzamenti, the district attorney said he "was right hard up against it ... [because he] had no evidence" against Sacco or Vanzetti. Ruzzamenti declined to go along with a plan that would have placed him undercover in the jail, so Katzmann suggested an alternative: that Ruzzamenti rent a room in the house where the Sacco family was staying, "establish friendly relations" with the distraught Rosina Sacco, and "secure confidential communications from her as to any criminal activities of her husband."[17]

Katzmann told the informer that he would not be ready to implement the plan for a few days. In fact it never got off the ground. In mid-January 1921, finding "nothing developing," Ruzzamenti returned to his home in Pennsylvania. Katzmann later admitted meeting briefly with Ruzzamenti but denied initiating the contact and denied discussing "any plan of work for him to follow."[18] (In the two weeks between Ruzzamenti's arrival and departure, Angelina De-Falco tried to activate her acquittal-for-cash scheme; perhaps Katzmann decided that was enough unsavory business for the moment.)

Sacco may not have known about Ruzzamenti, but he did know about Carbonari and DeFalco. He was worried. He continued to hope that the upcoming trial would vindicate him. When the guilty verdicts came down in July 1921, his hopes collapsed and his inner resources gave out.

Aldino Felicani initially became concerned about Nick because he was complaining of stomach problems. Felicani asked an Italian-speaking internist who knew Sacco to examine him at Dedham Jail. "You have got the wrong [kind of specialist]," Dr. Gualtiero De Amezaga told Felicani after the exam. "You better get an alienist, because I think this man has a case of dementia." (Alienists were psychiatrists, treating people "alienated" from sanity.) De Amezaga said that Sacco could not grasp the gravity of his situation and believed his wife was being manipulated "through magnetic influence."[19]

At De Amezaga's request, Dr. William Boos examined Sacco on October 14, 1921. "The prisoner answers questions readily and intelligently, and in conversation he appears quite normal," Boos reported. Nevertheless Sacco complained of strange physical symptoms—heat around the heart, buzzing in the head—and he believed people were trying to poison him. Boos concluded that Sacco was "suffering from a mental obsession of a persecutional character . . . not rare in prisoners of an introspective nature, who have nothing to divert their mind."[20]

Four days later alienist Dr. Edward Lane also examined Sacco. "I am very tough," Nick told him. "Any other man would be dead. I used to hear knocks. They have a couple of spies. I have got a charge of dynamite. They do it to make me nervous. . . . They have brains and try to persecute me. They want to make me sick or crazy. I never cry." Lane reported that Sacco "told of hearing noises overhead and of seeing a face at the cell window. . . . He experiences also feelings of numbness and prickling in his legs. He is positive that these feelings are caused by some substance placed in his food. . . . He is certain this stuff is meant for him and 'they'...want to break him down....At one time he noticed these bad feelings after partaking of food brought by his wife, and for a time he believed she had been induced to tamper with his food. He said he now thinks she would not do it. When asked who 'they' are, he stated at different times officers, authorities, the State, bankers, capitalists. He stated that...he believed once someone put a noxious substance in his ear while he slept."[21]

Lane concluded that Sacco was hallucinating, suffering from chronic paranoia, and that the condition was incurable.[22] But the alienist did not recommend hospitalization. Sacco remained in the shadows of his cell.

∽ Bartolomeo Vanzetti was thirty-two — "a very dark swarthy guy, with flowing mustache, and deep, liquid brown eyes, with a full head of hair," a deep voice, and an air of calmness — when he arrived at Charlestown State Prison in August 1920.[23] Miles from Dedham, the state prison differed from the county jail in almost every way. It was older and much bigger.[24] And although it had been constructed at the start of the nineteenth century with input from renowned architect Charles Bulfinch, by 1920 it was unanimously considered a disgrace. That year, the Massachusetts commissioner of correction reported that Charlestown was the only unsatisfactory prison in the state. "It is antiquated, out of date and hard to keep clean. It is in a congested and dirty location. There are no adequate hospital facilities. There is no congregate dining room, with the result that men are obliged to eat all their meals in their cells. ...The absence from the cells of any kind of plumbing makes necessary the obnoxious and unhealthy 'bucket system.'... Many repairs are immediately necessary....It is the recommendation of this Department that this property be immediately sold."[25]

That was the *official* opinion. Unofficially, the prison got even worse reviews. Charlestown was judged "unfit for humans" in 1921, "barbaric" in 1923, and the "worst in America" in 1925, when the Massachusetts Prison Association expressed outrage that the facility was still standing.[26]

Vanzetti, unlike Sacco, had already been sentenced for a crime, and so he was permitted — required — to work. He spent "7 hours in a gassy [paint] shop, 40 minutes [outdoors] in an overcrowded smoky, dusty yard, 16 hours in a small cell...except the days of the Lord when I must stay from 21 to 23 hours ...in my cage."[27]

Despite the miserable conditions at Charlestown, the truth about Vanzetti's time there is paradoxical and discomfiting. Prison robbed him of his freedom, and it liberated him.

Here was a man who had been pulled out of school early by his father and who had toiled ever since without achieving professional or financial security. In prison, food, clothing, shelter, and work were provided. After work shifts, he had nothing but time, and he was more inclined than Nick to use it for study. Bartolo burned with what he called the "fever of knowledge." In prison, his fields of study broadened, and so did his circle of friends and correspondents, to include writers and political activists whom he never would have encountered under ordinary circumstances. Prison was a brutal endurance test, but for Vanzetti it was also the gateway to intellectual awakening and a rich inner life. An alienist who examined Vanzetti upon his arrival at Charlestown noted that the new prisoner was "a man of much greater intelligence than one would infer from the kind of work that he has followed in this country."[28]

Most of the prison staff treated him well. In time he became "a very favorite convict in that prison," Gardner Jackson noted. "He was a trustee, they gave him privileges, and he worked in the library. The warden . . . was devoted to Vanzetti, was convinced that he was an innocent man." Other prisoners looked up to him. A released convict who had worked by his side in a prison workroom later told Elizabeth Evans that Vanzetti was "Christ-like."[29]

In his many years as an itinerant worker, Bartolo had somehow always managed to get books. In prison, he became an insatiable reader. His reading list expanded beyond anarchist philosophers. He would study "Longfellow's, Paine's, Franklin's and Jefferson's works," if only his English were better, he wrote Elizabeth Evans, just days after the Dedham trial ended. Later, he wrote friends that he was reading Tagore, Dante, Anatole France, Thoreau, and Emerson. When he was transferred out of Charlestown temporarily, he was upset that the books he took with him were not returned. He had lost, among others, a volume of Marcus Aurelius.[30] He regularly read several newspapers and magazines, and supporters were always happy to send him more.

Bartolo knew that his lack of formal education made it hard for him to understand much of what he read. Still he never gave up trying, and he maintained a sense of humor about his self-directed endeavors.

~ As the men's first full year in prison, 1921, was winding down, Nick's condition briefly improved. After Thanksgiving he wrote Bartolo that he had had a visit from "my Rosie and the children. . . . You can imagine how happy I felt to see them so joyful and so gay and in the best of health. . . . I am very sorry that no one comes and sees you, no one comes to see me neither, but Rosie."[31]

Some prisoners received an unexpected Christmas gift that year. President Warren Harding commuted the sentences of socialist Eugene Debs and twenty-three other prisoners serving time for war-related convictions. Sacco and

Vanzetti received a different kind of Christmas surprise. Their lawyers had filed a motion for a new trial on the grounds that the verdicts were against the weight of evidence. Webster Thayer, the original judge, rejected the motion on Christmas Eve.[32]

~ The next year, the sheriff of Norfolk County yielded to incessant requests by Fred Moore and gave Nick special permission to work in Dedham Jail. It was a "great happiness" to be able to work again, Sacco told Elizabeth Evans. "I am joy whin I am work," he wrote a friend. He was dyeing shoe leather for heels. He was "a very good workman" who chatted in "pretty good" English with other prisoners in the shop, according to jail officer Amos Loring.[33]

Yet when Evans visited Sacco a month later, the happy experiment had ended. "He said, 'Oh, they threw things at me in the workshop and [my] life was in danger.'" On November 13, Loring explained, a heel had been thrown from one prisoner to another, who tossed it over his shoulder. "It went in Sacco's direction, but I understood that it was not intended for him." Despite the apparently minor provocation, Sacco "was persuaded . . . that his life was in danger if he stayed in the shop, so," said Evans, "he lost what might have been his chance for sanity."[34]

He never worked in the jail again.

Sacco went on an eight-day hunger strike that month, and the situation degenerated from there. In mid-February 1923, he began a second hunger strike.[35] He told Evans he was on strike against his lawyers. He said that they "were not using the diligence that they should, that he wasn't going to sit down and bear it. . . . 'No, no,' he said, 'free or die.' With that look in his face like a fanatic. He had never had that before. You could [not] reason with him. . . . It is his counsel, Mr. Moore, he has found fault with, not with the judge or process of law, but only . . . with Mr. Moore, who, he says, has taken too much time. [He] says he is going to send him back to California. . . ." Then, Evans said, Nick "lost interest in earthly affairs and turned his face to the wall to die. . . . [H]ow to proceed with the [case] of a person who was insane was now the problem."[36]

A week into the hunger strike, jail physician Dr. Arthur Worthington began visiting Sacco every day. He treated physical symptoms—headache, leg pains, general weakness, "pains in his bowels," a "decided sour peculiar odor" to his breath. He found Nick "of more than the average intelligence in the criminal. . . . [H]e reads the Literary Digest." Inspired one day by a spray of violets in Worthington's buttonhole, Sacco reminisced about Italy where, he told the doctor, "all the violets had a great fragrance and it was a delight to go out into the fields." Worthington said Sacco was calm and rational, but Worthington was not a psychiatrist, and he agreed that a patient with paranoia could conceal the condition from a non-inquisitive doctor.[37]

Sacco continued refusing food. Concern mounted. There was no doubt that Sacco's mind was "disturbed and shocked" by his long ordeal, Vanzetti confided to his sister. Aldino Felicani talked to Sacco "over and over. I saw him . . . almost every day. I wanted him to break his fast. The authorities were very cooperative with me at the time because they didn't like this business at all. The publicity was terrific." "[Q]uite a few" hunger strikes had been staged previously at Dedham Jail, but none had lasted as long as Sacco's, according to Oliver Curtis, a longtime officer there. Curtis believed that without intervention Nick might well continue to the point of death.[38]

Meanwhile no legal arguments could be scheduled because one of the prisoners was not well enough to participate. Lawyers discussed separating the two cases, but now Vanzetti was opposed, even if it might help him. "I am innocent and I am fully convinced of Sacco's innocence," he wrote his sister. "[F]or this reason I would like to share the fate that would be decided at a joint proceeding."[39]

Supporters vehemently disagreed about what to do. On March 14, Moore wrote an urgent letter to the defense committee insisting that "we cannot wait any longer in instituting proceedings, if necessary involving an admission upon our part that Nicola Sacco is insane in order that proper steps may be taken to assure him of proper medical attention, thus avoiding his carrying out his avowed intention to starve himself to death." Moore said this was the "uniform decision" of himself, all three McAnarney brothers, and two additional lawyers, William Thompson and Arthur Hill, and that it was reached only after "full and detailed consultation. . . . I appreciate fully the reluctance of your Committee and of Mrs. Sacco and of Mr. Vanzetti to sign any papers making such allegations," Moore continued. "On the other hand, there is a duty that we owe as members of the bar to our client not to allow him to commit suicide."[40]

Vanzetti felt "furious but impotent" at the lawyers' decision. The committee's response was unambiguous. "[W]e flatly refuse to allow you to go ahead and carry out the plans outlined in the letter. If you do so it will be against our express wishes."[41]

"We felt," the committee later elaborated, "that the Commonwealth had deprived comrade Sacco of his liberty, that they were responsible for his safe care, and that we would not allow them to escape that responsibility" by initiating insanity proceedings.[42]

Moore was desperate. Twenty-nine days into the hunger strike, on March 15, he contacted Harold Williams, Katzmann's successor as district attorney. A psychiatrist hired by the defense had found Sacco incapable of "consistently advising with his counsel," Moore reported. Medical attention was essential, but Mrs. Sacco and the defense committee would not consent to it, so Moore was turning the matter over to the DA. "[T]ake such steps as you may deem appropriate."[43]

A sanity hearing was scheduled for the next day.

And so it was that on March 16, 1923, a familiar cast of characters gathered in a familiar setting, Superior Court in Dedham, Judge Thayer presiding, to decide whether Nicola Sacco was or was not crazy. The prisoner himself was not there. Due to "progressive starvation," he was physically unable to come and mentally unable to participate; he was in "a condition of comparative indifference to whatever may take place in court."[44] Moore, Thompson, and Hill were there to represent him.

Insanity, the district attorney argued, was "not sufficient reason for indefinite continuance of motions."[45] Thompson countered that treatment was by no means a delaying tactic, and that Sacco's insanity would hopefully prove temporary. Thayer ordered the appointment of two psychiatrists to examine Sacco and report back within a day.

Three psychiatrists in all, one for the defense and two for the court, visited Nick that afternoon. They found him weak but calm, insisting that the state was torturing him by poisoning his food, polluting the air in his cell, and circulating electric currents under his bed. Thayer ordered that he be admitted to Boston Psychopathic Hospital for ten days' observation.[46] (The hunger strike was always seen as a symptom of Sacco's insanity, rather than the other way around, that temporary insanity might be a symptom of hunger. Years later, however, unrelated experiments would show that otherwise healthy male volunteers on an extended semi-starvation diet experienced psychological changes, including social introversion, depression, emotional instability, hypochondria, and hysteria.)[47]

Because Sacco had not eaten for so long, Moore told Thayer, his "life is at stake. It is only a question of days." But once in the hospital and threatened with force-feeding, Sacco finally began to eat—broth and gruel every hour for the first two days, then a normal diet. He relented, he said, because after a month without food he didn't have the strength to resist attempts to force-feed him. There may have been an additional reason. His son, Dante, had vowed to go on a hunger strike, too, if his father didn't eat.[48]

Nick at first responded well to the environment at Boston Psychopathic Hospital, even if it did include a police guard outside his room. He received daily medical care. He had many visitors. He put weight on quickly. He referred to his previous delusions as "all a mistake." He was friendly to the doctors, and spoke to them with enthusiasm about his family, his love of the outdoors, and his knowledge of the shoe manufacturing business. He told them he had dodged the draft because he was "afraid of war," and that he "never kill anybody." He denied that the hunger strike had been a suicide attempt.[49]

Yet the impulse to self-destruct did not go away. On March 21, Sacco "managed to knock his head several times against a heavy chair. . . . [He] said that he wanted to end it all." Stitches were needed to close the self-inflicted forehead wounds. "I was trying to smash my skull and I would do it the next time," Nick told Elizabeth Evans, who recalled that "his head was all bandaged." Despite this violent outburst, hospital director Dr. Macfie Campbell reported on March 26 that Sacco showed "no evidence of insanity of any type," and that the head banging indicated only "a transitory condition of emotional tension."[50]

Defense attorneys could not reconcile Campbell's diagnosis with the earlier findings of the court-ordered psychiatrists. The lawyers requested and received an extension of Sacco's hospital stay.

Sacco remained at Psychopathic until April 22. More psychotic episodes occurred while he was there. On April 7, after a visit from Rosina, he charged out of bed and "called for his wife, and his mother. He said that he heard his wife in the next room . . . and that she was being kept from him." He heard voices: the voice of his wife upstairs, another voice telling him there were roses for him in a hotel lobby, more voices at night. On April 12, he was restrained after suddenly lunging forward from his chair; he said he had heard Rosina calling out Dante's name. On April 19, he "became violent and unmanageable," and continued that way on and off for four days. Rosina's frequent visits caused Nick's "most powerful delusions and hallucinations," according to psychiatrist Ralph Colp, Jr., who analyzed Sacco's behavior decades later. "It was as if every visit of Rose—however much her husband desired it—could only be unbearable to him."[51]

Elizabeth Evans visited Sacco at Boston Psychopathic as often as five times a week. She found him getting worse instead of better. "[H]e had this perfectly fatal idea in his mind," she recalled, "like a fixed point, like an automaton, when he spoke to me about smashing his head. . . . 'I did not smash my head hard enough. The next time I will dash my brains out . . . and make my protest.'"[52]

Evans pleaded with him to fight within the legal system. It was useless. "There is nothing [I can say] that would appeal to him—for his little boy, for his loyalty to Vanzetti. . . . 'No, free or die. I do make my protest.' Well, that is

Elizabeth Glendower Evans in 1919. Evans provided financial support to the defense committee and moral support to the defendants. The Schlesinger Library, Radcliffe Institute, Harvard University.

not the talk of a reasonable man." "The pleas of his loved ones, of his friends, and of all his comrades are in vain," Vanzetti noted.[53]

Dr. Campbell at last began to take the suicide threats seriously.[54] He recommended transferring Sacco to another psychiatric hospital for treatment, and on April 22, the day before his thirty-second birthday, Nick was admitted to the Bridgewater State Hospital for the Criminally Insane.

Nick stayed at Bridgewater for five months, throughout the spring and summer of 1923, and it turned out to be a surprisingly benign interlude in his prison ordeal. Instead of the solitary confinement of his cell at Dedham and his room at Psychopathic, he bunked in a hospital ward. He polished floors, he exercised, and best of all, he worked outdoors. Patients from what was called the insane division helped cultivate more than eight hundred acres at the State Farm in Bridgewater. They grew corn, potatoes, and beans; baled hay; and tended pigs, chickens, and beef and dairy cattle. Nick may have worked on the farm or he may have tended a garden on the hospital grounds. Either way, he was working outdoors, the best therapy for him. He was "in a very much improved, both physical and mental, condition," Moore wrote a supporter.[55]

Black clouds did not vanish completely. Nick said he would not hesitate to attempt suicide again if he couldn't get justice. But at the Bridgewater hospital he ate well, dressed neatly, made friends with other prisoner-patients, and

Mary Donovan, secretary of the defense committee from 1924 to 1927, frequently visited Vanzetti in prison. Lilly Library, Indiana University, Bloomington, Indiana (detail of original image).

was "quiet, cautious, pleasant, and agreeable." He told the doctors, "My mind is clear. I am not crazy." He even became hopeful again about chances for a new trial. He received only sporadic medical attention, but didn't seem to require more.[56]

The irony, of course, was that successful treatment meant a return to Dedham Jail. In September Nick was discharged from the hospital and returned to his cell at Dedham.

⁓ Back in darkness again, there was a bright spot. Sacco was given permission to study English in prison with a tutor. In the autumn of 1923, he began to receive weekly visits from Cerise Carman Jack. "I was so glad to hear from you that after our lesson you went back home happy and cheerful, and so I Mrs. Jack!" Nick wrote her. "And I think that you should not bother yourself to buy a dram[a] play because it will be really a drama play right here every once a week!"[57]

Betty Jack (later Betty Wirth) sometimes accompanied her mother to Dedham Jail, and when Betty turned sixteen and got a driver's license in 1925, she

Cerise Carman Jack, circa 1897. Jack began giving English lessons to Sacco in 1923; she also befriended Rosina Sacco and her children. Rockwood Studios photograph from *The Mortarboard*, 1898; courtesy of the Barnard College Archives (detail of original image of Banjo and Guitar Club).

started visiting Sacco on her own. "We went over vocabulary words," Betty Jack recalled. "Occasionally we'd go through a primer. But a great deal of the time was spent just talking. We didn't talk about the case. We talked about trees, flowers, fruits, farming—the things he loved and associated with Italy. We talked about his family. He was very, very gentle. He was kind beyond words. He was very concerned about his family." Betty had no qualms about entering the jail. She found the security procedures lenient and the guards friendly. "My feeling was the guards were sympathetic" to Sacco.[58]

Cerise Jack, a member of the New England Civil Liberties Committee, had attended the Sacco-Vanzetti trial and visited both prisoners. Her husband, botanist John Jack, was a professor of dendrology at Harvard. The family lived on twenty acres in Walpole, Massachusetts, which Professor Jack and his students used as an experimental farm. More than a thousand apple trees grew there, and two thousand peach trees.[59]

Virginia MacMechan, circa 1915. In prison, Vanzetti studied English with MacMechan; he also fell in love with her. Courtesy of Virginia Mallen (detail of original image).

This magical place, Folly Farm, provided an anchor to the Saccos. Nick loved to picture it in his mind's eye. "I could [imagine] your dear household, the green grass, the beautiful flowers and the lovely fruit trees that only Mr. Jack can take care," he wrote.[60] And "[O]h, how I wish to be out here to help you to gather all the peaches that they hung on the trees."[61] For Rosina and the children, Folly Farm provided a retreat when they needed one. Dante often visited the Jack family, just to "wander in the orchards" and play. He enjoyed spending time "with his comrade Betty," and was happy that the Jacks wanted him to visit the farm during his summer vacation.[62]

With their breadwinner in prison, the Saccos had to rely on the kindness of friends. People helped in different ways. Some left food on the back porch of the family's house.[63]

In such unpredictable circumstances, Folly Farm became a source of nutritional as well as emotional comfort. During the growing season, Cerise and Betty Jack brought Rosina fresh produce from the farm at least twice a week. Then, when Cerise and Betty visited Nick, they could bring him firsthand news of his family as well as treats from the orchards. Sacco's letters to the Jacks are filled with thanks for apples, berries, peaches, cherries, flowers, honey. "I have given to my family the little box honey that you send to me because I knew that they do love it," Sacco wrote Mrs. Jack. "I do loved it myself but I do enjoy more by give it to my family."[64]

Nick took pleasure in giving gifts to Rosina and the children. Knowing this, friends often brought little items for him to pass along. (Surprisingly prison authorities allowed this. Gardner Jackson believed that Sacco, like Vanzetti at Charlestown, had become "a favored guy" with sympathetic prison staff.) Daughter Ines was a toddler in the early years of her father's imprisonment. "Everytime that she does come see me," Nick wrote, "she always hug me, kiss me, and [keep] on asking me if I have something for her, because she know that I do always prepare for her some little thing which my friends they bring to me." In one touching letter, Nick tells Cerise Jack of a visit from Rosina and Ines. "[B]efore I could come out from my cell, [Ines] run into my cell and embrace me and kiss me several time. After [a while] I told her I had something for her that Mrs. Jack brought. . . . So I take her . . . little hand . . . and get your little beauty cradle. I wish you could see her how glad she was when she saw it—she jump upon my legs and she hug me, she kiss me [again], and then she asked me, Why don't you come home papa and play with me out in the yard?"[65]

"Oh, she is a bright little dear child," Nick wrote another friend. "I could not describe to you how much I do love her."[66]

To Vanzetti, Sacco wrote that son Dante, who became a teenager during his father's imprisonment, "will bring you a great surprise; he is quite a boy now, almost as big as his mother, and he seemed to me that he does love his mother very much and certain it does bring a relief to me. I love him so much." In Dedham, Sacco and his son were allowed to play a poignant version of catch, throwing a ball back and forth to each other, sight unseen, over the wall that enclosed the prison yard, Nick in confinement on one side of the high brick wall, Dante free on the other side.[67]

In the presence of his family and his anarchist comrades, Sacco put up a brave front. He was less guarded with Cerise Jack and Elizabeth Evans, his closest American friends. He confided his bleakest moods to them, feeling perhaps that it would burden them less than it would the others. He often told Elizabeth Evans, who was sixty-five at the time of his arrest, that she was like a mother to him. "[O]nly my poor dear mother she used succeed to know from me once in a while the pain that I was suffering when I used be sik. And that is why I am telling you sincere from the deep of my heart, because since the day that I have meet you, you been occupied in my heart my mother her place . . . that this terrible life it is insupportable, and I feel so nervous and tired of this miserably life that I hate to see my own shade."[68]

With Cerise Jack, he reminisced about happier times and often referred to himself as a poor recluse. He told her he was weary of his misery and worried about Rosina: she "looks very tired and depressed." He apologized for lack of progress in his studies. "I have tryed with all my passion for the success of this beautiful language, . . . to know and to be able to read and write correct English. But woe is me! It wasn't so, no, because the sadness of these close and cold walls . . . had more than once exhaust my passion."[69]

— Bartolomeo Vanzetti had no dependents to support, no informants to distrust. He did not suffer the same torments as his co-defendant. Unlike Nick, who gave up on the legal process early, Bartolomeo engaged in it, giving advice to Fred Moore. Vanzetti was practical, and his suggestions were "really wonderful," Gardner Jackson observed.[70]

In addition to devouring books, Vanzetti tried his hand at writing. He completed a short autobiography, *The Story of a Proletarian Life*. He wrote poetry, articles, booklets, and even attempted a novel, "more for exercise than for anything else." He multitasked. "I am overloaded of works," he wrote Elizabeth Evans. "Today, at noon, instead of eat my [lunch] I have finished the translation—from English into Italian of a quite long article. Actually I have to answer to eight or ten letters. . . . Beside that I intend to write the last letter upon 'Syndicates and Syndicalism.'" If people praised his literary efforts, he was astonished. "My poor writings find favor and approval," he marveled.[71]

He began studying arithmetic. He enjoyed singing and planned to use a gift of Christmas money to buy a guitar. There is some evidence that he dabbled in drawing. And of course he continued his prison labor. "I have obtained the promotion to work in the yard (shovel coal)," he wrote Mrs. Evans, "and already feel much better."[72]

Vanzetti corresponded with old friends. The intimate tone of his letters to the Brini family reveals deep mutual affection. When the Brinis sent Vanzetti a Christmas present of five dollars in 1923, Beltrando reported that even little Zora, his younger sister, "had saved her $1.00 up secretly to send to you." (Beltrando also wrote that he would never forget the details of December 24, 1919, the day he had helped Vanzetti sell fish.)[73]

Vanzetti corresponded with new friends, too. As his predicament became more widely known and the number of supporters multiplied, he wrote more and more. He corresponded with some of the best-known political activists in America, including Roger Baldwin and Eugene Debs. Vanzetti idealized Debs and said he loved him "as I love my father and my masters."[74]

Surely there were days when he admired Debs much more than he did his own father. Vanzetti described the Socialist leader, whom he called the greatest American, as someone "who has loved me more than my own father and whom I love with the heart of a son and disciple."[75] This hints at the irreparable breach that now split the family. The already strained relations between Vanzetti *père et fils* had broken down completely. Mr. Vanzetti, while believing his son innocent, nevertheless was so upset by the younger man's atheism and anarchism that, he told his daughters, "I don't understand him any more. I don't know how to speak to him any more." He stopped writing to his imprisoned son in 1922. For his part, the son thereafter addressed almost all of his letters home to his sister Luigia. Their father, he told her, was hostile to principles of freedom.[76]

One of Bartolo's most wide-ranging correspondences was with Alice Stone Blackwell, a member, as Vanzetti put it, of "one of the most distinguished families of America."[77] Blackwell's parents had been abolitionists and Blackwell herself, a born reformer, edited women's rights publications, helped organize the women's suffrage movement, and was a founding member of the Massachusetts League of Women Voters.

Blackwell also translated works by international poets, which was the starting point for her friendship with Vanzetti. While their first letters focused on poetry, the correspondence quickly moved on to other subjects: political prisoners, defense propaganda, the judge, the lawyers.

Blackwell was sixty-four years old in 1922 when she met Vanzetti. She became like a mother to him, offering both emotional support and sound advice. She praised him for being brave and inspiring, intellectually curious, and impressively self-disciplined for attempting to cut down on his smoking in prison. "You cannot know how good your friendship is to me," he told her.[78]

— In letter after letter for more than three years, Blackwell tried to coax Vanzetti into talking about his deceased mother. "I wish you would tell me more about your mother." "Do not forget that some day you have promised to tell me about your mother." "Long ago you promised to tell me some day about your mother, and you have never done it." "[I]f you find it too hard to write, perhaps [I can visit], and then you may find it possible to speak to me about her. It is easier to speak than to write."[79]

Blackwell doggedly persisted, but Vanzetti was incapable of complying with her request. "My heart is the tabernacle in which my mother, and she was brave, lives," he wrote Blackwell. "If a good hour will strike me, I will tell you of her. Not now, it is impossible now." And later, "I hold my mother's memory as the sacrest thing to me. I feel an unspeakable responsibility at the very thought to speak of her to you. . . . It would be a torture to me now, for I would really like to speak of my mother with the tongue of an archangel."[80]

Many years later psychiatrist Ralph Colp, Jr., speculated that Vanzetti may have suffered from depression due to unconscious guilt over the death of his mother.[81] True or not, Bartolo's intense feelings do spark a question: Was this bachelor ever romantically involved with women?

Until now, the answer to this question in the literature of the case has been a unanimous no. There is "no evidence of personal love by Vanzetti for a woman," according to one study. "Vanzetti is not known to have shown an interest in women in America," according to another. Beltrando Brini told a writer that "to my knowledge, he never had a girlfriend. Never interested." In 1914, when he was twenty-six years old, Vanzetti wrote an aunt in Italy: "The intention of taking a wife has never crossed my mind, nor have I ever had a lover, and if I have been lovestruck, it has been an impossible love, which I had to smother in my breast."[82] Vanzetti put his passion into politics. "Anarchy is my beloved," he wrote, and anarchism is "as beauty as a woman for me, perhaps even more. . . ."[83]

What is wrong with this picture?

According to the official "Inmate's History and Record," an intake form filled out when he entered Charlestown State Prison, Vanzetti had been indulging in sexual activity "Since 18"—in other words, since 1906, when he lived in Turin.[84]

Who were his partners? During his jailhouse interrogation, Vanzetti was initially evasive about his whereabouts on May 2, 1920, the Sunday before his arrest, finally telling Katzmann, "I am ashamed. I am sure I slept in Boston but I had a woman with me—that is why I did not want to tell you. . . . I don't know where we stayed in Boston; she took me to a place. It is a woman I met that night; a woman who goes with everybody. I met her in Hanover Street. She asked me to come with her."[85]

Resorting to streetwalkers, at least in 1920, and naturally reticent about it, Vanzetti longed for something more. "Am I without a lover? Yes, but I would like to have a lover," he wrote Elizabeth Evans from prison in 1924. "Have I not, by nature, by instinct, the faculties and, therefore, the right of love? Of course yes, but it would be better if not, for having them but not the freedom to realize them, it all become an excruciable laughing stock."[86]

Vanzetti had known Virginia MacMechan for more than a year when he wrote those pained words.

About the time that Nick received permission for visits from an English-language tutor in 1923, Bartolo received similar permission. His teacher at Charlestown State Prison was to be Virginia MacMechan of Sharon, Massachusetts, a friend of Cerise Jack and the wife of businessman Tom MacMechan.

The MacMechans had no children of their own, but Virginia was close to her young niece and namesake. Virginia MacMechan (later Virginia Mallen) recalls her aunt as loving and gentle, well-spoken, beautiful, elegant, and kind. She was also a deeply spiritual person, a Christian Scientist. She was, her niece remembers, "not simply religious; she was devout. She *walked* the faith." Her faith gave her strength, and she seemed absolutely fearless.[87]

Bartolo had left his own Catholic faith behind him long ago. He was impressed by Virginia, if not by her religion. His new teacher was scholarly and modest, he told his sister.[88]

In his first known letter to MacMechan, on August 26, 1923, he thanked her for sending a "special delivery" (apparently a letter and a book), and recounted his elation and sense of freedom after spending hours reading anarchist newspapers. He worried when she didn't reply right away. But when he did hear back from her, he said he was "content that you have done just what I like you to do in such circumstances. A player of golf and of tennis, friend of mine! . . . Indeed, I never thought such a thing possible — but it is."[89]

Vanzetti had a tendency to express himself in highfalutin "ritzy literary words." To MacMechan, who was correcting his writing and editing his autobiography, he blamed his "pedantic style" on the "old phraseology" of Italian as well as on his "blessing ignorance" of English. Her teaching, he said, was "providential." They were getting along well, but who knew how long that would last? "[W]e have a discussion now," he wrote, "soon we will begin to quarrel."[90]

After working with Vanzetti for several months, MacMechan sailed for Europe with a friend on May 10, 1924. On the trip, she planned to visit Vanzetti's family in Villafalletto. Vanzetti asked his sister to welcome "my American friend . . . with an open heart."[91] To MacMechan herself, he wrote an astonishing letter the day before her departure. He refers to "the unforgetable May 7," and continues:

You understand that I cannot say in words my thoughts and my sentiments, and I pray you to believe that my heart was aching because of the incompleteness of my [previous] note. There were so many things that I would have said and told to you—and I was unable; unable. What would I say if I than[k]you with all my heart for your goodness to me? As nothing. I have never saw you so beautiful as the last time: Pale, tired, throb[b]ing, and yet so brave. I have been so near to you, I have felt you my dear, even more good and generouse than ever. Dear, you have glad[d]ened my soul; you have delivered my heart of the hate which contracted it, spasmodically. Do not be sad for me—I am blessing you. O, the great communion of our soul, Virginia, beloved one—I have touch your [wrap] in an unconsciouse impulse to grasp your hands. . . . My divine friend, forgive me of the poor goodby that I bided you, and believe that here I am with open arms and heart.

At the end of the letter, he wrote another message, this one in invisible ink:

My beloved Virginia: My soul was within your soul at the moment of sailing. I am with you night and day. I embrace you and cares[s] and kiss you and all you, my beloved Virginia into my arms.[92]

MacMechan never read the invisible postscript. And her planned visit to Villafalletto never materialized.

His aching letter belies the image of Vanzetti as romantically disinterested in women. Still, there he was, locked up, literally, smitten with a married woman of high morals and religious faith. When she visited him in prison after returning from Europe, there was so much to say that they ended up speaking a lot but saying very little.[93] His hopeless love was poignant, and safe.

Only two later letters from Vanzetti to MacMechan are known to exist.[94] However, between 1924 and 1927, he often wrote about her to others, especially Alice Blackwell and Cerise Jack, and tried to send messages to her through them. He told Blackwell that MacMechan was "more than a friend." She was "really a noble spirit & of a superior mind. Not only a little of the English language have I learnt from her, but also knowledge & truth."[95]

Vanzetti said that MacMechan sent him notes "almost daily" in 1923, and that she promised to send him many postcards from Europe in 1924.[96] None of her correspondence with him is known to survive.

— Vanzetti's inner resources and his large and diverse circle of friends helped him stay sane in prison. But in October 1924, after a major legal setback, he began insisting that Mussolini's Fascist government in Italy was plotting to kill him, that Fascist convicts had been planted at Charlestown, and that they were "just waiting for an opportunity to do him harm." Therefore he asked to be allowed to carry a gun for self-protection. "The deputy warden was greatly surprised that so intelligent a man as Vanzetti should even expect that a prisoner would be allowed to carry a revolver."[97]

The situation with the "fascista thugs" was getting "worse and worse," Vanzetti wrote Jeremiah McAnarney in late October. "I beg you, Mr. [McAnarney,] to [plead] my rights before the authority—and to do it soon—otherwise it might be too late.... [A]t the extreme, I will take the law in my hands...and defend my life."[98]

Vanzetti had been a model prisoner until this point, but now he began exhibiting "outbursts of anger, coupled with insults and threats of violence toward his fellow prisoners." He paced his cell at night, and barricaded the door.[99]

On December 24, he was "abusive and threatening" to an inmate he said had laughed at him, and he said he felt "vibrations in his body" which meant an earthquake was coming. He said he had been "forsaken by everyone."[100]

Three doctors examined him at the end of December.

The psychiatrist for the defense, Dr. Abraham Myerson, arrived at Charlestown State Prison just as a "wildly excited" Vanzetti "was breaking the furniture of his room." He quieted down, and told Myerson that there was "an agreement between the American government and the Mussolini government not to set him free." He also said that because he was an atheist, the prison's Catholic chaplain did not like him and had turned the prison staff against him. Myerson concluded that the years of confinement, legal struggle, international press attention, and threat of imminent death, "together with the type of temperament often found in devotees of social movements (the lunacy fringe) have brought on a transient paranoid state. In my opinion he would be better off in a hospital than in his present environment."[101]

Doctors for the Commonwealth agreed. They concluded that Vanzetti had developed "a hallucinatory and delusioned state of mind," was dangerous as well as insane, and should, like Sacco before him, be transferred to the Bridgewater State Hospital for the Criminally Insane.[102]

So Vanzetti began the new year in a mental hospital. On January 2, 1925, he was taken to Bridgewater under police guard. He told the admitting physician he wasn't crazy and didn't know why he had been sent there. He reassured Cerise Jack, "[T]here are no reason of allarm since I am not crazy at all."[103]

He may, in fact, have been crazy like a fox. Vanzetti may have staged his symptoms for the express purpose of being hospitalized. Perhaps he thought that, like Sacco, he would benefit from the comparative freedom at Bridgewater. This appears to be the meaning behind a cryptic message he sent his sister in October 1924. "I will try to get as much sunshine and fresh air for myself as I can," he told her. "... I want to come out stronger and tougher than ever for the struggle of life and for my grand dream. So, in the future, don't believe everything that news about me might appear to signify."[104]

What little information exists about Vanzetti's hospital stay is contradictory and comes almost entirely from his own letters. He complained about persecution. He said he was kept isolated for weeks, then allowed into the day-room where speaking was forbidden. He said he was kept indoors even in good weather until, "after many protests," he was allowed to go into the yard, but only when no one else was there. He said he was sent without explanation to "a worse ward of the institution where the dangerous were." He worried that he had developed stomach ulcers.[105] He chafed under restrictions on his correspondence.

But he also acknowledged receiving special privileges. "[T]hey let my door open, give me two cups of milk a day, and the permission to keep books in my room." He was allowed to have visitors daily. Friends came bringing cigars and home-cooked Italian food. One day Beltrando Brini visited and played his new violin for Vanzetti, who was as proud of the boy as any father would have been.[106]

Vanzetti was discharged suddenly from Bridgewater in the spring of 1925. While there, according to the medical director, he showed no "abnormal mental reactions. He has been quiet, well oriented, and has given us no trouble. He has shown no evidence of hallucinations or delusions." His return to Charlestown State Prison came so unexpectedly that he left personal belongings behind at Bridgewater, and was upset when they were not returned.[107]

After his release from the hospital, Vanzetti continued to include cryptic messages in his letters. When he told his sister, "I am well and if you hear that I am ill, don't believe it," was he thinking about staging another breakdown? When he later told her that "the will of the enemy can be influenced," was he thinking about attempting to threaten or bribe officials? And when he told Alfonsina Brini that an unfavorable decision by the state's highest court would create the greatest judicial scandal in America, "and also something else. Finally," was he predicting violence?[108]

The meaning behind his coded messages is uncertain. He obfuscated to get by prison censors, only to end up with language so vague that it confused the recipients. "I can explain myself only by hints, which you always interpret differently from the way in which I am trying to give them," Vanzetti complained to his sister. But, he continued, no doubt adding to her puzzlement, "I have made a firm decision to take the law in my own hands, to make my own justice. This does not necessarily mean desperation, suicide, or murder—it means, however, that I want to win."[109]

For all his bravado, back at Charlestown Vanzetti struggled to remain optimistic. "I am in the twilight, the sky is dark, there are lightnings and thunder," he wrote one correspondent. But, he added, "I like the storm." For the rest of his imprisonment, with one brief exception, Vanzetti managed to weather what he called his "psychologic storms." His fellow prisoners welcomed him back to Charlestown as a hero, he said, yet he saw himself as "only a hard bone which refuses to fool himself."[110]

I don't care how it ends, if it would only end.
~ Nicola Sacco

13 | BATTLES IN AND OUT OF COURT

The wheels of justice grind slowly. If by starving himself Nick Sacco had hoped to speed up the legal process, it didn't work. Time and effort were needed for appeals. Defense lawyers prepared and argued five supplementary motions for a new trial, all based on new evidence, between 1921 and 1923.

The first—the Ripley motion, filed on November 8, 1921—was based on an affidavit by Jeremiah McArnarney about his conversation with jury foreman Walter Ripley shortly after the trial. Ripley told the lawyer that he had brought into the jury room three of his own .38 caliber shells, similar to shells from Vanzetti's revolver, and that jurors had discussed them.[1] It was improper for jurors to consider anything not accepted as evidence in open court, the defense argued in the motion. Ripley himself was unavailable for comment. Three days after he spoke to McAnarney, he was found dead in his office. Foul play was suspected at first. But negative tests for poison on his lunchbox and coffee bottle, combined with results from the medical examiner, showed that the foreman, who had just turned seventy, died of a heart attack brought on by natural causes.[2]

An affidavit by William Daly was later added to the Ripley motion. Daly had known Ripley for more than thirty years. The two men ran into each other on the day Ripley was reporting for jury selection. Daly mentioned that he did not think that Sacco and Vanzetti were guilty. Ripley's response, according to Daly, was blunt: "Damn them, they ought to hang them anyway."[3]

The second supplementary motion—the Gould-Pelser motion, filed on May 4, 1922—was based on affidavits by Roy Gould, a peddler, and Louis Pelser, a shoe worker. Gould said that he had been at the scene of the crime in South Braintree; that the getaway car passed within a few feet of him; that the bandit sitting next to the driver fired at him, the bullet piercing his coat; and that police had his name as a potential witness but did not question him. After being located by Fred Moore and after viewing Sacco and photographs of Vanzetti, Gould swore that neither defendant was the man he had seen in the car. Pelser, who at trial had identified Sacco as the man he saw shoot Berardelli, signed a statement retracting the identification.[4]

The third supplementary motion—the Goodridge motion, filed on July 22,

1922—contended that Carlos Goodridge's identification of Sacco as a bandit in the getaway car should be discredited, because new evidence showed Goodridge was a perjurer, a thief with a criminal record in New York, a fugitive from justice living under an assumed name, and a man of "violent malice" toward Italians.[5]

Like the Pelser affidavit, the fourth motion—the Andrews motion, filed on September 11, 1922—involved a retraction. At the trial Lola Andrews had identified Sacco as a man she spoke to in South Braintree. Andrews now signed an affidavit saying that police and the assistant district attorney had intimidated her into giving testimony that was "in its entirety unqualifiedly false and untrue."[6]

The fifth and final supplementary motion prepared while Fred Moore was still in charge of the defense—the Hamilton-Proctor motion, filed on April 30, 1923—focused on ballistics. Albert Hamilton, a "micro-chemical investigator and crimin[o]logist" hired by Moore to examine trial exhibits through a compound microscope, said that neither Bullet III, which had killed Berardelli, nor the Fraher Winchester shell from the crime scene, had been fired from Sacco's gun. He further said that, contrary to the trial testimony of a gun shop repairman, Vanzetti's revolver did not have a new hammer.[7] In affidavits supporting the motion, Augustus Gill charted microscopic measurements he had made of markings on Sacco's gun, the mortal bullet, and some test bullets. Gill, a professor of technical chemical analysis at Massachusetts Institute of Technology (MIT), determined that the measurements showed "conclusively that the 'mortal' bullet never passed through the barrel of Sacco's pistol."[8]

An affidavit by state police captain William Proctor was later added to the Hamilton motion. At trial Proctor had testified that the bullet that killed Berardelli was "consistent with being fired by [Sacco's] pistol." Now Proctor said he had found no evidence that the bullet came from Sacco's gun, that he had so informed the staff of the district attorney's office before the trial, and that his questioning had been prearranged to permit him to use the vague expression "consistent with." The mortal bullet "passed through some Colt automatic pistol," Proctor swore in his affidavit, "but I do not intend by that answer to imply that I had found any evidence that [it] had passed through this particular Colt automatic pistol and the District Attorney well knew that I did not so intend and framed his question accordingly. Had I been asked the direct question: whether I had found any affirmative evidence whatever that this so-called mortal bullet had passed through this particular Sacco's pistol, I should have answered then, as I do now without hesitation, in the negative."[9] (Defense lawyers had badly miscalculated in not asking Proctor such a direct question.

Thomas McAnarney later explained they thought his wording was "a catch," and that "he would follow it up . . . [with] reasons, explaining exactly that it was the [mortal] bullet.")[10]

Proctor also said that the district attorney and his staff had "repeatedly" asked him about the mortal bullet, and that he had "repeatedly" told them there was no evidence that it came from Sacco's gun. In a brief counteraffidavit, Katzmann ignored the substance of Proctor's allegations, denying only that he had asked for incriminating evidence "repeatedly," and had been told "repeatedly" that Proctor would "be obliged to reply in the negative."[11]

No further word on the subject would be forthcoming from the captain. Proctor died four months after filing his affidavit.[12]

~ Fred Moore was a busy man. He obtained the Gould, Pelser, and Andrews affidavits. He was behind the Goodridge investigation and the hiring of Hamilton. He was generating publicity, drumming up donations, hiring investigators, and seeking two new trials, one for both defendants, one for Vanzetti alone on his earlier conviction.

Nevertheless the defense committee, especially founder Aldino Felicani, was growing increasingly dissatisfied with the erstwhile labor lawyer. Sometimes Felicani and Moore disagreed about strategy, but mostly they disagreed about money.

Early contributions to the defense committee had arrived in small amounts from Italian anarchists: "ten cents . . . fifteen cents . . . I don't think any contributions of more than a dollar came in at the [beginning]," Felicani said. Later, a supporter recalled, "Collections were made on every [local] job where Italians worked," and laborers came "week after week on payday to lay down on the desk the donations which they had collected." Vanzetti told Alice Blackwell that people "have taken the bread out of their children's mouths to help us."[13]

With Moore's arrival and the involvement of labor activists, important additional contributions began arriving from union locals and workmen's circles around the country. Donations were steady but still small — "five dollars, two dollars, and so on."[14]

Elizabeth Evans and the fellow liberals she attracted to the case made larger contributions. Evans, Roger Baldwin explained, was connected to "all the so-called best people in Boston. They were untouchables and they could do a job for civil liberties just because they were untouchables." By 1923 Moore was surprised to realize that "the best support" for his defendants was coming from what he had thought would be the least likely source, "the finest of the old New England puritan stock . . ., the oldest of the old Back Bay stock of Boston."[15]

A total of more than half a million dollars was collected from all sources over the seven years of the case. Felicani, the treasurer of the defense committee, controlled the purse strings. He kept meticulous itemized records of all contributions and expenses, and was adamant about making them public. Moore opposed such transparency. Sacco, Vanzetti, and Rosina Sacco trusted Felicani implicitly, and sided with him on most matters. The records were published, and Moore ended up "in a position of no control [over spending] at all."[16]

Felicani believed that Moore was basically honest but wanted open access to funds to support a possible drug habit and to employ his friends as investigators or propagandists, and he insisted that Moore turn in expense accounts regularly. Felicani realized that Moore was working "all the time [on] new motions for retrial, new evidence, [and] new witnesses," yet the treasurer balked at bankrolling the wide-ranging investigations because they "cost a lot of money."[17] (There may have been an additional reason for the foot-dragging. Members of the defense committee as well as Sacco and Vanzetti themselves reportedly opposed attempts to identify the real South Braintree bandits, taking "the position that they are not police-informers.")[18]

For his part, Moore believed that members of the defense committee were honest but unimaginative, lacking the vision to see the broader implications of the case and to diversify their base of support. Felicani and comrades were "devoid of ideas . . .," Moore told Elizabeth Gurley Flynn. "They haven't the same form of physical and mental virility that some other people have."[19]

The friction between Moore and Felicani was reaching a boiling point. In July 1922, after he filed the first three supplementary motions, Moore pushed Felicani and the committee to form "a definite policy for the future. . . . One thing certain, the present policy, or rather, I should say lack of policy must not continue. It can only lead to disaster." In response, the committee told Moore that the "enormous sum of money" spent to date was a scandal, and that it was "time to come to a conclusion."[20]

It was the beginning of the end of Moore's tenure, but the long goodbye would drag on for two years. "I frankly confess that my capacity has been taxed to the limit," Moore told Eugene Lyons, but "I am going through on this case if it is the last case I ever try."[21] He desperately courted more donors. The defense owed money to medical experts, to ballistics experts, to investigators and printers and stationery shops, and unfortunately, Moore complained, "I am devoting time to the money angle that I should be devoting to the case." By the end of September 1923, he told Carlo Tresca that checks were bouncing, the committee was not bringing in money, and "unless a new attitude is manifested upon the part of all persons . . ., I shall have to sever my relations with the defense" after the conclusion of hearings on the motions.[22]

— Fred Moore and William Thompson were both lawyers, but any similarity ended there. Moore was an outsider's outsider, Thompson the ultimate insider: graduate of Harvard College and Harvard Law School, lecturer at the law school and member of the Harvard Club, senior partner in his law firm, and vice president of the Boston Bar Association. He was, in short, as Sacco put it, "a nice old Mayflower."[23]

Thompson had had a glancing familiarity with the Sacco-Vanzetti case from the start. As relations between Moore and the defense committee deteriorated, Thompson was prevailed upon to assume more responsibilities. He did so cautiously, agreeing only to work on some motions.

When Thompson began helping out in March 1923, Moore was alternately relieved and irritated. He worried that Thompson did not sufficiently believe in his new clients, telling him, "I wish you might feel as strongly as I do that these men are innocent."[24] What really bothered Moore was that "every scrap of information" Thompson would use in arguing the Hamilton motion "was done in [my] office," and while Thompson deserved to be paid, "the men who carry up the brick and mortar should also be taken care of."[25]

Under state law, the judge who would rule on supplementary motions would be the same judge who had presided at the original trial. On October 1, 1923, as hearings on the motions began, Webster Thayer ascended the bench in a nearly empty courtroom and listened to people tell him why Nicola Sacco and Bartolomeo Vanzetti should or should not receive a new trial.

The defendants — Sacco, just released from the hospital, and Vanzetti, temporarily transferred from Charlestown — sat side by side in the familiar cage, reunited for the duration of the hearing.

Thompson wowed them. Vanzetti wrote him immediately "to express you my gratitude. . . . I feel positive that if we have knew you from the beginning of this shame, at this time we would have been fred." And Sacco told Cerise Jack that he felt hopeful again; "today Mr. Tompson . . . did relief [my] soul."[26]

— Work on the supplementary motions had consumed two years. Another year would pass before the judge ruled on them. Vanzetti tried to reassure his family that the delays were not unusual. Meanwhile friction between Moore and the defense committee continued growing like a bad case of fungus.

By one estimate Moore had personally raised at least one-third of the defense money.[27] Yet he had little control over how it was spent, and he thought the committee was wasting it by financing protest demonstrations instead of hunting down new evidence. For their part, committee members distrusted the "hocus-pocus of motions and affidavits." They blamed Moore for all delays, unwilling to recognize that some were beyond his control. Within the committee, discord was also growing, between the "hot-headed and desperate Italians" and the privileged New England liberals. The atmosphere, Eugene Lyons observed, was "surcharged with emotion and at moments touched with hysteria."[28]

In April 1924 Fred Moore came up with a way to sidestep the conflicts. He formed an alternative defense committee, dubbing it the Sacco-Vanzetti New Trial League. He referred to it as the "American group."[29] Stalwarts Elizabeth Evans and Alice Blackwell supported it. A small group of Irish-American socialists, new to the cause, invigorated it. Other members came from several union locals, the New England Civil Liberties Committee, and the Communist Party of Boston.

Felice Guadagni was a go-between for the two committees. He promised cooperation. "Between us and the american friends," he wrote Moore, "cant be any intentional misunderstanding." He assured Moore that the original defense committee had no objections to the new group.[30]

He was dead wrong. The existence of two committees was an "impossible situation" for Felicani. Moore "had to go. I wouldn't tolerate anything like that. . . . [W]e [on the original committee] knew Sacco and Vanzetti and they didn't."[31]

For Sacco, Moore's perceived duplicity was the last straw. In August 1924, he erupted in a blast of anger and threats. Stop using my name on anything associated with the New Trial League, Sacco wrote Moore:

> I do not want have anything to do any more with the New [Trial] League. . . . [G]et out of my case. . . . Of course it is pretty hard to refuse a such sweet pay. . . . If it is not the truth, why did you not finish my case then? . . . [Y]ou been [deluding] me many times. . . . I would not be surprise if somebody will find you some morning hang on lamp-post.[32]

In bitter antagonism, Sacco signed the letter, "Your implacable enemy, now and forever."

The battle of the dueling committees lasted only a few months. The New Trial League dissolved, and its members joined or rejoined the original defense committee. In its brief lifetime, the league had two important achievements. It published the English version of Vanzetti's autobiography. And it brought Mary Donovan to the committee.

Donovan, the Socialist daughter of an Irish immigrant and a factory inspector for the Massachusetts Department of Labor, said she had learned how "to be fearless" from an older brother. Donovan's factory inspection district included Dedham, and during the Sacco-Vanzetti trial, she had sat in on the proceedings when her schedule allowed. After she left the New Trial League, she became part of the defense committee's inner circle, a valuable bridge between Italian workers and American Brahmins. "I became the errand boy and the spokesman," she recalled. "There had been a wall built up by Moore and his friends between the Italians and the so-called Americans," and it was time "to break it down."[33]

She also became Vanzetti's pal, visitor, and correspondent. For a while in 1924 she visited him at Charlestown State Prison every week. Despite the dreary surroundings and dismal prospects, "we laughed," she said, "at little nothings."[34]

∼ Nick and Bartolo marked time behind bars, waiting for Judge Thayer to rule on the motions. "There was nothing new to talk about," Mary Donovan said. The "newspapers either ignored us or gave us adverse publicity." That changed one warm autumn evening. As Donovan was coming home after a late inspection, she "saw the newspaper headlines at the subway station, 'Judge Thayer Refuses Latest Sacco-Vanzetti Motion.'"

It was October 1, 1924. One year to the day after the start of hearings on the five supplementary motions, the judge denied all of them.

Regarding the Ripley motion, Thayer found "that the mere production of the Ripley cartridges and the talk or discussion about them did not create such disturbing or prejudicial influence that might in any way affect the verdict," and that "if this motion for a new trial based upon the hearsay statements made by a deceased juror to a counsel for the defendants ... [should be arbitrarily granted], it would result in smirching the honor, integrity and good name of twelve honorable jurors, by a decision that never could be justified."[35] Thayer said nothing about Ripley's alleged "hang them anyway" remark.

Regarding the Gould-Pelser motion, Thayer found, first, that information from the newly discovered eyewitness Gould stating that neither Sacco nor Vanzetti was the man he had seen in the bandit car was "simply" cumulative, and that eyewitnesses were irrelevant anyway. "For these verdicts did not rest, in my judgment, upon the testimony of the eyewitnesses. . . . The evidence that convicted these defendants was circumstantial and was evidence that is known in law as 'consciousness of guilt.'" (This contradicted his instructions to the Dedham jury: The "real issue that you must determine is a very narrow one. It is one of identity.")[36]

As for Pelser's retraction of his identification of Sacco, Thayer found it "not at all satisfactory or trustworthy." (Pelser had since retracted his retraction. He said he had been drunk and manipulated by Moore into saying something he didn't mean.)[37]

Regarding the Goodridge motion, Thayer found that Goodridge's prior criminal convictions in 1893 and 1908 "could not have been used at the trial" because they were too old, that Goodridge's use of an assumed name was "immaterial," and that in any case the defense had already "successfully impeached" Goodridge's "reputation for truth and veracity" at the trial. Thayer then addressed a matter "exceedingly unpleasant to me" and reprimanded Moore. The attorney had tracked Goodridge to Maine, had had him detained at police headquarters there for two nights without authorization, and had threatened him with arrest under an old indictment in New York unless he admitted that he had made a deal with the district attorney to identify Sacco in Dedham in return for some benefit. This "bold and cruel attempt to sandbag Goodridge" was a "most atrocious invasion of his rights," as well as an attempted smear against the office of the district attorney. "I have tried to look at this conduct of Mr. Moore with a view of finding some justification or excuse of it," Thayer continued. "I can find none."[38]

In the matter of the Andrews motion, Thayer found that Lola Andrews's retraction of her identification testimony of Sacco had "beyond doubt" been obtained through Fred Moore's "intimidation, coercion and duress" and "should not receive any consideration whatever in a court of justice." (Moore had located Andrews's teenage son in Maine, brought him to Boston, and staged a late-night confrontation where the son, Moore, and two associates took turns pressuring Andrews to retract her "terrible lie" and threatening to release "damaging evidence" about her past if she refused.) Moore's unprofessional conduct was an attempt to "defeat and take away the rights of the Commonwealth." While the judge regretted being compelled to criticize Moore, he said the attorney "has no one to blame but himself."[39]

Finally, regarding the Hamilton-Proctor motion, Thayer said, "With experts disagreeing [about whether or not the mortal bullet was fired by Sacco's gun], I must use my best judgment as I am able to from my own observation, and from that observation I am not convinced that the claim of Mr. Hamilton is correct. Therefore, on this particular issue I find as a fact that the defendants have not maintained the burden of proof that the law requires."[40]

As for Captain Proctor's claim that the district attorney questioned him in a way to imply falsely that he believed the mortal bullet was fired through Sacco's gun, Thayer said "I do not believe that the interpretation of counsel for the motion is the true one. Neither do I believe that Captain Proctor would like this interpretation, for if it is true it places him in the very unfortunate position of testifying intentionally to something that was false."[41]

As a mournful melody from a street piano filled the air that October evening, Mary Donovan scanned the headlines at the newspaper stand, then left the subway station and trudged home. The somber music, she recalled, suited her mood.[42]

As long as the motions were alive, supporters had been hopeful. "Victory Is in Sight!" the defense committee had trumpeted. Now, with all five motions defeated, Vanzetti tried to cheer his family. "I assure you," he wrote his sister, "and I beg you to reassure [all our friends and relatives], that there is no reason to be discouraged. Quite the contrary," because appeals to higher courts would now be possible.[43]

~ A few weeks after ruling on the motions, Judge Thayer traveled to New Hampshire to attend a football game at his alma mater, Dartmouth College. There on the field he chatted with a group of acquaintances, including attorney James Richardson, a member of the 1917 Massachusetts Constitutional Convention and a professor of law at Dartmouth. Thayer "immediately went into the subject of the Sacco-Vanzetti case," Richardson later recalled. "Judge Thayer said . . . 'Did you see what I did with those anarchistic bastards the other day. I guess that will hold them for a while. . . . Let them go to the Supreme Court now and see what they can get out of them.' . . . [W]hat he said on that day was a surprise to me and I wouldn't have believed it possible." Thayer's attitude, Richardson recalled, was "violent."[44]

~ Fred Moore had been trying to extricate himself from the case ever since his New Trial League collapsed. Elizabeth Evans informed members of the moribund league on September 12 that Moore had resigned "to clear the air," but the announcement was premature because, in the absence of alternative arrangements, Moore stayed on as counsel.[45] William Thompson was dragging his feet about making a full-time commitment, and defense committee coffers were empty.

Committee members begged Thompson to help. To get off the hook, he agreed to take the case for twenty-five thousand dollars up front, a demand he expected they would be unable to meet. Instead, they raised five thousand dollars, borrowed twenty thousand, and presented him with a check. He "smiled ruefully . . . [and said] 'I thought sure you couldn't raise it. . . . I can't say that I'm glad!'"[46]

And with that, Fred Moore drove off into the sunset.

To his admirers, he had been a "brilliant lawyer, quixotically devoted and self-sacrificing." His work had been heroic; his mistakes, exaggerated. He "subordinated . . . legalistic procedure to the larger needs of the case as a symbol of class struggle. If he had not done so, Sacco and Vanzetti would have died six years earlier [than they did], without the solace of martyrdom."[47]

In the parallel universe of his detractors, however, Moore's approach had been a "grave error," and the defendants' martyrdom a meaningless reward. Sacco for one "had no ambition to be a martyr. He wanted to go home . . . to his wife, his children and his job."[48]

— The first task William Thompson confronted in his new role as lead attorney for the defense was to appeal Thayer's decisions on the Ripley, Gould, and Hamilton-Proctor motions to the Supreme Judicial Court for the Commonwealth of Massachusetts. The Pelser, Goodridge, and Andrews decisions would not be appealed.

With the legal work in progress, 1925 was a quiet year for the two prisoners. Supporters began talking about alternative endgames — executive clemency or deportation. Vanzetti cautioned friends not to get carried away by optimism. He feared that even Thompson's best efforts were doomed to fail.

The quiet year screeched to an abrupt halt on November 18. An inmate at Dedham Jail smuggled a handwritten, one-sentence note to Nick Sacco: "I hearby confess to being in the South Braintree shoe company crime and Sacco and Vanzetti was not in said crime."[49]

Slipped between the pages of a magazine, the astonishing note was delivered to Sacco by a prison trusty, who found him a few minutes later, "leaning against the wall [of his cell] trembling, with the paper in his hands . . ., and tears in his eyes. He asked me, 'What is this?' I said, 'Can't you read English?' He said he would telephone his friend and get him to take the paper to Mr. Thompson."[50]

The author of the confession was Celestino Madeiros, 23, a Portuguese immigrant from Massachusetts, a bouncer and a thief who, during an attempted bank robbery a year earlier, had shot and killed a teller. Convicted of murder for that crime, Madeiros was in Dedham Jail awaiting the results of an appeal.[51] He had been trying to confess for a while. Suspicious of jailhouse spies, Sacco had ignored his earlier attempts to talk, and a deputy sheriff had likewise ignored his previous request to forward a written confession to a Boston newspaper.[52]

Thompson interviewed Madeiros at the jail two days later. Sacco sat in on the interview, begging Madeiros to tell the truth "for Christ's sake." According

Celestino Madeiros confessed to participating in the South Braintree crime and exonerated Sacco and Vanzetti. His confession led to an entirely new theory of who the real perpetrators might have been. Courtesy of Historical and Special Collections, Harvard Law School Library (detail of original image).

to Madeiros, very early in the morning of April 15, 1920, four Italians in a Hudson picked him up by prearrangement at the boardinghouse where he lived in Providence, Rhode Island. They drove to South Boston, where they met someone in a saloon "to get information . . . about the money," then back to Providence, and then on to South Braintree, where they spent time in a speakeasy. At some point they also drove to woods in Randolph, Massachusetts; transferred from the Hudson to a Buick brought there by another Italian; and later transferred back to the Hudson after they "did the job at South Braintree." Madeiros said he had known the men for "three or four months" and had seen them in a Providence saloon "two or three nights before" April 15, when they persuaded him to join them. His assignment was to sit on the backseat of the getaway car with a gun and to use it if necessary to "hold back the crowd in case they made a rush." Madeiros said he had never been in South Braintree before April 15. He was eighteen years old at the time and "scared to death when I heard the shooting begin." He said one of the Italians was about thirty-five years old; one, about forty; two, in their twenties; and all, professional gangsters "engaged in robbing freight cars in Providence" who had "done lots of jobs of this kind."[53]

Madeiros refused to tell "the last names of the gang." He did tell the two first names that he said he could remember—Mike and Bill—but also said those names were meaningless since "they change them whenever they want to." The men were supposed to meet him the night after the crime in a Providence saloon to split the money, but "they did not come." He later searched for them in New York and Chicago, "hoping to find them in cabarets spending the money," but never found them, and did not know where they were. He said the mastermind of the South Braintree job was "the oldest of the Italians in Providence," and "Sacco and Vanzetti had nothing to do with this job."

Thompson sent a copy of his interview notes to the assistant district attorney. He planned to wait until Madeiros's appeal in the bank murder case had played out, then file a motion for a new trial for Sacco and Vanzetti based on the confession.

Perhaps optimism was not unreasonable after all.

∼ "Let them go to the Supreme Court now and see what they can get out of them." That was a defiant Webster Thayer's alleged challenge to the defense, issued on a college football field in 1924. William Thompson now took up the challenge, appearing before the justices of the Supreme Judicial Court of Massachusetts on January 11, 1926.

It was the role of the court to consider questions of law, not questions of fact. It would review, "in effect, the conduct of the trial judge. . . ." It would *not* review "whether the facts as set forth in the . . . record justified the verdict." [54] Thompson hoped he could find a way to "open the door" to a consideration of evidence. If he failed, Elizabeth Evans worried, who "can doubt that the lower court will be upheld? Supreme Court judges, after all, are only human beings; there is such a thing as pride of profession." [55]

Thompson argued that Judge Thayer had made error after error at the trial and in his subsequent rulings, primarily concerning the admission or exclusion of evidence. The errors were unjustifiable, prejudicial, "seriously detrimental," and amounted to an "abuse of judicial discretion." [56]

Thompson's appearance before the court was a local media event. Newsmen covered his arguments "from A to Z." (The defendants themselves were not present. Thompson "said we didn't have the right [to be there], and we didn't want to ask for any special privileges," Vanzetti explained to his sister, adding that he suspected Thompson concocted this reason as an excuse to avoid having police guards in the court.) Alice Blackwell attended the morning session, but could not reenter in the afternoon; "every seat in the courtroom was full, and there was a small crowd outside. . . . Mrs. Evans said Mr. T. made a splendid argument." [57]

Oral arguments ended on January 13. Their lives at stake, Bartolomeo and Nick nervously awaited the decision of the Supreme Judicial Court as well as the results of the Madeiros appeal. Nick was doing "pretty good," Rosina told Cerise Jack in January, "but I cant see just how he can stand it for when I think of it I just go crazy." A month later, "[w]e are still waiting for the decision," said Bartolo. "There is much optimism in Boston, not so much in me." A month later still, Rosina thought a decision would come at any moment, "and they tell me it looks O.K." By April Bartolo acknowledged, "The delay is terrible, but I hope it will end soon."[58]

In May, it finally did. "We have examined carefully all the exceptions in so far as argued," the justices of the Supreme Judicial Court concluded in a ninety-page decision, "and finding no error the verdicts are to stand and the entry must be *Exceptions overruled*." Judge Thayer had not, in the court's opinion, abused his judicial discretion, nor had he violated any of the defendants' constitutional rights.[59]

The gist of the opinion, said Eugene Lyons, "was that Thayer might be mistaken — it had no power to inquire on that issue — but right or wrong, his judgement must stand. It was legal."[60]

The court's decision was the last stroke, Vanzetti mourned. (He didn't know how many more last strokes still lay ahead.) To Virginia MacMechan he confided that "Nick, poor Nick, he has been so confident and trustfull — want to drop at once every legal defense. He won't do nothing more. . . . [But] I believe that the legal defense should be carry to the last."[61]

Thompson petitioned for a rehearing of the court's decision, and was quickly turned down.

~ Gloom descended in the wake of the court's decision, but hope still glimmered in the form of the Madeiros confession.

Thompson hired Massachusetts corporate lawyer Herbert Ehrmann to investigate the confession's validity. Believing it to be "a call which I could not refuse,"[62] Ehrmann spent the next few months tracking down leads. He met with cops and robbers in police stations and prisons from Providence, Rhode Island, to Leavenworth, Kansas. His inquiries led to a completely new theory about the South Braintree bandits.

Briefly, it went like this. The actual perpetrators in South Braintree were professional criminals, "a menace to the community," the so-called Morelli gang of Providence: American-born brothers Joe Morelli, Mike Morelli, and Frank (Butsey) Morelli, plus associates Tony Mancini, Steve Benkosky, and Celestino Madeiros.[63] (Two other Morelli brothers, Fred and Pasquale, did not participate.) Mike Morelli was in charge of the two cars used on the job; he stayed in the woods where the cars were switched, and was not at the crime scene. Police in both Providence and New Bedford, Massachusetts, knew the Morellis well as gangsters who robbed freight cars and used informants to find out which shipments of shoes and textiles from which factories were being loaded onto which freight cars.[64] Four of the Morellis, including Joe and Frank, had previously been indicted on charges of stealing shoes shipped from the Rice & Hutchins and Slater & Morrill factories in South Braintree. On the day of the crime, all of the Morelli brothers except Fred had been at liberty.[65]

Sergeant Ellsworth Jacobs of the New Bedford Police Department had originally suspected the Morellis of committing the South Braintree crime. Jacobs was familiar with the brothers' rap sheet; he knew Mike Morelli had transferred a license plate from one car to another around the time of the crime; and, when he approached Frank Morelli and three companions for questioning in a restaurant shortly after the crime, he noted that they behaved strangely, one of them reaching for his hip pocket as if to draw a gun. His supervisor on the force seemed to share the sergeant's suspicions. But Jacobs "dropped the matter after the arrest of Sacco and Vanzetti."[66]

Joe Morelli resembled Nicola Sacco so strikingly that several eyewitnesses who were shown Morelli's photograph identified it as a picture of Sacco.[67]

Madeiros's motive for confessing was "to save Sacco and Vanzetti because he knew they were perfectly innocent." Also, Madeiros said, "I seen Sacco's wife come up here [to Dedham Jail] with the kids and I felt sorry for the kids." While Madeiros freely confessed to his own participation, he refused to provide additional information to identify the Morellis, even after they had been implicated by other sources.[68]

Comparing multiple points of evidence against Sacco and Vanzetti to evidence against Madeiros and the Morellis—character, opportunity, motive, and a first-person confession, as well as possible identification of all five of the bandits described by witnesses—Ehrmann concluded that the gangsters, not the laborers, had done the deed.

The Supreme Judicial Court reversed Madeiros's murder conviction in March 1926, but he was quickly retried and reconvicted. Now Thompson was free to go public with the South Braintree confession. Within a week, he filed a motion for a new trial for Sacco and Vanzetti.

Under Massachusetts law, the judge who would rule on the new motion would be the original trial judge. Once more the decision would be Webster Thayer's.

— Interest in the case was growing. Reporters from New York, Chicago, and Pittsburgh crowded into the Dedham courtroom alongside their Boston colleagues on Monday, September 13, 1926, to hear Thompson argue that Sacco and Vanzetti were entitled to a new trial on the basis of new evidence.

Thompson and assistant district attorney Dudley Ranney began by reading the eighty-plus affidavits they had assembled for the motion. Validating the Madeiros confession were three people who said he had told them about his involvement in South Braintree. Discrediting the confession was a jail officer who said that Maderiros had consulted a financial report of the Sacco-Vanzetti Defense Committee before confessing.[69]

There was new evidence in other areas as well. The president of a men's haberdashery company had measured Sacco's hands and said in an affidavit that they were "smaller than the average, the left hand being noticeably smaller than the right," thus casting doubt on Mary Splaine's 1921 identification of Sacco as the bandit with a "good sized" left hand, "a hand that denoted strength." Two employees of Slater & Morrill—Minnie Kennedy and Louise Hayes Kelly—said in affidavits that they had seen the driver of the getaway car in South Braintree; that they had described him to police investigators; that they had told the assistant district attorney they were "positive that neither [Sacco nor Vanzetti] was the man we had seen," and that they had then "never heard again from Mr. Katzmann or anyone connected with his office."[70]

Of all the new evidence, none was as explosive as that concerning alleged arrangements between former district attorney Fred Katzmann and agents in the Boston office of the Bureau of Investigation, part of the U.S. Department of Justice. As early as January 1921, the Boston Post had reported that "labor unions here and in the mill cities . . . have declared that the two men are being 'railroaded' by the Department of Justice."[71] The allegation now gained momentum.

Lincoln Wadsworth, the gun shop supervisor who had testified at the trial, said in an affidavit that from 1916 to 1919 he had been a special agent investigating radicals for the Department of Justice, and that in that capacity he had been informed that Sacco and Vanzetti were "under surveillance by the Boston office of the Department" and were known to agents "as leading communists and radicals."[72]

Fred Weyand, a special agent in the Boston office from 1917 to 1924, said in his affidavit that he and other undercover agents had attended pretrial defense committee meetings, but "no evidence was obtained . . . which warranted proceedings against anybody." Weyand continued:

The Boston agents ... hoped to be able to secure the necessary evidence [of the defendants' anarchism] from their testimony at their trial for murder, to be used in case they were not convicted. ... [Agent William] West furnished Mr. Katzmann information about the Radical activities of Sacco and Vanzetti to be used in their cross-examination. ...

I am also thoroughly convinced, and always have been, and I believe that is and always has been the opinion of such Boston agents of the Department of Justice as had any knowledge on the subject, that these men had nothing whatever to do with the South Braintree murders, and that their conviction was the result of co-operation between the Boston agents of the Department of Justice and the District Attorney. It was the general opinion of the Boston agents ... that the South Braintree crime was committed by a gang of professional highwaymen.[73]

Lawrence Letherman, another former agent in the Boston office, also said in an affidavit that "before, during, and after the trial," the department had planted informers on the defense committee "to get sufficient evidence against Sacco and Vanzetti to deport them," but failed to do so. Letherman went on:

It was the opinion of the Department agents here that a conviction of Sacco and Vanzetti for murder would be one way of disposing of these two men. It was also the general opinion of ... the agents ... that Sacco and Vanzetti, although anarchists and agitators, were not highway robbers, and had nothing to do with the South Braintree crime.[74]

Disputing these claims, former Bridgewater police chief Michael Stewart said in an affidavit that he had been the chief investigator for the state on the Sacco-Vanzetti case and that, from the time of the crime until the end of the trial, the "only official of the United States Government with whom I ever came in contact" was an immigration inspector on a deportation case.[75]

This meant nothing: Katzmann, not Stewart, was the person whom the former agents said had cooperated with Justice. In his affidavit, however, Katzmann said nothing at all about the Weyand and Letherman allegations. Katzmann's "absence of denial of the [agents'] statements" was, said Thompson, "extraordinary."[76]

The reading of dueling affidavits in the courtroom went on for two and a half days. Finally Thompson began oral arguments. Regarding Madeiros and the Morellis, he told the judge that if state investigators had obtained at the outset "the evidence we have got and you had been the committing magistrate, you would have held the Morellis."[77]

Claims of evidence-sharing between the Department of Justice and the district attorney provoked Thompson's passionate outrage:

> Mr. Katzmann asked your Honor to admit those questions concerning Sacco's radicalism on the ground that he wanted to test the sincerity of Sacco's claim that he was a radical at all, and it was on that ground that your Honor admitted those questions. . . .
>
> What does your Honor think now? That was not [Katzmann's] reason. That is one way in which he was paying part of his bargain with the United States officials. . . .
>
> Mr. Katzmann . . . has remained silent. . . . Nothing that I can say is more eloquent than that silence."[78]

Thompson was if possible even more outraged about the Justice Department's refusal to make available (in those pre–Freedom of Information Act days) the extensive correspondence on the matter which Weyand and Letherman had said could be found in department files:

> Now you never in the world can convince the common sense of mankind that it is justifiable to send two men to the electric chair when it stands unanswered and uncontradicted in the case that there is documentary evidence in the possession of your national government having the greatest possible bearing upon the innocence or guilt of these men and on the methods by which they were entrapped, and [the government refuses] to produce it.[79]

"We have heard much here . . . of the rottenness of Massachusetts," assistant district attorney Ranney responded. "Let me remind Mr. Thompson that though we are public servants in the employ of the Commonwealth, we are still human beings and we have hearts. The bitter, untrue accusations cut like the thrust of a bayonet."[80] (Ranney "suffered awfully, all through the case," according to Sara Ehrmann, Herbert Ehrmann's wife. Ranney later told Herbert Ehrmann that if he had been a juror, he would have found the prosecution's case "not proven.")[81]

The Madeiros confession should be disregarded, Ranney argued, because its author was a "surly, morbid brute," a perjurer whose failure to remember details about South Braintree was not credible if he had really been there. As for former agents Letherman and Weyand, they were, in Ranney's view, disloyal whistle-blowers who "betray the secrecy of their department." In any event, Ranney said, cooperation between state and federal agencies in criminal prosecutions was common practice, and no illegal act had been committed.[82]

The hearings wrapped up on September 17, 1926, five days after they began. The defense team was optimistic. According to Herbert Ehrmann, "[W]e honestly believed that the sheer weight of our evidence would carry Judge Thayer, however unwilling."[83]

⁓ Sacco and Vanzetti continued doing what they had been doing for six years: waiting. Bartoloemo considered going on a hunger strike. Nick, impatient for news, asked Elizabeth Evans for a progress report.

Vanzetti heard the bad tidings first. "I learn the new and last refusal of murderer Thayer this morning while going to the yard," he wrote Mary Donovan. "Peoples here have heard it by radio last night, at 10 p.m."[84]

In a lengthy decision filed on October 23, Thayer found Madeiros not believable. Regarding character and reputation, "Madeiros is, without doubt, a crook, a thief, a robber, a liar, a rum-runner, a 'bouncer' in a house of ill-fame, a smuggler, and a man who has been convicted and sentenced to death for . . . murder," the judge said.[85] Regarding Madeiros's story, it was full of discrepancies and improbabilities.

Thayer insinuated that Madeiros had been bribed into confessing. Madeiros had seen a copy of the financial report of the Sacco-Vanzetti Defense Committee. (There was disagreement about whether he had seen it before or after submitting his first written confession.)[86] Thayer asked rhetorically: "Is it not quite likely that Madeiros desired, before he made his confession, to ascertain whether or not this large [legal fund] had been raised and expended . . .? . . . Who pumped this curiosity into him? . . . Was Madeiros given to understand that he would receive the same aid if he had the power of this organization behind him?" Thayer further speculated that Madeiros might have confessed in order to buy time, to delay his execution so he would still be available to testify if there were a new trial for Sacco and Vanzetti.[87]

"I am forced to the conclusion," Thayer wrote, "that the affidavit of Madeiros is unreliable, untrustworthy and untrue. To set aside a verdict of a jury affirmed by the Supreme Judicial Court of this Commonwealth on such an affidavit would be a mockery upon truth and justice. Therefore . . . this Motion for a new trial is hereby denied."[88]

Thayer then addressed what he called charges of "conspiracy," "fraudulent conspiracy," and "collusion" between the Department of Justice and the district attorney. (Thompson had not used such legally loaded terms, referring to the cooperation as a "bargain" or "arrangement.")[89] Thayer characterized the charges as a symptom of "a new type of disease . . . [which] might be called 'lego-psychic neurosis' or 'hysteria' which means: 'a belief in the existence of something which in fact and truth has no such existence.'... [T]he Court is rather of the opinion that the disease is absolutely without cure."[90]

The defense request to see relevant files of the Department of Justice appeared to Thayer to be nothing more than a fishing expedition. Is it conceivable, Thayer asked incredulously, that the attorney general of the United States would stoop so low as to withhold exonerating evidence, and the district attorney would conspire with government agents to convict innocent men? No, he concluded, such a scenario was not conceivable, and he could not believe it. As for the files Thompson could not obtain from the Department of Justice, Thayer was "inclined to believe" that, "in all probability," Thompson could have obtained them if only he "had used a little more tact and diplomacy." Thayer said he "would be absolutely unwarranted in finding ... that there was ... a fraudulent conspiracy. This being true, the Court would be unwarranted in granting a new trial."[91]

Then the judge went on to justify his own conduct in 1921. The fact that the defense did not make "a single request for instructions" at the close of evidence amounted, Thayer said, to an "almost unprecedented compliment to the Court of his fairness and impartiality." That, plus the fact that the defense took "not a single exception" to the judge's charge to the jury, "ought to be fairly conclusive that these defendants had a fair and impartial trial." Repeatedly, and inaccurately, Thayer said that the Supreme Judicial Court of the Commonwealth had affirmed the jury's verdict. In fact, said Felix Frankfurter, the court "never approved the verdict; nor did it pretend to do so. The Supreme [Judicial] Court passed on technical claims of error, and 'finding no error the verdicts are to stand.' Judge Thayer knows this, but laymen may not."[92]

Thayer's decision ran on for fifty-five pages, "most unusually long, and perhaps unnecessarily so," the judge himself conceded. He could simply have denied the motion without explaining his reasons. Instead, as even Thayer supporter Robert Montgomery acknowledged, "the spirit of the opinion was that of an advocate and ... the tone was in some parts of it somewhat alien to judicial utterance. This was unfortunate."[93]

~ With Thayer's decision, a backlash began, and it appeared almost immediately. Three days after the decision, the *Boston Herald* reversed its editorial position and called for a new trial for Sacco and Vanzetti. Thayer's decision contained errors and innuendoes, and sounded "the tone of the advocate rather than the arbitrator," the newspaper said. The Justice Department files ought to be examined, and Madeiros ought to "be placed on the stand in open court. . . . He may be lying, but the criterion here is not what a judge may think about it but what a jury might think about it."[94]

One person surely unimpressed by the *Herald*'s stand was Alvan Tufts Fuller, governor of Massachusetts, a man making a name for himself, like his predecessor, Calvin Coolidge, as a law enforcement hard-liner. In an interview published at the end of 1926, Fuller said that, despite "all manner of pressure," he maintained his belief in the deterrent effect of capital punishment. He criticized "newspaper sob-sisters" for ignoring the plight of victims. He criticized law enforcement officials for leniency, and he criticized the law itself for providing "so many appeals."[95]

⁓ A year that had begun in hope for the two prisoners ended in failure. It was rumored that William Thompson might meet the same fate as Fred Moore, but such talk was quickly squelched. "All of us realize that no better man than Mr. Thompson could have been choised as our defender," Vanzetti wrote. "Our pessimism is related solely to the sistem."[96]

Thompson began working on a new appeal to the Supreme Judicial Court.

To a supporter Nick confided that "more than once the death has appear more sweet than the life itself."[97] Christmas gifts from the Jack family—apples and candy and flowers, a book for Dante and a dollhouse for Ines—briefly lifted his spirits, but a family visit broke his heart.[98] The children looked well, but "my poor dear Rosina, her health has hardly left on her poor soul, and it does immensely sad my soul."[99]

At Charlestown, Bartolomeo tried to steel himself for the worst. He wanted to "look the reality straight in its face," he said, because "unfounded optimism . . . cannot help us." Thanksgiving was "miserable" and Christmas, "my sixth Hell-Christmas in prison," was "bitter."[100]

Neither Sacco nor Vanzetti knew if he would live to see another Thanksgiving or Christmas. Jointly from their separate prisons, they issued a year-end rallying cry to supporters:

> [O]ur hearts wish is that the new year may give us Liberty or Death.
> . . . Death! Well, what of it? It can destroy us two, but not the Idea. . . .
> Comrades, . . . we salute you. We would salute you with full-throated,
> steady voices and gladdened hearts even strapped to the electric chair.

> Salve,
> *Nicola Sacco*
> *Bartolomeo Vanzetti*[101]

14 | CLINGING TO RAZOR BLADES

Once upon a time, at the dawn of the twentieth century in the town of Torre-maggiore, a child known as Nando gathered fresh vegetables in his father's sunny fields and picked wild roses for his mother. Likewise, in Villafalleto a boy called Bartolo swam in the river and listened to the sounds of beating insect wings and trilling nightingales.

As 1927 began, those days were long ago and far away, and memories of happier times flickered ever more faintly for Bartolomeo Vanzetti, now 38, and Nick Sacco, 35. Locked away for more than six years, they felt grim fate closing in. "[O]ften I feel numb and blunt as if dying," Vanzetti wrote from Charlestown. Sacco described life in Dedham as "living death." Their sympathizers hoped that public pressure for a new trial would finally sway decision makers. To think in such a delusional way, Bartolo warned Mary Donovan, is "'to cling to rasors' blades.'" His pessimism grew when three prisoners on death row were executed at Charlestown at the beginning of the year. "Now, after that," Bartolo recounted, "everybody said that Sacco and Vanzetti will go. Most of my fellow prisoners were glad of it, and . . . [t]he friendly ones have not had the courage to look into my face."[1]

— Defense lawyers William Thompson and Herbert Ehrmann were still fighting for their clients. On January 27, they appeared before the Supreme Judicial Court to appeal Judge Thayer's October denial of the Madeiros motion. Assistant district attorney Dudley Ranney represented the Commonwealth.

Thayer's lengthy decision gave the defense plenty of ammunition for argument. Not only had the judge's rulings been "so erroneous and injurious as to entitle the defendants to a rehearing of the motion," Thompson contended, but the rehearing should take place "before another judge" because Thayer had become "incapable of dealing either logically or impartially with this motion." The judge had misstated facts. A "particularly dangerous" misstatement was his assertion, "made eleven times," that the Supreme Judicial Court had put its stamp of approval on the jury verdict; that court had reviewed the judge's work, not the jury's. Thayer had ignored "every statement in any affidavit tending to establish the truth of [the Madeiros] confession or the contention of the defendants with reference to the Federal agents." The judge's reasoning showed "that his mind was moved by irrational, hostile, and unjudicial considerations."[2]

On the other side of the adversarial divide, Ranney argued that Thayer's decision "not to believe Madeiros was entirely natural and logical," that the failure of the defense to get access to pertinent files of the Department of Justice was due to Thompson's own "complete lack of tact and diplomacy, amounting to obstinacy," and that Thayer had committed no abuses of judicial discretion.[3]

The justices of the court listened to arguments for two days, then took the appeal under consideration.

— Heading for its last chance within the Massachusetts court system, the case was getting a big break in a different court, the court of public opinion. This was due in large part to two men: Gardner Jackson and Felix Frankfurter.

Jackson had been a cub reporter at the *Globe* in 1921. He did not cover the Dedham trial, but he came to believe it had been a frame-up, and began helping the defense committee. "Aldino Felicani and Mary Donovan got hold of me and pleaded with me . . . to think up a campaign so that we could [get] public opinion more aroused and have some recourse other than through legal processes," Jackson later recalled. His idea — "a very obvious simple thing," as he described it — was to get hundreds of thousands of Americans to sign petitions asking the governor of Massachusetts to review the case. The committee approved the plan, and from then on Jackson devoted his life to saving Sacco and Vanzetti. He "worked unceasingly," said Mary Donovan. "He knew every reporter in Boston, he knew about publicity, the things of which we knew nothing."[4]

Jackson himself believed that someone else had a greater impact on public opinion: Felix Frankfurter, who, he said, aroused "intellectuals all over the world."[5]

An Austrian immigrant and Harvard Law School graduate, Frankfurter was a renowned and controversial professor at that institution. (He had co-authored the *Report Upon the Illegal Practices of the United States Department of Justice* in

1920.) Outraged when he heard of Proctor's affidavit and Katzmann's evasive response to it, Frankfurter decided to review the record of the Sacco-Vanzetti trial. "[M]y whole antecedents propelled me into action," Frankfurter recalled. The result of his review was *The Case of Sacco and Vanzetti, A Critical Analysis for Lawyers and Laymen.*[6]

"This is no ordinary case of robbery and murder," Frankfurter began. "More issues are involved in it than the lives of two men." Frankfurter noted unreliable eyewitness testimony; questionable tactics of police, prosecutors, and judge; and the "collusive effort" of the district attorney and the Department of Justice, "prejudicial methods ... not denied by the prosecution." He found that Katzmann's conduct in the Proctor episode violated "the standards which the ... Supreme Judicial Court has laid down for district attorneys." And he portrayed Thayer's latest decision as "unmatched ... for discrepancies between what the record discloses and what the opinion conveys. [The lengthy] document cannot accurately be described otherwise than as a farrago of misquotations, misrepresentations, suppressions, and mutilations." It was "infused by a spirit alien to judicial utterance."[7]

Frankfurter's analysis appeared almost simultaneously as a book and as a magazine article in the March 1927 issue of *Atlantic Monthly*. At the time, the case was still before the Supreme Judicial Court. A critic later condemned both the "indecorous" timing and "specious" reasoning of Frankfurter's analysis, charging that it amounted to nothing less than a brief for the defense.[8]

Frankfurter's work was perhaps *the* major turning point in public opinion. It made "a gigantic sensation" in Boston, said journalist H. L. Mencken. In Washington, justices of the United States Supreme Court took note. Chief Justice William Howard Taft regretted that Frankfurter's "perverted view of the facts had reached so many readers." Associate justice Louis Brandeis told fellow justice Oliver Wendell Holmes, Jr., that Boston's "Beacon Street [was] divided" over the case, and Holmes remarked that with "Frankfurter potently abetting" the case had turned Boston into a "perturbed teapot."[9]

Brandeis's comment gave no hint of a surprising fact: he was deeply involved with Frankfurter's work.

Brandeis, sometimes called "the people's attorney," was well-known as an advocate of economic and social reform when he was appointed to the high court in 1916. He was a longtime friend of both Elizabeth Glendower Evans and Felix Frankfurter. The friendships continued after Brandeis ascended to the bench, as did his interest in reform. "[A]lmost as soon as he joined the Court, Brandeis arranged to maintain contact with politics and public causes," writes biographer Philippa Strum.[10]

Frankfurter never earned more than twelve thousand dollars a year as a professor at Harvard Law.[11] On his salary, extra expenses were a hardship, whether they were personal or related to public service activities that Brandeis, his mentor, wished him to undertake. So, beginning with two hundred fifty dollars in 1916[12] and increasing over time to more than three thousand dollars a year,[13] the independently wealthy Brandeis supplemented Frankfurter's income. Frankfurter at first declined to accept the money, but, Brandeis wrote him, "I ought to feel free to make suggestions to you, although they involve some incidental expense. And you should feel free to incur expense in the public interest."[14] The much younger Frankfurter was "half brother, half son" to Brandeis and his wife, the associate justice said, and his "public service must not be abridged."[15]

Brandeis "bombarded" Frankfurter with suggestions about public service matters.[16] In 1927, one of those matters was the Sacco-Vanzetti case. Brandeis sent Frankfurter comments about his case analysis and about the governor.[17] He worried that Frankfurter was going to end up in debt. "I have realized that S[acco]. V[anzetti]., inter alia, must have made heavy demands for incidental expense, as well as time," Brandeis wrote in June, "& meant to ask you when we meet whether an additional sum might not be appropriate this year. Let me know."[18]

The Brandeis-Frankfurter funding arrangement was not widely known, but it "was not secret," says Strum, "nor did either man [or the law school] consider it unethical."[19] Secret or not, the intimate behind-the-scenes involvement by a sitting justice of the United States Supreme Court in an active legal case certainly had the potential for conflict of interest, and seems astonishing today.

On the lighter side, Elizabeth Evans's friendship with members of the Brandeis family led to an implausible, if long-distance, connection of convicted murderers to an associate justice. When Sacco wrote letters to Evans during the summer vacations that she spent with the Brandeis family on Cape Cod, he sometimes included greetings for Mrs. Brandeis, and Vanzetti extended his regards to both the justice and his wife.[20]

— Waiting.

In the first few months of 1927, everyone involved with Sacco and Vanzetti was waiting for the Supreme Judicial Court to reach a decision on the request for a rehearing. The waiting was unbearable for Rosina Sacco. In February, living with her children and an Italian woman friend in one part of an old house, Rosina became "very sick, and lay in bed at the hospital for one entire month," her husband said.[21]

Nick had long since stopped sharing details of prison life with his wife, to spare her the pain. But, he told Cerise Jack in March, Rosina was more depressed than ever. "I fear that they will succeed to kill Rosy before Nick and I," Bartolo worried.[22]

~ On April 5, 1927, the Supreme Judicial Court put an end to all the waiting and handed down its decision: Exceptions overruled. There would be no rehearing.

"The granting or the denial of a motion for a new trial of an indictment for murder rests in the judicial discretion of the trial judge," the justices wrote, "and his decision will not be disturbed unless it is vitiated by errors of law or abuse of discretion. . . . No error of law or abuse of discretion appeared in the denial of the motion; the denial was, in substance, a finding that the [newly discovered] evidence submitted was not worthy . . . and that a new trial was not necessary to prevent a failure of justice."[23]

Further, the justices continued, "It is not imperative that a motion for a new trial of an indictment for murder based on newly discovered evidence be granted, even though the evidence is newly discovered, and, *if presented to a jury, would justify a different verdict* [emphasis added]." To grant a new trial, "it would be necessary to decide that no conscientious judge, acting intelligently, could honestly have taken the view expressed by the trial judge," and this was a decision the justices would not make.[24]

Once again, a defense supporter said, the court had "sustained Judge Thayer's right to be wrong."[25]

Supporters were "stunned," said Mary Donovan. "We did not know which way to turn now."[26]

News of the decision "ran round the city in the late afternoon like wildfire." Public safety officials, fearing retaliation by defense sympathizers, posted extra guards throughout the Supreme Judicial Court building, around other public buildings in Boston, and at the justices' homes.[27] Donovan took a devastated Rosina Sacco home with her to avoid reporters.

William Thompson was "badly shaken" and undecided about his next move. Nevertheless, the following day he visited Vanzetti and reassured him that he would keep on fighting to the very end.[28]

~ Sacco and Vanzetti reacted differently to the court's ruling. Vanzetti dashed off a flurry of letters. Feeling doomed "in this black hour," he urged his friends to be brave, and he thanked them for their goodness.[29] In the gloom, his thoughts turned to Virginia MacMechan. He thanked Cerise Jack for "the good you have done for Nick, to his family and to me," and then asked her for a favor: "I wonder about our dear friend, Virginia MacMechan—here I enclose a note to her, begging you to address it to her."[30]

Unlike his co-defendant, Sacco seemed oddly at peace with the court's decision. It confirmed his conviction that he could get no justice in a capitalist society, and it brought him a step closer to the death he said he sought.

Dr. Abraham Myerson, the psychiatrist who had examined Sacco for the defense during the1923 hunger strike, examined him again, two days after the court's decision, in an attempt to find out why he opposed a clemency appeal and what would make him change his mind.

Sacco was reading a book on the natural history of the Ten Commandments when Myerson entered his cell. The prisoner, Myerson observed, had "a library not to be duplicated in any cell in any jail I have ever been in."[31] Doctor and patient discussed various Italian newspapers that were also in the cell, Sacco being a "quite objective" evaluator.

Sacco told Myerson that exercise was "the one thing that kept him from breaking down in the jail."

On the subject of anarchism, Myerson found Sacco's ideas "hazy" but a source of comfort to him nonetheless. "[H]e had philosophy and he had faith. . . . He was proud to die for his faith, and if he had to die, he was not afraid to die." Sacco told Myerson there were "good people in Massachusetts and good people throughout the U.S., [but they were] not powerful enough." He admitted that "capitalist states were right in their own way" to deport anarchists. "It was a fight and a war, and [governments] were taking steps to save their ideas and ideals in their society, and that was why they had deported [Italian anarchists], and that was why they were going to put him and Vanzetti out of the way."

On the subject of crime, Sacco said he "believed in expropriation, but not in expropriation for any individual or for himself, because that was robbery, banditry; that he never could in his philosophy or in his character have taken a pistol and robbed a lot of workmen of their payroll. . . . He had been guilty of no crime, and to spend the rest of his life in a jail [an interim goal of clemency advocates] was something he did not wish to do."

On the urgently time-sensitive matter of a clemency appeal, Sacco would not budge. "He said, 'I have always been against [continuing the legal] battle. I have yielded [in the past] because of the pleadings of the Committee, my friends, my wife, and because Vanzetti wanted to fight. Vanzetti has a different philosophy than mine. . . . I told them I would have freedom or death. . . . Vanzetti is a good, true friend and comrade, but he has a different philosophy than

Sacco and Vanzetti on the April day that Webster Thayer sentenced them to die "by the passage of a current of electricity through your body." Courtesy of the Trustees of the Boston Public Library/Rare Books (International Newsreel Corp.).

I have.'" When Myerson argued that the survival instinct was part of the laws of nature, Sacco parried that "nature does not reach into his cell. . . . [H]e felt that there was nothing further to do, and that his freedom must come either as a result of a popular pressure . . ., or else he must die."

— The defendants' options in state courts were played out. "I think that we will be sentenced soon," Bartolo warned his sister in a letter he wrote one day after the decision of the Supreme Judicial Court.[32] It happened before she received the letter.

On Saturday morning, April 9, 1927, almost seven years to the bloody day that Frederick Parmenter and Alessandro Berardelli lost their lives on the streets of South Braintree, Nicola Sacco and Bartolomeo Vanzetti sat side by side once more in a metal cage in Norfolk County Superior Court, and faced Webster Thayer. Police surrounded the courthouse. Reporters and spectators crowded inside. Some were hostile, Mary Donovan recalled, but most were friendly, and weeping, "like myself, unashamed."[33]

"Nicola Sacco, have you anything to say why sentence of death should not be passed upon you?" asked the clerk of court, following custom.

"Yes, sir," Sacco began. Acknowledging his broken English ("I am not an orator"), he praised his co-defendant—a man "more familiar with the language," "a kind man to all the children," and a man whom "you know he is innocent." At its heart, Sacco continued, this was a case of class warfare:

I know the sentence will be between two class, the oppressed class and the rich class, and there will be always collision between one and the other. . . . That is why I am here today on this bench, for having been the oppressed class. Well, [Judge Thayer,] you are the oppressor. . . .

I am never been guilty, never—not yesterday nor today nor forever.[34]

"Bartolomeo Vanzetti, have you anything to say why sentence of death should not be passed upon you?" the clerk asked again. Vanzetti rose.

Yes. What I say is that I am innocent, not only of the Braintree crime, but also of the Bridgewater crime. That I am not only innocent of these two crimes, but in all my life I have never stole and I have never killed and I have never spilled blood. . . . And it is not all. . . . I have struggled all my life, since I began to reason, to eliminate crime from the earth. . . .

I struggled all my life to eliminate . . . the exploitation and the oppression of the man by the man, and if there is a reason why I am here as a guilty man, if there is a reason why you in a few minutes can doom me, it is this reason and none else."[35]

Vanzetti noted that defense sympathizers included "the flower of mankind of Europe, the better writers, the greatest thinkers . . . , the greatest scientists, the greatest statesmen . . ." and wondered: "Is it possible that only a few on the jury . . . are right against what the . . . whole world has say it is wrong . . .?" He continued:

We have proved that there could not have been another Judge on the face of the earth more prejudiced and more cruel than you have been against us. We have proven that. Still they refuse the new trial.[36]

Vanzetti retraced his grievances against his former attorneys, John Vahey and Fred Moore. He spoke of being tried during a time of "hysteria of resentment and hate against the people of our principles," and charged that any deals made to keep the Dedham jury from learning of his prior conviction had been useless. "In fact, even the telephone poles knew at the time of this trial at Dedham that I was tried and convicted in Plymouth."[37] He spoke for forty-five minutes, then with moving eloquence he closed:

> I would not wish to a dog or to a snake, to the most low and misfortunate creature of the earth — I would not wish to any of them what I have had to suffer for things I am not guilty of. But my conviction is that I have suffered for things that I am guilty of. I am suffering because I am a radical and indeed I am a radical. I have suffered because I was an Italian, and indeed I am an Italian. I have suffered more for my family and for my beloved than for myself, but I am so convinced to be right that if you could execute me two times, and if I could be reborn two other times, I would live again to do what I have done already. I have finished. Thank you.[38]

In "an atmosphere charged with electricity," Vanzetti sat down; his words had "set every person in that courtroom tingling." Herbert Ehrmann remembered seeing "tears in the eyes of practically everyone," including the prosecutors.[39]

While the defendants were making their statements, Judge Thayer gazed out a window. Now it was his turn to speak. The case had reached the stage, he said, where "there is only one thing that this Court can do. It is not a matter of discretion. It is a matter of statutory requirement, and . . . that is to pronounce the sentences." And so Thayer sentenced, first Sacco, then Vanzetti, to "suffer the punishment of death by the passage of a current of electricity through your body within the week beginning on Sunday, the tenth day of July."[40]

He "did not, as was customary, say, 'And may the Lord have mercy on your soul.'"[41]

"You know I am innocent," Sacco cried out. "That is the same words I pronounced seven years ago. You condemn two innocent men."[42]

His wife was spared the painful scene. Sacco had asked her to stay away.

Everything was over in an hour. Court adjourned in time for lunch.

— Bartolo was not satisfied with his statement in the courtroom. He had forgotten to say something important. The next day he put it in writing and gave it to friends.

"I have talk a great deal of myself but I even forgot to name Sacco," he wrote. His co-defendant was a "lover of work, . . . lover of nature and of mankind . . . [who] has never dreamt to steal, never to assassinate."[43]

People who compared the two men often decided that Sacco was the less intelligent one. Of the differences between them, Vanzetti now observed that "I may be more witfull, as some have put it. I am a better babbler than he is, but many, many times . . ., remembering his heroism I felt small small at the presence of his greatness."[44]

— If living in prison under sentence of death can ever be considered a good experience, then the sentencing of Sacco and Vanzetti had two benefits.

It galvanized public support. The men's courtroom speeches, worthless as legal documents, were priceless for public relations. The defense committee quickly printed and distributed the speeches in pamphlet form. Letters and telegrams urging a new trial began pouring into the office of the governor.

The second benefit was reunion. Except for short stretches during courtroom proceedings, Sacco and Vanzetti had been separated for seven years. Now, for whatever time remained, they would be housed in the same prison.

Each was a living bundle of contradictions: Bartolo, an optimistic pessimist, an atheist who studied religion, an anarchist with lingering faith in authority; and Nick, a supposedly "mentally shallow" man who nevertheless read philosophy, a loving family man who believed in class war.[45] There were times when they got on each other's last nerve. Nick in particular could annoy his comrade and other allies with his rigid obstinacy.

Mostly, however, the two men respected each other, understood each other, and were loyal to each other. When Vanzetti's spirits flagged, Sacco had reassured him: "[C]ourage my dear friend, because this fight we are going to win." When Sacco refused to see visitors, Vanzetti had begged their forbearance for "our good Nick—he is exhausted and disgusted; and you, surely, understand too much to not forgive him." Even when a misunderstanding between Sacco and Mary Donovan resulted in her being banned from the jail, and she and Vanzetti could no longer see each other, still Vanzetti urged forgiveness. "Sometime I get impatient or harsh or resented from Nick," he wrote her. "Then I think that I might be worse had I been seven years segregated [from wife and children] as he is. And then I . . . get ashamed of my conduct with him and regret it. . . . [H]e does not intend to offend."[46]

So when sentencing reunited these two uniquely bonded friends at Dedham Jail in April, despite the grimness of the occasion it was a welcome change of pace. Spring had arrived, the sun was shining, and yard time was permitted. "Here there is more air and sun than in Charlestown," Vanzetti wrote Donovan, "and [Nick and I] have a daily walk together in the yard." Smoking was permitted and, said Vanzetti, "I smoke like a Turk. Fruits and candy are allowed and we have fruits." Friends brought plants and flowers, too, including the mayflowers which reminded Vanzetti "of Plymouth and of the woods . . . which I love so much."[47]

Best of all for Nick, Rosina was feeling better, "as nice as I have always dream her," he said.[48]

A friend brought a set of bocce balls to Dedham Jail. "Vanzetti and I we began to play two . . . games every day," Sacco wrote. The first two day he had [beat] me, the second two day we [were tied] and this morning I had him [beat]." Vanzetti measured distances with a handkerchief; Sacco teased him that the wind was blowing in his favor. "[S]ince I began to . . . play balls in the yard I am another man," Vanzetti told a friend; "it [is] better to me than hundreds of sermons." The two prisoners also held friendly singing contests, which Vanzetti, with his "wonderful rich baritone," apparently won, once delivering a jail yard rendition of "Let Me Call You Sweetheart" in what an unobserved officer called the "sweetest voice I ever heard."[49]

The irony of the situation — condemned men at play — was not lost on them. "[I]t is hell!" Sacco wrote Elizabeth Evans, "but nevertheless, the humble men they always find something to smile [about], even when they are waiting the electric chair."[50]

Bartolo wrote his last known letter to Virginia MacMechan that April. The visitation policies at Dedham were unpredictable, he said. He understood she had tried to visit him and been turned away. He would try to arrange it so that she could come with one of the lawyers. "If you would come with him in such circumstance, it would be better than nothing, but I would hardly have time to look in your eyes, we would hardly have time to exchange a word. . . . But I will do my utmost to find a way for your admittance."[51] Whether he succeeded, and what they said to each other, is not known.

— As they played bocce in the valley of the shadow of death, Sacco and Vanzetti simultaneously wrestled with the decision of whether to petition the governor for a review of the case.

In truth, only Vanzetti wrestled. He agonized over it. "That work," he said, "devoured my flesh." His expectations ricocheted wildly. He urged his sister to send a petition to the governor from the family in Italy, "otherwise he might think that you don't care about us — and that would be very bad." Vanzetti would not sign an official pardon request form, but agreed to write a petition — not because he hoped for clemency, he explained, but "out of respect for [our lawyers] . . . and out of solidarity and gratitude to the thousands of petitioners who had asked for 'a complete and public investigation.'"[52]

Sacco did not go through a similarly tortured decision-making process. When he told Dr. Myerson that he opposed a continuation of the legal battle, he wasn't kidding. Even when his lawyer's wife pleaded with him to sign the appeal for the sake of his family, he wouldn't do it. "Excuse me!" he told Mrs. Ehrmann. "I no love Rosina if [I'm] not true first to myself!" "I am innocent. I cannot, even for the sake of my family, say that I am guilty. I cannot beg for mercy."[53] When he heard that the *Boston Herald* had called him fanatic and insane for refusing to sign, "it weren't pleasant news," he said, but still he held his ground.[54]

On May 3, 1927, Vanzetti signed his petition. The defense team transmitted it to Governor Alvan Fuller on behalf of both clients, asking him to "ignore the absence of Sacco's signature," due, they said, to his "condition of complete dejection and despair."[55]

"We, Bartolomeo Vanzetti and Nicola Sacco, confined in the jail at Dedham under sentence of death . . ., hereby pray you to exercise the power conferred upon you . . . publicly to investigate all the facts of our cases and set us free from that sentence . . .," the petition began. "[W]e are asking not for mercy but for justice. . . . Our present request is made first and foremost on the ground of our innocence. We had nothing whatever to do with the South Braintree crime."[56]

The fourteen-page petition reviewed the reasons for a new investigation, and then, against the advice of counsel, the petitioners closed with a defense of their unpopular beliefs:

> We are anarchists, believers in anarchy, which is . . . a philosophy that . . . aims to human progress and happiness. . . . We call ourselves Libertarians, which means briefly that we believe that human perfectability is to be obtained by the largest amount of freedom, and not by coercion. . . . [W]e are opposed to every theory of authoritarian communism and socialism. . . . On principle we abhor violence. . . . [W]e are willing to suffer and to die [for our beliefs], but not for the low and sordid South Braintree crime."[57]

~ Alvan Tufts Fuller, in whose hands the fate of Sacco and Vanzetti now rested, was a self-made multimillionaire descended from ancestors who had sailed to America on the *Mayflower*. When his father died, the teenage Fuller had dropped out of school to help support his mother. He opened a bicycle shop and prospered, along the way becoming a champion cyclist. Then, boldly envisioning the potential of the "horseless carriage," he imported the first automobiles to Massachusetts. His car business, once derided as Fuller's Folly, had grown to include successful auto dealerships throughout New England. In 1914 Fuller entered politics. Accepting no salary, he served as a state legislator, United States congressman, and lieutenant governor.[58]

When the Sacco-Vanzetti petition landed on his desk in 1927, Fuller was in his second two-year term as governor of Massachusetts. To his supporters, he was a generous philanthropist, visionary entrepreneur, and effective leader with a record of solid accomplishments.[59] To his detractors, however, he was "Babbit enthroned," a "crude, illiterate, self-confident, purse-proud creature."[60]

Pressure on Fuller to act intensified after Judge Thayer set the executions for the week of July 10. More than 750,000 people signed a petition that was delivered to the State House.[61] The document did not impress officials (they reportedly burned it), but the thousands of appeals from individuals were harder to ignore, especially those from Bishop William Lawrence of the Episcopal Church, Dean Roscoe Pound of Harvard Law School, and other leaders of the Boston establishment.

The governor did not have legal authority to grant a new trial. He did have the option to exercise mercy and grant some form of clemency. He could commute the death sentences to life imprisonment, or to time served. He could pardon the prisoners and release them. Or he could let the existing sentences stand.

The defense committee wanted Fuller to appoint an impartial committee to advise him, and it also wanted public hearings. "[W]e really wanted a [de facto] second trial," Aldino Felicani said.[62]

Lizzie Borden, another famous Massachusetts murder suspect, died on

June 1, 1927. On the same day Fuller appointed a blue-ribbon committee to advise him on the Sacco-Vanzetti case, and he staffed it with three of Boston's éminences grises: Abbott Lawrence Lowell, the president of Harvard University; Samuel Stratton, the president of MIT; and Robert Grant, a retired probate court judge.

Thompson was thrilled. He brought the good tidings to his clients at Dedham Jail, and a relieved Vanzetti immediately conveyed the news to his sister.

— A. Lawrence Lowell, 71, was the scion of an old Massachusetts family prominent in scholarship, business, and the Boston aristocracy. The mill towns of Lowell and Lawrence were named for his ancestors. (Lowell himself had once been a director of the Plymouth Cordage Company, Vanzetti's former employer, as well as a vice president of a national Immigration Restriction League commitee.) Lawyer, professor, historian, and author, Lowell had been president of Harvard since 1909. Although he had some concerns about the fairness of the Sacco-Vanzetti trial, Lowell didn't want to spend the summer of 1927 reviewing the case. "I never undertook anything with greater repugnance than this [advisory committee] job," he admitted. But it was a public duty he said he felt unable to reject.[63]

Robert Grant, 75, said he felt the same way. "How the Governor happened to select me [for the committee], I have never ascertained," Grant recalled. But when asked to participate, despite "my lack of enthusiasm . . . as the matter was one of public service, I would not refuse." Grant led a sort of double life. He was a retired judge and a member of the Harvard Board of Overseers; he was also a novelist and friend of literary figures such as Edith Wharton and Charles Scribner. (It was Grant who advised Scribner to publish Ernest Hemingway's novel, *The Sun Also Rises*, despite its then-shocking profanity. "You *must* publish the book," Grant wrote Scribner in 1926. "But I hope the young man will live to regret it.")[64]

Samuel Stratton, 66, rounded out Fuller's committee. Unlike his two associates on the panel, Stratton was neither a native Bostonian nor a lawyer. He had taught physics, mathematics, and engineering at universities in Illinois and had for more than twenty years directed the National Bureau of Standards in Washington, D.C. Since 1922 he had been serving as president of the Massachusetts Institute of Technology, to mixed reviews. Stratton was, in the opinion of an admirer, "direct and engaging . . . respected by everyone," while to critics he was "irascible," a poor communicator with failing eyesight and hearing, soon to be kicked upstairs to a face-saving figurehead position.[65]

"This committee was accepted," said Felicani. "[I]ntellectuals welcomed this." There were some skeptics, and some questions about Grant's impartiality, but most people believed "everything was going to be hunkey-dory because the president of Harvard University was appointed."[66]

— Execution was set for the week of July 10. By June 29, advisory committee members had not yet held their first meeting. To give them more time, Fuller granted the prisoners a one-month reprieve, postponing execution to August 10. (Celestino Madeiros, reconvicted of murder and sentenced to death, was included in the reprieve.)

Nick and Bartolo, still confined at Dedham Jail, learned about the postponement on June 30. In Nick's eyes, it meant only one thing, "thirty-one more day living death."[67]

That night, as midnight struck, Sacco and Vanzetti "were suddenly awakened, told to dress quickly, well manacled, . . . and thus hurriedly transferred from the Dedham jail to the State Prison in Charlestown." In the darkness and confusion, Vanzetti lost treasured books and mementos. Whether or not the timing of the surprise transfer showed "vindictive slyness," as the defense committee charged, it shook the prisoners.[68] They lost the privilege of daily yard time. They also lost the privilege of seeing friends; with the exception of Felicani, only lawyers and relatives would henceforth be allowed to visit them.

— Members of the advisory committee convened in early July. They conducted their inquiry in the same place—the State House—and during the same time frame as the governor held his inquiry, so witnesses often went directly from one to the other on the same day.

Fuller conducted his review in complete secrecy. Everything that transpired before him was off the record; whatever is known about it was learned unofficially and after the fact.

The advisory committee chose partial secrecy. It shielded Thayer, the jurors, Chief Justice Walter Hall of Superior Court, and, to some extent, Katzmann, and no "information [was] given to counsel for Sacco and Vanzetti as to what may have been thereby disclosed." The committee permitted other witnesses to be questioned on the record, and Katzmann agreed to be questioned by the defense. An incomplete transcript of committee hearings tells all that can be known for certain about proceedings before the panel.[69]

Evidence of Judge Thayer's prejudice went on the record at this time. Attorney George Crocker testified to having heard Thayer speak of Sacco and Vanzetti as dangerous "reds and anarchists." Dartmouth professor James Richardson testified to having heard a "violent" Thayer speak of "anarchistic bastards." *Life* magazine editor Robert Benchley testified to having heard secondhand of Thayer saying "that he would like to get a few of those Reds and hang them." *Globe* reporter Frank Sibley testified to having observed Thayer's "air of prejudice and scorn," and to hearing him refer to the defendants as "damn fools" and to Fred Moore as a "long-haired anarchist from California." International News Service reporter Elizabeth Bernkopf testified to having heard a "decidedly antagonistic" Thayer frequently speak to her of Moore as a "long-haired anarchist from the West" who couldn't intimidate him. Federated Press reporter John Nicholas Beffel swore that he had heard a "thoroughly angry" and "flushed" Thayer excoriate Moore and threaten to "show 'em!" when he gave his charge to the jury. And Boston Federation of Churches representative Lois Rantoul, a relative of President Lowell, testified to having heard a "vehement" Thayer, with "complete intolerance" for Moore, tell her not to believe certain pro-defense testimony.[70]

Assistant district attorney Ranney countered that if Thayer were as prejudiced as the defense claimed, "it would be indicated somewhere in that [trial] record, and that, search as you will from the first page to the last of that record, you will find no betrayal of that prejudice." Ranney argued that a decision in favor of the defendants would "destroy our courts."[71]

A putative clash of the titans occurred on July 13 and 14, when Thompson and Ehrmann questioned Katzmann in tension-filled sessions before the committee. The former district attorney said he could not recall much of the information he was asked. Making good use of double negatives, he said he was "not prepared to say [that federal agents] did not" inform him pre-trial about the suspects' radical politics. The most Katzmann would concede was that he could not positively deny that Proctor told him he thought the suspects were innocent.[72]

Two witnesses called before the committee—Lincoln Wadsworth and Jeremiah Gallivan, both former law enforcement officials—unburdened themselves.

Wadsworth was the gun shop supervisor who in 1921 had testified that Berardelli's gun was of the same type and caliber as Vanzetti's, and who in 1926 went public with his past as a special agent investigating radicals for the Department of Justice. Wadsworth now told the committee that his conscience was "disturbed" because "I had created the impression that there was a possibility that [Vanzetti's gun] was [Berardelli's] pistol. Well, that is just a possibility. There are a number of possibilities." In fact, Wadsworth said, "there are thousands of times more chances that it was not [Berardelli's gun] than that it was." He said he "absolutely" did not intend to give the impression that it was

Berardelli's gun, but that the assistant district attorney "did not seem to want to have that at all."[73]

Gallivan was chief of the tiny Braintree police department in 1920. He had played a minor role in the original investigation, and did not testify at the trial, but now he told the committee that a cap which the prosecution had entered in evidence at the trial had been misrepresented. The cap, found at the scene of the crime, had a torn lining. The prosecution had argued that the cap was Sacco's. Thayer later said that the prosecution claimed Sacco tore the lining by hanging the cap from a nail at the factory where he worked, and Katzmann later said that the cap "alone was enough to warrant conviction of the defendant Sacco." Now Gallivan told the advisory committee that he was the one who had torn the lining, while searching for a label or name tag that might help him identify the owner. "That cap was whole when it was given to me, but I am the fellow that tore it." Gallivan said that when he turned the cap over to a state police officer, he explained the rip in the lining, but he had "no knowledge" of whether the officer had passed that information along to the district attorney's office. He was coming forward with the information now, he said, because "[t]here's a right and a wrong to this thing, that's all there is to it."[74]

At this late date, Thompson and Ehrmann acquired for the first time two critical pieces of potentially exculpatory evidence that had been around for years. In June 1927 they obtained reports of witness interviews conducted in 1919, immediately after the attempted Bridgewater robbery. And in July they obtained minutes of the 1920 inquest into the South Braintree murders, which had been conducted two days after the crime. (It seems inconceivable that the documents were not made available to the defense at a much earlier stage. The Bridgewater notes apparently belonged to the shoe manufacturer who had hired private detectives to interview witnesses, and the South Braintree notes were retained by the district attorney who, Ehrmann said, had "the right to hold [them] in secrecy" under Massachusetts law at the time.)[75]

The two new pieces of evidence revealed discrepancies between what people had said immediately after the crimes and their later trial testimony. The defense team hastened to point out the differences. Concerning Bridgewater, the 1919 notes showed "all four of the principal witnesses describing both the car and the bandits in a manner entirely different from the description given at the [Plymouth] trial."[76] As for South Braintree, the 1920 inquest minutes showed that witness Shelley Neal, who testified at trial to seeing one bandit car at South Braintree, had originally testified to seeing two bandit cars — corroborating the two-car version of Madeiros.[77]

Two of the most controversial episodes that played out before the advisory committee and the governor involved the defendants' alibis.

Vanzetti's alibi for the attempted robbery at Bridgewater had been that he was selling eels in Plymouth before, during, and after the crime. Governor Fuller told Aldino Felicani and Gardner Jackson that if only he could see something in writing to document this alibi, "things would be just solved." A wild hunt through the warehouses of Boston fish dealers for an eight-year-old receipt ensued, ending successfully when, against all odds, "up in a loft, in a bunch of old papers covered with dust," Felicani and Ehrmann found a receipt for eels shipped from Boston to "B. Vanzetti, Plymouth, Massachusetts" during the time frame in question. Ehrmann "was beside himself" with relief, believing this was "exactly the evidence which the governor had wanted." But it was delivered to Fuller, and that, said Ehrmann, "was the last we heard of the eel receipt."[78]

As for Sacco's alibi, he had said that on April 15, 1920, he was in Boston applying for a passport, shopping, and socializing with other patrons at an Italian restaurant. President Lowell, interviewing two Italians who said at trial that they had talked to Sacco at the restaurant that day, told them they had to have been mistaken. Lowell had personally researched the date of a banquet the witnesses said had taken place that day, and he found that it occurred one month *after* April 15. The two witnesses were flummoxed, but later located the back issue of an Italian newspaper with coverage of the banquet. It had indeed taken place on the day in question. The witnesses had been correct all along. Two different banquets honoring the same person had been held a month apart; Lowell had learned only about the second one. He apologized to the witnesses, but no account of the episode was included in the minutes of the committee hearing. The "carelessness of the Committee's investigation in a matter of life and death, and their gross error that ensued, was covered over by silence,"[79] said Ehrmann.

Speaking off the record were an unknown number of witnesses who appeared before the governor, and at least thirteen who appeared before the advisory committee. Nearly forty additional witnesses spoke to the committee on the record. The most unusual interrogations of all were surely those that took place when A. Lawrence Lowell, Samuel Stratton, Robert Grant, and, separately, Governor Alvan Fuller left the gilt-domed State House on Beacon Hill and made their way to Charlestown State Prison to speak to the condemned men.

Among the participants, only Vanzetti has left firsthand impressions of these encounters, true collisions of parallel universes.

The committee members arrived at the prison on July 8. They "interviewed us in a conversational form," Vanzetti reported, and then "they interviewed Madeiros." The two college presidents were "possibly impartial and well-intentioned." Grant, on the other hand, was "so contrary and hostile to us and our principles that he could not . . . be fair with us and see the facts with unbiased vision."[80]

Two weeks later Governor Fuller visited the prison. Sacco, the realist, "didn't want any part of it. . . . He refused to talk." But Vanzetti spoke to Fuller at length, going over the whole case and telling his life story. The tête-à-tête of the penniless convict and the millionaire governor was extraordinary, and Vanzetti grew enthusiastic in spite of himself. "[W]ith me he stayed an hour and a half, and he will come back again," Vanzetti wrote one friend. Fuller "sat down and talked to me like a brother, smiling and joking," he told another. "That man will never send us to the chair." Fuller also spoke briefly with Madeiros.[81]

The governor took time out to give an official Boston welcome to triumphant transatlantic aviator Charles Lindbergh, and then, true to his word, he returned to the prison, this time around nine o'clock at night on July 26. Vanzetti again spoke to him at length. He seemed "well-intentioned," Vanzetti wrote Alice Blackwell, and "he gave me a good heartfelt handshake before he left. I may be wrong, but I don't believe that a man like that is going to burn us."[82]

— July simmered. In the outside world, as one young Bostonian noted in his diary that summer, flagpole sitting was all the rage, knickers for men were making a fashion comeback, the Red Sox were having an amazing season, and pugilism was as popular as ever, with millions of Americans tuning in to a blow-by-blow radio broadcast from Yankee Stadium of a boxing match between two big Jacks, Dempsey and Sharkey.[83]

On the inside, Nick and Bartolo began a hunger strike to protest the secrecy of the hearings and the treatment of witnesses.

A rush of would-be gawkers and morbid thrill-seekers were beginning to make their way to the state prison. "They think they can get a glimpse of Sacco and Vanzetti. They are disappointed when they learn that the law forbids [them from seeing] a person doomed to die."[84]

On the Fourth of July Nick read the "wonderful letters" of Abraham Lincoln. He found "so much worth of good" in them that he almost forgot it was "my last four July. It is too sad to think of it I know," he wrote Elizabeth Evans, but "if the friends and comrades . . . get themselves as ever in the old past weakness illusion, I think they will be too late and sorrow for it tomorrow."[85]

Bartolo had not seen a member of his family since leaving Italy almost twenty years earlier. On the edge of the abyss, convinced of Judge Grant's unfairness, hoping for the best but expecting the worst, he longed to see someone from home before he died. In July he asked that one of his sisters come to America.[86]

Nick, too, had not seen any relatives from Italy in years, but his wife and children were a constant presence for him. Daughter Ines, now nearly 7, asked Mary Donovan, "Do you think they are going to kill my father? If they do, I would never stop crying as long as I live." Donovan suggested she write her father a letter.[87]

In July, she did. It pierced his heart. "My Dear Ines," he replied on July 19:[88]

I will bring with me your little and so dearest letter and carry it right under my heart to the last day of my life. When I die, it will be buried with your father who loves you so much, as I do also your brother Dante and holy dear mother.

You don't know Ines, how dear and great your letter was to your father. It is the most golden present that you could have give to me. . . .

It was the greatest [desire of] my struggling life that I could have lived with you and your brother Dante and your mother in a neat little farm, and learn all your sincere words and tender affection. . . .

The same I have wished to see for other poor girls, and their brothers, happy with their mother and father as I dreamed for us — but it was not so and the nightmare of the lower classes saddened very badly your father's soul. . . .

You do not know Ines, how often I think of you every day. You are in my heart, in my vision, in every angle of this sad walled cell, in the sky and everywhere my gaze rests. . . .

With the most affectionate kiss and ineffable caress from him who loves you so much. . . .

Your Father

— Partisans of every stripe were eager to share their opinions of the case.

"Give 'em the juice, burn them, if they're guilty," advised the Reverend Billy Sunday, a popular Christian evangelist. "I'm tired of hearing these foreigners, these radicals, coming over here and telling us what we should do," the preacher said after paying a visit to the governor in June.[89]

"[E]nemies of our country" were involved in the case, said Frank Goodwin, registrar of motor vehicles for Massachusetts. "If there is any criticism to be made of the laws of Massachusetts, it is that this case has been allowed to drag on so long."[90]

On July 27 the advisory committee delivered its report to Fuller. He embargoed it for later release, and continued his own deliberations.

"[E]ven in the closing days of the case the Governor's mail is still bulky with communications advising him [either] to sustain the courts or pardon the two Italians," the press reported. "The largest petition for clemency received yesterday was from Belgium, containing the signatures of 10,000 workers of Brussels."[91]

For bookies, the uncertainty was good business. By Tuesday, August 2, with execution scheduled to take place in eight days, "hundreds of men, personally indifferent to the fates of the two condemned men . . ., placed bets on the outcome of the governor's decision affecting them."[92]

— The *New York Times* predicted that instead of being executed, Sacco and Vanzetti would receive a new trial. Defense committee members were cautiously hopeful. They worried that Fuller was moving beyond issues of fairness and judicial indiscretion to determining the defendants' guilt or innocence by himself, "an issue clearly beyond his competence."[93] At the same time, they were encouraged by leaked tidbits of information. For the defense committee had a mole in the State House, a 1927 version of Deep Throat.

A mystery man had phoned Gardner Jackson after the first day of hearings. "'I want to help you,'" the voice said. "'I do not want you to try to identify who I am and trace this call. I am in a position where I am privy to what's going on in the governor's mind. I will try to call you as nearly every night after the hearings as I can, to tell you what his reactions are so that you can, with Felicani, guide the bringing of witnesses.'" The unidentified source was as good as his word, and secretly reported in "almost every night." (Jackson said he never traced the calls, but the man subsequently "did reveal himself to me." It was Clement Norton, superintendent of the Commonwealth pier, whose State House office was close to the governor's.)[94]

Fuller was expected to announce his decision on Wednesday, August 3. To carry the news quickly, telegraph wires were installed in the State House press gallery. The day was "one of taut nerves and strained expectation." Fuller was said to be working in seclusion at a downtown hotel, finalizing his text. He arrived at the State House around eight o'clock in the evening, and conferred with public safety officials. Hours passed. Finally, shortly before midnight, the governor's secretary emerged and began handing out envelopes to the press. "[B]efore I could rip the flap open," a witness recalled, "Louis Stark, ace correspondent of the *New York Times*, had torn his envelope apart and dived to the last page of the five-page document. To the telegraph operator across the hall, who was waiting with his finger on the key, Stark shouted: 'They die!'"[95]

"I believe with the jury, that these men, Sacco and Vanzetti, were guilty, and that they had a fair trial," the last paragraph read. "I furthermore believe that there was no justifiable reason for giving them a new trial."[96]

With Ehrmann at his side, Thompson was at home, waiting by the phone for news. "It must be true that hope springs eternal," Ehrmann said, "because we still had the capacity to be stunned by what we heard." Mary Donovan went to break the news to Rosina Sacco at a friend's apartment where she was hiding out from reporters. Donovan found her waiting beside a dying fire. "She knew what the decision was before I could tell her. 'What will we do? What will we do?' [she repeated.] I could only put my arms tighter around her."[97]

The eleven surviving members of the Dedham jury "considered the judge fair," Fuller wrote. Further, the "Supreme Judicial Court . . . establish[ed] that the proceedings were without legal flaw. . . . [F]rom a layman's standpoint . . . I am convinced that [the trial was fairly conducted]. . . . I am further convinced that the presiding judge gave no evidence of bias in denying [the motions] and refusing a new trial. . . . I give no weight to the Madeiros confession. . . . I believe with the jury that Vanzetti was guilty [in Bridgewater] and that his trial was fair. I found nothing unusual about this [Bridgewater] case except . . . that Vanzetti [waived the privilege of telling his own story to the jury and] did not testify. . . . The delays that have dragged this case out for six years are inexcusable. . . . I find no sufficient justification for executive intervention."[98]

In Maine on that summer day, Judge Thayer played eighteen holes of golf at the Cliff Country Club.[99]

On Cape Cod, Justice Brandeis wrote Felix Frankfurter that Fuller's decision was "a complete surprise to all of us." The *New York Times*, which on August 2 had predicted the likelihood of a new trial, on August 5 reported that the "apparent last-minute finding of Governor Fuller came as a shock to those who thought they were aware of his intentions. They put the change in the Governor's decision as apparently made between 3 p.m. Tuesday [August 2] and that midnight."[100]

In that nine-hour window, President Calvin Coolidge had announced that he would not run for office again in 1928. The implication was that Coolidge's withdrawal prompted an ambitious Fuller to think that he now had a shot at the presidency, that one law-and-order governor of Massachusetts could follow another to the White House, and that a decision against clemency would demonstrate his hard-liner bona fides. But Fuller surely knew (although the public as yet did not) that the advisory committee opposed clemency, and it's unlikely that he would have ignored the recommendations of a committee that he himself had appointed.

— The people to whom the governor's negative decision mattered most still did not know of it. On Thursday morning, August 4, with execution six days away, a somber trio of William Thompson, Rosina Sacco, and Aldino Felicani entered Charlestown State Prison to break the news to the prisoners.

Thompson was "depressed" and Mrs. Sacco "appeared to be on the verge of collapse."[101] Felicani was in anguish. "I finally related to them that they were going to die. Vanzetti took it very hard. He looked at me for some minutes with his eyes growing larger . . ., as if losing his mind. He would not believe it. The illusory effect of the Governor's visit kept him from realizing that this was the end. Sacco was not surprised at all. He accepted the outcome as part of the revolutionist's struggle against the ruling class. He had only one regret — not being on the outside to express his feelings with action." As for Madeiros, he seemed to take the news with equanimity. " 'I'm a criminal anyhow,' " he told Felicani, " 'But it's a shame for them.' "[102]

Vanzetti dashed off a batch of letters. The governor's "conviction will not make us guilty — we are and will remain innocent," he told Elizabeth Evans. To his family in Italy, he swore innocence. "Do not be ashamed of me. . . . I have written my tombstone with twenty years of life dedicated to justice and freedom. . . . [N]one of my enemies will be mourned the way I will be mourned. . . . I want you all to sing rather than weep for me, and let me live in your hearts."[103] Luigia Vanzetti was at that moment en route to America to see her brother.

In the evening of that interminable day, Thompson and Ehrmann withdrew as counsels for the defense. Thompson felt he had become a lightning rod for criticism that could hurt his clients in last-minute appeals. Arthur Hill, who had helped out on previous motions, took over as chief counsel.

— The embargoed report of Lowell, Grant, and Stratton was finally released to the press on Sunday, August 7. (It is usually called the Lowell report in recognition of its author, but Grant told one magazine editor that the report was substantially his work, and another editor said the report "was really the work of Stratton.")[104] The committee's findings were by now a foregone conclusion, but the eighteen-page report shed light on the reasoning behind the findings.

Concerning Judge Thayer's conduct at Dedham, the committee found that the court record "gives the impression that the Judge tried to be scrupulously fair" and that the jurors interviewed agreed that such had been the case. "They state that . . . they perceived no bias . . . [and each] felt sure that the fact that the accused were foreigners and radicals had no effect upon his opinion." Acknowledging testimony from the hearings, however, the committee simultaneously rebuked the judge, and excused and forgave him: he "was indiscreet in conversation with outsiders during the trial. He ought not to have talked about the case off the bench, and doing so was a grave breach of official decorum. But we do not believe that he used some of the expressions attributed to him, and we think there is exaggeration in what the persons to whom he spoke remember. Furthermore, we believe that such indiscretions in conversation did not affect his conduct at the trial or the opinions of the jury."[105] (Or, as a Massachusetts state senator put it fifty years later, "Webster Thayer was the doggonest loudmouth in America. Whether it had any effect on the trial is another thing.")[106]

Because of defense contentions that the judge had exercised his discretion wrongly, if not illegally, the committee studied the motions which Thayer had denied, admitting that there "can be no doubt that the Judge has been subjected to a very severe strain. . . . [W]hile there is no sufficient evidence that his capacity to decide rightly the questions before him in this case has been impaired, nevertheless he has been in a distinctly nervous condition."[107]

Concerning the Ripley-Daly motion, the committee found "no evidence" that the cartridges which foreman Walter Ripley carried into the jury room "did influence the opinion of the jury," and further that William Daly "must have misunderstood" or misremembered his friend Ripley's hostile statement about the defendants. Concerning the Gould motion, the committee found that eyewitness Roy Gould's post-trial statement that neither Sacco nor Vanzetti was the man he had observed at the crime scene was "merely cumulative" and balanced by other witnesses. Concerning the Proctor motion, the committee found that, despite the defense claim that Captain Proctor's ballistics testimony was "devised to mislead the jury . . ., it must be assumed that the jury understood the meaning of plain English words [such as 'consistent with']." Finally, concerning the Madeiros motion, the committee found the confession of Celestino Madeiros "worthless."[108]

Regarding charges of collusion between the district attorney and the Department of Justice, the committee found no indication that information in department files "would help to show that the defendants are not guilty." As for former police chief Gallivan's testimony that he had torn the hole in the lining of the so-called Sacco cap, the committee found the information "so trifling a matter . . . by no means a ground for a new trial."[109]

In sum, "the Committee are of opinion that Sacco was guilty beyond reasonable doubt of the murder at South Braintree. . . . *On the whole,* we are of opinion that Vanzetti also was guilty beyond reasonable doubt [emphasis added]".[110]

Criticism was immediate and widespread.

"The evidence . . . seems to us at this distance incredibly thin," British political scientist Harold Laski wrote to his friend Oliver Wendell Holmes; Laski accused A. Lawrence Lowell of almost criminal narrow-mindedness. Boston investment banker John Moors had expected impartiality from Lowell, a close friend, but now Moors reluctantly concluded that the Harvard president "was incapable of seeing that two wops could be right and the Yankee judiciary could be wrong."[111]

Philosopher John Dewey of Columbia University summed up what troubled so many about the report: the committee looked at each piece of evidence in isolation, when the main issue should have been "whether, taking *all considerations together,* there was or was not reasonable ground for doubt as to a miscarriage of justice."[112]

However, not everyone found the report troubling or its authors narrow-minded. Chief Justice William Howard Taft admired Lowell, Grant, and Stratton for their courage. Taft told Grant that the case for clemency showed an "utter lack of substance," and he told Lowell that his work had been of "inestimable value," all the more so since it had been complicated by "one of the agents of government, the Judge, [who] had made an ass of himself outside the court."[113]

15 | GROUNDSWELL

Governor Fuller made the advisory committee report public on Sunday, August 7, 1927. That same day some five thousand people gathered on Boston Common to demand justice for Sacco and Vanzetti.[1] Thousands more demonstrated in cities across the United States — Pittsburgh, Los Angeles, Detroit; and around the world — Paris and London and Moscow and Rio; also in Morocco and Uruguay, South Africa and Sweden.

The approaching execution date was triggering a desperate endgame in the streets as well as in court. The defense committee was divided. Should sympathizers lie low and let the lawyers continue working within the system, a tactic that so far had failed? Or should sympathizers stir up as much protest as possible, in the vague hope of convincing the governor that reasonable people still had reasonable doubts, and that commutation to life imprisonment would allow for development of new evidence and possibly avoid a fatal mistake?

Defense lawyers had squelched street protests a year earlier, when the case was before the Supreme Judicial Court. Thompson and Frankfurter were "opposed to any demonstration or meetings. . . . They feared it would 'prejudice the court,'" Mary Donovan recalled. "We were between two forces, Sacco and Vanzetti urging action, [and] the lawyers urging restraint."[2] In the spring, when the case went to the governor, the lawyers continued urging restraint.

Once the governor denied clemency and Thompson severed his official ties to the defense committee, the anarchists saw nothing left to lose. Felicani rented a hall, lined up speakers, and distributed flyers for a mass meeting.

And still he was pressured into calling it off.[3] The lawyers were orchestrating a frantic round of last-minute appeals.

Conflicted on the matter, Bartolomeo had long wanted it both ways. "Only the will and the action of the people . . . could . . . give us freedom," he told Alice Blackwell. "This is not to say that the legal defense and the reason are useless.

They are useful, if . . . accompanied by action, extra-legal action." But, while he wanted the defense committee to organize demonstrations, "of course, the committee should not appear as the initiator."[4]

Nick was not conflicted. "[You are] the only hope that can save us from the electric current. . . . Give us freedom," he urged the "International Proletariat" in May, and he reiterated this belief often. "[I]f the voice of our comrades and friends does not become a mighty one and is not backed with the will to do whatever is necessary," then, he said, he was doomed.[5]

Plans to storm Charlestown State Prison and liberate the two anarchists were supposedly in the works.[6] No such plans materialized but, as peaceful protests multiplied, so, too, did acts of violence. Bombs went off in New York, Philadelphia, and Baltimore on August 6; a bomb exploded and another was defused in Chicago on August 8 and 9; and a powerful explosion destroyed the home of Dedham juror Lewis McHardy on August 16. Governor Fuller reportedly declared that Sacco-Vanzetti sympathizers "should be held jointly responsible" for the McHardy bombing, but no suspects were arrested.[7]

— Arthur Hill held a strategy session on Friday, August 5. Ehrmann sat in, along with Felix Frankfurter, Pittsburgh lawyer Michael Musmanno, and other sympathetic attorneys who would help out in the final push. They decided to zero in on one issue: judicial prejudice.

On Saturday, August 6, the defense filed a motion in Norfolk County to revoke the death sentence and grant a new trial because, in violation of the United States Constitution and the Constitution of the Commonwealth of Massachusetts, "the Honorable Webster Thayer . . . was so prejudiced . . . that the defendants . . . have never had such a trial . . . as constitutes due process of law." The lawyers requested that a judge other than Thayer be assigned to hear the motion. The request was denied by Chief Justice Hall of Superior Court, citing "precedent and established practice [requiring] that the said motions . . . should be heard by the judge who had presided at the original trial."[8]

This set the stage for one of the most controversial episodes of the entire case, the moment when, on Monday, August 8, Judge Thayer sat in judgment on Judge Thayer. "[T]here is not any [prejudice] now and never was at any time," he reportedly said. In open court he denied the request for a new trial on a technicality, ruling that the "the Court had no jurisdiction to entertain the said motion," because it came too late, after sentencing.[9]

In a terse written statement the following day, Thayer, without explanation, declined to revoke sentence or issue a stay of execution. Then he went home to Worcester and took his dog for a walk.[10]

— Jeannette Marks read the papers. In the editions of August 9, she saw the defense committee's appeal to "artists, authors, teachers . . . and other . . . professional men and women to come to headquarters in Boston." Marks, a college professor on summer vacation far from the action, pondered what to do. If she stayed away, she might regret it later. If she went, it could be "perhaps the last thing any of us could do for them."[11]

Marks went to Boston. She was not alone. A groundswell of support for the condemned men arose at the eleventh hour. Laborers and Italian anarchists had been supporting Sacco and Vanzetti from the start. A handful of prominent individuals had also been early supporters, especially Elizabeth Evans from the Brahmin orbit and John Dos Passos and H. L. Mencken from the literary world. Now people in great numbers and from all walks of life joined them.

Vanzetti was astonished. For years he had been telling his family back home that supporters held him in high esteem. Finally he felt justified in reporting that, with some exceptions, all Americans are "on our side. Catholics, Episcopalians, Presbyterians, Quakers, free thinkers, atheists, the intelligentsia, professors, scientists, writers, almost the whole national press, and, most important, the best part of the American people and the students at almost all of the colleges and universities." It was truly amazing. "I never expected such general efforts from persons of every class in my behalf," he marveled to a friend; "[even] the business men, at least many of them, are in our behalf." Indeed, he told Mary Donovan, the support "of the intellectuals and of the middle class and prominent persons and clergies . . . seems to me more active and energetic than the proletarian and unionist protest."[12]

Boston "became alive with all the literary figures from all over the country," Gardner Jackson recalled, and many "of them were milling around our little [defense committee] offices." American writers Dorothy Parker, Katherine Anne Porter, and Edna St. Vincent Millay, among others, joined the protests. To Porter, it was "as miscellaneous, improbable, almost entirely unassorted a gathering of people to one place in one cause as ever happened in this country." To Judge Grant, on the other hand, it was just so much radical chic, "young intelligentsia from New York [parading] like dancing dervishes before the State House."[13]

An emotional but mostly orderly cycle developed at the State House: protesters marched; police warned them to disperse and arrested them when they didn't; sympathizers bailed them out; and they went right back to the picket line.

The celebrity intellectuals drew press attention, as did Powers Hapgood, a handsome young Harvard graduate of privileged background who had been

Police break up a demonstration of "Sacco backers" at the State House. Efforts to save the condemned men grew more frantic as the execution date neared. Library of Congress, Prints & Photographs Div., NYWT&S Collection.

working as a coal miner and labor organizer since his 1921 graduation. He came to Boston on behalf of the Sacco-Vanzetti Conference of Chicago, a group that represented thousands of unionized workers. "Brother Hapgood" was a romantic figure and an irresistible media magnet.[14]

The participation of the latecomers gratified some longtime supporters. It was, in Jackson's opinion, a small "recompense for all of us who had worked with this" for years. But Eugene Lyons saw the belated support as hypocritical, motivated primarily by a middle-class desire to "save our institutions."[15]

These opposing viewpoints hint at the long-running feud dividing Communists and members of the defense committee. (An informer for the state, working undercover at the hotel where several organizations had set up shop in the final days of the case, reported bitter infighting between "Socialists, communists, radicals, liberals, Reds, anarchists, etc.," all there for the ostensibly common purpose of saving Sacco and Vanzetti.) To the Communists, the replacement of Moore by Thompson "sold the class birthright of the Sacco-Vanzetti case for a mess of liberal milk and pap," and blinded the defense committee, a group with the "dignity of gnomes," to the need for militant proletarian action. In the alternate narrative of the defense committee, Communists were trying to wrest control away from committee leaders for their own material gain and publicity. The "martyrdom of Sacco and Vanzetti was far more important [to Communists] than the actual rendering of justice," Jackson believed.[16]

— As Marks, Hapgood, and others flocked to Boston, the *New York Times* devoted four pages of its August 9 edition to the case, and in Detroit carmaker Henry Ford, an opponent of capital punishment, declared that "Sacco and Vanzetti should not be executed."[17] Workers staged protest strikes in Rochester, Philadelphia, Indianapolis, Baltimore, Tampa, and other American cities.

Abroad on that same day, protesters marched, too. Laborers went on strike in Copenhagen, bombs exploded in Buenos Aires, activists called for a boycott of American goods in Lyon, and police had to guard American property in London and Berlin and Paris, in Melbourne and in Santiago, Cuba. "The whole world revolts at this [pending] execution," Harold Laski wrote Oliver Wendell Holmes from France.[18]

The case had re-ignited a perennial debate: Does it make any difference what foreigners think about America?

Yes, argued civil rights attorney Morris Ernst. President Coolidge should heed the "clamor from abroad . . . because we should remember that this country's protests in the Dreyfus case and in connection with the Russian pogroms were heeded." No, countered Senator William Borah of Idaho; international opinion was irrelevant. When Borah was asked to appeal to Coolidge, he declined, adding that "international protest does not concern me in the least." He later elaborated that "it would be a national humiliation, a shameless, cowardly compromise of national courage, to pay the slightest attention to foreign protests or mob protests at home."[19]

Borah's comments raised eyebrows. He was, after all, chairman of the Senate Foreign Affairs Committee. His words may have gratified those Americans who thought that foreigners should mind their own business, but they infuriated international allies. Writing from Switzerland and later England, Laski told Holmes of the "immense damage [the case] has done to the good name of America" in Europe. "What has angered thinking people most is the incredible remark of Borah. . . . As one Frenchman said to me, 'if we have to mobilize five thousand troops to protect American lives and property [from protesters in Paris], we are at least entitled to consideration.'"[20]

Nowhere were the international ramifications of the Sacco-Vanzetti case more complex than in the defendants' native land. Benito Mussolini and his Fascist party had ruled Italy since 1922. On August 5, 1927, Michele Sacco, Nick's father, sent Mussolini what the *New York Times* described as "a pathetic telegram," begging the Italian leader to intervene in the case. Mussolini replied that "for a long time past I have been assiduously occupying myself of the situation of Sacco and Vanzetti. I have done everything compatible with international law to save them from execution."[21]

The claim is usually seen as posturing on the part of someone who essentially kept silent on the case. In fact, says historian Philip Cannistraro, Mussolini "actually did more than his predecessors to assist Sacco and Vanzetti." Beginning in 1922 Mussolini repeatedly questioned his ambassadors to America about the progress of the case and instructed them to approach both federal and Massachusetts officials "in favor of our fellow countrymen." William Thompson adamantly advised the Italian consul in Boston against such meddling. Nevertheless, with hope running out in 1927, Mussolini still sought to intervene behind the scenes. "[B]y all means approach the president of the United States on behalf of Sacco and Vanzetti," he telegraphed Italy's ambassador, Giacomo De Martino, on April 9. "[T]he governor could commute the sentence and release our nationals.... [The] repercussions would be especially positive in Italy," he telegraphed consul Agostino Ferrante on July 23. A day later he contacted American ambassador Henry Fletcher, requesting that he urge the governor toward clemency.[22]

Similarly, President Antonio de Fragoso Carmona of Portugal urged clemency for Celestino Madeiros. Carmona's argument was that capital punishment was not permitted in Portugal and that the execution of Madeiros, a Portuguese citizen, might provoke anti-Americanism. His request, "like all other communications received at the State Department bearing on the case," was forwarded to Governor Fuller.[23]

If "the courts and governor . . . listened to domestic and foreign influence," the Washington Post editorialized, then "they wronged the people of the United States."[24]

In the end, pressure from abroad, whether from laborers or luminaries, from presidents or people on the street, hurt Sacco and Vanzetti more than it helped. Their last lawyer, Arthur Hill, believed they "could have been saved if it hadn't been for the agitation in their behalf, the public demonstrations around the world."[25]

Governor Fuller actually pinned the blame for the outcome of the case on foreign support. "Perhaps without such pressure from outside another solution [such as a pardon] might have been possible," Fuller told a reporter in Germany in 1930. In any case, he continued with dubious logic, "the widespread support that Sacco and Vanzetti enjoyed abroad proved that there was a conspiracy against the security of the U.S.A. and that we should have to defend ourselves with every means at our disposal."[26]

~ Wednesday, August 10, 1927. Without a stay of execution, Sacco and Vanzetti (and Celestino Madeiros) would die after midnight.

Defense lawyers headed for the summer home of Associate Justice Oliver Wendell Holmes to petition for a writ of habeas corpus. "They . . . said all that they had to say," Holmes wrote Laski, "and I declined to issue the writ. . . . [T]he result has been already some letters telling me that I am a monster of injustice." In his official memorandum, Holmes said he did not have authority to interfere with the proceedings of a state court "unless it appears that the Court had not jurisdiction. . . . I cannot think that prejudice on the part of the presiding judge however strong would deprive the Court of jurisdiction."[27]

The defense presented an identical petition to Judge George Anderson of the United States Circuit Court of Appeals. He also denied it. "I am unable to take a different view [from that of Holmes]. . . . I have on this record no right to interfere with the legal processes of the Courts of Massachusetts."[28]

Eleven United States congressmen and governors petitioned the Department of Justice to break its secrecy and make public information in its files about Sacco and Vanzetti.[29]

~ In New York on August 10, police "redoubled their vigilance" around public buildings and subway lines, and insurance underwriters handled a spike in inquiries about "explosion insurance." In Toronto Sacco-Vanzetti demonstrators picketed the American consulate. A protest strike shut down the city of Montevideo, Uruguay, for twenty-four hours. By contrast, in Torremaggiore, Sacco's hometown, things were quiet on August 10. Residents told a reporter they believed that protest "would be entirely useless and indeed injurious to chances of clemency."[30]

Governor Fuller could still grant a stay. He held meetings all day long—with former state attorneys general and with his executive council. Reporters packed the State House waiting for an announcement. Protesters kept marching.

In the eye of the storm, in the bleak death house at Charlestown State Prison, Nick and Bartolo waited.

Nick had aged far beyond his thirty-six years. Eyes sunken, cheeks pinched, lips pursed, he wore an almost otherworldly expression of weariness. On a hunger strike once more, he had not had anything to eat or drink for more than three weeks. He could barely stand.[31]

In contrast, Bartolo seemed stronger. He wrote short final notes of gratitude to his supportive mother surrogates. He had already sent his farewells to Mary Donovan, thanking her for "the good spirit you . . . have that comfort me." Vanzetti admired Donovan's courage, and the two had become good friends. He consoled her when, in April, she was fired from her state job, a job she had had held for twelve years. He gave her gardening advice and folk remedies for seasickness ("Eat plenty of garlic"), and encouraged her in her study of the Italian language. He even sent her a sentimental poem in invisible ink, along with instructions on how to make the ink herself, "if you want to tell me something that you do not wish the censor knows."[32]

As for another important woman in his life, sister Luigia, she had not yet arrived. Without a stay of execution, Bartolo would not see her before he died.

The minutes ticked by with excruciating ineluctability. The freelance executioner from New York arrived at the prison, entering by a service gate to avoid reporters. Michael Musmanno visited the prisoners and heard ominous "experimental noises emanating from the execution chamber." It was the executioner, checking and rechecking the chair. The prisoners donned "dark blue trousers slit in the side where the electrodes were to be strapped, and short-sleeved white shirts, to make it easier to reach the arms."[33]

Security was tight. Streets near the prison were blocked off. An army of policemen, mounted state troopers, and harbor police in river patrol boats were all on duty. "Never before had a penal institution been so armed and garrisoned. . . . [T]he eyes of the world were on Boston that night."[34]

Evening came. Darkness fell. "Everybody in the prison, from the warden down, was uneasy, tense."[35] At the State House, members of the governor's executive council broke for supper. When they reconvened at half past eight, they listened to Arthur Hill plead for a stay. It was ten thirty when he finished. Ninety minutes to midnight.

Hundreds of sympathizers who had come to Boston maintained vigil at a church, not for religious reasons but because the Church of St. John the Evangelist welcomed them, whereas no landlord with a hall to rent in Boston would.

Over on Hanover Street, in Boston's heavily Italian North End, up two flights of narrow stairs, in the bare-bones office that constituted defense committee headquarters, a core group of longtime supporters waited for news. In more hopeful days, the office had been bustling and noisy, filled with the strains of men singing Italian arias as they stuffed envelopes with news bulletins. Now, everyone was subdued and tense.[36]

Rosina spent all day there. Around nine o'clock, she "quietly fainted." She was helped to a friend's nearby apartment, where she lay on a couch, borrowed someone's watch, and with an awful sense of dread kept checking the time.

"It's ten o'clock. They said we would hear by this time."

"It's half past eleven. They said if there was news we'd be sure to know it by this time."[37]

"Nobody knew what to do. Nobody knew what to think. Messages came, messages were sent, there was nothing authoritative."[38] Shortly before midnight, the suspense ended. Supporters received word, reliably confirmed: the governor was granting a stay of twelve days.

Someone at the State House notified the prison. The warden hurried to the prisoners in their death house cells. "It's all off, boys!" he called out. With apparent relief, he returned to his office and passed out cigars to reporters and would-be witnesses.[39]

At midnight the governor put out a formal statement: "The courts of the Commonwealth are actively engaged in the work of considering and deciding the various motions and petitions filed by the counsel in these cases. . . . To afford the courts an opportunity to complete the consideration of the proceedings now pending and render their decision thereon, I have recommended to the Executive Council that the sentences of Sacco, Vanzetti and Madeiros be respited for 12 days, or until midnight on Monday, Aug. 22, 1927. The [Executive] Council has unanimously adopted this recommendation."[40]

The prisoners were moved out of the death house in the morning.

— After rejecting any form of clemency just seven days earlier, Fuller now was approving a temporary stay. He said it was because the courts needed more time to consider pending actions. There may have been another reason as well.

Viola Fuller, the governor's wife, was a devout Catholic. Fuller, himself a Baptist, was "well known for his generous donations to Boston archdiocesan charities."[41]

In public, William Cardinal O'Connell, archbishop of Boston, appeared uninterested in the plight of Sacco and Vanzetti. "[H]e knew better than to take secular sides," a writer observed. Yet, in an apparently little-known after-dinner reference to the case in April, O'Connell had told a group of Holy Cross alumni that the governor had "the right to examine the whole status of a case," and that he should use "every human aid that he can possibly gather, so that no human life will be taken while there is a reasonable doubt as to the perpetration of a crime."[42]

The cardinal continued to maintain a public stance of non-involvement as the execution date neared. In private, however, he was sending and receiving urgent messages on August 10, messages that, as historian Rosario Joseph Tosiello documents, apparently originated at the Vatican.

The first was a telegram from the Apostolic Delegation in Washington, D.C.: "Card. Gasparri requests if possible your charitable intercession in favor of Sacco Vanzetti /stop/ Please answer by telegram."[43]

Cardinal Gasparri was secretary of state to Pope Pius XI.

"We have already done so and will continue as long as there is hope," O'Connell replied.[44]

The same day, O'Connell "wrote an intercessory note to his friend Governor Alvan T. Fuller." He asked the governor, in the name of mercy and compassion, to do whatever he could for the prisoners "even at this last moment": "I have been implored by people whose request I cannot ignore to do whatever is possible in this matter and I offer you my application for clemency trusting that it may be favorably received."[45]

O'Connell's plea to the governor may have been sent in response to pressure from the Vatican, via the Apostolic Delegation. Tosiello notes that three days earlier, on August 7, 1927, the Vatican newspaper, *L'Osservatore Romano*, began daily coverage of developments in the case, after having ignored it for years. An editorial in the paper expressed "hope [that the appeals process] can open . . . the ways of justice or clemency."[46]

If O'Connell's letter did influence Fuller to grant the stay on August 10, neither party would have wanted it known. "As I am a citizen of Mass. and a friend of Gov. Fuller," O'Connell wrote Patrick Cardinal Hayes of New York, "I feel that my position would be misunderstood by all even the general public though I have taken care to act privately."[47]

~ Twelve more days for Sacco and Vanzetti. "What could be done in that time? . . . [W]e discussed every possibility," Mary Donovan recalled. "It seemed strange, later on as we looked back on that night, that people who had gone through seven years of continued disappointments could [still] have had such high hopes."[48]

The lawyers strategized, but the defense committee had had enough. On August 11 it issued *The Final Fight*. In bold type and blunt language, the broadside called for action in the streets:

> We call upon you to hold meetings in a nation wide protest. . . . On Monday, August 22, the day of the execution we urge you to participate in a general strike. . . . Do everything in your power to prevent this tragic, judicial murder. Bombard Governor Fuller and President Coolidge with letters and telegrams of protest. . . . [G]ather in Boston. . . . Come and help save Sacco and Vanzetti. . . . In the name of everything worth while in life save them![49]

"Do everything in your power," the broadside urged. It was an impotent plea. The people to whom it was addressed had no power to stop the death train carrying Sacco and Vanzetti.

But soon it will be night. Now is the time to
leave this place, for we have seen it all.
— Dante Alighieri, *Inferno*

16 | BRINK

If Robert Elliott, who grew up in northern New York, had met Italian-born Nicola Sacco and Bartolomeo Vanzetti under normal circumstances, the three of them might have had a good old time, swapping stories and reminiscing about their similar rural roots. But they did not meet under normal circumstances. When their paths crossed in 1927, Elliott was a professional executioner.

Born in 1874, just four years before Thomas Edison and his business partners founded the Edison Electric Light Company, Elliott grew up fascinated by "electricity and its wonders." Incandescent lamps, phonographs — and who knew what other marvels the future would bring?[1]

In the late nineteenth century, the search was on in America for a less error-prone and hopefully more humane method of capital punishment than the gallows. In 1888 the New York legislature approved electrical execution.[2] Two years later convicted murderer William Kemmler became the first person to die by the new technology when he was strapped into an electric chair at Auburn Prison in northern New York and electrocuted.[3] Coincidentally, that was the same year that sixteen-year-old Robert Elliott decided to become an electrical engineer.

Starting out as an electrician at a "light plant" in Brockport, New York, Elliott advanced quickly, and by 1898 was chief electrician at Clinton Prison in Dannemora. Although Clinton was one of three prisons in New York with an electric chair, "it never occurred to me when I accepted the post," Elliott said, "that [operating machinery for executions] was to be part of my work."[4]

Elliott "threw the switch" on a prisoner for the first time in 1905 at Sing Sing. He had gone there only "to assist at a double execution," but Edwin Davis, New York's official executioner, needed to train backup help, and told a surprised Elliott to "take care of the first one." "Since that morning," Elliott said years later, "I have thrown the switch that has sent three hundred and eighty-seven people into the next world."[5]

Elliott went into business for himself as an electrical contractor in 1921. No longer a prison employee, he freelanced as a circuit-riding electrocutioner for several states, including Massachusetts, which in 1898 had followed New

York's lead and approved "death by electricity," situating its new electric chair at Charlestown State Prison. Elliott's payment in New York was one hundred fifty dollars per job, presumably comparable to his payment in other states.[6]

Sacco and Vanzetti almost met Elliott at Charlestown on August 10, 1927. When the governor granted a reprieve until midnight of August 22, Elliott left for home.

— Twelve more days.

Defense lawyers immediately brought two bills of exceptions focusing on judicial prejudice to the Supreme Judicial Court. Five days later, on August 16, the court heard arguments on the bills.

Arthur Hill maintained for the defense that Judge Thayer "could not sit" to hear a motion for a new trial based on his own prejudice (as he had done on August 6). "Both common sense and legal principle show that no man can judge fairly such questions. . . . [Thayer] was not obliged to sit. . . . His failure to [retire from the case] was an abuse of discretion which can be corrected by this Court."[7]

Massachusetts attorney general Arthur Reading countered that the defense had not offered any evidence that bias had been communicated to the jury "which in any way could affect the fairness of the trial." In what is arguably the most Kafkaesque statement in the six thousand pages of the case record, Reading also said that Judge Thayer "was not bound to find that he [Judge Thayer] was prejudiced, and so disqualified. He was entitled . . . to take into consideration . . . his own knowledge on the question of whether he was or was not in fact prejudiced, and his action in deciding to hear the motion is a decision that he was not disqualified by prejudice."[8]

— Thousands of "Sacco Backers" demonstrated on the Common on Sunday, August 14. It "was like an armed camp in terms of cops [on foot] and cops on horseback," Gardner Jackson recalled. The speakers included Arturo Giovannitti, one of the heroes of the 1912 Lawrence strike.[9]

Things were quieter in Worcester. The *Boston Post* juxtaposed an article on the protests with a photo of Judge Thayer in his shirtsleeves, holding a golf club. "He's a real golfer, too," the caption read, "shooting an 84 only the other day."[10]

Rosina visited Charlestown that Sunday. Take "good care of yourself," Nick told her. "Eat good fresh food and do not worry about me." He himself had not had anything to eat for the past twenty-eight days. Friends worried that he would have to be carried to the electric chair. "You want your wife to eat well," Bartolo called from the adjacent cell. "Why don't you do so yourself?" The next day a prison doctor arrived with a pump and tube for force-feeding, and Nick gave in. "What [else] is there for me to do?" he asked the doctor. "You are strong and I am weak." He sipped a cup of soup. "So . . . life begins to revive slow and calm, but yet without horizon."[11]

Dante went to Charlestown the next day with his mother. Sacco was overcome with emotion at the sight of his fourteen-year-old son. He couldn't get over how tall the boy had grown. Never forget those who helped us, father counseled son; they "have done their best." Three days later, still so weak from the hunger strike that he couldn't complete the task in one sitting, Sacco wrote Dante a long letter of farewell. Seven years of separation had not changed his "heart-beat of affection. . . . [D]on't cry, Dante, because many tears have been wasted. . . . [I]nstead of crying, be strong, so as to be able to comfort your mother . . . and help the weak ones. . . . And you will also not forget to love me a little for I do — O, Sonny! thinking so much and so often of you."[12]

— August 18, the date of Nick's letter to Dante, the justices of the Supreme Judicial Court placed their written decision on the bills of exceptions in a safe, and left town. The decision was made public the next day: Exceptions overruled. The judges sidestepped the question of judicial prejudice, noting that "a motion for a new trial in capital cases comes too late if made after sentence has been pronounced" and therefore the "conduct of the trial judge . . . need not be discussed because . . . neither the judge nor any of his associates had jurisdiction to entertain the motion."[13]

Michael Musmanno had "the grim task of informing Sacco and Vanzetti that our last appeal [in state courts] had been refused."

Musmanno later said the prisoners knew immediately by the expression on his face that the news was bad, and that Vanzetti merely "lifted his hand in token of silence." But contemporary accounts reveal that the lawyer thought Vanzetti went temporarily insane when he heard the news. "Mobilize a million men!" he screamed. He continued shouting through the night. Prisoners complained that his "loud outcries" disturbed them.[14]

— In 1908, when her brother left Italy, Luigia Vanzetti had been a teenager. Now in her midthirties, prone to depression, she had never married. She looked after her father and his household, and knew little of the world beyond Villafalletto.

Unreasonably, Luigia blamed herself for her brother's predicament. From his prison cell, Bartolo had tried to disabuse her of these self-punishing theories. Even if he had stayed in Italy, he reassured her, life was so unpredictable that "I could have died of melancholy or a thousand other illnesses." Even if she "had been free to dedicate [herself] completely to my defense, things wouldn't have turned out . . . any differently." He constantly advised her to have courage, to stay well, to go out, and to conquer her pessimism, for his sake if not for her own. "If you and others waver," he asked, "what would I do?"[15]

Bartolo had asked Luigia to write the governor on his behalf and to drum up support in Italy, but throughout most of his long ordeal, he had not wanted her to visit. "I don't think it's necessary," he wrote her after the Dedham trial. "What could you do, a foreigner who doesn't know the language?" Later, he told her it would be "useless" to come. "You would find yourself in an unfamiliar world, and could do no more than what our comrades and friends are doing and will do."[16]

On the threshold of death, Vanzetti changed his mind. In July he requested that one of his sisters come to America, and on August 19, Luigia, small and frail, landed in New York.

Hundreds of sympathizers met her ship, as did the paparazzi of the day, a "whole army of newspapermen" and photographers with "flash guns . . . going full speed."[17]

To Aldino Felicani, who, with Rosina Sacco and friend Jessica Henderson, met Luigia at the dock, she appeared "pathetic . . ., tired, discouraged, bewildered and lost . . . a true expression of grief." (Katherine Anne Porter memorably described her as a "corpse walking.") Wearing a religious medal around her neck, Luigia told reporters that she would ask her brother to "see a priest and return to the faith of his childhood, of those happy days before he left us and became a radical and an atheist."[18]

Warden William Hendry bent the rules when Luigia arrived at Charlestown; he unlocked Vanzetti's cell so brother and sister could embrace. Luigia collapsed, the warden caught her, Rosina ran for water, then Bartolo and Luigia spent their allotted hour reminiscing. It was almost too much for Vanzetti. "[S]ince I saw her my heart lost a little of its steadyness," he confessed to Jessica Henderson the next day. "The thought that she will have to take my death to our mother's grave, it is horrible to me."[19]

To Luigia herself, "dearest sister," he wrote a last letter to express what a joy their reunion had been. "But I think it was a terrible mistake to make you cross the ocean to see me here. You cannot know how much I suffer to see you witness my agony."[20]

— A power failure occurred at the prison around this time. It happened in the middle of the night. Prisoners "feared that the place had been bombed and for a time there was a hubbub, more prisoners being awakened and joining in the furor." In the darkness, flashlight-toting guards quickly repaired a problem "in the oiling system of a dynamo."[21]

The brief electrical blackout was considered a coincidence, unrelated to the upcoming executions. But Gardner Jackson and Mary Donovan each revealed years later that the electrical tampering had been deliberate, part of a half-baked plan concocted by others to delay the executions and possibly even to spring the men from prison.[22]

~ While desperate anarchists with revenge fantasies devised unworkable plans for prison escapes, equally desperate defense lawyers turned their attention to the federal courts. Among their many daunting obstacles was the calendar. It was August and, along with everyone else, judges and government officials were on vacation. Defense lawyers used boats, trains, and automobiles to chase them down.

The endgame of legal maneuvers flew by in a blur.

On Friday, August 19, lawyers presented a habeas corpus petition to district court judge James Morton. He denied it the following day. Previous denials of the same petition by Justice Holmes and Judge Anderson "are entitled to great weight," Morton said, and the "federal questions involved are not in my opinion of sufficient substance or doubt to justify me" in granting the petition.[23]

That evening Michael Musmanno set off for Washington, D.C., to file petitions for a review of the case by the United States Supreme Court when it reconvened in the fall. In the meantime, any one of the nine Supreme Court justices could grant a stay of execution. Defense lawyers called on the three justices within their reach: Holmes in Beverly, north of Boston; Brandeis in Chatham, on Cape Cod; and Harlan Stone, on an island in Penobscot Bay in Maine. Holmes would not grant a stay: "If the proceedings were void in a legal sense . . . I might issue a habeas corpus. . . . [But no] one who knows anything of the law would hold that the trial . . . was a void proceeding." Stone concurred with Holmes. Brandeis declined to act—officially, because "of the relation of members of his family with the case"; unofficially, no doubt, because of the conflict of interest presented by his own relations with Felix Frankfurter and Elizabeth Evans.[24]

Chief Justice William Howard Taft was out of the country, vacationing in Canada. Musmanno made arrangements to charter a plane and fly to a point somewhere on the United States–Canadian border, where he hoped Taft would agree to meet him and hear the request for a stay. Taft declined, citing the "absence of jurisdiction in our Court." Musmanno also made repeated requests for permission to fly to the summer White House in the Black Hills of South Dakota, to plead with President Coolidge to intervene, but those efforts were rebuffed as well.[25]

— On August 21, the last Sunday before the scheduled execution, hundreds of picketers maintained their march at the State House, and twenty thousand people, the largest crowd yet, gathered on Boston Common. There was some dispute over whether they were there to show solidarity with Sacco and Vanzetti, or to enjoy the concert and baseball game that were going on at the same time.[26]

The quietest place in Boston that Sunday was probably Charlestown State Prison.

Bartolo wrote letters. Two of his addressees could not have been more jarringly disparate. To industrialist Henry Ford, Vanzetti expressed gratitude for suggesting "the commutation of our death sentence to life imprisonment, so as to give the possibility of presenting eventually new discovered evidence. . . . I have always claimed my entire innocence and I will die affirming it." To young Dante Sacco, Vanzetti was more personal. Dante should feel no shame, only pride, because his father was a good man, "not a criminal, but one of the bravest men I ever knew. Some day . . . if you come brave enough, you will take his place in the struggle [for liberty and justice] . . . and . . . vindicate his (our) names. . . . Dante, remember always these things; we are not criminals; they convicted us on a frame-up. . . . Now Dante, be brave and good always. I embrace you."[27]

Rosina Sacco and Luigia Vanzetti, accompanied by Michael Musmanno, visited Nick and Bartolo that Sunday morning. They promised to return in the afternoon. When they did not appear by half past five, the two discouraged prisoners wrote a joint letter urging their supporters to be "as of one heart" and to continue the good fight: "Just treasure our suffering . . . for future battles."[28]

— Monday arrived, August 22, 1927, the final day of the final reprieve. Defense attorneys reflexively continued going through legal motions. Since the previous reprieve of August 10, every one of their efforts had failed. Barring a miracle, the last grain of sand in the Sacco-Vanzetti hourglass would fall at midnight.

Around the world people took to the streets. There was a bombing in Argentina and "feverish interest" in Germany. Twelve thousand demonstrators gathered in Hyde Park in London. There was a call for general strikes in Australia and in Paraguay. Protesters marched in Mexico and Switzerland.[29] In

Weathered.

Opposing views of Massachusetts justice. Top: James North in the August 22, 1927, issue of the *Washington Post*. Bottom: Fred Ellis in the July 22, 1927, issue of the *Daily Worker*. Courtesy of the *Washington Post* (North) and the *Daily Worker* Photographs Collection, Tamiment Library, New York University (Ellis).

WITCHES SALEM 1692

LABOR BOSTON 1927

HAVE A CHAIR!

July 22, 1927

Paris, police were reported to be mobilizing against "Sacco outbreaks," as if support for the prisoners was spreading like the plague.[30]

In the United States police were on red alert. Officers in Chicago received instructions "to rush every Sacco-Vanzetti assemblage and to be liberal in the use of tear bombs." Special guards were assigned to protect monuments and government buildings in Washington, and bridges and subways in New York. In Allegheny County coal-mining country, violence turned fatal when Private John Downey of the Pennsylvania State Police was shot and killed while dispersing a gathering of Sacco-Vanzetti sympathizers.[31]

In Boston, at the center of the action, demonstrators maintained their State House protest. (A bystander told Mary Donovan he would "be damn glad when they fry those wops tonight and get this thing over.") The protest was noteworthy, according to the *Globe*, for the "absence of roughness and discourtesy on the part of the police and the submissive attitude of the pickets." *Globe* editors had by then decided that Frank Sibley, who had covered the case from the start, could no longer be objective, and had reassigned him. "The day of the execution," Gardner Jackson recalled, "Sib was assigned to cover a flower show out at the Armory."[32]

Defense sympathizers consumed by their lost cause might have been surprised to realize that there *was* a flower show at the Armory, that life outside their pressure cooker was going on as usual. They might have been surprised, too, by opinions in the parallel universe of opponents where, notes historian Eric Foner, "the cab drivers, shop clerks and subway guards of Boston—except in the Italian North End—supported the execution of the 'damn Reds.'" Such sentiments were not confined to Boston. "The condemned men should be reprieved until Nov. 1, until after the crops are all in," one Leroy Stafford Boyd of Arlington, Virginia, wrote in a letter to the editor of the *Boston Evening Transcript*. Then "the governor of each New England state should advertise a homecoming week [for Southerners of New England ancestry]. . . . And on the day of the execution in Boston, with the city filled with Mississippians and Texans, swear in twenty-five thousand of them as policemen, and if any Red shows his head, put a bullet in him and throw his body into the Charles River."[33]

— Luigia Vanzetti and the woman she called her sister in misfortune, Rosina Sacco, tried to keep busy. They made an appearance before a large and sympathetic audience at the Scenic Auditorium. Though neither one spoke, their mere presence was said to have transformed a "very quiet" meeting into "a yelling, cheering mob."[34]

They called on Cardinal O'Connell, a "logical thing," Aldino Felicani explained, since Luigia was so religious. Luigia appealed to the cardinal for his help, but was said to have understood that the prelate's role was "strictly spiritual."[35]

Rosina and Luigia also went to the State House to plead with Governor

Fuller. According to Michael Musmanno, who interpreted for them at this interview and who later reconstructed the scene, Mrs. Sacco appealed to Fuller as a family man: "My husband was always good and faithful to me. He was devoted to his home. Is that the way bandits act? . . . Governor, help my children! Do not kill their father! Please, please, have mercy and have justice. . . . Won't you see how innocent Nick is?"[36]

For her part, Luigia Vanzetti appealed to the governor as a religious man: "[My brother's] innocence is assured. Of that there can be no doubt. God has recorded that on the books; the only problem in this long case has been to have those in authority read God's handwriting. . . . On my knees, oh, Governor! I implore you, do not let America become known as the land of cruelty instead of mercy. I beg of you, I pray you for mercy!"[37]

Musmanno himself was overwrought, and his version of the encounter may be exaggerated. Yet there can be no doubt that at this point, on August 22, with the scheduled execution mere hours away, the women were in anguish. The governor said he was impressed by the two women, but had no doubts about the prisoners' guilt. "There is nothing, absolutely nothing I can do and remain true to the oath of my office."[38]

~ Although Governor Fuller was not about to change his mind, he stayed in his office until midnight on August 22, making himself available to just about anybody who wanted to see him.

The visitors streamed in.

Poet Edna St. Vincent Millay met with him, then sent a follow-up letter begging the governor to ask himself: What would Jesus do? Jesus would not, she believed, have walked "the way in which your feet are set! . . . There is need in Massachusetts of a great man tonight. It is not yet too late for you to be that man."[39]

Congressman Fiorello La Guardia of New York met with Fuller. Ten years earlier the two men had served together in the United States House of Representatives. Now, La Guardia told reporters, "There is about one chance in a thousand" for a successful appeal.[40]

Paul Kellogg, editor of the social policy journal *Survey*, met with the governor. Together with five other prominent citizens, he asked for a stay until doubts could be resolved. Fuller accused the group of being manipulated by Felix Frankfurter.[41]

Attorneys Arthur Garfield Hays, Francis Fisher Kane, and Frank Walsh met with Fuller to ask for a stay until federal government files on the case could be examined, because former federal agents had sworn they contained evidence material to the case. (One day earlier, acting United States attorney general George Farnum had consented to make the files available to senior state officials, upon request.) "I know more about the case than you do," Fuller told the group. He appeared fixated on the significance of Vanzetti's failure to testify on his own behalf at the Plymouth trial. "Isn't it your experience," Fuller asked, "that an innocent man insists upon taking the stand?"[42]

All day long current and former defense attorneys filed into Fuller's office to ask for a stay: Arthur Hill, William Thompson, Herbert Ehrmann, and Michael Musmanno. The governor asked Musmanno why Vanzetti did not take the stand at Plymouth—"the same question he had asked scores of times, and, though it had been answered time and again, still, with maddening repetition, he continued to put it."[43]

Nearly a thousand letters and telegrams, most urging clemency, also swamped Fuller's office that day.

— Inside Charlestown State Prison, Monday, August 22, 1927.

Early morning.

Mrs. Consuelo Aruda arrived to say goodbye to her brother, Celestino Madeiros. This hapless half-forgotten thug, whose written confession on a slip of paper had tied his fate inextricably to that of Sacco and Vanzetti, wanted to see his mother before dying. He had waited all weekend for a visit from her, but she did not come, and now his sister explained that their mother was "in a state of collapse and has been so since a week ago." The brother and sister conversed in Portuguese. He gave her a message for his mother. "Mrs. Aruda was in tears when she left and said that her brother had also showed some emotion."[44]

Midmorning.

Rosina Sacco and Luigia Vanzetti arrived for the first of three visits they would make to the prison that day. The women entered the death house "with faltering steps," the *Globe* reported, and left an hour later showing "evidences of great sorrow."[45]

Midafternoon.

Robert Elliott arrived. The practiced professional did an equipment check on the heavy wooden electric chair with its straps, high back, broad arms, rubber-padded headrest, and legs bolted to the floor:

I make certain [for each execution that the chair] is hooked up and that no wires are broken. I inspect the adjusting screws, test the strength of the straps, and determine whether the buckles work freely. A strap did break during an execution, and I try to prevent a repetition of this.

Then I look to see if the mask is where it should be, and ascertain whether its strap and buckle are sound. The mask, usually a black leather band with an opening for the nostrils and mouth, serves a double purpose: that of shielding the face and holding the head in place. . . .

A pail of brine—nothing more than a solution of common salt and water—is prepared. In this are soaked the sponges of the electrodes to insure a good contact. . . .

My next step is to test the apparatus. This is accomplished in either of two ways. One is to attach a board of electric lights to the wires leading to the chair. . . . The other is to put the two electrodes in a bucket of water, with perhaps a pinch of salt, and close the circuit.[46]

The atmosphere inside the prison was tense, said Elliott. Nerves were almost at the breaking point.[47]

Late afternoon.

Rosina and Luigia visited again, then William Thompson arrived. He had received a message that Vanzetti wanted to see him before he died. Lawyer and client spoke of battles they had fought, and of the future. "[T]he thought that was uppermost in his mind," Thompson said, "was the truth of the ideas in which he believed for the betterment of humanity, and the chance they had of prevailing."[48]

Vanzetti gave Thompson "his most solemn reassurance, . . . with a sincerity which I could not doubt, . . . that both he and Sacco were absolutely innocent of the South Braintree crime, and that he (Vanzetti) was equally innocent of the Bridgewater crime." Vanzetti said he understood more clearly than ever that he would not have been convicted "had he not been an anarchist, so that he was in a very real sense dying for his cause. He said it was a cause for which he was prepared to die. He said it was the cause of the upward progress of humanity. . . . He said he was grateful to me for what I had done for him. . . . He asked me to do what I could to clear his name."[49]

They talked about Christianity. The condemned man "asked me whether I thought it possible that he could forgive" his persecutors. Thompson replied that he did not know, but suggested that Vanzetti try, "for his own peace of mind, and also because an example of such forgiveness would in the end be more powerful . . . than anything else. . . ." Vanzetti said he would think about it.[50]

Aware that Vanzetti's failure to testify at the Plymouth trial had become a "positive obsession" for Governor Fuller, Thompson asked Vanzetti if he would release his Plymouth attorneys from confidentiality restrictions so they could disclose any information they had about Vanzetti's guilt. Vanzetti "readily assented to this," as long as Thompson "or some other friend" were also present.[51]

"At parting he gave me a firm clasp of the hand [through the bars] and a steady glance, which revealed unmistakably the depth of his feeling and the firmness of his self-control."

Before leaving the death house, Thompson said farewell to Sacco, in the adjacent cell. The two men had often disagreed about strategy. Now Sacco told Thompson that "he hoped that our differences . . . had not affected our personal relations, thanked me for what I had done for him, showed no sign of fear, shook hands with me firmly [through the bars], and bade me goodbye. His manner also was one of absolute sincerity."

Thompson went directly to his office and wrote an account of the conversations. Then he and Herbert Ehrmann headed to the State House to tell Fuller he was free to question Vanzetti's Plymouth attorneys. By then, however, it was late, and "nothing further (to our knowledge) occurred" with respect to this matter.[52]

Five o'clock.

Suppertime at Charlestown. Even Madeiros, who had been a hearty eater behind bars, had no special requests for his last meal. A light supper was brought to the three prisoners in the death house. No one was hungry.[53]

In streets around the prison, the "Biggest Police Detail Ever" assembled: more than seven hundred officers in uniform and in plainclothes; on foot, motorcycle, and horseback; from riot and bomb squads; from city, state, and even railroad forces. Harbor police patrolled the rivers. Firemen stood ready with high-pressure hoses to use if needed.[54]

Sympathizers maintained a deathwatch outside the police cordon. Amazingly, Joe Morelli later claimed to have been among them. Morelli, the professional criminal and Nick Sacco look-alike whom the defense had accused of taking part in the South Braintree murders, said he stood unrecognized in the dense crowd of people near the prison that night, hoping, like them, for a reprieve.[55]

Six o'clock.

Bartolomeo Vanzetti, the autodidact who had kept up such an extensive correspondence with so many people during seven years behind bars, sat down to write his last known letter. It was a message for lecturer and liberal activist Henry Wadsworth Longfellow Dana, namesake of his famous literary grandfather. Vanzetti thanked him for "all that you have done for Nicola, I, and for our families." He asked Dana for a final favor: "What I wish more than all in this last hour of agony is that our case and our fate may be understood . . . and serve as a tremendous lesson . . . so that our suffering and death will not have been in vain. . . . I wish and hope you will lend your faculties in inserting our tragedy in the history under its real aspect and being."[56]

Aldino Felicani arrived at the prison while Vanzetti was writing this letter. By law, someone was required to claim the bodies of electrocuted prisoners before they died. "It was up to me to do that," said Felicani, the friend who had supported them untiringly for seven years.[57]

"Gardner Jackson and his sister . . . accompanied me to the jail. The whole city was an armed camp. . . . My heart was beating fast. The trip . . . was made in silence. . . . We reached the jail. The atmosphere that prevailed was suspense and fear. . . . Inmates appeared to be watching in the shadows. . . . Everyone, at the entrance, in the lobby, in the office, was busy with the details of the execution. I entered the office. The warden, Mr. Hendry, was there. He was drunk. I asked him what the procedure was and he gave me the papers to sign. It was in such a manner that I claimed the bodies of my friends, who were then still alive."[58]

Seven o'clock.

Rosina and Luigia returned for a few final moments of farewell. LEAVE-TAKING PATHETIC, one headline summed up; DOOMED MEN STRETCH ARMS THROUGH CELL BARS IN EFFORTS TO EMBRACE WIFE AND SIS-TER. Starting at seven "and continuing throughout the evening," radio station WBET aired live coverage of execution night.[59]

Eight forty-five.

Warden Hendry went to the death house. The latest petition for a writ of habeas corpus had been denied. Any faint glimmer of hope for an eleventh-hour reprieve was gone. Hendry stopped at each cell. "I am sorry," he told each prisoner, "but it is my painful duty to inform you that you have to die tonight. Your lawyers have exhausted their efforts."[60]

Madeiros, asleep when Hendry went to his cell first, awakened, listened, and went back to sleep. Sacco was writing a letter to his father when Hendry went to his cell next. He told the warden he wanted to be sure his father received the letter, and Hendry promised he would personally see that it was mailed. Sacco thanked the warden "for this and other kindnesses" during his imprisonment. Vanzetti, in the last cell, was pacing back and forth. He had been at Charlestown, and known Hendry, the longest. He appeared momentarily shocked when Hendry gave him the news. Then Vanzetti too thanked the warden for his kindnesses, and resumed pacing.[61]

Prison chaplain Father Michael Murphy accompanied Hendry. All three condemned men rejected his entreaties to return to their faith before dying.

Nine forty-five.

Father Murphy went back to the death house cells with Hendry, but his ministrations were again rejected.[62] The prisoners, he told a reporter, said they preferred to die as they had lived.

Ten o'clock.

In the presence of Robert Elliott, prison electricians tested the chair one last time.

Eleven fifteen.

Michael Musmanno rushed into the warden's office. Only now admitting defeat, he wanted to say goodbye to the prisoners. It was too late. He was turned away. "Tears streamed down the face of the lawyer" as he left the prison, according to press reports.[63]

Midnight.

The official witnesses headed to the white-walled, brightly lit death chamber: five government doctors, three corrections officials, and a "newsgatherer" selected by lot, William Playfair of the Associated Press. Scores of other reporters waited across the prison yard in a guards' building.[64]

A few months earlier, when Nick and Bartolo were still at Dedham Jail, they had spoken to Phil Stong, a reporter for the North American Newspaper Alliance. The interview had proceeded uneventfully until the moment came for Stong to leave. Then, said Stong, Vanzetti, quietly and in imperfect English spoke the words that, over time, would become the most famous epitaph for the Sacco-Vanzetti case:

> If it had not been for these thing, I might have live out my life talking at street corners to scorning men. I might have die, unmarked, unknown, a failure. Now we are not a failure. This is our career and our triomph. Never in our full life can we hope to do such work for tolerance, for joostice, for man's onderstanding of man, as now we do by an accident. Our lives—our words—our pains—nothing! The taking of our lives—lives of a good shoemaker and a poor fish peddler—all! The moment you think of belong to us—that agony is our triomph!"[65]

The moment was now.

"When more than one person is ticketed for death on the same night, the order of their going is determined in advance. The weakest—that is, the one least able to stand up under the ordeal of waiting his turn—is first. The others follow according to their physical and mental condition."[66] Thus Robert Elliott described the procedure for deciding the order of multiple executions, a procedure that in Charlestown dictated the prisoners' cell assignments: Celestino Madeiros in cell 1, Nicola Sacco in cell 2, Bartolomeo Vanzetti in cell 3.

"The death march began three minutes after twelve," Elliott recalled. "With a guard on each side, Madeiros entered the death chamber in a semi-stupor. . . . He spoke not a word."[67] He was strapped down. Elliott "threw on a current of 1400 to 1900 volts. Three times the current was thrown on and off, and at 12:09:35 [a.m.], four examining physicians declared officially that Celestino Madeiros was dead."[68]

Behind a screen stood "three green slabs awaiting three corpses."[69] The body of Madeiros was removed from the chair and placed on one of the waiting slabs. He was twenty-five years old when he died.

One telegraph operator was sitting near the death chamber; another, in the guards' building where the press was hunkered down. "Within a minute of the time that Madeiros had died, the ticker . . . flashed out the news. Instantly other tickers . . . went into action, and within a matter of minutes the news went racing across the world."[70]

Nicola was next. To Bartolo, he called out, "Goodbye." Then he walked "slowly but steadily" into the death chamber. Elliott noticed that Sacco was "deathly pale. It was obvious that he was under a terrific mental strain."[71]

Nick "sat down without protest." Many years had passed since the day he had sat down in another chair, posing for a portrait in a photographer's studio, exuding youthful ambition and confidence. Many years, too, since he had mastered his shoemaking craft, since he had fallen in love, since he had carried his son in his arms. "As the guards swung about to adjust the straps [and apply the electrodes], Sacco sat bolt upright in the chair of death. Casting about wildly with his eyes, he cried [out] in Italian, 'Long live anarchy!' "[72]

"Everything was now ready," Elliott said, "except the placing of the mask over his face. But the mask could not be found. The guards and I searched frantically for it. I could feel beads of perspiration starting out on my forehead. Meanwhile, Sacco continued to speak. 'Farewell, my wife and child and all my friends,' he cried in broken English."[73]

"Then, seeming to become cognizant of the witnesses as individuals . . ., he went on politely, 'Good evening, gentlemen.' "[74]

"As Sacco was saying these things," Elliott recalled, "a guard strode back into the room with the mask. It had been caught in Madeiros's clothing, and carried from the chamber when his body was taken out for autopsy. Had it not been for Sacco's talking, the incident might have been noticed. As it was, the only reporter present failed to observe what had happened, and no mention was made of it in the newspapers. I have often since been thankful that the little Italian was so talkative as he sat in the chair awaiting the end."[75]

Guards slipped the recovered mask over Nick's face. He called out to his dead mother, "Farewell, mia madre." An "extra heavy current" was administered, 1,800 to 2,000 volts.[76] At 12:19:02 a.m., Nicola Sacco was pronounced dead, and his body removed from the chair. He was thirty-six years old when he died.

The guards went to the cells for the last time. They unlocked the third cell, and "escorted Vanzetti over the twenty short steps to the door of the death chamber." Elliott noted that the last prisoner was the "most composed. . . . When guards came for him, he shook their hands." He thanked Warden Hendry "for everything you have done for me."[77]

Vanzetti took his place in the heavy chair. The survival skills he had developed as a lonely teenager far from home had served him well throughout his life, and now, staring death in the face, he stayed calm. As the guards adjusted straps and electrodes, Vanzetti spoke to the witnesses: "I wish to tell you I am innocent, and never committed any crime, but sometimes some sin. I thank you for everything you have done for me. I am innocent of all crime, not only of this, but all. I am an innocent man."[78]

Bartolo must have spent his final hours on earth thinking about his conversation with William Thompson, for he pronounced his last words with great precision: "I wish to forgive some people for what they are now doing to me."

Guards slipped the mask over Vanzetti's face, and "current was applied," 1,400 to 1,800 volts. At 12:26:55 a.m., Bartolomeo Vanzetti was pronounced dead, and his body removed from the chair. He was thirty-nine years old when he died.

~ Robert Elliott, another job professionally done, took a taxi back to his hotel.[79]

The special police forces stationed around the prison went off duty.

In Detroit, Sacco-Vanzetti sympathizers in Cadillac Square clashed with police. Anarchist Attilio Bortolotti was clubbed on the head. He went to the offices of the *Detroit News* later and learned that the executions had taken place as scheduled. "I don't know how I got home that night," Bortolotti said.[80]

In New York, protesters in Union Square sobbed uncontrollably when the executions were announced. Valerio Isca and his comrades eventually "went home to Brooklyn on the subway. When we emerged at the Montrose [Avenue] station, we were still crying."[81]

There were tears, too, in the Italian neighborhood of Federal Hill in Providence. The executions were a "moment of great defeat," Thomas Longo recalled.[82]

It rained all night in Boston. At home with her family, waiting by the phone for news, Cerise Carman Jack felt "emotional [and] sad." Powers Hapgood was devastated. "[N]othing has ever ravaged my soul and feelings" like the executions, he wrote his parents.[83]

Aldino Felicani and Gardner Jackson walked the dark streets of Boston in silence that night. So did Felix Frankfurter and his wife. When a radio loudspeaker blared out the announcement of the deaths, Marion Frankfurter collapsed.[84]

Luigia Vanzetti, at the apartment where she had taken refuge, cried in silence. With her, Rosina Sacco wept without restraint. Her "piercing cries" were said to echo through the neighborhood.[85]

In Worcester, the worst downpour the city had experienced in years started right after midnight. For twelve hours it pummeled Judge Thayer's hometown with such torrential intensity that it sounded like "so many little bullets, hitting the houses in a steady stream." Sewers backed up. Streets flooded.[86] By early afternoon the deluge had finally stopped, but a different kind of storm was beginning.

. . . remind our friends of me. I speak no more.

— Dante Alighieri, *Inferno*

17 | AFTERLIVES

Supporters hoped that the funeral of Sacco and Vanzetti would be a call to action. To stay a step ahead of the funeral planning, worried public safety officials put a wiretap on Felix Frankfurter's home phone and planted an undercover agent on a pro-defense committee.[1]

In confidential reports dated August 24, the informer communicated first that nervous Boston undertakers and landlords were refusing to allow the bodies of Nick and Bartolomeo to be carried onto their property, and then that "Joseph Langone, undertaker on Hanover Street, . . . has been engaged," and the manager of the National Casket Company would let police know when the bodies went to Langone's. (The body of Celestino Madeiros was sent to a funeral home in New Bedford.)[2]

Calling hours began at Langone's on Thursday evening. Mourners streamed through the funeral parlor in Boston's North End. A fracas broke out when police arrested Mary Donovan for displaying anti-Thayer posters. A touch of carnival atmosphere emerged: children boosted each other up "to have a peep at the two dead faces," and tour guides on sightseeing buses pointed out "the place where Sacco and Vanzetti are lying in state." Mostly, though, people were solemn and silent as they "shuffled past the open caskets [to view the] emaciated bodies, paste-gray faces, the quiet of death in a small room lit only by candles."[3]

All told, one hundred thousand people crossed the marble step at the entrance to the funeral parlor and went inside to pay their respects. In three days they wore the marble down more than a quarter of an inch.[4]

— The funeral was to take place on August 28, a Sunday, chosen so that as many mourners as possible could come to Boston. When the day dawned, windy and gloomy, a chill in the damp air made it feel more like November. At two o'clock the corpses left Langone's in side-by-side hearses. The Sacco family and Luigia Vanzetti followed, hidden behind the drawn curtains of their car.[5]

Spectators crowded at open windows in buildings along the route to watch the procession. Thousands more lined the curbs — more than two hundred

Police, mourners, and side-by-side hearses proceed along the rain-slicked streets of Boston on August 28, 1927, as spectators crowd the route. More onlookers perch on a fire escape, upper left. Library of Congress, Prints & Photographs Div., NYWT&S Collection.

thousand, said the *Boston Post*. They tossed so many flowers at the cortege that "the streets became red with the blossoms."[6] Another large crowd, estimated to number anywhere from six thousand to fifty thousand people, marched behind the hearses.[7]

Rain began to fall. Entrepreneurial taxi drivers offered to ferry carloads of people to the cemetery for a dollar a head.[8]

Spectators and policemen skirmished all along the eight-mile route, and in the end only two hundred people made it all the way to the cemetery. Inside a small chapel, Mary Donovan read Gardner Jackson's brief farewell address, vowing "to accomplish that better world . . . for which you died." Then, against the wishes of Luigia Vanzetti, the caskets were rolled into the cemetery's crematorium and fed to the flames.[9]

Felicani escorted the grieving relatives back to "where they were living. I spent some time with them, and then went home. That was all."[10]

— Evidence that controversy would outlive Sacco and Vanzetti appeared the very next day. On August 29, Massachusetts attorney general Arthur Reading addressed his peers at a meeting of the National Association of Attorneys General in Buffalo.[11] He told them that the trial of Sacco and Vanzetti had been fair. The attorney general of Louisiana introduced a resolution praising Massachusetts for its actions in the case.

A day later, the resolution was withdrawn. Other attorneys general would not approve it.[12] Reading would soon fare no better than his resolution. Within six months he was charged with extortion, and eventually impeached and disbarred.

— Webster Thayer remained on the Superior Court bench and continued hearing cases. It "was frequently reported that he would begin to talk about the [Sacco-Vanzetti] case to his personal friends, and even to strangers, on any or no provocation."[13]

If, as rumored, Thayer hoped for an appointment to the Supreme Judicial Court of Massachusetts, he was disappointed; it did not come. Instead, he received a steady stream of letters—some threatening, but many, he claimed, laudatory, praising him for "the great courage required to go through what I went through for seven long years under the most vicious attacks."[14]

In the early morning hours of September 27, 1932, a powerful bomb exploded at Thayer's Worcester home. The house was completely destroyed; miraculously no one was seriously injured. Thereafter Thayer continued to work, but was always accompanied by a bodyguard. Less than a year after the explosion, Thayer became ill in court, was brought to his club, and died there of a stroke at age seventy-five. Despite a large reward for information about the bombing, no one was apprehended, and the unsolved case was closed in 1949.[15]

Thayer was the "most bitterly attacked judge in the history of the United States," the *Boston Globe* reported upon his death. He "was known all over the world for just one reason": the Sacco-Vanzetti trial. William Thompson said he believed that Thayer did not mean to be bad, but was blinded by his "fear of reds . . . [and] thought that he was rendering a great public service."[16]

— Fred Moore, Thayer's nemesis, having failed to win acquittal for Sacco and Vanzetti, left Boston under a cloud of ignominy in 1924.

Moore hit the road alone; after a brief marriage, he and his current wife had separated. He had a few hundred dollars of borrowed money in his pocket and, on the backseat of his car, stacks of novelty signs for license plates that he planned to sell along the highway.[17] Moore was reported to be in New York in 1925; in Colorado in 1927.[18] How he supported himself is unclear. "He had no more law practice; for a while he eked out a miserable existence selling law books.... [He lived] in a 'little hotel room.'"[19]

By 1931 Moore was back home in California, where he made a public appearance in San Francisco at a meeting of radicals. In 1933, at the age of fifty-one, Fred Moore died of cancer at his mother's home in Los Angeles.

Moore's early successes on behalf of the IWW had long ago been eclipsed by his failure in Boston. He died in obscurity, his passing unnoticed except for a short memorial tribute in an anarchist monthly. There, a T. H. Bell noted that "Fred here in Los Angeles remained as radical as ever, ... always ready to help a worker in trouble."[20] If Moore could have spoken on his own behalf, he might have echoed the courtroom remarks of his former IWW colleague, George Vanderveer: "I speak with feeling of [downtrodden] men, for I know what life can do to them."[21]

~ For William Thompson, the Sacco-Vanzetti case was "the most transforming event of his life." He continued to practice law, but also made time to lobby for causes important to him: a well-qualified judiciary and legislative protection for the Bill of Rights. In 1930 he was asked to run for the United States Senate, but declined.[22]

In 1934, Thompson, then 70, observed that he thought "people are rather tired of hearing about the Sacco-Vanzetti case." He died a year later, mourned by an official of the Boston Bar Association as "the recognized leader of the bar of the Commonwealth." Elizabeth Evans asked Dante Sacco to attend the funeral with her. Thompson, she said, "was your father's great champion, and I feel indebted to him down to the ground of the floor."[23]

The fight to save Sacco and Vanzetti "seriously impaired [Thompson's] health and brought on the illness from which he never recovered," the *Boston Herald* reported. "The case shortened his life," defense committee member Joseph Moro concurred. "I'm sure of it."[24]

~ Prosecutor Frederick Katzmann went into private law practice when his term as district attorney ended in 1923, partnering at first with John Vahey, his opponent at Vanzetti's first trial. Katzmann also became president of a local savings bank. In 1953, while arguing a civil case, the former district attorney had a heart attack and collapsed in the same Dedham courthouse where he had tried Sacco and Vanzetti. He died that night.[25] He was in his late seventies.

Katzmann went to his grave without ever speaking publicly about the Sacco-

Vanzetti case or his role in it, although he thought about the case all the time. He told one of his law partners that he was certain of the defendants' guilt, but "if I had my life to live over, I'd never want to go through that again."[26] His house had been under guard for years, and he believed the strain drove his wife to an early death.

— If Thayer had aspired to serve on the state's highest court, and Katzmann, as rumored, to become the attorney general of Massachusetts, Governor Alvan Fuller had bigger dreams. He hoped to run for president or vice president on the Republican national ticket in 1928. He was passed over for both jobs. "Senator Borah took the position that to put [Fuller's] name on the Republican ticket would compel them during the campaign . . . to defend . . . [his] refusing to commute the death sentence of Sacco and Vanzetti."[27]

Fuller's role in the case continued to shadow his political life. When Fuller's gubernatorial term ended in 1929, Gardner Jackson accosted him on his ceremonial exit from the State House and thrust a copy of *The Letters of Sacco and Vanzetti* into his hands. When Fuller sought the ambassadorship to France that year, he was unsuccessful. SACCO CASE SAID TO PRECLUDE HIS BEING AMBASSADOR THERE, a headline explained. The *New York Times* predicted that Fuller would be offered another foreign post. He wasn't. In 1930 he withdrew from a primary race for a United States Senate seat. He was a favorite son candidate for vice president in 1932; it was a courtesy nomination that went nowhere. Two years later, Fuller made one last stab at running for office, trying again for the governorship, then abruptly withdrew from the race.[28]

The self-made multimillionaire devoted much of the rest of his life to philanthropy and art collecting. In 1958, as he sat in a Boston movie theater watching the on-screen characters of Nellie Forbush and Emile de Becque grapple with love and racism in *South Pacific*, Fuller collapsed and died of a heart attack.[29] He was eighty. He had lived long enough to see an Italian American win his old job. In a development that surely would have surprised Sacco and Vanzetti, Foster Furcolo was elected governor of Massachusetts in 1956, the first Italian American to hold the office. Others would follow: John Volpe in the 1960s and Paul Cellucci in the 1990s.

As early as 1930 Fuller told a reporter in Germany that "the whole [Sacco-Vanzetti] affair has been forgotten long ago. No one in America thinks of it any more." Memories were longer than he realized. After Fuller's death, when the Boston Museum of Fine Arts exhibited his art collection, protesters marched to remind people "that one of Governor Fuller's masterworks . . . had been the execution of Sacco and Vanzetti."[30]

∼ Of the three men Fuller named to his advisory committee, Harvard University President A. Lawrence Lowell was the most conspicuous target for critics. Every August, on the anniversary of the executions, Lowell received letters "of bitter, personal abuse." He left Harvard in 1933, but return to private life brought no respite from the attacks. When the university celebrated its tercentenary in 1936, twenty-eight alumni published a scathing critique of the advisory committee's deliberations.[31] Lowell died in 1943, at the age of eighty-six.

Samuel Stratton, one of Lowell's two colleagues on the governor's advisory committee, was the group's only scientist. In 1931 Stratton, 70, was speaking to a reporter about his close friend Thomas Edison, who had died that day, when Stratton himself, "sitting in his parlor overlooking the Charles River, . . . without any sign of pain or fatigue," had a heart attack and dropped dead. He "departed this life, with a eulogy of Edison on his lips."[32]

Robert Grant, the third member of the committee, published his autobiography in 1934. It included a chapter on the Sacco-Vanzetti case, thus making Grant the only government-affiliated person involved in the case to speak about it publicly at any length. He said committee members were "free from doubt on the two vital issues — the fairness of the trial and the guilt of the two men." Grant saved some of his harshest words for Felix Frankfurter, who caused "world-wide hysteria" with his "one-sided article."[33] Frankfurter was appointed to the United States Supreme Court a year before Grant died at the age of eighty-eight in 1940.

∼ If supporters of Sacco and Vanzetti really "lost their sense of proportion," as Justice Oliver Wendell Holmes believed, much of the credit — or blame — belonged to Italian printer Aldino Felicani and wealthy reporter and Colorado native Gardner Jackson.[34] The two men came from radically different backgrounds, but forged a friendship on the barricades that lasted a lifetime.

Felicani bought his own printing company, Excelsior Press, in 1925. He published material for the defense committee and, between 1927 and 1967, he also published three different anti-Fascist journals. His sons eventually took over management of the printing business, but Felicani, despite advancing age, continued to work on his journal six days a week. "As long as I have a pencil in my hand and ink in the machine, we'll keep it going," he told an associate. "It's our mission.'"[35]

Aldino Felicani died in 1967 at the age of seventy-six, but his influence lives on. The former treasurer of the defense committee was, it turned out, a man who threw away nothing. In 1979 Felicani's sons presented their father's enormous collection of original case-related documents to the Boston Public Library, where they constitute the bountiful core of the institution's Sacco-Vanzetti archive.

For Gardner Jackson, working on the Sacco-Vanzetti case proved to be "the major directional influence in my life." Jackson gave more than fifty thousand dollars of his own money to support defense efforts. Defeat left him emotionally shattered and, he believed, professionally "marked." He worked on and off for several newspapers, for the Department of Agriculture during the New Deal, and for a labor union, but felt "sunk in such gloom." Jackson never stopped speaking out in defense of Sacco and Vanzetti. He died suddenly of a heart attack in 1965, at the age of sixty-eight, memorialized as a "crusading newsman" who led " 'lost' causes."[36]

— Carlo Tresca and Elizabeth Gurley Flynn began an intense and stormy relationship after meeting during the Lawrence strike in 1912. Tresca and Flynn continued working for radical causes all their lives, but not together. They drifted apart politically and romantically. "Carlo had a roving eye that had roved in my direction in Lawrence but then, some ten years later, was roving elsewhere," Flynn said. By 1925 they had parted, Tresca having fathered a child by a woman who not only was married to another man but also was Flynn's younger sister.[37]

Flynn officially joined the Communist Party in 1937. She died on a visit to Russia in 1964.

Tresca devoted himself to fighting Fascism, primarily in the pages of his newspaper. He was constantly involved in bitter feuds — with Communists, with Italian-American supporters of the Fascist government in Italy, and with other Italian-American anarchists, especially followers of Luigi Galleani.[38] Tresca defied death threats for years, but fate caught up with him on a January evening in 1943 when he was gunned down on a New York street corner. Despite an intensive investigation, no one was ever brought to trial for the murder.[39]

— Luigi Galleani, inspiration for Sacco and Vanzetti and rival of Tresca, was deported to Italy in 1919. Anarchists were as unwelcome there as they were in America, and Galleani was imprisoned for seditious activities, later sent into internal exile, jailed again, and finally released. He died in Italy in 1931, at the age of seventy, "still under police surveillance."[40]

Mario Buda, who had been with fellow Galleanisti Sacco and Vanzetti on May 5, 1920, escaped the trap police set for him, and is believed to have detonated the deadly Wall Street bomb that September. Two months later he was back in Italy, where he renewed his anarchist connections. Like Galleani, Buda was arrested for anarchist activities in his native land and sent into internal exile. Unlike Galleani, however, Buda, upon his release, worked undercover for the Mussolini government, as an agent provocateur "among anarchists, communists, and antifascists of Switzerland and France."[41] He died in Italy in 1963.

The lives of at least two other anarchists encountered in these pages took no less surprising turns. Arturo Giovannitti did a brief stint in Hollywood in 1931, writing dialogue for MGM movies dubbed in Italian.[42] And Ella Antolini, the beautiful "Dynamite Girl" arrested in 1918 with a suitcase full of explosives, later went to work at the upscale Priscilla of Boston bridal shop, where in 1956 she helped make gowns for members of the royal wedding of Grace Kelly and Prince Rainier of Monaco. Antolini had learned how to sew years earlier, while serving out her prison sentence at the Missouri State Penitentiary.[43] Giovannitti died in 1959; Antolini, in 1984.

— Elizabeth Glendower Evans remained an active reformer. When she celebrated her eightieth birthday in 1936, she was feted in the press as "one of the most unusual persons in Massachusetts" for fighting injustice despite being sometimes labeled a "misguided zealot." She died a year later, eulogized for her philanthropy and her lifelong activism.[44]

Other American supporters of the defendants lived out their lives in relative anonymity, without the public recognition bestowed on the better-known Evans.

Cerise Carman Jack, who tutored Nick in prison, befriended his family and stayed in touch with them after he died. Rosina was fond of her. "[I] allways hoped you was coming out to see us," Rosina wrote her in 1932. "I must say I will be very glad to see you." Cerise Jack committed suicide in 1935. Her daughter, Betty Jack Wirth, had "very little faith in the legal system for a long time" after the executions.[45] A teacher and world traveler, Betty Wirth died in 2006, a few months shy of her ninety-seventh birthday.

Virginia MacMechan, Vanzetti's tutor and inspiration for his hopeless love, kept her involvement private; her nieces and nephews had no idea that their aunt had once been caught up in the case. MacMechan died of cancer in the 1950s.[46]

For Mary Donovan, secretary of the defense committee, love appeared unexpectedly. Ivy Leaguer and union organizer Powers Hapgood had come to Boston for eleventh-hour demonstrations to save Sacco and Vanzetti. After the funeral, an exhausted trio of Hapgood, Donovan, and Aldino Felicani went to the countryside for a few days of rest on the farm where Donovan's father and sister lived. Mary's "courage and fighting spirit is wonderful," Hapgood wrote his parents. "I'm getting more and more in love with her."[47]

On December 28, 1927, four months to the day after the funeral of Sacco and Vanzetti, Donovan married Hapgood and moved with him to Pennsylvania, where he briefly worked to unionize coal miners. Donovan ran unsuccessfully for governor of Massachusetts on the Socialist ticket a year later. In 1932 in Indiana, where the couple eventually settled, Hapgood also ran unsuccessfully for governor on the Socialist ticket.

The couple had two children, the first, a girl, Barta, born in 1929. Her arrival was "one of the few completely right things that seem to have come out of the Sacco-Vanzetti tragedy." Barta's unusual first name was chosen to honor Bartolomeo, a man, Hapgood explained to his parents, whom Mary loved dearly. Indeed, speaking of the childless Vanzetti in 2001, Barta, then a woman of seventy-one years, conceded that at times "I feel like I am his child."[48]

Powers Hapgood died in a car crash near Indianapolis in 1949, when he was only forty-nine years old. Mary Donovan outlived her husband by many years. In 1973, at the age of eighty-seven, having participated in "most reform movements of the twentieth century," she died during the Watergate hearings.[49]

— Giovanni Vanzetti did not write a letter to his son for most of the last five years of Bartolomeo's life. Perhaps the estrangement intensified the father's grief. In 1929 a visitor to Villafalletto found Mr. Vanzetti "broken." Before the executions, he had been "erect as an oak tree, his voice firm." Now he "sits dazed and rigid in a chair in front of his home from morning to evening, like a statue. He seldom speaks to anyone." He said he was "waiting for my Creator to call me." Giovanni Vanzetti, 82, died four years after the death of his eldest child.[50]

Luigia Vanzetti's trip to America in 1927 had been unbearable. She had lost her brother and, worse if possible, he died outside the Church. Her father had instructed Luigia to "bring Barto home with you." She did—in ashes. As time passed, Luigia "suffered and cried so much that something went out in her brain," sister Vincenzina said. "She kept getting more and more depressed." Luigia dedicated her life to her brother's memory. She began to assemble the letters that Bartolo had been writing to the family since he first left Villafalletto at age thirteen, but she died in 1950, before the letters were published in Italy.[51]

— Rosina Sacco soldiered on. She did not do so alone. Ermanno Bianchini was a member of the defense committee who had fallen "hopelessly in love" with her. The two began living together as man and wife sometime in 1928. By

December of that year, she was using the name Bianchini, and referring to Ermanno as her husband.[52]

People gossiped. An article about the "secret marriage" appeared in print, prompting Elizabeth Evans to write a letter to the *Springfield Republican* in January 1932: "There has been nothing secret about Rosie's marriage. She said plainly . . . that she wanted all her husband's friends [to know] that she was marrying for the sake of her children. The man she has married is a gallant, upstanding mechanic, one of the early [members of the] Sacco-Vanzetti defense committee, and a man whom the children respect and love." The letter apparently had the unintended effect of calling more unwanted attention to the marriage. Shortly after Evans wrote it, *Time* magazine "revealed" the marriage of "Mrs. Rose M. Sacco, relict of Nicola Sacco . . .; and one Ermano Bianchini; 18 months after her husband was electrocuted."[53]

Rosina had a cheerful nature, with "not a malicious bone in her body," according to one of her grandsons. She didn't complain and, if she was upset, she didn't show it. She sewed her own clothes, made her own pasta, grew her own vegetables, tended flowers in a "beautiful" garden that was "neat as a pin," and raised chickens. Ermanno adored his wife, protected her, and took care of her and the children. The couple tried to have children together, but Rosina was never able to carry another pregnancy to term.[54]

Rosina, Ermanno, Dante, and Ines lived in Watertown, west of Boston on the banks of the Charles River. Dante and Ines were "wonderful kids, very well thought of," their next-door neighbor recalled , and people "were friendly but not nosy." When Gertrude Winslow paid a Christmas visit to the family one year, she found them "happier than one would have believed possible . . .!"[55]

Dante Sacco had "not one peep of interest in radical affairs," Elizabeth Evans observed in 1932. "He just has nothing to do with them, which greatly disappoints his mother and stepfather, who are hot radicals still." In this behavior he resembled many other children of Italian-American radicals, steering clear of the movement that had animated their parents.[56] Dante became a parts manager for a regional airline, married, and had three sons.[57] Ines also married, and had two sons.

In middle age, Rosina and Ermanno bought and managed a poultry farm. In old age they moved to a nursing home, and it was there that Rosina received the awful news that she had outlived her son, who died in 1971 of complications following surgery. Ermanno died in 1985. In 1989, more than sixty years after her first husband was executed, Rosina Zambelli Sacco Bianchini, 92, suffered a fall in the nursing home, and died. Her long life had been as full of drama as the plot of any of the Italian operas she loved so much.

Rosina Sacco's greatest achievement was to give her children the semblance of a normal life. She accomplished it by doing her best to lock out the past and live in the present. She seldom spoke about the case to her children; they in turn seldom spoke about it to their children; and family members almost never discussed it with outsiders who, they believed, would misinterpret and misquote them, invade their privacy, and exploit them for personal gain. The fears were not groundless. In one of his rare forays into the Sacco-Vanzetti universe, Dante attended a wake for Aldino Felicani, only to be so "pestered" by people there that he "got disgusted and left."[58]

In such circumstances withdrawal and silence were reasonable survival tactics. But they had drawbacks. For one thing, they were not sustainable. "No one can hide forever," Aldino Felicani acknowledged in 1960, when NBC was preparing to broadcast a drama based on the case.[59] Suppressed emotions re-emerged in other contexts. Dante sometimes threw a football to his sons back and forth over the roof of their house, re-creating in a way the games of catch he had once played with his father back and forth over the jail yard wall.

Surely the most damaging drawback of the family's silence was the way some people interpreted it as an admission of Sacco's guilt. Writer Upton Sinclair said that the family's silence must conceal "some dark secret." Writer Francis Russell went further, saying that the "only conclusion" he could draw from "the silence of the Sacco family is . . . an implication of guilt."[60]

Using this reasoning, one might just as easily conclude that Frederick Katzmann's lifelong silence about the case was also an admission of dark secrets, also an admission of guilt — in his case for withholding exculpatory evidence, colluding with federal intelligence agents, or suborning perjury.

In fact, any number of explanations for the silence of the Sacco family are plausible, including a fear of being misinterpreted or a desire to avoid reopening old wounds each time a new request for information surfaced.

The experience of losing a parent publicly and violently, of embodying a cause that is not your own, of being famous for something you know little about, of being idolized or demonized by strangers — this is an experience that perhaps only two other people in America have ever experienced in such a public way: Michael and Robert Meeropol, the sons of Julius and Ethel Rosenberg. Michael was ten and Robert six when their parents were executed for espionage in 1953.

Robert recalls in his memoirs, *An Execution in the Family*, that even at the age of six, he resolved to keep a low profile to avoid attracting attention. The brothers, who went by the name of their adoptive parents, Meeropol, spent years living in fear of being identified as the Rosenberg sons. As adults, having

chosen to reveal their identity, Robert says he felt uncomfortable and coated with "emotional residue" whenever he received special attention from his parents' supporters simply because of his lineage.[61] Similar feelings might have animated the Sacco family's aversion to the spotlight.

~ Frederick Parmenter and Alessandro Berardelli are the ghosts who still haunt the Sacco-Vanzetti case; their widows and children, the invisible victims.

Hattie Parmenter was seriously ill when her husband was murdered. Son Richard was twelve; daughter Jeannette, seven; and Hattie had cancer.[62]

Her husband had been "a man of sterling qualities, generous to a fault, Christian in every way, and ready at all times to help those who were unfortunate and needed aid." Now that his own family was in need, who would help them? Of Fred's twelve siblings, none was prepared to take in the children should Hattie die. "They had young families themselves," Jeannette Parmenter Murphy recalled in 2004. "My mother was discouraged. But she was a brave woman." To protect the children, Hattie "never talked about the events" in South Braintree or Dedham.[63]

Hattie Parmenter succumbed to her illness in 1925; her sister took in the orphaned children. Richard would become an engineer; Jeannette, a teacher. Jeannette said her brother "always felt cheated out of life. He needed a father." Still, Jeannette would come to believe that the evidence against Sacco and Vanzetti had not been strong enough to justify their conviction for killing her father.[64]

Sarah Berardelli, the other widow of South Braintree, was only twenty-eight when, an hour after the murders, a newspaper reporter located her and told her that her forty-four-year-old husband had been killed. She was "prostrated by the news."[65]

Parmenter was laid to rest in Brockton, Massachusetts. Photograph by Randy Ross.

Eight years earlier, Sarah Bisnovich had fallen in love with Alessandro Berardelli, then a barber in Waterbury, Connecticut, and had eloped with him in defiance of her family's wishes.[66] Sarah was a Jewish immigrant from Russia whose native language was Yiddish; her husband came from a small town in southern Italy and was almost surely Roman Catholic.[67] A justice of the peace performed the wedding ceremony. The cross-cultural marriage was no less happy for being unusual. Sarah and Alessandro had two children: Jacob Michelangelo (Jack), born in 1913, and Ida, born two years later. By 1920 Sarah was working at the Slater & Morrill factory, lining and stitching shoes, and she "always used to wait at the gate for [Alessandro] when he got through working." She was not at work on the day her husband was killed, however, most likely because Ida was hospitalized at the time with scarlet fever.[68]

Berardelli was a "family man in the true sense of the word, going to any extreme for his wife and children; he took a great pride in his family," a former employer recalled. Ironically, since Sarah married outside her faith without her family's approval and was at first disowned by them, Alessandro seems to have been comfortable following the customs of his wife's religion. The couple "resided in the Jewish section of nearly every city [they] lived in"; Alessandro visited the synagogue and observed "the Jewish feast [days and fast days] . . . the same as his wife"; and he even spoke some Yiddish.[69] In fact Alessandro Berardelli must have converted to Judaism at some point, because Sarah buried her husband in a Bisnovich family plot in a Jewish cemetery. His anglicized name, Alexander Berardell, and a Hebrew name, Abraham son of Abraham, a name typically given to converts, are both carved on his gravestone.

Sarah never recovered from the shock of losing her husband; she was "emo-

Berardelli was buried alongside his wife's relatives in a family plot in Connecticut. The location as well as the inscription indicate the strong likelihood that he had converted to Judaism. Photograph by Werner Hirsch.

tionally unsettled for the rest of her life." She moved back to Connecticut to be near her Bisnovich relatives, took a job in a mattress factory, and briefly considered putting her children in an orphanage.[70] In 1923 her relatives arranged for her to marry Nathan Albert, an Austrian immigrant and widower with three children whose wife had died in an influenza epidemic. Sarah made a brief reappearance in the news in 1927 when she was reported to have asked Governor Fuller to spare the lives of Sacco and Vanzetti, a report she quickly denied. Like Rosina Sacco and Hattie Parmenter, Sarah Berardelli never discussed the events of April 15, 1920, with her family.[71] Son Jack Berardelli joined the Merchant Marine. Daughter Ida married happily, became a housewife, and raised three children. Sarah Bisnovich Berardelli Albert died at the age of sixty, in 1952.

On April 15, 2010, near the spot where Frederick Parmenter and Alessandro Berardelli had been gunned down ninety years earlier, Braintree officials dedicated a monument to the memory of the two men, whose names "history has forgotten."[72]

∼ Robert Elliott — electrician and beloved husband, father, and Sunday school superintendent — executed thirty-five people in 1927 alone, including Sacco and Vanzetti, and close to four hundred people in six states over the course of his long career, including Bruno Richard Hauptmann, convicted kidnapper of Charles Lindbergh's baby.[73]

A powerful explosion tore through Elliott's New York home on May 18, 1928. Fortunately no one was seriously injured. In a familiar denouement, no culprit was ever identified. Elliott said he was targeted because he was "society's agent of legal death," but he didn't think that Sacco-Vanzetti sympathizers were behind the bombing.[74]

One of the great compartmentalizers of all time, Robert Elliott did his job even though he actually opposed capital punishment, believing it did not deter criminals. Except when electrocuting people, Elliott said, his life was "prosaic and pleasant."[75] He died in his own bed in 1939, at the age of sixty-five.

The Massachusetts electric chair served its deadly purpose sixty-five times over a span of forty-six years. The state used its old oaken killing machine for the last time in 1947. Beginning in the 1970s a series of judicial rulings eventually eliminated the death penalty under Massachusetts law.[76]

Another kind of hot seat outlasted the electric chair in Massachusetts, but not by long. The metal courtroom cages where defendants in capital cases had once been confined during trial were banned in 1963. Governor Endicott Peabody called the cages "a relic from colonial days [with] no place in the dispensing of twentieth century justice."[77]

— Speaking of relics, Charlestown State Prison was already more than a century old and "unfit for humans" when Vanzetti arrived there in 1920. Not much had improved twenty-six years later when Malcolm Little, later Malcolm X, was sent there to serve time for robbery. "I could lie on my cot and touch both walls," Malcolm recalled in his autobiography. "The toilet was a covered pail," and the cells still had no running water.[78] (Coincidentally, Malcolm, like Vanzetti, experienced an intellectual awakening at Charlestown.)

Charlestown was finally razed in 1957, and Bunker Hill Community College later erected on the site. The school enrolled its first class of students in 1973.[79]

Dedham Jail, Sacco's "hell hole," had become so overcrowded by the 1980s that two prisoners were being crammed into cells barely big enough for one. The jail was closed in 1992. For years it sat vacant, unheated, deteriorating, a tomb for squirrels and birds with a bad sense of direction.

As rundown as it was, the jail had a valuable asset: a prime location in a leafy neighborhood of historic homes near the center of picturesque Dedham. Eager developers submitted plans for the site to the state. The winning proposal called for adaptive reuse, preserving the façade of the jail but rehabbing the dark interior into luxury condos. Thus it was that granite-walled Dedham Jail became Stoneleigh, its cramped cells transformed into two- and three-bedroom units with large windows, open floor plans, balconies, and a community fitness center.[80]

The highest opening price for a unit at Stoneleigh was less than than the lowest opening price for a unit at another building with a role in the Sacco-Vanzetti story: the former headquarters of J. P. Morgan & Co., at the corner of Wall and Broad streets in Manhattan. After September 11, 2001, the New York financial district began to evolve into a mixed-use commercial and residential area. The former House of Morgan became Downtown by Starck, the first luxury condominium on Wall Street.[81] The scars that pockmark its façade are the only reminder of the day in 1920 when someone, perhaps Mario Buda, tried to blow it up.

— It was an open secret among members of the Massachusetts bar that the Sacco-Vanzetti case had exposed "serious imperfections in our methods of administering justice."[82] The chief imperfection was in the state's appellate procedures:

> A single judge of the Superior Court now presides over murder trials and passes not only on questions of law included in the trial of the indictment, but upon mixed questions of law and fact arising on motions for a new trial. The Supreme Judicial Court on appeal passes only on questions of law. As the verdict on such an indictment involves the issue of life and death, . . . the responsibility [is] too great to be thrown upon one [trial judge]. If he errs . . ., the result is irreparable.[83]

After the executions of Sacco and Vanzetti, reform efforts began almost immediately. It took years for them to succeed. Procedures were finally changed in 1939. Henceforth, when considering an appeal of a first-degree murder conviction, the Supreme Judicial Court could review both the law and the evidence, and could order a new trial "if satisfied that the verdict was against the law or the weight of the evidence, or because of newly discovered evidence, or for any other reason that justice may require."[84]

The impetus for the change was the worldwide perception that "a miscarriage of justice had occurred when Sacco and Vanzetti were executed."[85]

History never lets bygones be bygones.
~ Arthur M. Schlesinger

18 | TWO MYSTERIES

Surprisingly, Nicola Sacco and Bartolomeo Vanzetti, long dead, can still get people all riled up.

Pandemonium erupted at a public hearing in 1959. The Massachusetts legislature was considering a bill requesting Governor Furcolo to grant a posthumous pardon to Sacco and Vanzetti. Emotions ran wild on both sides of the issue, with one official predicting that a pardon would jeopardize "our judicial system and our very way of government." The legislature rejected the bill.[1]

Passions flared anew in 1977. Governor Michael Dukakis proclaimed the fiftieth anniversary of the executions to be Sacco and Vanzetti Memorial Day in Massachusetts, and declared "that any stigma and disgrace should be forever removed from [their] names." The proclamation was based on a legal analysis citing substantial ground for doubt that the trial had been fair. It provoked outrage among opponents, and the state senate voted to condemn the governor.[2]

More recently, organizers of a 2001 art exhibit, *Ben Shahn and the Passion of Sacco and Vanzetti*, were rebuffed by a potential sponsor for supporting "those radicals," and the exhibit's curator was shunned at a Harvard luncheon after speaking about President Lowell. And in 2006 the developer who converted Dedham Jail into Stoneleigh abandoned plans to place a historical marker about Sacco and Vanzetti on the building's grounds because neighbors found it "inappropriate to celebrate the life of two anarchists."[3]

Many people had once naively hoped that debate over the case would end with the funeral. "The chapter is closed. . . . Now let us go forward," the *Boston Herald* exhorted after the executions. Yet collective amnesia would not take hold. Instead, as Justice Brandeis accurately predicted, "the "end of S.V. is only the beginning" (a fact that puzzled Justice Holmes, who observed that a "thousand-fold worse cases of negroes come up from time to time, but the world does not worry over them").[4]

The reason why an old case still stirs controversy may be this basic: some people believe that Sacco and Vanzetti were innocent victims of prejudice run amok; others believe that they were cold-blooded murderers who got what they deserved, and despite the adamancy of partisans on both sides, doubt persists.

— The central mystery remains. Did Nicola Sacco and Bartolomeo Vanzetti commit robbery and murder on April 15, 1920?

Clues to the truth must lie in the evidence, but which evidence? Statements and items introduced at trial in 1921 constitute the only "real" evidence. Post-trial, new information continued to surface, during the six-year appeals process and later, in the years from 1927 to the present, when personal documents and official files became newly available. None of it was ever presented to a jury.

IDENTIFICATIONS

Presentation of identification testimony took up the most time at trial. Seven witnesses identified Sacco as someone they had seen before, during, or after the crime in South Braintree, but "[n]ot one of the witnesses against Sacco was at all times [including pre-trial] consistently positive in the identification."[5] More than four times as many witnesses—thirty-one—contradicted or refuted the seven witnesses who identified Sacco. Four witnesses identified Vanzetti as someone they had seen right before or soon after the crime; eight witnesses contradicted or refuted them. No witness identified Vanzetti as being at the scene while the crime was in progress.

Three new eyewitnesses came forward after the trial. All swore in affidavits that neither Sacco nor Vanzetti was among the bandits they had seen.

In the end all the identification witnesses probably cancelled each other out. Judge Thayer conceded as much in 1924 when he noted that, since the defense had called more witnesses than the prosecution, the verdicts "did not rest" on eyewitness testimony.[6]

ALIBIS

Nine witnesses backed up Sacco's alibi; six witnesses corroborated Vanzetti's alibi. No new alibi witnesses came forward after the trial.

CONSCIOUSNESS OF GUILT

Evidence in this category grew more important as the trial progressed. Arguments centered on two facts: that Sacco and Vanzetti were armed when arrested, and that they lied when interrogated.

These facts were undisputed, but the reasons behind them were a matter of fundamental disagreement. The defense claimed that Sacco and Vanzetti carried guns for self-defense and "to shoot in the woods," and that they lied to protect themselves and their comrades from political harassment and possible deportation. No, said the prosecution; the guns showed that Sacco and Vanzetti were criminals, and the lies showed that they were concealing criminal acts.

More than half a century after the trial, in 1977, the Massachusetts State Police released records that cast doubt on the prosecution's consciousness-of-guilt argument, and showed that some of the defendants' "lies" were not lies after all.

When Katzmann cross-examined the defendants at trial, he read aloud a long list of responses from their jailhouse interrogations and got them to admit that they were lies. He read from what was assumed to be an accurate transcript of the interrogations, but he never introduced it as evidence, and the defense never had a copy of it. The transcript surfaced in 1977 as part of the police files. It shows, William Young and David Kaiser point out in *Post-mortem*, that Katzmann misquoted or distorted statements from the interrogations.[7] For example, at trial Katzmann chided Vanzetti for not remembering how many times he had slept in Boston, and he reproached Sacco for asserting he had worked on the day of the crime, but the transcript shows that under interrogation Vanzetti had actually been more certain, and Sacco less certain, than Katzmann accused them of being.[8]

Minutes of the secret grand jury proceedings also surfaced after 1977. In them, Young and Kaiser discover "that Sacco simply did not make the most damaging statement attributed to him — namely, that he had been working on 15 April." On the contrary, according to the testimony of a state police officer who heard him, Sacco, when questioned after his arrest, said that on April 15 "he was in Boston . . . [m]aking some arrangement about his passport . . . [t]o go to Italy" — exactly what he would later claim at trial.[9]

Still, didn't the fact that Sacco and Vanzetti were armed when arrested show consciousness of guilt? In 1927 Katzmann himself conceded that such behavior was commonplace. "It has been my experience," he told members of the governor's advisory committee, "that Italians carry some sort of weapons."[10]

Carrying weapons and using them are two completely different matters. Judge Thayer told jurors that if they believed the defendants tried to reach for their weapons when arrested, as the prosecution contended, that was evidence of consciousness of guilt. Sacco and Vanzetti both denied going for their guns.[11]

The account of the men's attempted gun grabs originated with Brockton policeman Michael Connolly, who testified at the Dedham trial that, when arrested, both defendants tried to draw their guns — Vanzetti, on the streetcar; Sacco, twice in the police car. However, Connolly had not made this claim earlier — not at Vanzetti's Plymouth trial, not to the grand jury, and not in a statement he gave to Chief Stewart a mere twelve days before the Dedham trial began. The fact that Connolly had at least three opportunities before Dedham to speak about the attempted gun grab but said nothing casts deep doubt on his later claim.[12]

PHYSICAL EVIDENCE

Jurors never knew that fingerprints had been taken from the Buick, or that the crime-scene cap had been found more than twenty-four hours after the crime, and had been torn by a policeman, not by Sacco.

Of the physical evidence jurors did learn about, none was more persuasive than the ballistics evidence.

Vanzetti was carrying a .38-caliber Harrington & Richardson revolver, serial number G-82581, when he was arrested. (Captain Proctor recorded the serial numbers of both men's guns on an undated property list.)[13] Prosecutors argued that Vanzetti's revolver was the same gun "that poor Berardelli tried to draw from his pocket to defend himself. . . . [S]ome person took that revolver off the person of the dying Berardelli. . . . Sacco . . . took the gun and it eventually came into the possession of his co-defendant Vanzetti."[14]

Even at trial in 1921, corroboration for this theory was slim. No witness had seen Berardelli with a gun on the day of the crime, or seen a bandit take a gun from him. In addition, three defense witnesses testified to a completely different ownership trail for Vanzetti's gun.

In 1927 former gun shop employee Lincoln Wadsworth told members of the governor's advisory committee that his trial testimony had been misleading, and that "there are thousands of times more chances" that Vanzetti's gun was not Berardelli's "than that it was."[15]

There could have been no question that Berardelli's gun and Vanzetti's gun were one and the same if they had had the same serial number. A match could not be attempted, however, because, as Wadsworth explained in 1927, the shop's "records were very incomplete. . . . [T]here was no record of this serial number [on Berardelli's gun] in court. There was nobody had the number in their possession; nobody knew it. . . . [The .38-caliber Harrington & Richardson model was very] common and very cheap, and there are thousands and thousands of them in existence today. . . . [T]he only way you can distinguish them is by their serial number. . . . [But the] number of the [Berardelli] revolver . . . was never on the record."[16]

Or so everyone believed for years. Then, in 1977, with the release of police files, a startlingly different possibility emerged from the notes of Michael Stewart.

Chief Stewart had conducted several interviews in early 1921 to gather evidence for trial. In one such interview on January 31, Sarah Berardelli told

Stewart that her husband had been "employed by the Slater & Morrill people [for] about six months previous to his death," which would mean that he had gone on the factory payroll around October 1919. She also said that the gun her husband used "was given to him by Mr. Parmenter and was the property of the firm." In another interview on February 12, Mrs. Berardelli clarified that Parmenter gave her husband a gun to use on paydays.[17]

Stewart's notes never surfaced in the courtroom. If they had, jurors would also have learned that on February 16, Stewart "found on the revolver book of C.A. Noyes Hardware Company in Brockton a[n] entry showing that on October 10, 1919 F.A. Parmenter purchased a Harrington and Richardson, *32 calibre*, nickel finish, centre fire revolver *No. 394717* [emphasis added]."[18]

The purchase date coincides with the time frame of Berardelli's start date and with the time frame when Parmenter had to replace a gun that had disappeared from the factory.[19] Thus the gun that Parmenter bought at Noyes Hardware may well have been the same gun that he loaned Berardelli on paydays. If this is so, then prosecutors knew but suppressed the fact that Berardelli's gun and Vanzetti's gun had different serial numbers and were of different calibers.

~ Sacco was carrying a .32 caliber Colt automatic pistol, "the all-time best seller in Colt pocket automatics," when he was arrested.[20] The prosecution contended that, of four bullets removed from Berardelli's body, the one that had actually killed Berardelli—the bullet marked "III" by the doctor who extracted it from the guard's body, and the only one of the six bullets removed from both bodies that "was assuredly of Winchester manufacture"—this bullet, and only this bullet, had been fired by Sacco's gun.[21]

This was the single most damning argument to emerge from the entire trial. If Bullet III came through Sacco's Colt, then Sacco must be guilty of murder (unless someone else had used his gun, a claim which no one ever made).

At trial in 1921, expert witnesses disagreed about Bullet III. "[F]irearms identification in 1921 was in an embryonic stage," notes forensics investigator James Starrs.[22]

The controversy surrounding Bullet III intensified after the trial.

In 1923 Captain Proctor withdrew his testimony that Bullet III was "consistent with being fired by [Sacco's] pistol," saying he had found no "affirmative evidence whatever that this so-called mortal bullet had passed through the particular Sacco's pistol." The same year that Proctor recanted, Albert Hamilton, an expert witness on ballistics matters hired by the defense, also swore in an affidavit that Bullet III had not been fired by Sacco's gun.[23]

Four years later, in 1927, the defense shocked members of the advisory committee by suggesting that the prosecution had tampered with the bullet.

William Thompson and Herbert Ehrmann made the charge in a letter they sent to Governor Fuller on June 15, 1927. The attorneys raised doubts about the authenticity of certain shells introduced as evidence, then continued: "We also think the mortal bullet is under the same suspicion. It was evidently not fired through Sacco's pistol; but it may well have been fired through some Colt automatic 32 calibre pistol and substituted for the No. 3 bullet actually taken by Dr. Magrath from Berardelli's body. The marks on the base of it were evidently not made by the same man that marked the other three bullets taken from Berardelli's body."[24]

Thompson and Ehrmann repeated the allegation of doubts about the authenticity of the mortal bullet in a brief for the advisory committee, and Ehrmann restated it again in oral arguments to the committee. Somebody had disposed of the real Bullet III, Ehrmann implied, and replaced it with a bullet test-fired through Sacco's gun. He couldn't imagine "that the District Attorney or [the medical examiner] would be a party to substituting any exhibits," Ehrmann said, but "I do not have such hesitation about suggesting it as concerning the police."[25]

"It was a desperate theory," one commentator has observed, "for it made it clear that Sacco could be innocent only if the Commonwealth itself was guilty of a grave crime."[26]

"Are you suggesting that the Colt bullet was invented for the occasion?" Judge Grant asked Ehrmann in disbelief. The advisory committee roundly rejected the theory as "devoid of truth" and characterized the case as "rather desperate on its merits when counsel feel it necessary to resort to a charge of this kind."[27]

Defense lawyers *were* desperate in the summer of 1927. Nevertheless, the substitution theory may explain otherwise inexplicable testimony. Six bullets were pumped into the victims. Bullet III was the only one fired by a Colt. The other five were fired by a different gun. However, no witness saw one bandit shoot two guns, and the only witness who claimed to have seen two bandits shoot Berardelli did not identify Sacco or Vanzetti. Thus, "[t]here is no testimony which accounts for the single bullet from Sacco's Colt."[28] If one gunman fired all the bullets, then, say Young and Kaiser, the inauthenticity of Bullet III is "[v]irtually conclusive" and probably due to substitution of a test-fired bullet for the original Bullet III by police officers.[29]

In 1927, 1944, 1961, 1982, and, most recently, 1983, various experts examined the aging ballistics evidence in the Sacco-Vanzetti case. The 1982 tests were inconclusive, and details of the 1944 tests are unknown. In the other cases, experts determined that Bullet III was fired by Sacco's Colt (which would be true whether it had been fired at the crime scene or during testing).[30]

A flaw in the bullet substitution theory has been pointed out by James Starrs, who reviewed the firearms evidence in 1986. If a test-fired bullet was substituted for the actual Bullet III, then the defense experts who swore that the Bullet III they examined did not come from Sacco's gun either erred or lied.[31]

— In 1937 Sergeant Edward J. Seibolt of the Boston Police Department mentioned to a cub reporter for the *Boston Globe* that he had worked on the Sacco-Vanzetti case and that "we switched the murder weapon in that case. . . . [W]e suspected the other side of switching weapons, so we just switched them back."

Seibolt's statement came to light in 1988 when Charles Whipple, the cub reporter in question, who had gone on to become an editor and ombudsman for the newspaper, spoke about it publicly for the first time. Whipple said he had kept silent because the sergeant had said he would deny making the statement and because "I was timid in those days."[32]

Only one "murder weapon" had ever been entered in evidence. That was Sacco's gun, and its identity was never in dispute. Sergeant Siebolt's tale of reciprocal weapon switching may refer to an episode in 1924, when it was discovered that a new barrel had been inserted into Sacco's pistol, and that Sacco's old barrel had been inserted into a new pistol belonging to defense expert Albert Hamilton, even though both pistols had supposedly been under lock and key in the custody of the court.[33] The prosecution implied that Hamilton had boldly made the switch while disassembling and reassembling three pistols in open court during hearings in November 1923, in order to provide grounds for another motion for a new trial. The defense implied that unknown persons had obtained access to the locker and cupboard where the guns were stored and made the switch to prevent new test firings. The real perpetrator of the switch was never positively determined.[34] Siebolt's mind-boggling statement to Whipple lends credence to the disturbing possibility that both sides tampered with Sacco's pistol.

— In time, as the case grew older and colder, hearsay and rumor superseded evidence. It began most famously when Fred Moore and, later, Carlo Tresca were said to have told others that they had come to believe that Sacco, and perhaps Vanzetti, had been guilty all along.

Neither Moore nor Tresca ever spoke publicly or wrote about this. Moore relayed his doubts in a conversation with Upton Sinclair, whom he met in Denver when the writer was researching *Boston*, his documentary novel about the case. Moore had told William Thompson in 1923 that he believed "strongly" in his clients' innocence, but in 1927 he told Sinclair that "he had come reluctantly to the conclusion that Sacco was guilty of the crime for which he had died and that possibly Vanzetti also was guilty."[35] Moore offered no reason for his change of opinion other than to say that some anarchists raised money by stealing, and that criminal lawyers succeeded by "inventing alibis and hiring witnesses." Moore conceded that neither the defendants nor their friends had ever admitted the slightest hint of guilt.

Sinclair next interviewed Moore's ex-wife, who was "astounded" at Moore's assertion of his former clients' guilt. "I worked on the case with him all through the years, and I knew about it as intimately as he did," Lola Moore told Sinclair. "He never gave me a hint of such an idea. . . . Fred is embittered because he was dropped from the case, and it has poisoned his mind." William Thompson telegraphed Sinclair: "Judge McAnarney trustworthy and well informed emphatically contradicts Moore's confession to you,."[36]

Like Moore, Carlo Tresca was a Sacco-Vanzetti supporter who defected from the ranks. Tresca had, along with Elizabeth Gurley Flynn, recommended Moore to the defense committee. In 1942 journalist Max Eastman, having heard "whispers" of Sinclair's discoveries, asked Tresca to tell him the truth about Sacco and Vanzetti. "Sacco was guilty but Vanzetti was not," Tresca replied. Then the men's private conversation was interrupted, the discussion ended, and, writes Eastman, "I had no opportunity to see Carlo alone again before he was . . . shot by an assassin. . . . But that quick and simple answer from such a source settled the question for me." Tresca made similar statements to at least two other people during the same time period, but Roger Baldwin and Beatrice Tresca, Carlo's daughter, said Tresca never expressed any doubts about Sacco's innocence to them.[37]

Why might the former loyalists have changed their minds?

Moore had lost a high-profile case, and been fired. He had been publicly reprimanded by the judge. His legal career had tanked. He had ample reason to be embittered, as his ex-wife described him.

As for Tresca, he had quarreled about strategy with other anarchists, particularly followers of Luigi Galleani. Tresca was not a hero to all Italian anarchists, as Eastman claimed. On the contrary, historian Nunzio Pernicone points out that, toward "the end of his life, Tresca became disillusioned and embittered because of the terrible treatment that he received from some fellow anarchists ... [who,] mainly for reasons of political rivalry, had waged a relentless campaign to destroy [his] standing in the movement. Their attacks, which ... reached a peak in 1938, took a heavy spiritual toll. ... It is probably no coincidence, therefore, that every known instance of Tresca's pronouncing Sacco guilty occurred after the climax of [the] campaign against him."[38]

— Believers in split guilt—the theory that Sacco was guilty and Vanzetti was not—seek affirmation by comparing statements of the men themselves. Vanzetti's letters are "startlingly different from Sacco's in the unmistakable explicitness of [his] assertions of innocence and denials of guilt," New York attorney James Grossman wrote in 1962. "Sacco has been parsimonious even in general expressions of his own innocence."[39]

Sacco was indeed parsimonious in *writing* about his innocence. This author has found only two such written references. In a 1920 note to fellow prisoner (and jailhouse informer) Domenic Carbonari, Sacco said, "I have been arrested but I am innocent. They have accused me of having committed a terrible crime, simply because I have been the defender of the workers and also because I am an Italian." And in a 1924 letter to Vanzetti, Sacco wrote that "we are still on our feet—of course, because we are always keep in our soul the hope and faithful in our innocent."[40]

This taciturnity is balanced by two overlooked facts. Sacco, who struggled with English, wrote far fewer letters in general than his more linguistically gifted comrade (fifty-eight letters by Sacco, compared to one hundred forty-seven by Vanzetti, in the volume of their correspondence in English). And Sacco's *spoken* declarations of his innocence were far more extensive than the single one cited by Grossman.

He said in conversation that "he had never killed any man," Carbonari reported in 1920.[41]

"I am innocent!" Sacco cried out in the courtroom in 1921. "They kill an innocent m[a]n! They kill two innocent men!"[42]

"He said he did not do it, and the police framed him," said a doctor who examined him in 1921.[43]

"Luigi," Sacco told visiting attorney Luigi Quintiliano in 1922, "continue to assert our complete innocence. You will never regret it. I am innocent of this crime as my Ines and my Dante could be."[44]

"[I] never kill anybody," and "I am innocent," he told doctors at Boston Psychopathic Hospital in 1923.[45]

"I am never been guilty, never—not yesterday nor today nor forever," he said in court before being sentenced in 1927.[46]

"I am innocent. I cannot, even for the sake of my family, say that I am guilty," he told his lawyer's wife in 1927.[47]

Unlike Vanzetti, Sacco did not declare his innocence in the final moments of life. Was this a sign of guilt? Or was it a sign that, like a later death row prisoner who lived to tell the tale, he had long since "stopped bothering to tell people he was innocent; no one who believed in him seemed able to do anything about his plight anyway [, and] most people simply . . . would not accept the possibility that he was innocent"?[48]

The one person who more than anyone should have known whether Sacco was guilty or innocent was his co-defendant, and Vanzetti's opinion was clear. "I am innocent and I am fully convinced of Sacco's innocence [and] for this reason I would like to share the fate that would be decided at a joint proceeding," Vanzetti wrote his sister in 1923. Since Vanzetti repeatedly expressed his intention to fight for exoneration, it's unlikely he would have wanted "to share the fate" of Sacco if he believed Sacco were guilty.[49]

Vanzetti addressed the subject again in his final days. "From the Death House" on August 21, 1927, he wrote Dante Sacco that "all that I know of your father, he is not a criminal. . . . [E]ach one who will say otherwise of your father and I, is a liar. . . . [R]emember always these things; we are not criminals; they convicted us on a frame-up. . . ." The following day, his last, Vanzetti solemnly reassured William Thompson "with a sincerity which I could not doubt, . . . that both he and Sacco were absolutely innocent of the South Braintree crime."[50]

— Luigi Galleani believed that "revolutionary expropriation" was not theft. In an egalitarian society, he wrote, "theft has no meaning. . . . Therefore, among anarchists, no question of principle concerning theft exists. . . . [If] revolutionaries attack a bank . . . [and] deliver their loot to insurrectionary committees to further the revolutionary movement in their community . . . you cannot disapprove."[51]

Or, as Katherine Anne Porter put it: "Anarchy—another variation on the Robin Hood myth."[52]

Fred Moore had told Upton Sinclair that "some of the anarchists [raised] funds for their movement by robbery. It was strictly honest from the group's point of view—that is to say, they kept none of the money for themselves." Anarchists interviewed by Paul Avrich spoke of bank robberies and train robberies, as well as fencing of stolen merchandise, counterfeiting, and arson to collect insurance money.[53] In this context, might Sacco and Vanzetti have committed the crime in South Braintree but considered themselves innocent because they handed the money over to support their radical movement?

In 1920 Sacco told Mary Heaton Vorse that he would be glad to die for the cause of anarchism, but "they have arrested me for a gunman job. . . . Do I want to go back to gorilla days, shooting men in the back? Why should they say I do things like that, when I love all people . . . the same."[54]

Sacco made similar remarks to a psychiatrist seven years later. He believed in expropriation, Sacco told Dr. Abraham Myerson, but he also said "that he never could in his philosophy or in his character have taken a pistol and robbed a lot of workmen of their payroll."[55]

Vanzetti addressed the issue of expropriation as well. "I wished with all my faculties that the social wealth would belong to every [human being]," he wrote Elizabeth Evans in 1921. "But this do not mean robbery for a[n] insurrection. The insurrection . . . do not need dollars. It need love, light, spirit of sacrifice, ideas, conscience, instincts. . . . And all this . . . can be seeded . . . in many ways, but not by robbery and murder for robbery."[56]

These private statements, made by Nick and Bartolomeo to a journalist, a doctor, and a friend, underscore the unlikelihood of their committing murder for money, whatever the cause. Even if Sacco and Vanzetti did believe that assassination and theft could be justified for the greater good, their likeliest targets would have been symbolic ones — capitalist institutions, politicians, industrialists. Their least likely target would have been the payroll cash of fellow workers. The idea may not be unthinkable, but it is illogical.

In an effort to trace the stolen payroll, Fred Katzmann asked the U.S. Department of Justice to find out if anarchists had come into any large sums of money after the holdup. The department did not make its files public before the executions, but it did provide a summary to reporter W. G. Gavin. His story, published nine hours before Sacco and Vanzetti died, recounts that the "Boston office [of the Department of Justice] . . . sent an inquiry to the New York office and was informed that the radicals there had not come into any large sums."[57]

Thus it was the United States government that ended up making a strong argument against South Braintree as a crime of anarchist expropriation.

— Over the years various people have concluded that this or that nugget of information — a letter, a fire, a scratch mark — revealed the whole truth about Sacco and Vanzetti. It is frustrating to realize that, as James Grossman once noted, "whatever conclusion we adopt, all the facts will never lie comfortably side by side no matter how much we try to make them fit each other."[58]

The men were armed when arrested, but said they needed guns — Vanzetti for protection when carrying money, Sacco for his night job. They lied when interrogated, but said they did so to protect their comrades. Some witnesses identified them; many more could not.

Their weapons were linked to the crime, but in Vanzetti's case the link turns out to have been almost surely false. Sacco's case is less certain. Generations of forensics experts have determined that Bullet III was fired through Sacco's gun. This cannot be ignored. Nor can it be ignored that it was the defense that requested the test firing, and that Sacco approved since he "was not afraid."[59] How was it possible that only one of the six bullets that hit the victims was fired from a Colt? No witness saw a bandit with two guns, and the only witness who reported seeing Berardelli shot by two bandits did not identify Sacco or Vanzetti.

The questions don't stop. What happened to the stolen money? Why didn't police keep the fingerprints from the Buick? Who were the other three bandits? Why were they never identified and brought to trial? Were Sacco and Vanzetti ruthless enough to shoot Parmenter and Berardelli? If so, why weren't they ruthless enough to shoot their arresting officers and escape? "Do you suppose for one minute that the kind of fellows who would . . . murder two men in broad daylight, . . . would . . . let a cop grab them? . . . [T]hat sort would go for their rods in a flash and try to smoke their way out," said Sergeant Ellsworth Jacobs of the New Bedford police. Sacco did not have "the courage to commit such an act as the Braintree murder," an acquaintance told police.[60]

"It was never intimated . . . at the trial nor at any time subsequent thereto, that Sacco and Vanzetti had any prior experience at holdups or any association with bandits," Supreme Court Associate Justice William O. Douglas observed in a 1969 study of the case. "There was no claim that the money obtained by the robbery . . . ever found its way into their pockets. There was no claim that their financial condition was in any way changed after April 15. There was no claim that after the murders either Sacco or Vanzetti altered his manner of living or shifted his employment" or went into hiding. In fact, on April 16, 1920, "the day after the murder he's supposed to have done, Sacco was in his garden early as usual and was at his [factory] bench when the seven o'clock whistle blew."[61]

In 1996 Joseph Kadane and David Schum undertook an exhaustive scientific study of evidence from the case, using complex mathematical equations, chains of reasoning, and probabilistic analyses. Their bottom line: Vanzetti was innocent, and the case against Sacco was not proven.[62]

Beyond the screeds of partisans on both sides of the divide, beyond a reasonable doubt, we still know only pieces of the truth about Sacco and Vanzetti. The whole truth remains exasperatingly elusive. The guilt of Sacco and Vanzetti seems unlikely, but neither their guilt nor their innocence can be proven. The case is still an unsolved mystery.

— And one mystery leads to another. If Sacco and Vanzetti did not rob and kill on April 15, 1920, who did?

Members of the criminal underworld, according to Massachusetts state police captain William Proctor. Professional criminals, according to former federal agents Fred Weyand, Lawrence Letherman, and, they claimed, their colleagues. People behaving "with typical gangster ruthlessness," said Herbert Ehrmann.[63]

Joe Morelli and his four brothers — Mike, Frank, Fred, and Pasquale — were, by any standard, professional criminals.

Joe, the oldest, age 39 in 1920, was the boss of the Morelli gang at the time of the South Braintree crime. He boasted of his gang leadership. Between stretches of jail time, Joe Morelli was accused of engaging in "robbery, murder, counterfeiting, dope peddling, living off prostitution, [and] rum-running." The *Providence Evening Bulletin* called him a "white slaver," a term that police officers also used to describe his brother Mike Morelli, "known as a 'pimp'" and "an astute car thief."[64]

Joe may have been the boss in 1920, but it was his brother Frank (Butsey) Morelli who was "the toughest of the mob," "the most dangerous of the brothers," "a tough stone killer, an old don who wouldn't give the right time of day to anybody he didn't like." Tough guy Frank was also "a good dresser and always appeared to be supplied with money." He would go on to become the first organized crime boss of New England.[65]

All the brothers lived in Providence except Mike, and he lived only thirty miles away in New Bedford. Together with various accomplices, the Morellis were "notorious freight car thieves in the immediate post–World War I years."[66]

In October 1919, Joe, Fred, and Pasquale Morelli were arrested in Providence and accused of stealing from freight cars at the city train yards. Their preferred merchandise, their "specialty," was shoes and textiles. They knew exactly where to find what they wanted because, in the factory towns where the shipments originated, they posted lookouts to tell them into which cars the goods were loaded. When the cars reached Providence, a member of the gang pried open the locked trains "with a brake-pin and . . . rolled out the boxes . . . for Joe to collect . . . when the coast was clear." Joe sent some of the loot to New York to be fenced.[67]

In December 1919, and again in March 1920, Joe, Fred, and Pasquale — "Joseph

Morelli et als."—were indicted on multiple counts related to the railroad heists, including the theft of several hundred pairs of shoes shipped from the Rice & Hutchins and the Slater & Morrill factories in South Braintree, a town where they were said to have employed lookouts. On May 10, Frank Morelli was also indicted, and his case consolidated with that of his brothers. Their trial began the next day. They were found guilty on several counts, and in June 1920 all the brothers except Mike were sentenced to terms of from two to ten years in federal prison in Atlanta, Georgia.[68]

On April 15, the day that robbers hijacked the Slater & Morrill payroll and murdered the guards, Fred Morelli was in jail, but his four brothers were "out on bail or otherwise at liberty."[69]

Unbeknownst to investigators in South Braintree, police officers in New Bedford were already suspicious about the possible involvement of the Morellis in the events of April 15. Sergeant Jacobs had noticed that someone was switching Rhode Island license plate number 154E from one car to another. Before April 15, Jacobs spotted the plate on a Buick that Mike Morelli was driving. The observant officer noticed it again on the Buick on April 15, but on April 24 he spotted it on a Cole 8 auto parked outside a restaurant where Frank Morelli was meeting with associates. That group, said Jacobs, became "extremely nervous" when he questioned them about the license plate, one man reaching "for his hip pocket . . . [as if] he was going to draw a gun."[70]

"At the time of the South Braintree murder and payroll robbery," Jacobs would later swear in an affidavit, "I suspected the Morrells [sic] and discussed my suspicions with then Inspector [Raphael] Pieraccini [of the New Bedford Police Department] who seemed to share them. However, as I had no definite evidence I dropped the matter after the arrest of Sacco and Vanzetti."[71]

There the matter rested, and there it probably would have rested forever had it not been for Celestino Madeiros, and the trail that led from his confession to the Morellis.

— Herbert Ehrmann's first assignment after joining the defense team in May 1926 was to investigate Madeiros's confession. Since, on April 15, 1920, Madeiros had been living in Providence, and had subsequently worked in nearby Seekonk, Massachusetts, Ehrmann began his inquiries in those towns, and immediately hit "pay dirt in Providence." Madeiros had said that the men who recruited him for South Braintree were "engaged in robbing freight cars in Providence. . . . They had been stealing silk, shoes, cotton, etc., from freight cars and sending it to New York." Police officers in Providence now told Ehrmann that a gang fitting that description did indeed operate in the city: the

Morelli gang. Once the Providence police established that most members of the gang had been at liberty on April 15, "it was possible," said Ehrmann, "to believe in Madeiros."[72]

Ehrmann built a circumstantial case alleging that the five bandits in South Braintree had been Joe and Frank Morelli, plus accomplices Tony Mancini, Celestino Madeiros, and Steve "the Pole" Benkosky as driver, with a sixth bandit, Mike Morelli, stationed in the woods to handle the exchange of getaway cars.[73]

No jury would ever have the opportunity to consider the Morelli/Madeiros hypothesis. On October 23, 1926, Judge Thayer denied the motion for a new trial. The five criminals whom Ehrmann had placed in the murder car would never be called to testify about South Braintree.

But if hearsay can be believed, both Frank Morelli and Joe Morelli eventually confessed to taking part in the crime. (Of the other three bandits whom Ehrmann placed in the car, Madeiros had already confessed; Benkosky was murdered before Ehrmann's investigation began; and Mancini, doing time for murder, told Ehrmann that "there isn't anything I know" about South Braintree, but that Sacco and Vanzetti were "not stick-up men.")[74]

Frank Morelli's confession came by way of Vincent Teresa, a high-ranking figure in the New England underworld who turned informant and testified against several other mobsters before entering the federal witness protection program in the 1970s.[75] In *My Life in the Mafia*, Teresa recounts that Frank Morelli told him he was at South Braintree.

Frank, known as Butsey, "had an adopted kid, Buddy. That boy was his life," said Teresa. The son was unaware of his father's criminal enterprises. When, in the 1950s, a Boston newspaper reported that Butsey, then ill and retired, "had been behind the robbery-murder in the Sacco-Vanzetti case, Butsey sued. . . . 'What they said was true, but it's going to hurt my kid,'" he told Teresa. "'We whacked them out, we killed those guys in the robbery. . . . These two greaseballs [Sacco and Vanzetti] took it on the chin.'" To Teresa's question "Did you really do this?," Butsey looked "right into my eyes, and said: 'Absolutely, Vinnie. These two suckers took it on the chin for us. That shows you how much justice there really is.'"[76]

Joe Morelli's confession came by way of Morris Ernst, a lawyer in New York who in the 1930s and 1940s took a stab at investigating the Morelli hypothesis on his own. "I have had talks with Joe Morelli," Ernst said. "I have had letters with him. I have seen him with his counsel. . . . I listed up hundreds of questions [to ask him]. . . . I went up to Providence and sat with Morelli for hours,

Joe Morelli told Morris Ernst that he got rid of the South Braintree money boxes by tossing them here, in Canada Pond on the border between Providence and North Providence. Photograph by Rey Tejada.

and I examined him. . . . [He] stated details [about the South Braintree crime] no one could have known but somebody on the job."[77]

Joe Morelli described for Ernst the source of the stolen cars and license plates, the escape route from South Braintree, the switch from one car to another, and the size and material of the money boxes. Morelli also said that he had gotten rid of the boxes, which were lying where he had thrown them, at the bottom of Canada Pond, a small but deep body of water, spring-fed and sandy-bottomed, on the border between Providence and North Providence. "When he told me where the money box[es were] thrown," Ernst recalled years later, "I said . . . that this would not exclude Sacco and Vanzetti because he might have been with them on the job. . . . I forget his exact words, but it was complete disdain. These 'guys [knew] nothing about this.'"[78]

— Morris Ernst had a symbiotic relationship with Joe Morelli. Ernst wanted information from the gangster, and Morelli wanted Ernst to help him find, of all things, a publisher for his autobiography. In 1939 Morelli told Ernst that, while in prison, he had written the story of his life, including the Sacco-Vanzetti case.

Morelli demanded twenty-five thousand dollars for his opus, a sum that neither Ernst nor a publisher would come close to matching, and so, said Ernst, "I failed, I didn't snatch [the manuscript] or get it away from him."[79]

Eleven years later, a reporter for the *Providence Journal* made another attempt to get the mobster's remarks on the record, but that effort also failed. Joe Morelli was by then terminally ill (although even "when he was dying he still had a couple of broads hustling upstairs," according to a policeman). Morelli agreed to talk to reporter Ben Bagdikian about Sacco and Vanzetti, but he slipped into a coma before Bagdikian arrived, and never regained conscious-ness. He died the next day.[80]

Ten more years passed. In 1960 writer Francis Russell tracked down Helen Morelli, Joe's granddaughter, in Providence. She said she had the autobiogra-phy, but she would not agree to show it to Russell. A year later, however, Rus-sell claimed that he "finally manage[d] to learn the contents of Joe Morelli's document." How this occurred, he did not explain. According to Russell's un-corroborated account of the manuscript, Joe Morelli said that he planned the South Braintree crime with five men — Sacco, Vanzetti, Mario Buda, Ricardo Orciani, and Ferruccio Coacci — but that the five double-crossed him by pull-ing off the job ahead of schedule, without him. Also according to Russell, Joe said that security guard Alessandro Berardelli "was another of his confeder-ates," and that the five holdup men "killed Berardelli because he recognized them."[81] (If Coacci had been there, Berardelli would indeed have recognized him, because Coacci had worked at Slater & Morrill and was "well acquainted with Officer Baradilli [sic]." But, as assistant district attorney Harold Williams had admitted at trial, the prosecution could not "place [Coacci, Buda, or Or-ciani] in South Braintree.")[82]

Russell's account of "Morelli's document" is unverifiable. But nearly forty years later, in 1998, the Harvard Law School Library acquired a copy of a man-uscript purportedly by Joe Morelli.[83] Unfortunately the manuscript, once as elusive and sought-after as an ivory-billed woodpecker, settles nothing. It shows Morelli's familiarity with the South Braintree case, but this knowledge was known to have been acquired at least in part from books.[84] It contains confusing contradictions, referring at one point to the South Braintree crime as poorly planned, and at another as perfectly planned. Morelli also says that Sacco and Vanzetti were well-known as professional criminals, a characteriza-tion at total variance from the record.[85]

~ Despite the criminal records of the Morellis and the lack thereof for Sacco and Vanzetti, there are gaps in the case against the Morelli mob. The fact that the Morellis had previously used lookouts in South Braintree does not ad-equately explain how they — or others — could have timed and executed the April 15 heist so well.

For that, the criminals would have needed an inside man — if not a willing accomplice, then an unwilling one whom they could threaten.

~ Alessandro Berardelli sailed away from his homeland at the age of 14, ac-companied by an older married sister, Maria Lucia Berardelli, 21. When the siblings landed in New York on an October day in 1890, they carried all their worldly possessions in a single suitcase.[86]

Maria Lucia joined her husband, Pasquale Picchione, who had immigrated two years earlier. Their first child was born the following year. Maria Lucia then went back to Italy. Pasquale accompanied her, later returned to the United States, and then made at least one more round-trip to visit her in Italy. By the time Maria Lucia returned to the United States to stay in 1899, she had two more children. A year later, she gave birth to a fourth child.[87]

While his sister was in Italy, the teenaged Alessandro presumably spent at least some time with his brother-in-law. Pasquale Picchione had settled in Providence. In 1897 he was working there as a laborer, but within seven years he had become the proprietor of his own business, Pasquale Picchione Company, a tavern at 377 Atwells Avenue, in the Federal Hill section of the city.[88]

When Picchione opened his bar there, immigrants were already transforming Federal Hill into one of the largest Italian settlements in America. Atwells Avenue was the heart of the Hill, teeming with pushcarts and stores and apartments; crowded with families living, like the Picchiones did, in flats above their ground-floor businesses.[89] The avenue was a great location for a watering hole, and Picchione prospered.

July 4, 1907, was a glorious day for Picchione and for all Italian Americans, a double holiday, Independence Day and the centennial of Giuseppe Garibaldi's birth. Picchione led members of his mutual aid society as they marched with other Italian clubs and fraternal organizations in a "monster parade" through Providence.[90] His wife, his brother-in-law Alessandro, and his children may all have joined the happy holiday crowds along the route, excited by the pomp and circumstance.

Then sorrow struck. In 1909, nineteen years after she first arrived in America, Maria Lucia Berardelli Picchione died.

When he lost his sister, his only blood relation in America, Alessandro Berardelli was thirty-three and earning a living as a barber in Waterbury, Connecticut. In 1912 he married Sarah Bisnovich. The couple moved to Springfield, Massachusetts (where Alessandro joined a barber's union), then on to other towns before finally settling in Quincy. By then they had two children.[91]

Berardelli gave up barbering around 1919 and, after a short stint working at a factory owned by a former barber shop customer, he went into private security work. He was briefly employed by the Watts Detective Agency in Boston, but lost that job in less than a month due, said owner W. J. Watts, to "dishonesty and unsatisfactory character. . . . [H]e did not return money which he should have and . . . when he left he failed to square up [his] account with the agency."[92] Berardelli then went to work for another private investigator, Frederick Webster, who recommended him for special officer duty at Slater & Morrill, where he reported on employee theft.[93] "[H]e used to say quite a few pairs of shoes . . . and soles and things like that [were being stolen]," Sarah told Fred Katzmann. Her husband also "made several complaints about Italians in the factory for stealing."[94]

Slater & Morrill must have been satisfied with Berardelli's work, because the company put him on its payroll in the fall of 1919.[95] Soon Sarah was hired, too, as a stitcher.

In April 1920 Alessandro Berardelli became deeply troubled, according to his wife. He was "very nervous and talked a great deal about some bad men around the factory. He said they looked bad and he didn't like their actions." "He was quite suspicious there was too much going on inside the factory. The [police] were there very often."[96]

One night around April 12, Berardelli couldn't sleep. He woke Sarah "three times during the night and said that someone was walking outside." Their pet "dog . . . started barking," Sarah later recalled. "I thought I saw a shadow on the window. I was afraid to let [Alessandro] go to the window, and said, 'I will go myself.' I opened up the window. I stuck my head out through the window, but I didn't see anything."[97]

Sarah urged her husband to quit his job if he felt that he was in danger, but "he said, 'I am no coward, and I am going to stay on the job.'"[98]

On April 14 in South Braintree, one day before the crime, people saw Berardelli "in violent argument with two strangers, described as short and dark. All three spoke in Italian, and none of the [observers] understood that language. But they all agreed that the two strangers were 'laying down the law' to Berardelli most strenuously, obviously threatening him, and that Berardelli was resisting the argument in some timidity and shaking his head in obstinate refusal to some proposition."[99]

Back home in Quincy that evening, joking with his wife and a neighbor, Berardelli suddenly "said that they were having too good a time, that something was likely to happen. . . . He said that he felt too happy to have it continue" and, ominously, that "he was sure something was going to happen."[100] Then Berardelli "went to sleep early. He didn't feel good and he went to bed. He didn't have any supper."[101]

On the last day of his life, Berardelli left home at five thirty in the morning, "something he had never done before, as his usual time of leaving was seven thirty. . . . He said he had something to do, but didn't say what it was."[102] Berardelli kissed Sarah goodbye, "the first time in many months." He told her to take special care of their daughter when she came home from the hospital. Then mysteriously he said "as he went away that he hoped that everything would come out all right. [Sarah] . . . could not understand what it all meant. . . . [She] was apparently very much worried over his attitude and said that she was sure something was going to happen that day."[103]

~ The South Braintree bandits planned the job carefully. They possessed information that was not widely available.

They knew that Thursday was payday, even though it had been on Wednesdays until fairly recently.[104]

They seemed to know that Parmenter and Berardelli would be delivering the money on foot, even though they "always" delivered it by car.[105]

The paymaster and guard were alone on their delivery route on April 15, even though they had previously often been accompanied by others.[106]

Most significantly, the bandits seemed confident that no one would return fire. They claimed, according to Madeiros, that "they just had to show [their] gun and the man would give them the [box] right away." Indeed, unlike Parmenter, "Berardelli didn't hold onto his box." And while three of Berardelli's co-workers would later say that the guard carried a weapon "day after day," "invariably," and "always," no one actually saw him with a weapon on April 15. A co-worker who occasionally borrowed a gun from Berardelli said he heard that the guard "had not a revolver on him that day," a fact to which Aldeah Florence would later testify at trial.[107]

Did Alessandro Berardelli know his murderers? At the inquest Lewis Wade testified that he thought Berardelli was killed because he knew the man who shot him. Two other witnesses — Annie Nichols and James Bostock — testified that the gunmen spoke to Berardelli, and that he "acted to them as though he knew . . . them."[108] Madeiros also said that, on the morning of April 15, the bandits picked him up very early in the morning at his Providence lodgings, "about 4 a.m.," then drove to South Boston "to get information . . . about the money." "[S]omebody there . . . knew about this pay man that used to carry the money or would find out, or something of that kind."[109]

Through his deceased sister, Berardelli had, or had once had, ties to Providence. Did any members of the Providence-based Morelli gang know him? Under indictment and in need of money for legal defense in 1920, did the Morellis hatch a bold scheme to exploit Berardelli and his inside information? Did they intimidate him into cooperating, threatening to harm him or his family if he refused? Did the unlucky guard, worried about his sick daughter and working wife, give in and help the gang in exchange for a promised cut of the cash, only to be fatally double-crossed by men who wanted to be sure that he could never turn them in?

When the suspicious circumstances surrounding the timing and execution of the crime are coupled with Berardelli's failure to return fire and his anxiety beforehand—his comment about "bad men around the factory," his fear that he was being stalked, his refusal to act like a coward, his violent argument with threatening strangers, his sleeplessness and lack of appetite, his sense of impending doom, his early departure from home on the day of the crime, even the unaccustomed goodbye kiss and "final instructions" to his wife—it is hard to avoid concluding that Berardelli knew in advance that someone, either the Morellis or others, was going to commit a crime on April 15. Confirmation of a sort may have come from Joe Morelli himself who, in the version of his autobiography described by Francis Russell, called Alessandro Berardelli a confederate.

— Words matter.

People involved with the defense knew this instinctively. Early on, Fred Moore, who always had a sense that the world was watching his trials, encouraged journalists to present Sacco and Vanzetti in a favorable light. Later, Gardner Jackson and Aldino Felicani, newspapermen themselves, collected letters from the two prisoners because "[we] thought they showed how impossible it would be for men who had said the things [they] said in those letters to have been guilty of [a] grossly brutal . . . crime." *The Letters of Sacco and Vanzetti* was first published in 1928, as was the nearly six-thousand-page transcript of the trial record, its printing and free distribution to major libraries underwritten by a small group of wealthy men, including John D. Rockefeller, Jr., so "there can be no excuse for misrepresentation."[110] The transcript is the ubertext of the trial. The *Letters* have shaped the public image of the "good shoemaker" and the "poor fish peddler."

Important as these documents are, however, they go only so far in explaining why Sacco and Vanzetti continue to incite strong reactions.

The case acquired a unique emotional content. To their supporters, Nick and Bartolo became heroes in a morality play, worthy combatants in an epic battle of the underdog against the system. "Where the people's army marches now to fight, Sacco and Vanzetti will give us light," Woody Guthrie sang.[111]

Ironically, Webster Thayer, who hated everything that Sacco and Vanzetti stood for, made this possible. Every morality play needs a villain, and the judge was perfectly typecast for the role. Through his repeated denials of a new trial, his egregiously prejudicial comments off the bench, and his apparent preening for the media, Thayer virtually guaranteed that the men he called "anarchist bastards" would be immortalized. To compound the irony, the pre-sentencing statements that Sacco and Vanzetti each made to the judge now appear in anthologies of the greatest American speeches, alongside the words of Abraham Lincoln and Franklin Roosevelt.[112]

~ In his closing remarks at Dedham, Jeremiah McAnarney stated that "everything has been done as Massachusetts takes pride in doing, granting to any man, however lowly his station, the fullest rights to our . . . laws." In 1926 Judge Thayer cited this statement as "evidence of the fairness of Mr. Katzmann and the trial."[113] What it really seems to be evidence of is Thayer's wish for the trial to be *perceived* as fair. Thomas McAnarney told the Advisory Committee in 1927 that "Judge Thayer asked my brother to put that in his summation."[114]

The attempt at spin didn't succeed. There is near unanimity that the trial was unfair by the legal standards of 1921, and certainly by later legal standards. "Sacco and Vanzetti did not receive a fair trial": this unambiguous assessment is part of a recent exhibit at the Supreme Judicial Court of Massachusetts, an institution at the very heart of the case.[115]

Based on their words and behavior, both the judge and the jury foreman were not impartial. Further, a representative cross-section of the community did not sit on the Dedham jury, as would be required by law after 1965.[116]

Interrogating the suspects, Fred Katzmann did not tell them of the charges against them, or of their right to counsel, and he ignored Sacco's request for a lawyer. Such conduct would become explicitly unfair after 1966, when the Supreme Court's *Miranda* decision required that a defendant be told, among other things, of his "right to consult with a lawyer and to have the lawyer with him during interrogation."[117]

The prosecution suppressed evidence that could have helped the defense. Potentially exculpatory evidence included the names of uncalled witnesses (Roy Gould, Minnie Kennedy, Louise Hayes Kelly), fingerprint results, the serial number of Parmenter's new gun, Pinkerton detective agency reports on the Bridgewater investigation, and the minutes of the South Braintree inquest. Failure to disclose such evidence today would almost surely result in a new trial or a mistrial.

Judge Thayer defined reasonable doubt to the Sacco-Vanzetti jurors as doubt that "requires reasonable and moral certainty as distinguished from absolute certainty." In 1995 the Supreme Judicial Court of Massachusetts would rule that the term "moral certainty . . . potentially understate[s] the degree of certainty required to convict" and thus violates a defendant's right to due process.[118]

In 1969 Justice Douglas noted other troubling aspects of the Sacco-Vanzetti case: the elimination of lineups in the identification process, which encouraged false memory; the misleading implication that some ballistics testimony was more positive than the witness intended; and the "saturation" of the trial with the defendants' politics. All this, plus the absence of *Miranda*-type warnings, led Douglas to conclude that the case "certainly would have been reviewed by the United States Supreme Court on several federal grounds" if it had come to trial in the late 1960s.[119]

— In 1908, the year that Nicola Sacco and Bartolomeo Vanzetti joined the influx of more than 750,000 people from around the world pouring into the United States, the country was wrestling with immigration reform.[120] It still is.

In 1917 and 1918, when the United States was at war, Congress passed laws that criminalized the expression of ideas. Lawmakers wrestled with opposing concepts of civil liberties and homeland security. They still do.

In 1919, American workers staged more than thirty-six hundred strikes, including the police strike in Boston. Labor unions provoked an angry backlash in many quarters. They still do.

In 1932, law professor Edwin Borchard documented 65 cases of wrongful criminal convictions of innocent people, 62 of them in the United States. Wrongful convictions still haunt us, as the more than 250 prisoners exonerated on the basis of DNA evidence since the 1980s can attest.[121]

The polarization that set the Sacco-Vanzetti case at the fault line of liberalism and conservatism in America endures and deepens. Edmund Wilson said in 1928 that the case "revealed the whole anatomy of American life . . . and it raised almost every fundamental question of our political and social system."[122] It still does.

Vanzetti once predicted that he would be a "vanquished man, but a formidable shadow."[123] He was right. Like actual shadows, the figurative shadows cast by Sacco and Vanzetti grow longer over time.

Acknowledgments

There were times while working on this book when I felt quite alone, but in truth I never was. So many people helped in different ways. I could not have made it to the finish line without them.

Nunzio Pernicone and Edward Horowitz provided expert and incisive comments on the text. Russell Aiuto and Mary Collins also provided wise suggestions and sustaining encouragement. All unselfishly devoted precious time to the task, and the book is the better for their input.

I look up to librarians and archivists, and always have, but never more so than now. My heartfelt thanks go to Jennifer Harbster and the many other indefatigable reference librarians at the Library of Congress, Kimberly Reynolds and Susan Glover at the Boston Public Library, Jennifer Fauxsmith at the Massachusetts Archives, Edwin Moloy at the Harvard Law School Library, Rebecca Cape and Cherry Williams at Lilly Library of Indiana University, Ellen Shea and Johanna Carll at Schlesinger Library, and the librarians at Plymouth Public Library, Rhode Island Historical Society Library, Providence Public Library, Bunker Hill Community College Library, and the U.S. Department of Labor library. The Everett Helm Visiting Fellowship I received from Lilly Library helped make my research in Bloomington possible.

For speaking with me and generously sharing family stories and rare memorabilia, I am grateful to Spencer Sacco, grandson of Nicola Sacco; Jeannette Parmenter Murphy, daughter of Frederick Parmenter; Betty Jack Wirth and Conny Cross, daughter and granddaughter of Cerise Carman Jack; Barta Hapgood Monro, daughter of Mary Donovan and Powers Hapgood; James MacMechan and Virginia MacMechan Mallen, nephew and niece of Virginia MacMechan; Claire Finn Kiernan, Sacco family neighbor; and Cynthia Anthonsen Foster, wife of diarist Carl Anthonsen.

Many people over many years helped me learn about Alessandro Berardelli. I am indebted to them all: Gladys Mondshein, Stacey Dresner of the *Connecticut Jewish Ledger*, Marvin Bargar and Werner Hirsch of the Jewish Historical Society of Greater New Haven, Maria Medina of the Archdiocese of Hartford, and Doug Acree, whose generous assistance with genealogical research proved invaluable. I am indebted most of all to family members who spoke with me, especially Dina Chieffo.

I am obliged to historian Robert Hanson and to Superintendent Peter Perroncello and Captain Rick Donadio of the Norfolk County Sheriff's Office for information on Dedham, to John Chaffee for information on Plymouth, and to Simon Liu of the Rhode Island State Police dive team and the late Irving Irons for information on Canada Pond. I extend sincere thanks to Judge Nancy Gertner, Judge Peter Agnes, and Elizabeth Bouvier, Head of Archives at the Supreme Judicial Court of Massachusetts, for speaking or corresponding with me about the selection of jury foremen in Massachusetts.

When I translated material from the Italian, I did so hesitantly, and am grateful to those who guided me. Elena Papi checked my final translations with exacting care, and David Colbert, Cristina Marcantonio, and Bettina Petrarca Ponsart answered queries along the way.

Kind friends welcomed me on research trips and eased my journey: Sonia and Bill Valentine in Dedham, Margherita and Donald Pryor in Providence, and especially Paula Levine on my many trips to Boston. The family of the late Alfred Wellborn provided me with office space at a critical time.

Many thanks as well to Alejandro Anreus, Robert Barnes, Bronwyn Becker, John Cronin, Robert D'Attilio, William Faucon, David Ferris, Martin Finn, Dorothy Gallagher, Donald Graul, Judith Hammer, Stanley Hammer, Gail Jarrow, Jennifer Kirkpatrick, Sidney Kirkpatrick, Steve Klitzman, Alan Kraut, Susan McElhinney, Anne Meadows, Peter Miller, Sandy Mosshart, Emmett "Zip" Nanna, Liza Newman, Jim Oberman, Richard Pacia, Randy Ross, Norman Shore, Carol Shute, Mike Stanton, Allan Teichroew, Jean Kaplan Teichroew, Vincent Vespia, Ursula Vosseler, Jerilyn Watson, John Yemma, Carolyn Yoder, and Eugene Zepp.

To my agent, Regina Ryan, and my editor, Richard Pult: your confidence, unflappability, and wise guidance helped me more than you know.

Lastly, endless thanks to my family, who helped me over so many hurdles. My sister, Carolyn Gold, urged me to keep going despite setbacks. My son, Justin Tejada, the human thesaurus, provided sound editorial advice and never, ever failed to inspire. My husband, Rey Tejada, was my sounding board and anchor; this book is his achievement as much as mine.

Abbreviations Used in the Notes

AF	Aldino Felicani
ANB	*American National Biography*
ASB	Alice Stone Blackwell
BET	*Boston Evening Transcript*
BG	*Boston Globe*
BH	*Boston Herald*
BJW	Betty Jack Wirth
BPL	Boston Public Library, Rare Books and Manuscripts: Aldino Felicani Collection
Bulletin	*The Official Bulletin of the Sacco-Vanzetti Defense Committee of Boston, Massachusetts*
BV	Bartolomeo Vanzetti
CCJ	Cerise Carman Jack
CUOHROC: AF	Reminiscences of Aldino Felicani, 1954, Columbia University Oral History Research Office Collection
CUOHROC: GJ	Reminiscences of Gardner Jackson, 1955, Columbia University Oral History Research Office Collection
EGE	Elizabeth Glendower Evans
EGF	Elizabeth Gurley Flynn
FK	Fred Katzmann
FM	Fred Moore
GJ	Gardner Jackson
HBE	Herbert B. Ehrmann
HLSL	Harvard Law School Library: Herbert B. Ehrmann Papers
Il Caso	*Il caso Sacco e Vanzetti: Lettere ai familiari* (formerly titled *Non piangete la mia morte*)
Letters	*The Letters of Sacco and Vanzetti*
Lilly	Lilly Library, Indiana University: Hapgood Collections
LoC	Library of Congress, Manuscript Division: Cerise C. Jack Papers
LV	Luigia Vanzetti
MA/AG	Massachusetts Archives, AG1/Series 2062X, Attorney General's Office, Sacco and Vanzetti Case File, 1919–1976
MA/Inmate	Massachusetts Archives, HS9.01/Series 305, Mass. State Prison, Inmate Case Files, 1910–1941
MA/SP	Massachusetts Archives, PS11/Series 2084X, State Police, Sacco and Vanzetti Case File, 1920–1977
MD	Mary Donovan (later Mary Donovan Hapgood)

NS	Nicola Sacco
NYT	*New York Times*
Plymouth	*Background of the Plymouth Trial* (by Bartolomeo Vanzetti)
Proletarian	*The Story of a Proletarian Life* (by Bartolomeo Vanzetti)
Public Hearing	*Record of Public Hearing on the Resolution of Rep. Alexander J. Cella Recommending a Posthumous Pardon for Nicola Sacco and Bartolomeo Vanzetti, April 2, 1959*
Reel 3	*Sacco-Vanzetti Case Papers*, "Defense's Papers, Insanity Matters, 1923 and 1925," Microfilm, Reel 3, 0249.
RS	Rosina Sacco
SB	Sarah Berardelli
Schlesinger	Schlesinger Library, Radcliffe Institute for Advanced Studies, Harvard University: Elizabeth Glendower Evans Papers.
Transcript	*The Sacco-Vanzetti Case, Transcript of the Record of the Trial of Nicola Sacco and Bartolomeo Vanzetti in the Courts of Massachusetts and Subsequent Proceedings, 1920–1927*, volumes 1–6.
VMM	Virginia MacMechan
WGT	William Thompson
WP	*Washington Post*
WSJ	*Wall Street Journal*

NOTES

CHAPTER 1: SUDDEN DEATH

1. *Transcript*, 1: 489, 495; 519; 325, 327; 499, 505–06; 334, 336; 139.

2. "New York Manager Says Ruth Has Signed New Contract," *BET*, January 6, 1920.

3. "First Day of Trout Fishing" and advertisements, *BET*, April 15, 1920.

4. *Transcript*, 6:408.

5. Ibid., 1:137–38.

6. Francis Russell, *Tragedy in Dedham: The Story of the Sacco-Vanzetti Case* (New York: McGraw-Hill, 1962), 35; and *Transcript*, 1:171.

7. Rick Collins, "Forgotten Victims: Descendants Say Both Were Hard-Working Family Men," *Patriot Ledger*, July 27, 2005, www.southofboston.net/specialreports/saccovanzetti/pages/072705.shtml (accessed August 14, 2005).

8. SB to FK, February 12, 1921, 8, and SB to Michael Stewart, January 31, 1921, 1, MA/SP, Box 1, No. 7 (both).

9. *Transcript*, 6:411; and Charles Callanan and Jerome Sullivan, "Sacco-Vanzetti Live On — Long after Execution," *BG*, April 10, 1960.

10. *Transcript*, 1:112 (a medical examiner found the envelope in Berardelli's pocket); ibid., 6:412; SB to Michael Stewart, January 31, 1921, 2, MA/SP, Box 1, No. 7; and *Transcript*, 1:187.

11. *Transcript*, 6:430.

12. Charles Van Amburgh, "The Hidden Drama of Sacco and Vanzetti," *True Detective Mysteries*, part 1, April 1935, 12, and Michael M. Topp, *The Sacco and Vanzetti Case, A Brief History with Documents* (New York: Palgrave Macmillan, 2005), 1.

13. *Transcript*, 1:196.

14. Ibid., 1:267, 134.

15. Ibid., 6:462; ibid., 1:415; and ibid., 1:595–97.

16. Osmond K. Fraenkel, *The Sacco-Vanzetti Case* (New York: Alfred A. Knopf, 1931), 9; Herbert Ehrmann, *The Case That Will Not Die* (Boston: Little, Brown, 1969), 41; and Russell, *Tragedy in Dedham*, 43 (the driver was the fire chief).

17. *Transcript*, 1:661; Charles H. McCormick, *Hopeless Cases: The Hunt for the Red Scare Terrorist Bombers* (Lanham, MD: University Press of America, 2005), 88, 93, 107; and James J. Collins, "Braintree Had 3 Policemen, No Station at Time of Murders," *BG*, April 10, 1960.

18. Marcus Kavanagh, *The Criminal and His Allies* (Indianapolis, IN: Bobbs-Merrill, 1928), 349; and "The Bandit on Wheels," *BET*, April 22, 1920.

19. "Bandits Kill 2, Get $20,000," *BET*, April 16, 1920.

20. *Transcript*, 1:618.

21. Ibid., 1:651–654, 662, 666, 631, 635.

22. Ibid., 6:421, 418, 453, 460, 465, 403, 451.

23. Ibid., 6:397 (Nichols); ibid., 6:444 (Wade); and ibid., 1:196 (Bostock).

24. Ibid., 6:409, 411.

25. Ibid., 6:441, 453; and ibid., 6:451, 461.

26. Ibid., 6:426, 434, 436, 438. Witnesses who testified to seeing two cars were Shelley Neal, Edward Carter, John Mannex, and Thomas Treacy.

27. Ibid., 6:444 (Wade); ibid., 6:401–402 (Nichols); ibid., 6:417 (Colbert); and ibid., 6:445–446 (Langlois).

28. "Seeks a Big Reward for Braintree Gunmen," *BET*, April 20, 1920.

CHAPTER 2: "THIS HUMAN FLOTSAM"

1. BV to Mrs. L. N. Russell, September 18, 1925, in *Letters*, 174.

2. State Prison Inmate's History and Record (for BV), MA/Inmate, Folder 16102.

3. Federated Press, "Sig. Vanzetti Near Death," *Labor's News*, March 14, 1929, 8.

4. BV to Russell, September 18, 1925, in *Letters*, 170.

5. BV to CCJ, October 3, 1923, ibid., 101.

6. Roberta Strauss Feuerlicht, *Justice Crucified: The Story of Sacco and Vanzetti* (New York: McGraw-Hill, 1977), 14.

7. *Proletarian*, 9.

8. Eugene Lyons, *The Life and Death of Sacco and Vanzetti* (New York: International Publishers, 1927; repr., New York: DaCapo Press, 1970), 12. Citations are to the DaCapo edition.

9. BV to Mrs. M. O'Sullivan, October 7, 1926, in *Letters*, 208.

10. Ibid.

11. BV to Russell, in ibid., 171.

12. Ibid., 173.

13. *Proletarian*, 21.

14. Ibid., 9.

15. Ibid.

16. Ibid.

17. Ibid.

18. BV to his parents, December 23, 1902, in *Il Caso*, 38. Translations of letters from *Il Caso* by author.

19. June 10, 1903, in ibid., 39.

20. December 25, 1903, in ibid., 40.

21. March 3, 1906, in ibid., 45.

22. Feuerlicht, *Justice Crucified*, 18.

23. BV to his parents, June 10, 1903, August 15, 1903, January 3, 1905, January 28, 1906, and May 28, 1906, in *Il Caso*, 39, 40, 41–42, 44, 46.

24. BV to his parents, December 17, 1905, and January 28, 1906, in ibid., 42, 44.

25. BV to his parents, August 23, 1901, in ibid., 38; June 10, 1903, in ibid., 39; January 28, 1906, in ibid., 44; and November 23, 1904, in ibid., 41.

26. *Transcript*, 2:1690.

27. *Proletarian*, 10.

28. Ibid.

29. Feuerlicht, *Justice Crucified*, 18.

30. *Proletarian*, 11.

31. Ibid.

32. BV to ASB, June 21, 1925, in *Letters*, 156.

33. *Proletarian*, 21.

34. Ibid., 10.

35. Ibid., 11.

36. John Nicholas Beffel, "Eels and the Electric Chair," *The New Republic*, December 29, 1920, 127–128.

37. *Proletarian*, 11.

38. Ibid.

39. State Prison History Chart (for NS), MA/Inmate, Folder 17402.

40. Eugene Lyons, "Torremaggiore: A Glimpse of Sacco's Birthplace," *The World Tomorrow*, September 1921, 273.

41. Paul Avrich, *Sacco and Vanzetti: The Anarchist Background* (Princeton, NJ: Princeton University Press, 1991), 10.

42. NS to Gertrude Winslow, June 22, 1927, HLSL, Box 16, Folder 14.

43. *Transcript*, 2:1817; and History Chart (for NS), MA/Inmate, Folder 17402.

44. *Transcript*, 2:1817.

45. Lyons, *Life and Death*, 15.

46. NS to CCJ, February 26, 1924, in *Letters*, 15.

47. Ibid., 16.

48. Ibid., 15–16.

49. NS to EGE, November 23, 1923, in *Letters*, 10.

50. Avrich, *Sacco and Vanzetti*, 12.

51. Lyons, *Life and Death*, 16.

52. NS to EGE, n.d., in Elizabeth Glendower Evans, *Outstanding Features of the Sacco-Vanzetti Case, Together with Letters from the Defendants* (Boston: New England Civil Liberties Committee, 1924), 45.

53. *Transcript*, 2:1818.

54. U.S. Bureau of the Census, "Series C89-119. Immigrants, by Country: 1820 to 1970," *Statistical History of the United States from Colonial Times to the Present* (New York: Basic Books, 1976), 105.

55. I. W. Howerth, "Are the Italians a Dangerous Class?," *Charities, a Weekly Review of Local and General Philanthropy*, May 1904, repr., *The Italian in America: The Progressive View, 1891–1914*, ed. Lydio Tomasi (New York: Center for Migration Studies, 1972), 137.

56. Arthur H. Warner, "A Country Where Going to America Is an Industry," *National Geographic Magazine*, December 1909, 1063.

57. Niles Carpenter, U.S. Bureau of the Census, *Immigrants and Their Children, 1920* (Washington, DC: GPO, 1927), 324.

58. Ibid.

59. Madison Grant, *Passing of the Great Race, or The Racial Basis of European History*, 1st ed. (New York: Charles Scribner's Sons, 1916), 80; Grant, *Passing of the Great Race*, 3rd ed. (DeForest Grant, 1944), in Oscar Handlin, *Immigration as a Factor in American History* (Englewood Cliffs, NJ: Prentice-Hall, Inc., 1959), 184; Kenneth L. Roberts, *Why Europe Leaves Home* (Bobbs-Merrill, 1922; repr., New York: Arno Press, 1977), 113 (citations are to the Arno Press edition); and Grant, *Passing of the Great Race*, 1st ed., 80.

60. Alan M. Kraut, *The Huddled Masses: The Immigrant in American Society, 1880–1921* (Arlington Heights, IL: Harlan Davidson, 1982), 77, and Maldwyn Allen Jones, *American Immigration*, 2nd ed. (Chicago: University of Chicago Press, 1992), 177.

61. Benjamin Franklin, "Observations Concerning the Increase of Mankind," in Edmund S. Morgan, *Benjamin Franklin* (New Haven, CT: Yale University Press, 2002), 77.

62. U.S. Bureau of the Census, *Statistical History*, 105.

63. Grant, *Passing of the Great Race*, 1st ed., 15–16.

64. Ibid., 43.

65. Ibid., 65, 80, 82.

66. Roberts, *Why Europe Leaves Home*, 35, 54.

67. Ibid., 113, 97.

68. John Higham, *Strangers in the Land: Patterns of American Nativism, 1860–1925*, 2nd ed. (New Brunswick, NJ: Rutgers University Press, 1988), 160.

69. *Transcript*, 5:4904.

70. BV to LV, January 12, 1911, in *Il Caso*, 50.

71. Roberts, *Why Europe Leaves Home*, 54.

72. Edward Allsworth Ross, "Italians in America," *The Century*, July 1914, 444.

73. Ibid., 441.

74. Kraut, *Huddled Masses*, 19.

75. Ross, "Italians in America," 444.

76. Enrico C. Sartorio, *Social and Religious Life of Italians in America* (Boston: Christopher Publishing House, 1918; repr., Clifton, NJ: Augustus M. Kelley Publishers, 1974), 18–19.

77. Gino C. Speranza, "How It Feels to Be a Problem: A Consideration of Certain Causes Which Prevent or Retard Assimilation," in Tomasi, *The Italian in America*, 92.

78. Salvatore Mondello, *The Italian Immigrant in Urban America, 1880–1920, as Reported in the Contemporary Periodical Press* (New York: Arno Press, 1980), 15.

79. Howerth, "Are the Italians a Dangerous Class?," 135.

80. BV to LV, January 12, 1911, in *Il Caso*, 50.

81. Kraut, *Huddled Masses*, 158.

82. Fred L. Gardaphé, *Moustache Pete Is Dead! Evviva Baffo Pietro! The Fra Noi Columns, 1985–1988* (West Lafayette, IN: Bordighera, 1997), 3.

83. Peter Vellon, "Black, White, or In Between?," *Ambassador*, Fall 2000, 11.

84. Luciano Iorizzo and Salvatore Mondello, *The Italian-Americans* (New York: Twayne, 1971), 223, in Feuerlicht, *Justice Crucified*, 71, 445n8. States included Pennsylvania and North Carolina.

85. See Richard Gambino, *Vendetta: The True Story of the Largest Lynching in U.S. History* (New York: Doubleday, 1977; repr., Toronto: Guernica, 1998).

86. "An Act to Regulate Immigration," 47th Cong., 1st sess. (August 3, 1882), *U.S. Statutes at Large*, 214.

87. Ibid.

88. "An Act in Amendment to the Various Acts Relative to Immigration and the Importation of Aliens Under Contract or Agreement to Perform Labor," 51st Cong., 2nd sess. (March 3, 1891), *U.S. Statutes at Large*, 1085.

89. Ibid., 1084.

90. Barbara Miller Solomon, *Ancestors and Immigrants: A Changing New England Tradition* (Cambridge, MA: Harvard University Press, 1956), 99–101.

91. Ibid., 47.

92. Albert Shaw, ed., *Messages and Papers of Woodrow Wilson*, vol. 1 (New York: The Review of Reviews Corp., 1924), 95–96.

93. "An Act to Regulate the Immigration of Aliens into the United States," 57th Cong., 2nd sess. (March 3, 1903), *U.S. Statutes at Large*, 1214.

94. Ibid.

95. "An Act to Regulate the Immigration of Aliens into the United States," 59th Cong., 2nd sess. (February 20, 1907), *U.S. Statutes at Large*, 898–899.

96. "An Act to Amend an Act Entitled 'An Act to Regulate the Immigration of Aliens into the United States,'" 61st Cong., 2nd sess. (March 26, 1910), *U.S. Statutes at Large*, 264.

97. "An Act to Regulate the Immigration of Aliens to, and the Residence of Aliens in, the United States," 64th Cong., 2nd sess. (February 5, 1917), *U.S. Statutes at Large*, 875, 877.

98. Kraut, *Huddled Masses*, 174.

99. Higham, *Strangers in the Land*, 308.

100. Ibid., 310–311.

101. Ibid., 311.

102. "Immigration Act of 1924," 68th Cong., 1st sess. (May 26, 1924), *U.S. Statutes at Large*, 159. The new quota was two percent, based on immigrant population levels in 1890.

103. "This Evening's News," *BET*, June 6, 1921.

104. "An Act to Limit the Immigration of Aliens into the United States," (May 19, 1921), 6.

105. "Aliens in Wild Riot, 61 on *Canopic* Escape," *BG*, June 12, 1921.

106. Ibid.

107. "*Canopic*'s Italians to Be Freed Today," *BG*, June 13, 1921.

CHAPTER 3: CRIME WAVE

1. "Holdup Balked in Bridgewater," *BG*, December 25, 1919.

2. "Saves $40,000 in Gun Battle," *BH*, December 25, 1919.

3. *Transcript*, 6:363.

4. Ibid., 6:364–366.

5. Ibid.

6. Ibid., 6:368.

7. Ibid., 6:367.

8. Ibid., 6:371, 375.

9. Ibid., 6:378.

10. Ibid., 6:379–385.

11. Ibid., 6:382.

12. Ibid., 6:389–390.

13. Ibid., 6:389.

14. Coacci description by Officer John H. Scott, January 22, 1921, MA/SP, Box 1, Folder 5; and Avrich, *Sacco and Vanzetti*, 200.

15. HBE, *Case That Will Not Die*, 93.

16. "Memo by M. E. Stewart," May 31, 1921, MA/SP, Box 1, Folder 5.

17. Edward B. Simmons, *New Bedford Standard-Times*, August 23, 1952, quoted in Tom O'Connor, "The Origin of the Sacco-Vanzetti Case," *Vanderbilt Law Review*, June 1961, 993.

18. Van Amburgh, "Hidden Drama," Part 1, April 1935, 82.

19. "Memo by M. E. Stewart," May 31, 1921, MA/SP, Box 1, Folder 5. Unless otherwise noted, this memo is the source of information on Stewart's visits to Buda's house and Johnson's garage.

20. Avrich, *Sacco and Vanzetti*, 201.

21. *Transcript*, 5:4983–87.

22. "Red's Death Plunge, 14 Stories, Bares Long Bomb Trail," *NYT*, May 4, 1920, and A. Mitchell Palmer in Louis F. Post, *The Deportations Delirium of Nineteen-Twenty* (Chicago: Charles H. Kerr, 1923), 280.

23. CUOHROC: AF, 47.

24. *Transcript*, 2:1710.

25. Nunzio Pernicone, *Carlo Tresca, Portrait of a Rebel* (New York: Palgrave Macmillan, 2005), 116, and *Transcript*, 2:2048.

26. Elizabeth Gurley Flynn, *The Rebel Girl: An Autobiography, My First Life (1906–1926)*, (New York: International Publishers, 1973), 298.

27. *Transcript*, 2:1722, 1810–11, 1982, 2049.

28. "Red's Death Plunge," *NYT*, May 4, 1920.

29. William Young and David E. Kaiser, *Postmortem: New Evidence in the Case of Sacco and Vanzetti* (Amherst: University of Massachusetts Press, 1985), 167n40.

30. *Transcript*, 2:1883.

31. Ibid., 2:1822, 2057.

32. Ibid., 1:674–676.

33. Ibid., 1:676–678.

34. Ibid., 1:680–683.

35. Ibid., 1:715, 876.

36. Ibid., 1:751–752.

37. Ibid., 1:753.

38. Ibid., 1:752–753, 781, 756.

39. Ibid., 2:1724 and 1:752–53.

40. Ibid., 6:153.

41. Ibid., 6:156. The account of Stewart's interrogation of Vanzetti is based on the police chief's testimony at Vanzetti's first trial; see ibid., 6:153–157.

42. Ibid., 1:847. The account of Stewart's interrogation of Sacco comes from the joint trial of Sacco and Vanzetti; see ibid., 1:847–849, and 2:2110–11.

43. Ibid., 2:1725.

44. Ibid., 2:1845, 1726.

45. Ibid., 2:1725–26, 2113.

46. Ibid., 2:1742.

47. "Arrest Two Armed Suspects in Car," *BH*, May 6, 1920; and "Brockton Police Hold Two Suspects," *BG*, May 6, 1920.

48. "Hyde Park Man Under Arrest," *BG*, May 7, 1920.

49. Ibid.; "Three Arrested for Braintree Murders; Two Are Identified," *BH*, May 7, 1920; "Arrests for Braintree Murder," *BET*, May 7, 1920; and *Transcript*, 2:2061.

50. "Hyde Park Man Under Arrest," *BG*, May 7, 1920.

51. *Transcript*, 2:1607.

52. CUOHROC: AF, 53–54.

53. Obituary of Frederick Katzmann, *BG*, October 16, 1953; and Louis Joughin, "Beyond Guilt or Innocence: The Responsibility of History," in *Sacco-Vanzetti: Developments and Reconsiderations—1979, Conference Proceedings* (Boston: Trustees of the Public Library of the City of Boston, 1982), 9.

54. BV, "Awaiting the Hangman," *Bulletin*, August 1926, 1.

55. Avrich, *Sacco and Vanzetti*, 24.

56. *Transcript*, 2:1928, 1997.

57. Ibid., 2:1805.

58. BV, *Bulletin*, August 1926, 1.

59. BV and NS statements, MA/SP, Box 1, Folder 5.

60. *Transcript*, 2:1742–43.

61. Statement of Bert [*sic*] Vanzetti, 2, MA/SP, Box 1, Folder 5.

62. *Transcript*, 2:1812.

63. NS statement, 1, MA/SP, Box 1, Folder 5.

64. Ibid., 2–9.

65. Van Amburgh, "Hidden Drama," Part 2, May 1935, 111.

66. Cynthia Anthonsen Foster Papers, Carl Anthonsen diary, entry for May 6, 1920, MC 653, Schlesinger.

CHAPTER 4: "ORGANIZE! O TOILERS"

1. Kate Holladay Claghorn, *The Immigrant's Day in Court* (New York: Harper & Brothers, 1923; repr., New York: Arno Press, 1969), 6–7; and Avrich, *Sacco and Vanzetti*, 21.

2. History Chart (for NS), MA/Inmate, Folder 17402; and Avrich, *Sacco and Vanzetti*, 22.

3. Lyons, "Torremaggiore," 274.

4. Avrich, *Sacco and Vanzetti*, 22–23.

5. Bates Torrey, *The Shoe Industry of Weymouth* (Weymouth, MA: Weymouth Historical Society, 1933), 11, 117; and *Three Hundred Years of Shoe & Leather Making in Massachusetts* (Boston: Gill Publications, 1930), 5, 7.

6. William C. Hanson, M.D., *Hygiene of the Boot and Shoe Industry in Massachusetts* (Boston: Massachusetts State Board of Health, 1912), 4.

7. Joseph Moro in Avrich, *Sacco and Vanzetti*, 23; Art Shields, *Are They Doomed? The Sacco-Vanzetti Case and the Grim Forces Behind It* (New York: Workers Defense Union, 1921), 13; and EGE, "The Personal Side of Sacco and Vanzetti," *The Call Magazine*, [June 1921?], 5.

8. Avrich, *Sacco and Vanzetti*, 23.

9. *Proletarian*, 22.

10. Ibid., 12–13.

11. Ibid., 13; and BV to LV, January 12, 1911, in *Il Caso*, 49.

12. *Proletarian*, 13–14.

13. Ibid., 14.

14. Ibid., 14–17.

15. BV to ASB, January 24, 1924, in *Letters*, 115.

16. *Proletarian*, 17.

17. Ibid., 18.

18. John Chaffee, "A Small New England Mill Town," in *Beyond Plymouth Rock: America's Hometown in the 20th Century*, vol. 1, *Ties That Bind*, ed. John Chaffee (Plymouth: Plymouth Public Library Corp., 2002), 9; and Samuel Eliot Morison, *The Ropemakers of Plymouth, A History of the Plymouth Cordage Company, 1824–1949* (Boston: Houghton Mifflin, 1950), v.

19. Morison, *Ropemakers*, 3, 56.

20. Ibid., 68; and Richmond Talbot, "1900, The Dawn of the 20th Century," in Chaffee, *Beyond Plymouth Rock*, 6.

21. *Proletarian*, 18–19, and Shields, *Are They Doomed?*, 13; BV to Aunt Edvige, December 15, 1914, in *Il Caso*, 52; and Avrich, *Sacco and Vanzetti*, 39.

22. *Proletarian*, 22–23.

23. BV to Elvira Fantino, June 25, 1923, in *Il Caso*, 95.

24. BV to LV, [1908?], in ibid., 47.

25. BV to LV, January 12, 1911, ibid., 50; and BV to LV, n.d., ibid., 51.

26. History and Record (for BV), MA/Inmate, Folder 16102.

27. BV to LV, December 22, 1914, in *Il Caso*, 55; and BV to Aunt Edvige, December 15, 1914, ibid., 53.

28. Robert Knox, "Trial of the Century: Local Amnesia," in Chaffee, *Beyond Plymouth Rock*, 71.

29. BV to Beltrando Brini, June 17, 1922, BPL, Series 1, Box 2, Folder 6.

30. Beltrando Brini in Paul Avrich, *Anarchist Voices: An Oral History of Anarchism in America* (Princeton, NJ: Princeton University Press, 1995), 101.

31. U.S. Bureau of the Census, *Statistical History*, 168. In 1908 these workers worked 60.3 hours per week and earned $0.175 an hour.

32. Alexander M. Bing, *War-Time Strikes and Their Adjustment* (New York: E. P. Dutton, 1921; repr., New York: Arno Press, 1971), 165.

33. Patrick Renshaw, *The Wobblies: The Story of Syndicalism in the United States* (Garden City, NY: Doubleday, 1967), 33–34.

34. Paul Frederick Brissenden, *The IWW: A Study of American Syndicalism* (New York: Columbia University, 1920), 31.

35. Ibid., and Renshaw, *The Wobblies*, 74.

36. "What Is the Origin of the Term Wobbly?," posted May 1, 2005, Industrial Workers of the World website: www.iww.org/culture/official/wobbly (accessed September 21, 2009).

37. Preamble to the IWW constitution, in Renshaw, *The Wobblies*, frontispiece.

38. Melvyn Dubofsky, *We Shall Be All: A History of the Industrial Workers of the World*, 2nd ed. (Urbana: University of Illinois Press, 1988), 94.

39. John Clendenin Townsend, *Running the Gauntlet: Cultural Sources of Violence Against the IWW* (New York: Garland Publishing, 1986), 3–4.

40. Editorial, *San Diego Evening Tribune*, March 4, 1912, quoted in ibid., 34.

41. Townsend, *Running the Gauntlet*, 194.

42. Dubofsky, *We Shall Be All*, 340–341 (Everett); Ibid., 385–387 (Bisbee); and *The "Knights of Liberty" Mob and the IWW Prisoners at Tulsa, Okla.* (New York: National Civil Liberties Bureau, 1918), 6–7, and Earl Bruce White, "The United States v. C. W. Anderson et al.: The Wichita Case, 1917–19," in *At the Point of Production, The Local History of the IWW*, ed. Joseph R. Conlin (Westport, CT: Greenwood Press, 1981), 151–152 (Tulsa).

43. Renshaw, *The Wobblies*, 208–210, and Dubofsky, *We Shall Be All*, 455.

44. Ben Reitman in Brissenden, *The IWW*, 319, and Dubofsky, *We Shall Be All*, 289.

45. Renshaw, *The Wobblies*, 22.

46. Vincent St. John, *The IWW: Its History, Structure, and Methods* (Cleveland: IWW Publishing Bureau, 1913), 17–18.

47. Renshaw, *The Wobblies*, 134–135.

48. Philip S. Foner, *History of the Labor Movement in the United States*, vol. 4, *The Industrial Workers of the World, 1905–1917* (New York: International Publishers, 1965), 308; Dubofsky, *We Shall Be All*, 230; and A. N. Holcombe, "The Effects of the Legal Minimum Wage for Women," in *The Present Labor Situation, Annals of the American Academy of Political and Social Science* 69, no. 158 (January 1917): 36.

49. Maurice B. Dorgan, *History of Lawrence Massachusetts, With War Records* (Maurice B. Dorgan, 1924), 152.

50. "Clubs and Bobbins Used as Weapons in a Strike Started by Italians and Syrians," *BG*, January 12, 1912.

51. "Statement of Pres. Wood," in ibid.

52. Dorgan, *History of Lawrence*, 49.

53. Dubofsky, *We Shall Be All*, 230–231.

54. Foner, *History of the Labor Movement*, vol. 4, 309, 311–313; and Dubofsky, *We Shall Be All*, 232.

55. *ANB*, s.v. "Ettor, Joseph James"; Pernicone, *Carlo Tresca*, 49; and "Strikers Firm and Mills May Close," *BG*, January 14, 1912.

56. Renshaw, *The Wobblies*, 135; and Foner, *History of the Labor Movement*, vol. 4, 317.

57. "Strikers Driven Back by Troops but Close Mills," *BG*, January 16, 1912.

58. Avrich, *Sacco and Vanzetti*, 23–25.

59. Ibid., 24, and John Dos Passos, *Facing the Chair: Story of the Americanization of Two Foreignborn Workmen* (Boston: Sacco-Vanzetti Defense Committee, 1927; repr., New York: DaCapo Press, 1970), 66; citations are to the DaCapo edition.

60. Claire Finn Kirwan (Watertown neighbor of Sacco family) to author, telephone interview, February 7, 2000.

61. Avrich, *Sacco and Vanzetti*, 26.

62. Helen C. Camp, *Iron in Her Soul: Elizabeth Gurley Flynn and the American Left* (Pullman: Washington State University Press, 1995), 15–18.

63. EGE, "Memoir," [1936?], 2–4, Schlesinger, Reel 1.

64. Foner, *History of the Labor Movement*, vol. 4, 318–325.

65. Michael Miller Topp, "The Italian-American Left: Transnationalism and the Quest for Unity," in *The Immigrant Left in the United States*, ed. Paul Buhle and Dan Georgakas (Albany: State University of New York Press, 1996), 131; and Foner, *History of the Labor Movement*, vol. 4, 325–327.

66. Justus Ebert, *Trial of a New Society* (Cleveland: I.W.W. Publishing Bureau, 1913), 77.

67. Bill Haywood in Dubofsky, *We Shall Be All*, 253.

68. Dubofsky, *We Shall Be All*, 254.

69. Foner, *History of the Labor Movement*, vol. 4, 346; Brissenden, *The I.W.W.*, 293; and Joe Hill, "We Will Sing One Song," in *Songs of the Workers to Fan the Flames of Discontent*, 32nd ed. (Chicago: Industrial Workers of the World, 1968), 34.

70. NS to CCJ, December 14, 1923, in *Letters*, 13; and History Chart (for NS), MA/Inmate, Folder 17402, which gives a wedding date of Thanksgiving Day 1912.

71. Dubofsky, *We Shall Be All*, 247 (LoPezzi); Dorgan, *History of Lawrence*, 153 (Benoit); and Dorgan, *History of Lawrence*, 154, and Foner, *History of the Labor Movement*, vol. 4, 331 (Remi).

72. Ebert, *Trial of a New Society*, 87–88; and Renshaw, *The Wobblies*, 142.

73. Ebert, *Trial of a New Society*, 91–92.

74. Pernicone, *Carlo Tresca*, 45–47, 51, and Dorothy Gallagher, *All the Right Enemies: The Life and Murder of Carlo Tresca* (New Brunswick, NJ: Rutgers University Press, 1988), 33–37.

75. Carlo Tresca, in Pernicone, *Carlo Tresca*, 51.

76. Max Eastman, "Troublemaker," *The New Yorker*, September 15, 1934, 32.

77. Dorgan, *History of Lawrence*, 156.

78. Pernicone, *Carlo Tresca*, 55, and Foner, *History of the Labor Movement*, vol. 4, 348.

79. Dorgan, *History of Lawrence*, 157; and EGF, *Rebel Girl*, 151.

80. Ebert, *Trial of a New Society*, 125.

81. James P. Heaton, "The Salem Trial," in Tomasi, *The Italian in America*, 220–221.

82. EGE, "Memoir," 4.

83. EGF, *Rebel Girl*, 147.

84. Ibid., 146, 221, 302–303.

85. Roland Sawyer in *Public Hearing*, 89.

86. Pernicone, *Carlo Tresca*, 54.

87. Robert D'Attilio, "La Salute è in Voi: The Anarchist Dimension," in *Sacco-Vanzetti: Developments and Reconsiderations*, 78.

88. Avrich, *Sacco and Vanzetti*, 27.

89. Pernicone, *Carlo Tresca*, 61, and Dubofsky, *We Shall Be All*, 283–287.

90. *Transcript*, 2:1819; and "Strike Siege in Hopedale," *BG*, April 3, 1913.

91. "Will Offer Plan to Foss Today," *BG*, July 16, 1913; "Strikers Ask Places Back," *BG*, July 25, 1913; and "Three Boston Strikes," *BET*, June 2, 1913.

92. "Demands Rejected by Draper Company," *BG*, April 4, 1913; "Draper Waives Board's Offer," *BG*, April 8, 1913; and "Seek to Tie Up Every Plant," *BG*, April 15, 1913.

93. "Demands Rejected," *BG*, April 4, 1913.

94. Joseph Coldwell in Lyons, *Life and Death*, 33.

95. Sabino Sacco in Lyons, "Torremaggiore," 274.

96. Joseph Coldwell in Lyons, *Life and Death*, 33.

97. "Drapers Agree to Conference," *BG*, April 16, 1913.

98. EGE, *Outstanding Features*, 27.

99. NS to CCJ, December 6, 1923, in *Letters*, 11–12.

100. *Transcript*, 2:1606.

101. Talbot, "1900," in Chaffee, *Beyond Plymouth Rock*, 6; Morison, *Ropemakers*, 92–97; and BV to Aunt Edvige, December 15, 1914, in *Il Caso*, 52.

102. "Plymouth Has a Mystery Strike," *BG*, January 18, 1916; Morison, *Ropemakers*, 105; and BV to Aunt Edvige, July 12, 1915, in *Il Caso*, 56.

103. "Mill Strikers Reject Offer," *BG*, January 22, 1916; and "Strikers Tell Board Demands," *BG*, January 28, 1916.

104. Morison, *Ropemakers*, 107–108.

105. Shields, *Are They Doomed?*, 13.

106. Morison, *Ropemakers*, 113; BV, interview by Art Shields, *On the Battle Lines, 1919–1939* (New York: International Publishers, 1987), 34; and *Plymouth*, 6.

107. "Plymouth Mill Reopens Today," *BG*, February 3, 1916.

108. "Settle Strike at Plymouth," *BG*, February 16, 1916.

109. "Three Arrested for Braintree Murders," *BH*, May 7, 1920.

110. Dubofsky, *We Shall Be All*, 319–323, 326–327.

111. History Chart (for NS), MA/Inmate, Folder 17402.

112. Dubofsky, *We Shall Be All*, 332.

113. Pernicone, *Carlo Tresca*, 93; and D'Attilio, "La Salute è in Voi," 78.

114. "Babe Sets Record as Sox Win Twice," *BG*, September 9, 1919.

115. Joseph Slater, "Public Workers: Labor and the Boston Police Strike of 1919," *Labor History* 38, no. 1 (winter 1996–1997): 16, and Edwin U. Curtis, *Fourteenth Annual Report of the Police Commissioner for the City of Boston, Year Ending November 30, 1919* (Boston: Public Document No. 49, 1920), 15, repr. in *Boston Police Strike, Two Reports* (New York: Arno Press, 1971). In 1919 Boston policemen worked 73 to 98 hours a week and, after 6 years, maxed out at an annual salary of $1,400: Slater, "Public Workers," 15, and Francis Russell, *A City in Terror: 1919, the Boston Police Strike* (New York: Viking Press, 1975), 48.

116. U.S. Bureau of the Census, *Statistical History*, 179. The number of work stoppages reported was 3,630.

117. Slater, "Public Workers," 8–13.

118. Ibid., 16; "Firemen Will Do 'What Labor Demands of Us,'" *BG*, September 10, 1919; and "Park Police Refuse to Do Street Duty," *BG*, September 11, 1919.

119. Slater, "Public Workers," 26.

120. Frederick Manuel Koss, "The Boston Police Strike of 1919" (PhD diss., Boston University, 1966), microfiche, 245.

121. *Transcript*, 1:868.

122. EGE, *Outstanding Features*, 27.

123. *Transcript*, 2:1606–08.

124. Michael Kelley in EGE, *Outstanding Features*, 26.

125. *Proletarian*, 18–19; and Knox, "Trial of the Century: Local Amnesia," in Chaffee, *Beyond Plymouth Rock*, 76.

126. *Proletarian*, 19–20.

CHAPTER 5: CONSTRUCTING A CASE

1. "Three Arrested," *BH*, May 7, 1920.

2. HBE, *Case That Will Not Die*, 103, 149.

3. "Believe Bandit Chief Deported," *BG*, May 9, 1920.

4. *Brockton Times*, April 21, 1920, in Fred J. Cook, "Sacco-Vanzetti: The Missing Fingerprints," *The Nation*, December 22, 1962, 450.

5. Ibid.

6. "Believe Bandit Chief Deported," *BG*, May 9, 1920.

7. Simon A. Cole, *Suspect Identities: A History of Fingerprinting and Criminal Identification* (Cambridge, MA: Harvard University Press, 2001), 177–181; and Colin Beavan, *Fingerprints:*

The Origins of Crime Detection and the Murder Case That Launched Forensic Science (New York: Hyperion, 2001), xv.

8. "Asks Murder Warrants for Yegg Suspects," *BH*, May 9, 1920; Van Amburgh, "Hidden Drama," Part 2, May 1935, 106; Russell, *Tragedy in Dedham*, 97; Coacci's Trunk, report by Officer John H. Scott, n.d., MA/SP, Box 1, Folder 5; and FBI file on Sacco and Vanzetti, in Pernicone, *Carlo Tresca*, 118, 316.

9. "Three Arrested," *BH*, May 7, 1920; and "Police Obtain Clue to More of Bandit Gang," *BH*, May 8, 1920.

10. Felix Frankfurter, *The Case of Sacco and Vanzetti: A Critical Analysis for Lawyers and Laymen* (New York: Grosset & Dunlap, 1962), 12.

11. *Transcript*, 2:1861–62.

12. "Master Bandit Is Now Sought," *BG*, May 8, 1920.

13. "Police Obtain Clue," *BH*, May 8, 1920; and "Asks Murder Warrants for Yegg Suspects," *BH*, May 9, 1920.

14. "Three Arrested," *BH*, May 7, 1920.

15. "Hyde Park Man," *BG*, May 7, 1920.

16. "Master Bandit Is Now Sought," *BG*, May 8, 1920.

17. "Murder Charge against Sacco," *BG*, May 12, 1920.

18. "Hyde Park Man," *BG*, May 7, 1920.

19. "Arrest Two Armed Suspects in Car," *BH*, May 6, 1920; and "Police Obtain Clue," *BH*, May 8, 1920.

20. *Plymouth*, 31.

21. *Transcript*, 2:1743–44, 1932.

22. CUOHROC: AF, 49.

23. Ibid., 48, 49, 55.

24. Ibid., 51, 54.

25. *Plymouth*, 15.

26. CUOHROC: AF, 55.

27. *Plymouth*, 9.

28. Claghorn, *Immigrant's Day in Court*, 131, 123; and *Plymouth*, 15.

29. Claghorn, *Immigrant's Day in Court*, 129, 206, 133.

30. WGT and HBE to Gov. Fuller, June 15, 1927, in *Transcript*, 6:346 (Bridgewater), and Fraenkel, *Sacco-Vanzetti Case*, 13 (Braintree).

31. WGT statement to Advisory Committee, July 25, 1927, in *Transcript*, 5:5301–02.

CHAPTER 6: "CONSCRIPTION WAS UPON THEM"
1. Karin Goldstein, "Over Here: 1916–1918," in Chaffee, *Beyond Plymouth Rock*, 66–67.

2. David M. Kennedy, *Over Here: The First World War and American Society* (Oxford: Oxford University Press, 1980), 12.

3. Woodrow Wilson, Address to Congress, April 2, 1917, *Foreign Relations of the United States, 1917, Supplement I, The World War*, in *The Eagle and the Dove, The American Peace Movement and United States Foreign Policy, 1900–1922*, 2nd ed., ed. John Whiteclay Chambers II (Syracuse: Syracuse University Press, 1992), 112–113.

4. "The President's Appeal for Unity," in James A. Moss and M. B. Stewart, *Our Flag and Its Message* (Philadelphia: J. B. Lippincott Company, 1917), 16.

5. "An Act to Authorize the President to Increase Temporarily the Military Establishment of the United States," 65th Cong., 1st sess. (May 18, 1917), *U.S. Statutes at Large*, 76–78.

6. Ibid., 80.

7. Christopher Capozzola, *Uncle Sam Wants You: World War I and the Making of the Modern American Citizen* (New York: Oxford University Press, 2008), 23.

8. Kennedy, *Over Here*, 21–23, 37, 307.

9. Dubofsky, *We Shall Be All*, 350–351.

10. Bill Haywood to Frank Little, May 6, 1917, in Renshaw, *The Wobblies*, 217.

11. Ibid., 219; Dubofsky, *We Shall Be All*, 357; and Lowell S. Hawley and Ralph Bushnell Potts, *Counsel for the Damned: A Biography of George Francis Vanderveer* (Philadelphia: J. B. Lippincott Company, 1953), 226.

12. Paul Avrich, "Italian Anarchism in America: An Historical Background to the Sacco-Vanzetti Case," in *Sacco-Vanzetti: Developments and Reconsiderations*, 64.

13. Paul Avrich, *Anarchist Portraits* (Princeton, NJ: Princeton University Press, 1988), 167.

14. Paul Ghio, quoted in ibid., 168; and Carlo Buda via Charles Poggi in Avrich, *Anarchist Voices*, 132.

15. Avrich, *Anarchist Portraits*, 170.

16. Avrich, *Sacco and Vanzetti*, 59.

17. Charles Ashleigh, *Rambling Kid* (London: Faber & Faber Limited [1930?]), 201–202.

18. Kennedy, *Over Here*, 147; Ernest L. Meyer, *"Hey! Yellowbacks!" The War Diary of a Conscientious Objector* (New York: John Day Company, 1930), 4; and Thomas Wolfe, *Look Homeward, Angel: A Story of the Buried Life* (New York: Charles Scribner's Sons, 1929), 349–350.

19. "An Act to . . . Increase Temporarily the Military Establishment" (May 18, 1917), 78; and D'Attilio, "La Salute è in Voi," 79. At his Plymouth trial, however, Vanzetti said he had not "taken out first papers" for citizenship: *Transcript*, 6:155.

20. However, Sacco said he was planning "to get my citizen papers" before visiting Italy in 1920, "so I won't have any trouble when I come back to this country": NS statement, 8, MA/SP, Box 1, Folder 5.

21. *Transcript*, 2:1770.

22. Ronald Creagh, *Sacco et Vanzetti* (Paris: Éditions La Découverte, 1984), 97; Lyons, *Life and Death*, 37; Dos Passos, *Facing the Chair*, 67; and Avrich, *Sacco and Vanzetti*, 60.

23. BV to his father, sisters, and brother, July 26, 1917, in *Il Caso*, 57–58.

24. *Transcript*, 2:1869, 1820.

25. Avrich, *Sacco and Vanzetti*, 66.

26. EGE, *Outstanding Features*, 21; Dos Passos, *Facing the Chair*, 67; and D'Attilio, "La Salute è in Voi," 80, 83.

27. *Transcript*, 2:1877; BV to Aunt Edvige, December 15, 1914, in *Il Caso*, 53–55; and *Transcript*, 5:4916.

28. Joseph Moro in Avrich, *Anarchist Voices*, 114.

29. *Un Trentennio di Attivita Anarchica*, quoted in D'Attilio, "La Salute è in Voi," 80.

30. Carlo Valdinocci to Raffaele Schiavina, September 4, 1917, quoted in Avrich, *Sacco and Vanzetti*, 66, 227n29.

31. *Transcript*, 2:1820–22.

32. Avrich, *Sacco and Vanzetti*, 65, 70; and BV to his father, May 14, 1918, in *Il Caso*, 58–59.

33. George Creel, *How We Advertised America: The First Telling of the Amazing Story of the Committee on Public Information That Carried the Gospel of Americanization to Every Corner of the Globe* (New York: Harper & Brothers, 1920), 3–5.

34. Ibid., 114; 7, 85; 12, 76–77; and 134.

35. Capozzola, *Uncle Sam Wants You*, 42.

36. Creel, *How We Advertised America*, 181, 167.

37. Theodore Roosevelt, April 1917, in Chambers, *Eagle and the Dove*, 126–127.

38. John W. Chambers, introduction to *The Conscientious Objector*, by Walter Guest Kellogg (New York: Boni & Liveright, 1919; repr., New York: Garland Publishing, 1972); citations are to the Garland edition.

39. Introduction to Kellogg, *Conscientious Objector*, and Capozzola, *Uncle Sam Wants You*, 56.

40. Kellogg, *Conscientious Objector*, 6.

41. Ibid., 68, 70, 73.

42. Capozzola, *Uncle Sam Wants You*, 59.

43. Meyer, "Hey! Yellowbacks!," 36, 59, 138.

44. Roger Kahn, *A Flame of Pure Fire: Jack Dempsey and The Roaring '20s* (New York: Harcourt Brace & Company, 1999), 21, 24–25.

45. Ibid., 235, 200.

46. Obituary of Jack Dempsey, *NYT*, June 1, 1983.

47. Kennedy, *Over Here*, 165, and Capozzola, *Uncle Sam Wants You*, 9, 30.

48. Roberta E. Dell, *United States against Bergdoll: How the Government Spent Twenty Years and Millions of Dollars to Capture and Punish America's Most Notorious Draft Dodger* (Cranbury, NJ: A. S. Barnes and Company, 1977), 27.

49. Ibid., 65, 75, 77, 103, 124–27.

50. Ibid., 139, 141, 184.

51. Ibid., 139, 143, 157–165, 224.

52. Ibid., 244–49.

53. *BET*, May 3, 1924, quoted in introduction to Kellogg, *Conscientious Objector*.

54. Creel, *How We Advertised America*, 177. This number, or "very conservatively 245,000," was "more than of any other immigrant nationality": Philip M. Rose, *The Italians in America*, quoted in Antonio Stella, *Some Aspects of Italian Immigration to the United States* (New York: G. P. Putnam's Sons, 1924), 79.

55. Eben Putnam, preface to *Report of the Commission on Massachusetts' Part in the World War: The Gold Star Record of Massachusetts* (Boston: Commonwealth of Massachusetts, 1929), 2:xi.

56. Creel, *How We Advertised America*, 177.

57. Rose, *Italians in America*, quoted in Stella, *Aspects of Italian Immigration*, 79.

58. Some sources say Sacco quit; see EGE, *Outstanding Features*, 26. Others say he was fired; see Sacco bio by Officer John H. Scott, January 21, 1921, MA/SP, Box 1, Folder 5.

59. *Transcript*, 2:1967.

60. Ibid., 5:4916.

61. Kahn, *Flame of Pure Fire*, 264.

62. "Bergdoll's Proxy a Hero," *BG*, July 3, 1921.

CHAPTER 7: DRY RUN AT PLYMOUTH

1. Beltrando Brini in Avrich, *Anarchist Voices*, 103.
2. Michael Stewart in Russell, *Tragedy in Dedham*, 19.
3. Obituary of Webster Thayer, *NYT*, April 19, 1933; and Russell, *Tragedy in Dedham*, 98.
4. "Judge Rebukes Jury," *BET*, April 24, 1920.
5. *Transcript*, 6:49, 88, 21, 9–10.
6. Ibid., 6:90, 94, 25–28.
7. Ibid., 6:128–133.
8. Ibid., 6:116–117, 124, 30–31.
9. Ibid., 6:365–367.
10. Ibid., 6:65, 81, 90.
11. *Plymouth*, 22.
12. *Transcript*, 6:329, 263.
13. *Plymouth*, 18; and EGE, *Outstanding Features*, 18.
14. *Transcript*, 6:225–226, 244 (Fortini); 6:258 (B. Brini); and 6:305 (A. Brini).
15. Ibid., 6:224–226, 236.
16. Ibid., 6:316–117 (Longhi); and 6:254–255 (R. Balboni).
17. Ibid., 6:240 (DiCarli); and 6:281–282 (Malaquci).
18. Ibid., 6:251–253.
19. Ibid., 6:259–260.
20. Ibid., 6:227.
21. Ibid., 6:284, 288–289.
22. Ibid., 6:295, 301, 227.
23. Ibid., 6:248, 262; 292–293; 263; 248, 263.
24. The eight witnesses who put Vanzetti in Plymouth at the time of the Bridgewater crime were Mary Fortini, Carlo Balboni, Vincent Longhi, Rosa Balboni, John DiCarli, Terese Malaquci, Enrico Bastoni, and Beltrando Brini. Other witnesses who put Vanzetti in Plymouth later on the day of the crime were Margaretta Fiochi, Adeladi Bonjionanni, Emma Borsari, Esther Christophori, Vincenzo Brini, and Rose Forni (plus Mary Fortini and Beltrando Brini, who saw him more than once that day).
25. *Plymouth*, 21.
26. *Transcript*, 6:266, 271.
27. Beltrando Brini, quoted in Russell, *Tragedy in Dedham*, 22.
28. *Transcript*, 6:158.
29. Ibid., 6:171.
30. Ibid., 6:188–189.
31. Ibid., 6:105, 137–138.
32. Ibid., 6:364; 366; 60, 73.
33. Ibid., 6:143; 251, 293; and ibid., 2:1728.
34. Ibid., 6:140–141, 149.
35. Ibid., 6:146–148.
36. Ibid., 6:209.
37. Ibid., 6:220.
38. *Plymouth*, 34.

39. James Graham, quoted in Robert H. Montgomery, *Sacco-Vanzetti: The Murder and the Myth* (New York: Devin-Adair, 1960), 39–40.

40. *Transcript*, 6:244, 298–299, 274.

41. WGT and HBE to Gov. Fuller, June 15, 1927, in *Transcript*, 6:354.

42. Simon Sullivan in ibid., 6:356.

43. Ibid., 6:336.

44. CUOHROC: AF, 60.

45. "Vanzetti Convicted in Plymouth Court," *BG*, July 2, 1920.

46. WGT and HBE to Gov. Fuller, June 15, 1927, in *Transcript*, 6:356.

47. HBE, *Case That Will Not Die*, 114.

48. "Gives Slayer Life Sentence," *BH*, August 17, 1920.

49. "Twelve Years for Vanzetti Bandit," *BG*, August 17, 1920.

50. CUOHROC: AF, 58; and *Plymouth*, 36.

51. CUOHROC: AF, 58.

52. Montgomery, *Sacco-Vanzetti: The Murder and the Myth*, 20; and HBE, *Case That Will Not Die*, 115.

53. *Plymouth*, 36.

54. Shields, *On the Battle Lines*, 36; EGE, *Outstanding Features*, 6; and *Plymouth*, 36.

55. Cookie Stephan, "Selective Characteristics of Jurors and Litigants: Their Influence on Juries' Verdicts," in *The Jury System in America: A Critical Overview*, ed. Ruth James Simon (Beverly Hills, CA: Sage Publications, 1975), 104–105.

56. BV to ASB, June 18, 1925, Lilly; and *Plymouth*, 17.

57. CUOHROC: AF, 58, 60.

58. Pernicone, *Carlo Tresca*, 110; and CUOHROC: AF, 69–70.

59. EGF, *Rebel Girl*, 299–303.

60. Lyons, *Life and Death*, 66.

61. California Bar Association, Membership Records, e-mail from MEMREC@calbar.ca.gov to author, May 29, 2002; and *Transcript*, 2:2122.

62. Eugene Lyons, *Assignment in Utopia* (New York: Harcourt, Brace and Company, 1937; repr., New Brunswick, NJ: Transaction Publishers, 1991), 13; citations are to the Transaction edition.

63. Obituary of Marian L. Gore, *Los Angeles Times*, November 5, 2009; and Lyons, *Assignment in Utopia*, 14.

64. Mary Hunter to Dorothy Gallagher, February 1979; interview notes provided by Dorothy Gallagher to the author via Nunzio Pernicone.

65. T. H. Bell, "In Memoriam, Fred Moore," *Freedom: A Monthly Journal of Anarchist News and Opinion*, September 1933, 4.

66. Joseph Gordon to *The Workingman's Paper*, January 14, 1910, quoted in Townsend, *Running the Gauntlet*, 68.

67. Dubofsky, *We Shall Be All*, 175–183; and Hawley and Potts, *Counsel for the Damned*, 189.

68. Lyons, *Life and Death*, 31; and George Roewer in HBE, *Case That Will Not Die*, 153.

69. Dubofsky, *We Shall Be All*, 339–341, and Foner, *History of the Labor Movement*, vol. 4, 534–535.

70. Walker C. Smith, *The Everett Massacre: A History of the Class Struggle in the Lumber Industry* (Chicago: IWW Publishing Bureau, ca. 1920), 292, 295.

71. Hawley and Potts, *Counsel for the Damned*, 192.

72. Smith, *Everett Massacre*, 276

73. Ibid., 259.

74. Renshaw, *The Wobblies*, 22.

75. Philip Taft, "The Federal Trials of the IWW," *Labor History* 3, no. 1 (Winter 1962): 57–91.

76. White, "United States v. C. W. Anderson," 156 ("over a year"), and Renshaw, *The Wobblies*, 233 ("week or so").

77. White, "United States v. C. W. Anderson," 145–152, and *"Knights of Liberty" Mob*, 5–8.

78. Clayton R. Koppes, "The Kansas Trial of the IWW, 1917–1919," *Labor History* 16, no. 3 (Summer 1975): 339, and White, "United States v. C. W. Anderson," 153.

79. W. I. Fisher in *The One Big Union Monthly*, July 1919; and Forrest Edwards, William Clark, and Caroline Lowe in *The One Big Union Monthly*, September 1919.

80. Koppes, "Kansas Trial of the IWW," 345–347; and White, "United States v. C. W. Anderson," 158.

81. "A Hung Jury on Krieger's Guilt," *Tulsa Daily World*, November 11, 1919.

82. White, "United States v. C. W. Anderson," 158.

83. Ibid., 158–160, and Koppes, "Kansas Trial of the IWW," 353–356.

84. Koppes, "Kansas Trial of the IWW," 355, and White, "United States v. C. W. Anderson," 159.

85. White, "United States v. C. W. Anderson," 159.

86. EGF, *Rebel Girl*, 302–303.

87. CUOHROC: AF, 70, 72, 110.

88. Lyons, *Life and Death*, 68.

89. CUOHROC: AF, 91–92.

90. *Proletarian*, 19.

91. BV to his father, October 1, 1920, in *Il Caso*, 63–65.

92. FM to Elsie Hillsmith, January 25, 1921, BPL, Series 4, Box 32, Folder 21.

93. HBE, interview by Livia Baker, June 3, 1968, HLSL, Box 7, Folder 11.

94. CUOHROC: AF, 73–74.

95. Ibid.

96. "Guaranteed Mock Trial," *BET*, January 28, 1921, and "Clerk Squires Named in Trial," *BG*, January 28, 1921.

97. "Guaranteed Mock Trial," *BET*, January 28, 1921, "Clerk Squires Named," *BG*, January 28, 1921, and "Hints DeFalco Case Frameup," *BG*, January 29, 1921.

98. CUOHROC: AF, 75.

99. Ibid., 76.

100. Ibid., 76–77.

101. "Saw Skeletons on Posters and Fled," *BG*, February 1, 1921.

102. "Katzmann Denies He Knows Mrs. DeFalco," *BG*, February 2, 1921.

103. "Mrs. DeFalco Found Not Guilty by Court," *BG*, February 4, 1921.

104. Russell, *Tragedy in Dedham*, 121.

105. *Transcript*, 5:5051, and Frankfurter, *Case of Sacco and Vanzetti*, 8.

106. "What Does the Future Hold in Store for Us?," *Bulletin*, February 1927, 1.

107. Young and Kaiser, *Postmortem*, 43 (Tufts, Pelletier); Joughin and Morgan, *Legacy of Sacco & Vanzetti*, 315 (Reading).

108. CUOHROC: AF, 78.

CHAPTER 8: "TERRORIST PLOT IS SEEN"

1. "Eyewitness Depicts Crash and Scenes of Carnage in Its Train," *BH*, September 17, 1920.

2. "Wall St. Explosion Kills 30, Injures 300," *NYT*, September 17, 1920.

3. Avrich, *Sacco and Vanzetti*, 205–207; and Mario Buda, interview by Edward Houlton [*sic*] James ("Buda's Story"), February 14–16, 1928, HLSL, Folder 12, Box 21.

4. A. Mitchell Palmer, "The Case against the 'Reds,'" *Forum*, 1920, in David F. Trask, *World War I at Home: Readings on American Life, 1914–1920* (New York: John Wiley & Sons, 1970), 185–186.

5. Luigi Galleani, *The End of Anarchism?*, trans. Max Sartin and Robert D'Attilio (Orkney, Scotland: Cienfuegos Press, 1982), 8.

6. Errico Malatesta, "Il Programma Anarchico," 1920, in *Errico Malatesta: His Life & Ideas*, ed. Vernon Richards (London: Freedom Press, 1965), 27.

7. Galleani, *End of Anarchism?*, 16.

8. Marie Fleming, "Propaganda by the Deed: Terrorism and Anarchist Theory in Late Nineteenth-Century Europe," in *Terrorism in Europe*, ed. Yonah Alexander and Kenneth A. Myers (New York: St. Martin's Press, 1982), 8.

9. Ibid., 2, and Nunzio Pernicone, "Anarchism in Italy, 1872–1900," in *Italian American Radicalism: Old World Origins and New World Developments, Proceedings of the 5th Annual Conference of the American Italian Historical Association*, ed. Rudolph J. Vecoli (Staten Island, NY: AIHA, 1972), 16, 19, 28.

10. Malatesta, *Umanità Nova*, October 21, 1922, in Richards, *Errico Malatesta*, 58.

11. BV to ASB, November 13, 1924, in *Letters*, 133.

12. Avrich, *Anarchist Portraits*, 164; Philip V. Cannistraro and Gerald Meyer, eds., introduction to *The Lost World of Italian American Radicalism: Politics, Labor, and Culture* (Westport, CT: Praeger, 2003), 17; and Pernicone, "Anarchism in Italy," 13.

13. Philip S. Foner, *May Day: A Short History of the International Workers' Holiday, 1886–1986* (New York: International Publishers, 1986), 29–39.

14. Louis Post, *Deportations Delirium*, 12; and Emma Goldman, *Living My Life*, vol. 1 (New York: Dover Publications, 1970), 7–10.

15. Alexander Berkman, *Prison Memoirs of an Anarchist* (New York: Schocken Books, 1970), 59.

16. Harris M. Lentz III, *Assassinations and Executions: An Encyclopedia of Political Violence, 1865–1986* (Jefferson, NC: McFarland & Company, 1988), 23; and Pernicone, "Anarchism in Italy," 2.

17. James W. Clarke, *American Assassins: The Darker Side of Politics* (Princeton, NJ: Princeton University Press, 1982), 39, 53–55.

18. Malatesta, "Causa ed Effetti," September 22, 1900, in Richards, *Errico Malatesta*, 64; and Malatesta, *l'Agitazione*, September 22, 1901, in ibid., 62.

19. Galleani, *End of Anarchism?*, 51, 60.

20. "Act to Regulate the Immigration of Aliens," 57th Cong., 2nd sess. (March 3, 1903), *U.S. Statutes at Large*, 1214, 1221.

21. BV, *Proletarian*, 21, 23–24.

22. BV to Aunt Edvige, ca. 1919, in *Il Caso*, 63.

23. Attilio Bortolotti in Avrich, *Anarchist Voices*, 184; and Avrich, *Sacco and Vanzetti*, 27.

24. CUOHROC: GJ, 190–192.

25. EGF, *Rebel Girl*, 303–305.

26. Phil Stong, "The Last Days of Sacco and Vanzetti," in *The Aspirin Age, 1919–1941*, ed. Isabel Leighton (New York: Simon & Schuster, 1949), 170; Dos Passos, *Facing the Chair*, 56; and HBE to Upton Sinclair, June 9, 1928, HLSL, Box 14, Folder 8.

27. CUOHROC: GJ, 192.

28. CUOHROC: AF, 28–29.

29. Ibid., 31; and Luigi Galleani, "La Salute è in Voi" in Topp, *Brief History with Documents*, 63–65.

30. Thomas Tunney quoted in Beverly Gage, *The Day Wall Street Exploded: A Story of America in Its First Age of Terror* (New York: Oxford University Press, 2009), 209; and D'Attilio, "La Salute è in Voi," 89.

31. Fleming, "Propaganda by the Deed," 16, and Ulrich Linse, " 'Propaganda by Deed' and 'Direct Action,' " Two Concepts of Anarchist Violence," in *Social Protest, Violence and Terror in Nineteenth- and Twentieth-Century Europe*, ed. Wolfgang J. Mommsen and Gerhard Hirschfeld (New York: St. Martin's Press, 1982), 202.

32. Albert Parsons, *Alarm*, February 21, 1885, in Louis Adamic, *Dynamite: A Century of Class Violence in America, 1830–1930* (London: Rebel Press, 1984), 32.

33. Avrich, *Sacco and Vanzetti*, 99–100, and Gage, *Day Wall Street Exploded*, 96, 101.

34. *Cronaca Sovversiva*, March 13, 1915, quoted in Avrich, *Sacco and Vanzetti*, 101.

35. Ibid., 99–101.

36. "Dynamite at State House," *BG*, January 1, 1916.

37. Avrich, *Sacco and Vanzetti*, 102, and McCormick, *Hopeless Cases*, 2.

38. Avrich, *Sacco and Vanzetti*, 95, 104.

39. Ibid., 105.

40. CUOHROC: GJ, 191.

41. Jenny Salemme in Avrich, *Anarchist Voices*, 111.

42. Avrich, *Sacco and Vanzetti*, 108–111.

43. "Dynamite Girl Throws Light on IWW Plot," *Chicago Tribune*, January 20, 1918.

44. "Death Satchel in Girl's Hands Perils Scores," *Chicago Tribune*, January 19, 1918.

45. Avrich, *Sacco and Vanzetti*, 113.

46. McCormick, *Hopeless Cases*, 14; and Avrich, *Sacco and Vanzetti*, 118–122.

47. McCormick, *Hopeless Cases*, 17; and Avrich, *Sacco and Vanzetti*, 123.

48. Avrich, *Sacco and Vanzetti*, 125, and Young and Kaiser, *Postmortem*, 15.

49. Anthony Caminetti to H. J. Skeffington, May 13, 1918, quoted in Avrich, *Sacco and Vanzetti*, 126–127.

50. John Ryder quoted in Young and Kaiser, *Postmortem*, 16.

51. Anthony Caminetti, May 8, 1918, in ibid., 15.

52. D'Attilio, "La Salute è in Voi," 84.

53. "An Act to Punish Acts of Interference with the Foreign Relations, the Neutrality, and the Foreign Commerce of the United States . . .," 65th Cong., 1st sess. (June 15, 1917), *U.S. Statutes at Large*, 217–231.

54. "An Act to Define, Regulate, and Punish Trading with the Enemy . . .," 65th Cong., 1st sess. (October 6, 1917), *U.S. Statutes at Large*, 411–426.

55. "An Act to Amend . . . the Act Entitled 'An Act to Punish Acts of Interference with the Foreign Relations, the Neutrality, and the Foreign Commerce of the United States . . .," 65th Cong., 2nd sess. (May 16, 1918), *U.S. Statutes at Large*, 553–554.

56. "An Act to Exclude and Expel from the United States Aliens Who Are Members of the Anarchistic and Similar Classes," 65th Cong., 2nd sess. (October 16, 1918), *U.S. Statutes at Large*, 1012.

57. William H. Rehnquist, *All the Laws but One: Civil Liberties in Wartime* (New York: Alfred A. Knopf, 1998), 178.

58. Eric Foner, *The Story of American Freedom* (New York: W. W. Norton & Company, 1998), 177.

59. Sacco bio by Officer John H. Scott, January 21, 1921, MA/SP, Box 1, Folder 5; George Kelley in EGE, *Outstanding Features*, 26; *Transcript*, 2:1962; EGF, *Rebel Girl*, 304; Dr. Abraham Myerson, April 7, 1927, HLSL, Box 13, Folder 16; and Betty Jack Wirth, telephone interview with author, October 4, 2000.

60. EGF, *Rebel Girl*, 304; CUOHROC: AF, 64; Concetta Silvestri in Avrich, *Anarchist Voices*, 108; NS to FM, August 18, 1924, in *Letters*, 24; Upton Sinclair to WGT, June 16, 1928, HLSL, Box 14, Folder 8; and D'Attilio, "La Salute è in Voi," 88.

61. Lefevre Brini in Avrich, *Sacco and Vanzetti*, 38; BV to EGE, July 22, 1921, in *Letters*, 81; and Alfonsina Brini in Feuerlicht, *Justice Crucified*, 27.

62. BV to ASB, February 27, 1924, in *Letters*, 119–121; BV to ASB, November 13, 1924, in *Letters*, 132; and *Transcript*, 5:4922.

63. Melvyn Dubofsky, "Italian Anarchism and the American Dream: A Comment," in Vecoli, *Italian American Radicalism*, 55.

64. Elide Sanchini in Avrich, *Anarchist Voices*, 138; and Sebastiano Magliocca in ibid., 121.

65. D'Attilio, "La Salute è in Voi," 80; and *Transcript*, 2:1820.

66. BV to his father, May 14, 1918 and September 26, 1918, in *Il Caso*, 58–60; and *Transcript*, 2:1727.

67. Avrich, *Sacco and Vanzetti*, 107.

68. U.S. Bureau of the Census, *Statistical History*, 179. There were 3,789 recorded strikes in 1916; 4,450 in 1917; 3,353 in 1918; and 3,630 in 1919.

69. Avrich, *Sacco and Vanzetti*, 137.

70. Robert K. Murray, *Red Scare: A Study in National Hysteria, 1919–1920* (Westport, CT: Greenwood Press, 1955), 69.

71. Ibid., 69–71, and Avrich, *Sacco and Vanzetti*, 140–148.

72. "'Red' Blown to Bits as He Dynamites Palmer's House, Bombs in Seven Other Cities Spread Nation-Wide Terror," *WP*, June 3, 1919.

73. Ibid.

74. Ibid.

75. "Running Down the Terrorists," *BET*, June 3, 1919.

76. Post, *Deportations Delirium*, 38–41; "'Red' Blown to Bits," *WP*, June 3, 1919; "Capture 61 Suspected 'Reds' in Federal and State Dragnets; Dynamiter Here May Be Russian," *WP*, June 4, 1919; "Trail Reds in Secret," *WP*, June 7, 1919; "Unravels Bomb Plot," *WP*, June 11, 1919; and "Trailing 'Red' Chiefs," *WP*, June 9, 1919.

77. "Terror Reign Predicted for Fourth Fizzles," *San Francisco Chronicle*, July 5, 1919.

78. Post, *Deportations Delirium*, 49; David Williams, "The Bureau of Investigation and Its Critics, 1919–1921: The Origins of Federal Political Surveillance," *Journal of American History* 68, no. 3 (December 1981): 560–561; and Murray, *Red Scare*, 193.

79. "Know Dens of Crime," *WP*, June 4, 1919.

80. "Trail Reds in Secret," *WP*, June 7, 1919.

81. McCormick, *Hopeless Cases*, 3.

82. Post, *Deportations Delirium*, 44, 47.

83. Murray, *Red Scare*, 16.

84. Ibid., 165.

85. Ibid., 196, and Stanley Coben, *A. Mitchell Palmer: Politician* (New York: Columbia University Press, 1963), 215.

86. A. Mitchell Palmer quoted in Coben, *A. Mitchell Palmer*, 215.

87. A. Mitchell Palmer, "The Case against the 'Reds,'" in Trask, *World War I at Home*, 186.

88. Post, *Deportations Delirium*, 28; and Murray, *Red Scare*, 196–197.

89. "Bomb Factory of Radicals Raided by New York Officials," *San Francisco Chronicle*, November 26, 1919.

90. Murray, *Red Scare*, 207–209.

91. Post, *Deportations Delirium*, 80–81.

92. Zechariah Chafee, Jr., *Free Speech in the United States* (Cambridge, MA: Harvard University Press, 1941), 199, and Murray, *Red Scare*, 211–212.

93. Burke to Kelleher, December 27, 1919, in R. G. Brown and others, *To the American People: Report upon Illegal Practices of the United States Department of Justice* (Washington, DC: National Popular Government League, 1920), 37–40.

94. Post, *Deportations Delirium*, 155–157, and Chafee, *Free Speech*, 214–215.

95. "Decision Hits Fight on Reds," *BH*, May 6, 1920.

96. *Report upon Illegal Practices*, 4–8.

97. Ibid., 12, 18, 20, 22–23, 55.

98. Post, *Deportations Delirium*, 230–231.

99. Colyer et al. v. Skeffington, *The Federal Reporter* 265, August-September 1920 (St. Paul, MN: West Publishing Co., 1920), 79.

100. Post, *Deportations Delirium*, 166–167.

101. *Report upon Illegal Practices*, 7–8.

102. "May Day," *BET*, May 1, 1920.

103. Coben, *A. Mitchell Palmer*, 241; and Post, *Deportations Delirium*, 79.

104. A. Mitchell Palmer, "The Case against the 'Reds,'" in Trask, *World War I at Home*, 187–188.

105. Emmett T. Drew, "Summary Report in re Explosion of Bomb at Paterson N.J. on the Night of June 2, 1919," May 14, 1920, in Gage, *Day Wall Street Exploded*, 211, 365n10.

106. Avrich, *Sacco and Vanzetti*, 178–187, and Young and Kaiser, *Postmortem*, 19–21. See *Transcript*, 5:4983–87 for Elia's account.

107. "Red's Death Plunge," *NYT*, May 4, 1920; and *Transcript*, 5:4986.

108. "Red's Death Plunge," *NYT*, May 4, 1920; and Gage, *Day Wall Street Exploded*, 214.

109. A. Mitchell Palmer quoted in Post, *Deportations Delirium*, 280; and *Transcript*, 5:4985.

110. Avrich, *Sacco and Vanzetti*, 195.

111. Post, *Deportations Delirium*, 200.

112. Young and Kaiser, *Postmortem*, 125, 131.

113. *Transcript*, 5:4503–06.

114. Valerio Isca in Avrich, *Anarchist Voices*, 147.

115. "Kills 30, Injures 300," *NYT*, September 17, 1920; and "Property Damage Put at $2,000,000," *NYT*, September 18, 1920.

116. "Palmer Comes Here to Direct Inquiry," *NYT*, September 18, 1920.

117. "Secret Service Men Rushed to New York," *BH*; "Theories of Cause of Explosion," *WSJ*; and "Red Plot Seen in Blast," *NYT*, September 17, 1920 (all).

118. "Circulars Clue to Plot," *NYT*, September 18, 1920.

119. "Five Anarchists Sought by Flynn," *NYT*, September 19, 1920.

120. *Chicago Tribune*, repr. in ibid.

121. Murray, *Red Scare*, 81, and Avrich, *Sacco and Vanzetti*, 207.

122. McCormick, *Hopeless Cases*, 118, and Gage, *Day Wall Street Exploded*, 261.

123. Avrich, *Sacco and Vanzetti*, 205–207, 245n32.

124. Charles Poggi (quoting Frank Maffi) in Avrich, *Anarchist Voices*, 133.

125. Mario Buda interview, February 14–16, 1928, HLSL, Folder 12, Box 21.

126. "Dynamite for Wall Street," *WSJ*, September 17, 1920.

127. Kennedy, *Over Here*, 292.

128. F. Scott Fitzgerald, "Echoes of the Jazz Age," *Scribners Magazine*, November 1931, repr. in F. Scott Fitzgerald, *The Crack-Up*, ed. Edmund Wilson (New York: New Directions, 1956).

129. Warren Harding quoted in William E. Leuchtenburg, *The Perils of Prosperity, 1914–32* (Chicago: University of Chicago Press, 1958), 89.

130. "Wall Street Bomb Outrage Work of Boston Anarchists," *Daily News*, August 25, 1921.

131. Gage, *Day Wall Street Exploded*, 257.

132. FM to Eugene Lyons, August 29, 1921, BPL, Series 4, Box 33, Folder 10.

CHAPTER 9: DEDHAM: CURTAIN RISING

1. "Today's Globe Contents," *BG*, June 28, 1921, and "Heat Fells Nine," *BG*, July 5, 1921.

2. EGE, "Memoir," 1–2, Schlesinger, Reel 1.

3. EGE, "A New England Mooney Case," *La Follette's Magazine*, August [1921?]; CUOHROC: GJ, 202; and EGE, *Outstanding Features*, 27.

4. *Transcript*, 5:5047.

5. HBE, *Case That Will Not Die*, 460; and Moshik Temkin, *The Sacco-Vanzetti Affair: America on Trial* (New Haven, CT: Yale University Press, 2009), 213, 301n82.

6. *Transcript*, 5:4506.

7. CUOHROC: GJ, 115.

8. BV to his father, May 24, 1921, in *Il Caso*, 70–71.

9. BV to EGE, 1921, in *Letters*, 86–87.

10. D'Attilio, "La Salute è in Voi," 87; and Frank P. Sibley, "Police Seek Weapons at Trial," *BG*, June 14, 1921.

11. "Believe Bandit Chief Deported," *BG*, May 9, 1920; and Paul Avrich, "Sacco and Vanzetti's Revenge," in Cannistraro and Meyer, *Lost World*, 165.

12. EGF, *Rebel Girl*, 304.

13. Frank P. Sibley, "Three Dedham Jurors Chosen," *BG*, June 1, 1921.

14. Ibid.

15. Alan Rogers, "'Finish the Fight': The Struggle for Women's Jury Service in Massachusetts, 1920–1994," *Massachusetts Historical Review*, NA 2000, www .historycooperative.org/journals/mhr/2/rogers.html (accessed August 10, 2006).

16. *Transcript*, 1:3.

17. Michael A. Musmanno, *After Twelve Years* (New York: Alfred A. Knopf, 1939), 88–89; and *Transcript*, 1:2.

18. Sibley, "Three Dedham Jurors Chosen," *BG*, June 1, 1921.

19. Frank P. Sibley, "Jury for Trial at Dedham Completed," *BG*, June 4, 1921.

20. Frank P. Sibley, "Orders Sheriff to Get 200 for Jury," *BG*, June 3, 1921.

21. *Transcript*, 3:2280, 2282.

22. Sibley, "Orders Sheriff," *BG*, June 3, 1921, and "Jury for Trial," *BG*, June 4, 1921.

23. Sibley, "Jury for Trial," *BG*, June 4, 1921.

24. "Canned Music for Jury at Dedham," *BG*, June 6, 1921.

25. CUOHROC: AF, 91.

26. *Transcript*, 5:5047–49, 4992.

27. Ibid., 5:4992.

28. HBE, interview by Livia Baker, June 3, 1968, HLSL, Box 7, Folder 11.

29. *Transcript*, 5:4992. Robert Montgomery claims Thompson fabricated his account of Thayer's reaction to Moore; see Montgomery, *Murder and the Myth*, 290–293.

30. *Transcript*, 5:4924.

31. Ibid., 5:4929–30.

32. Peggy Lamson, *Roger Baldwin: Founder of the American Civil Liberties Union* (Boston: Houghton Mifflin, 1976), 171; CUOHROC: AF, 109; *Transcript*, 5:5061–62; and HBE, *Case That Will Not Die*, 154.

33. *Transcript*, 5:5061.

CHAPTER 10: DOCKET NOS. 5545 AND 5546

1. Frank P. Sibley, "Sacco-Vanzetti Defense Given the Right to Examine Pistols," *BG*, June 7, 1921.

2. *Transcript*, 1:76; see 1:62–80 for Williams' entire statement.

3. There were 172 witnesses by the author's count. Kadane and Schum count 169, but note the difficulty in establishing an accurate count due to spelling variations in names; see Joseph B. Kadane and David A. Schum, *A Probabilistic Analysis of the Sacco and Vanzetti Evidence* (New York: John Wiley & Sons, 1996), 13, 79.

4. *Transcript*, 1:333–337; and "Says She Saw Sacco at Scene of Killings," *BG*, June 12, 1921.

5. *Transcript*, 1:379–380.

6. Ibid., 2:1310, 1327 (Campbell); 2:1373–75 (Fay); 2:1377 (Labrecque); 2:1378, 1383 (Kurlansky); and 2:1601–02 (Allen).

7. Ibid., 1:499–501.

8. Ibid., 1:519–520; Harold Williams notes [February 1921?], in Young and Kaiser, *Postmortem*, 56–57, 171n32; and *Transcript*, 1:519.

9. *Transcript*, 1:294–295.

10. Ibid., 2:1168, 1172 (Constantino); 2:1150–53 (McCullum); and 2:1146 (Brenner).

11. Ibid., 1:206, 215–217.

12. Ibid., 1:257–259 (Nichols); 1:267 (McGlone); and 1:279 (Langlois).

13. Ibid., 1:265, 276, 284.

14. Ibid., 1:483 (DeBerardinis); and 1:178 (Carrigan).

15. Ibid., 1:195 (Bostock) and 1:329 (Behrsin).

16. Ibid., 2:1222, 1226 (Novelli); 1:1010–11 (Frantello); 2:1110 (Cerro); 2:1116 (Gudierres); 2:1098 (Iscorla); and 2:1191 (Liscomb).

17. Ibid., 1:223–224, 240, 244, 253.

18. Ibid., 1:464, 476.

19. Ibid., 1:545–546.

20. Ibid., 2:1356 (Magazu); 2:1353 (Arrogni); 2:1490 (Damato); and 2:1399, 1404 (Manganio).

21. Ibid., 1:973, 977 (Burke); 2:1342, 1348 (Chase); 1:1077, 1080 (Falcone); 2:1592 (Foley); and 2:1212 (Gatti).

22. Ibid., 2:1271 (Antonello); 2:1273 (Frabizio); 2:1571 (Cellucci); 2:1254 (Magnerelli); 2:1245 (Dominick DiBona); 2:1260 (Donato DiBona); and 2:1274 (Tobia DiBona).

23. Ibid., 2:2080, 2082.

24. Ibid., 2:1387 (Desmond); and 2:1368 (Dorr).

25. Ibid., 1:495, 490 (Dolbeare); and 1:427 (Faulkner).

26. Ibid., 2:1305 (Brooks); 2:1283 (Pratt); 2:1285 (Cash); 2:1295 (Wilmarth); 2:1284 (Katzmann); and 2:1276–77 (McNaught).

27. Ibid., 1:415–418.

28. Ibid., 1:595–597.

29. Ibid., 2:1372 (Victorson); 2:2000 (McCarthy); and 1:965 (Carter).

30. Ibid., 2:1728.

31. Ibid., 1:731–733.

32. Ibid., 2:1823–24.

33. Ibid., 2:1825–26, 1942, 1964.

34. Ibid., 2:1679 (Ricci); 2:1668 (Monello); 2:1991 (Guadagni); 2:1645 (Williams); 2:1662 (Bosco); 2:2266c (Andrower); 2:2024 (Dentamore); 2:1993 (Guadagni); and 2:2034–39 (Affe).

35. Ibid., 2:2021–24.

36. Ibid., 2:1680–83; and Frank P. Sibley, "Sacco or Vanzetti to Testify Today," *BG*, July 2, 1921.

37. *Transcript* 2:1701–03.

38. Ibid., 2:1495–97 (Rosen); 2:1523 (A. Brini); 2:1549 (Corl); 2:1670–74 (Mrs. Corl); and 2:1537–38 (L. Brini).

39. Ibid., 2:1549.

40. Ibid., 2:1626 (Bova); 2:1625 (Carbone); and 2:1587 (Guidobone).

41. Ibid., 2:1517–19 (Rosen); 2:1523–27 (A. Brini); 2:1538 (L. Brini); 2:1549 (Corl); and 2:1587 (Guidobone).

42. Ibid., 2:1617 (Millick); 2:1606–08 (Michael Kelley); 2:1612 (Leon Kelley); and 1:870 (George Kelley).

43. Ibid., 2:1618–19.

44. Ibid., 2:1629.

45. Ibid., 1:597 (Reed); 2:1555 (A. Brini); and 2:1803 (BV).

46. Ibid., 1:798.

47. Ibid., 5:5169, and *BH*, April 17, 1920, in HBE, *Case That Will Not Die*, photo.

48. *Transcript*, 1:854, 857.

49. Ibid., 2:1851, 2065.

50. Ibid., 1:133 (Hunting); and 1:103, 136 (Jones).

51. Ibid., 1:107 (Frazer); and 1:112–113 (Magrath).

52. Ibid., 1:195 (Bostock); and 1:882 (Fraher).

53. James E. Starrs, "Once More Unto the Breech: The Firearms Evidence in the Sacco and Vanzetti Case Revisited: Part 1," *Journal of Forensic Sciences* 31, no. 2 (April 1986): 645.

54. *Transcript*, 1:781; and Starrs, "Once More Unto the Breech: Part 1," 636, 651n55.

55. *Transcript*, 2:1858, 1895–96, 1899, 1900.

56. Ibid., 2:2058–59.

57. Ibid., 1:781; and Starrs, "Once More Unto the Breech: The Firearms Evidence in the Sacco and Vanzetti Case Revisited: Part 2," *Journal of Forensic Sciences* 31, no. 3 (July 1986): 1060.

58. List of property held by Capt. Proctor, MA/SP, Box 1, Folder 5.

59. FK, quoted by HBE in *Transcript*, 5:5319; and Ibid., 1:50.

60. Ibid., 1:76–77, 893.

61. Ibid., 1:894; EGE, *Outstanding Features*, 13; and *Transcript*, 5:5186.

62. FK, quoted by HBE in *Transcript*, 5:5319.

63. Ibid., 1:895–896.

64. Ibid., 1:919–920.

65. Ibid., 2:1414.

66. Ibid., 2:1466–68.

67. Ibid., 2:1428, 1437.

68. Ibid., 1:750, 752, 756.

69. Ibid., 1:78.

70. Ibid., 1:169–170.

71. Ibid., 1:196–200.

72. Ibid., 1:806–811.

73. Ibid., 1:814–815 (Wadsworth); 1:817–822 (Fitzemeyer); 1:824–825, 834–835 (Jones); and 1:825 (Jeremiah McAnarney).

74. Ibid., 1:815.

75. Ibid., 2:1556–58, 1567 (Atwater); 2:1635–37 (Slater); and 2:1629–30 (Falzini).

76. Ibid., 1:212 (Wade); and 2:1687, 1689 (Florence).

77. Frank P. Sibley, "Sacco Faces Sharp Grilling on Murder," *BG*, July 8, 1921.

78. BV to his father, June 1921, in *Il Caso*, 71–72.

79. *Transcript*, 2:1685; and Frank P. Sibley, "Sacco-Vanzetti Counsel Collapses," *BG*, July 3, 1921.

80. Russell, *Tragedy in Dedham*, 175.

81. *Transcript*, 6:158.

82. Ibid., 5:4993, 4996.

83. FM to Benjamin Legere, January 13, 1921, BPL, Series 4, Box 32, Folder 20.

84. *Transcript*, 1:752; Frank P. Sibley, "You're a Liar, Says Vanzetti," *BG*, June 18, 1921; and *Transcript*, 1:750.

85. Ibid., 1:842–847.

86. Ibid., 2:1701–02, 1728–29.

87. Ibid., 2:1703–10.

88. Ibid., 2:1981–83 (Nelles); 2:2047–49 (Quintiliano); and Pernicone, *Carlo Tresca*, 116.

89. *Transcript*, 2:1721.

90. Ibid., 2:1721–23, 1726.

91. Ibid., 2:1715, 1724, 1725–26, 1731–32, 1727.

92. Ibid., 2:1737.

93. Ibid., 2:1737–38.

94. Ibid., 2:1749–50, 1754–55, 1757–58, 1772–73, 1777, 1784, 1799, 1801–02.

95. Frank P. Sibley, "Told Untruths, Says Vanzetti," *BG*, July 6, 1921.

96. *Transcript*, 2:1779, 1758.

97. *Plymouth*, 11; and *Transcript*, 2:1748, 1750, 1757, 1773, 1769.

98. Frank P. Sibley, "Sacco in Boston, He Says, During Murder," *BG*, July 7, 1921.

99. *Transcript*, 2:1828, 1831.

100. Ibid., 2:1818, 1820–22.

101. Ibid., 2:1823–27, 1864.

102. Ibid., 2:1848–49, 1832–38.

103. Ibid., 1:752–753 (Connolly); and 1:780–781 (Spear).

104. Ibid., 2:1841–43.

105. Ibid., 2:1845.

106. Ibid., 2:1845, 1866, 1846, 1863, 1862.

107. Ibid., 2:1849.

108. Obituary of Webster Thayer, *NYT*, April 19, 1933; Frank P. Sibley, "Sacco Faces Sharp Grilling," *BG*, July 8, 1921; and HBE, *Case That Will Not Die*, 304.

109. *Transcript*, 2:1867–69.

110. Ibid., 2:1872–73.

111. Ibid., 2:1873–75.

112. Ibid., 2:1876–77.

113. Ibid., 2:1922.

114. Ibid., 2:1877–81.

115. Ibid., 5:5340; and Harold Williams quoted in David Felix, *Protest: Sacco-Vanzetti and the Intellectuals* (Bloomington: Indiana University Press, 1965), 78.

116. *Transcript*, 2:1882–91.

117. Ibid., 2:1895–96, 1900, 1911–12, 1914–16, 1918, 1924, 1945.

118. Ibid., 2:1947–48; and NS statement, 9, MA/SP, Box 1, Folder 5.

119. *Transcript*, 2:1915; ibid., 2:1899, 1912, 1914, 1916–17, 1926.

120. Ibid., 2:1894, 1915, 1948.

121. Ibid., 2:1914.

122. Sibley, "Sacco Faces Sharp Grilling," *BG*, July 8, 1921.

123. Frank P. Sibley, "Vanzetti Taken Ill, Trial Is Suspended," *BG*, July 8, 1921; *Transcript*, 2:1950; and ibid., 2:1957, 1959–60, 1962–63, 1967.

124. *Transcript*, 2:1967, 1964, 1962.

125. Ibid., 2:2010.

126. Ibid., 2:1972.

127. EGF, *Rebel Girl*, 305; and *Transcript*, 3:3437–38, 3472–73.

128. Lyons, *Life and Death*, 77; EGE, *Outstanding Features*, 29; and Gardner Jackson, "Sacco and Vanzetti," *The Nation*, August 22, 1928, 174.

129. *Transcript*, 2:1972.

130. Ibid., 2:2121.

CHAPTER 11: DEDHAM

1. "Celebrating Pilgrim Plymouth 1769–1995," *Twenty-Twenty: Plymouth's 400th Anniversary*, www.plymouthma400th.org/past.html (accessed October 26, 2009); and Frank P. Sibley, "Katzmann Closes State's Case," *BG*, July 14, 1921.

2. *Transcript*, 2:2122–23; see 2:2122–48 for Moore's summation.

3. Ibid., 2:2124.

4. Ibid., 2:2132–38.

5. Ibid., 2:2128–29, 2140.

6. Ibid., 2:2143–46.

7. Ibid., 2:2147.

8. Ibid., 2:2147–48.

9. Frank P. Sibley, "Identity the Issue, Says Sacco's Counsel," *BG*, July 13, 1921, and Sibley, "Katzmann Closes the State's Case," *BG*, July 14, 1921.

10. *Transcript*, 2:2149; see 2:2148–79 for McAnarney's summation.

11. Ibid., 2:2150 (Splaine); 2:2155 (Goodridge); 2:2165 (Levangie); 2:2174 (Andrews); and 2:2152 (Bostock, McGlone).

12. Ibid., 2:2171, 2174, 2151, 2157, 2175.

13. Ibid., 2:2160, 2171.

14. Ibid., 2:2177.

15. Ibid., 2:2168–70.

16. Ibid., 2:2166, and 1:920.

17. Ibid., 2:2170.

18. Ibid., 2:2162.

19. Ibid., 2:2161.

20. Ibid., 2:2175–76.

21. Ibid., 2:2175–78.

22. Frank P. Sibley, "Identity the Issue," *BG*, July 13, 1921.

23. *Transcript*, 2:2180, 2182; ; see 2:2179–2238 for Katzmann's summation.

24. Ibid., 2:2183, 2211.

25. Ibid., 2:1157, 1152, 2184.

26. Ibid., 2:2223.

27. Ibid., 2:2185.

28. Ibid., 2:2189.

29. Ibid., 2:2213 (Pelser); 2:2215 (Levangie); 2:2217 (Splaine, Devlin); 2:2219 (Andrews); and 2:2212 (Wade).

30. Ibid., 2:2181, 2192.

31. Ibid., 2:2196–97.

32. Starrs, "Once More Unto the Breech: Part 1," 635.

33. *Transcript*, 2:2225–27.

34. Ibid., 2:2229–30.

35. Ibid., 2:2230–31, 2264.

36. Ibid., 2:2206, 2198–2200.

37. Ibid., 2:2201–03.

38. Ibid., 2:2199, 2229, 2187, 2233.

39. Ibid., 2:2198, 2236–37.

40. Sibley, "Katzmann Closes the State's Case," *BG*, July 14, 1921.

41. *Transcript*, 5:4928.

42. Ibid., 5:5023.

43. Ibid., 5:4969.

44. Frank P. Sibley, "Real Issue Identity, Says Judge Thayer," *BG*, July 14, 1921; and *Transcript*, 5:4969–71.

45. Sibley, "Real Issue Identity," *BG*, July 14, 1921; and *Transcript*, 2:2239.

46. *Transcript*, 2:2241.

47. Ibid., 2:2243, 2251.

48. Ibid., 2:2253, 2241.

49. Ibid., 2:2249.

50. Ibid., 2:2251–52.

51. Ibid., 2:2259.

52. Ibid., 2:2263.

53. Ibid., 2:2263–64.

54. Sibley, "Jury for Trial at Dedham Completed," *BG*, June 4, 1921.

55. Seward Parker quoted in Edward B. Simmons, "Jurors Unshaken in Verdict Sacco and Vanzetti Guilty," *New Bedford Standard-Times*, November 12, 1950. Of the twelve jurors, Simmons interviewed seven; four others had died, and one could not be found.

56. Sibley, "Orders Sheriff to Get 200," *BG*, June 3, 1921.

57. Kadane and Schum, *Probabilistic Analysis*, 13.

58. "Foreman of Jury in Murder Trial Dead," *BG*, October 11, 1921; Van Amburgh, "Hidden Drama," Part 4, 83; and Simmons, "Jurors Unshaken."

59. Simmons, "Jurors Unshaken."

60. Elizabeth Bouvier (Head of Archives, Supreme Judicial Court), telephone interview with author, February 1, 2010; and *Transcript*, 1:49.

61. Reid Hastie, Steven D. Penrod, and Nancy Pennington, *Inside the Jury* (Cambridge, MA: Harvard University Press, 1983), 144.

62. Simmons, "Jurors Unshaken."

63. Ibid.

64. Frank P. Sibley, "Sacco and Vanzetti Both Found Guilty of Murder," *BG*, July 15, 1921.

65. *Transcript*, 2:2266; and Sibley, "Both Found Guilty."

66. HBE, *Case That Will Not Die*, 273; and *Brockton Enterprise*, July 15, 1921, quoted in Joughin and Morgan, *Legacy of Sacco & Vanzetti*, 220.

67. Frank Sibley to J. Weston Allen, October 27, 1921, MA/AG.

68. Alfred Atwood quoted in Simmons, "Jurors Unshaken."

1. BV to ASB, May 28, 1925, BPL, Series 1, Box 2, Folder 13.

2. NS to EGE, June 18, 1926, in *Letters*, 33.

3. Frederick G. Pettigrove, *An Account of the Prisons of Massachusetts* (Boston: Commonwealth of Massachusetts, 1904), 46; and *Annual Report of the Commissioner of Correction for the Year Ending November 30, 1920* (Boston: Commonwealth of Massachusetts, 1920), 128.

4. This and other observations based on author's tour of decommissioned jail, March 26, 1999.

5. FM to Luigi Antonini, May 14, 1924, BPL, Series 4, Box 37, Folder 5; and F. G. Pettigrove, *The Prison Officers' Hand Book* (Boston: Commonwealth of Massachusetts, 1905), 30.

6. Robert Hanson (Dedham historian) to author, telephone interview, March 25, 1999; *Reel 3*, 211; NS to CCJ, February 26, 1924, in *Letters*, 14–15; and NS to EGE, August 2, 1925, in *Letters*, 29.

7. Sabino Sacco, in Lyons, "Torremaggiore," 274.

8. EGE, "The Personal Side," 5; *Annual Report of the Commissioner*, 204; and Hanson interview.

9. Mary Heaton Vorse, *A Footnote to Folly, Reminiscences of Mary Heaton Vorse* (New York: Farrar & Rinehart, 1935), 333.

10. CUOHROC: AF, 64, 99, 49; CUOHROC: GJ, 208; Lamson, *Roger Baldwin*, 169; EGE, "The Personal Side," 5; and Shields, *On the Battle Lines*, 32.

11. Vorse, *Footnote to Folly*, 334; John Nicholas Beffel, "Eels and the Electric Chair," *The New Republic*, December 29, 1920, 129; and NS to Leonard Abbott, July 28, 1926, BPL, Series 1, Box 1, Folder 10.

12. Myerson, HLSL, Box 13, Folder 16; Vorse, *Footnote to Folly*, 334; EGF, *Rebel Girl*, 304; and NS to [?], n.d., BPL.

13. *Annual Report of the Commissioner*, 202; EGE, "The Personal Side," 5; and EGE, *Outstanding Features*, 28.

14. *Reel 3*, 193–194, 219–220; and Carbonari in Shields, *Are They Doomed?*, 10.

15. *Reel 3*, 193–194, 224.

16. FM to William West, January 13, 1921, BPL, Series 4, Box 32, Folder 20; and *Transcript*, 5:4369.

17. Ibid., 5:4493; see ibid., 5:4488–95, for Ruzzamenti's affidavit.

18. Ibid., 5:4494, 4611–12.

19. *Reel 3*, 276–278.

20. Dr. William F. Boos to Dr. G. De Amezaga, November 25, 1921, in *Reel 3*.

21. *Reel 3*, 261–262, 239–240.

22. Ibid., 269.

23. CUOHROC: GJ, 206.

24. Built in 1804–1805, the prison housed 483 inmates in 1920: Pettigrove, *Prisons of Massachusetts*, 18, and *Annual Report of the Commissioner*, 147.

25. *Annual Report of the Commissioner*, 17–18.

26. "George E. Curran Learns of Inadequacy of State Prison in Effort to Afford Pleasure," [unidentified newspaper], April 6, 1921, HLSL, clippings scrapbook of Sheldon Glueck;

"State Prison Is Unsuitable, Officials Harsh, Says Forbes," [unidentified newspaper], ca. February 1923, HLSL, Glueck scrapbook; *Boston Review*, February 14, 1925, HLSL, Glueck scrapbook; and "State Prison Scandal," *The Prison World*, February 15, 1925.

27. *Plymouth*, 38.

28. BV to EGE, winter 1923, in *Letters*, 110; and Dr. Frank M. D'Alessandro, *The Verdict of History on Sacco and Vanzetti* (New York: Jay Street Publishers, 1997), 439.

29. CUOHROC: GJ, 206; and EGE to Alice Brandeis, January 14, 1932, Schlesinger, Reel 2.

30. BV to EGE, July 22, 1921, in EGE, *Outstanding Features*, 31; BV to EGE, spring 1922, in *Letters*, 88; BV to Francis Bigelow, April 13, 1922, in *Letters*, 89; BV to Maude Pettyjohn, April 10, 1925, in *Letters*, 143–144; BV to MD, April 17, 1925, Lilly; BV to EGE, December 21, 1926, in *Letters*, 226; and BV to ASB, July 21, 1925, in *Letters*, 160.

31. NS to BV, November 30, 1921, in *Letters*, 6.

32. *Transcript*, 5:5547–63.

33. *Reel 3*, 167; NS to CCJ, October 23, 1922, in *Letters*, 7; and *Reel 3*, 233, 236.

34. *Reel 3*, 167, 232.

35. Ibid., 187; and Sacco-Vanzetti Defense Committee to *Il Martello* et al., March 1, 1923, BPL, Series 2, Box 6, Folder 18.

36. CUOHROC: AF, 116; *Reel 3*, 170–71; and EGE, *Outstanding Features*, 8.

37. *Reel 3*, 201–203.

38. BV to LV, March 15, 1923, in *Il Caso*, 91; CUOHROC: AF, 116; and *Reel 3*, 218.

39. BV to LV, March 15, 1923, in *Il Caso*, 92.

40. FM to AF and others, March 14, 1923, *Reel 3*.

41. BV to LV, March 15, 1923, in *Il Caso*, 91; and AF and others to FM, March 14, 1923, *Reel 3*.

42. Draft letter, Defense Committee to All Friends, [May 1923?], *Reel 3*.

43. FM to Harold Williams, March 15, 1923, *Reel 3*.

44. *Reel 3*, 2.

45. Ibid., 9.

46. Ralph Colp, Jr., "Sacco's Struggle for Sanity," *The Nation*, August 16, 1958, 65–66.

47. Ancel Keys et al., *The Biology of Human Starvation*, vol. 2 (Minneapolis: University of Minnesota Press, 1950), 864–865, 868.

48. *Reel 3*, 6; Colp, "Sacco's Struggle for Sanity," 66–67; and *Reel 3*, 152.

49. *Reel 3*, 180; Dr. C. Macfie Campbell to Webster Thayer, March 26, 1923, *Reel 3*; and Colp, "Sacco's Struggle for Sanity," 67.

50. Campbell to Thayer, March 26, 1923, *Reel 3*; draft letter, Defense Committee to All Friends, [May 1923?], *Reel 3*; and EGE, *Reel 3*, 168.

51. Campbell to Thayer, April 10, 1923, *Reel 3*; and Colp, "Sacco's Struggle for Sanity," 68–69.

52. *Reel 3*, 180–182.

53. Ibid., 183; and BV to LV, March 15, 1923, in *Il Caso*, 91.

54. Campbell to Thayer, April 10, 1923, *Reel 3*.

55. Colp, "Sacco's Struggle for Sanity," 69; *Annual Report of the Commissioner*, 97–98, 193, 205; and FM to T. M. Nagle, June 30, 1923, BPL, Series 4, Box 35, Folder 27.

56. Colp, "Sacco's Struggle for Sanity," 69.

57. EGE, *Outstanding Features*, 45; and NS to CCJ, February 12, 1924, in *Letters*, 13.

58. Betty Jack Wirth (daughter of Cerise Carman Jack) to author, telephone interview, October 4, 2000, and in-person interview, October 19, 2000, in Yarmouth Port, MA.

59. Ibid.

60. NS to CCJ, November 12, 1926, in *Letters*, 35.

61. NS to CCJ, September 2, 1925. This and other original letters from Mrs. Wirth's personal collection were given to the author and are now in the Cerise C. Jack Papers, Manuscript Division, Library of Congress.

62. Betty Jack Wirth, telephone interview, October 4, 2000; NS to CCJ, January 5, 1924, BPL, Series 1, Box 1, Folder 6; and NS to CCJ, July 5, 1925, LoC.

63. Spencer Sacco (son of Dante Sacco) to author, telephone interview, October 25, 1998.

64. Betty Jack Wirth, interviews, October 4 and October 19, 2000; and NS to CCJ, July 5, 1925, LoC.

65. CUOHROC: GJ, 208; NS to Mrs. Arthur Shurtleff, June 6, 1925, in *Letters*, 27; and NS to CCJ, March 30, 1925, LoC.

66. NS to MD, September 13, 1925, in *Letters*, 31.

67. NS TO BV, August 18, 1925, in ibid., 30; and Spencer Sacco, telephone interview, October 25, 1998.

68. NS to EGE, August 2, 1925, in *Letters*, 28–29.

69. NS to CCJ, December 29, 1922, BPL, Series 1, Box 1, Folder 3; NS to CCJ, December 16, 1924, LoC; NS to CCJ, March 17, 1925, LoC; and NS to CCJ, November 12, 1926, in *Letters*, 35–36.

70. CUOHROC: AF, 99; and CUOHROC: GJ, 207.

71. EGE, *Outstanding Features*, 35–36; and BV to LV, n.d., in *Il Caso*, 87.

72. BV to ASB, February 27, 1924, in *Letters*, 122; Camp, *Iron in Her Soul*, 107; BV to CCJ, n.d. (sketch of birds), LoC; and EGE, *Outstanding Features*, 35.

73. Beltrando Brini to BV, December 20, 1923, BPL, Series 1, Box 2, Folder 9.

74. BV to ASB, May 11, 1925, in *Letters*, 150.

75. BV to LV, April 15, 1925, and October 24, 1926, in *Il Caso*, 119 and 154; and BV to ASB, November 12, 1926, in *Letters*, 211.

76. Cesare Pillon, introduction to *Il Caso*, 15; and BV to LV, May 4, 1924, in ibid., 111–112.

77. BV to LV, October 20, 1922, in *Il Caso*, 85.

78. ASB to BV, November 28, 1922, July 20, 1923, July 25, 1924, and November 25, 1924, Lilly (all); and BV to ASB, May 21, 1926, in *Letters*, 197.

79. ASB to BV, June 29, 1923, November 24, 1923, July 25, 1924, and August 21, 1925, Lilly (all).

80. BV to ASB, September 15, 1924, in *Letters*, 128; and BV to ASB, June 21, 1925, in ibid., 156.

81. Ralph Colp, Jr., "Bitter Christmas: A Biographical Inquiry into the Life of Bartolomeo Vanzetti," *The Nation*, December 27, 1958, 490.

82. Joughin and Morgan, *Legacy of Sacco & Vanzetti*, 470; Eric Foner, "Sacco and Vanzetti," *The Nation*, August 20, 1977, 139; Beltrando Brini quoted in Feuerlicht, *Justice Crucified*, 24; and BV to Aunt Edvige, December 15, 1914, in *Il Caso*, 53. Daniel Lang/Levitsky calls this the "classic language of the closet": " 'Hearts That Grow Not Cold': Structures of Feeling and Vanzetti's Beloved Anarchy," in *Representing Sacco and Vanzetti*, ed. Jerome H. Delamater and Mary Anne Trasciatti (New York: Palgrave Macmillan, 2005), 79.

83. BV to Irene Benton, July 31, 1925, in *Letters*, 166; and BV to VMM, August 26, 1923, in ibid., 99.

84. History and Record (for BV), MA/Inmate, Folder 16102.

85. Statement of Bert [*sic*] Vanzetti, 9–10, MA/SP, Box 1, Folder 5.

86. BV to EGE, December 1924, in *Letters*, 135.

87. Virginia Mallen (niece of Virginia MacMechan) to author, telephone interview, November 19, 2002.

88. BV to LV, July 28, 1923, in *Il Caso*, 97.

89. BV to VMM, August 26, 1923, in *Letters*, 98–99; and BV to VMM, September 6, 1923, in ibid., 99–100.

90. CUOHROC: GJ, 207; BV to VMM, October 15, 1923, in *Letters*, 103; and EGE, *Outstanding Features*, 40.

91. BV to LV, April 6, 1924, in *Il Caso*, 110.

92. BV to VMM, May 9, 1924, BPL, Series 1, Box 2, Folder 10. Vanzetti probably made the invisible ink from the juice of a lemon or orange, as he would later instruct Mary Donovan to do; see BV to MD, n.d., Lilly. This author was able to read the postscript, still invisible in 1999, by putting it under black light.

93. BV to LV, October 5, 1924, in *Il Caso*, 117.

94. BV to VMM, May 15, 1926, and April 25, 1927, in *Letters*, 193–197 and 248–250.

95. BV to ASB, February 17, 1925, and April 13, 1924, Lilly.

96. BV to LV, July 28, 1923 and July 15, 1924, in *Il Caso*, 97, 115.

97. *Transcript*, 4:3484; and Dr. Abraham Myerson, "Report on the Case of Vanzetti, Examination Held at the State Prison on December 29 and 30 [1924]": Reel 3.

98. BV to Jeremiah McAnarney, October 20, 1924, in MA/Inmate, Folder 16102.

99. Myerson, "Report on the Case of Vanzetti," Reel 3.

100. *Transcript*, 4:3484–85.

101. Myerson, "Report on the Case of Vanzetti," Reel 3.

102. *Transcript*, 4:3485.

103. Colp, "Bitter Christmas," 494; and BV to CCJ, February 26, 1925, LoC.

104. BV to LV, October 5, 1924, in *Il Caso*, 118.

105. BV to Maude Pettyjohn, April 10, 1925, in *Letters*, 145; and BV to ASB, April 6, 1925, in ibid., 142.

106. BV to ASB, April 16, 1925, in *Letters*, 148; and BV to CCJ, February 26, 1925, Lilly.

107. *Transcript*, 4:3488; and BV to ASB, July 21, 1925, in *Letters*, 159–61.

108. BV to LV, September 16, 1925, in *Il Caso*, 128; BV to LV, January 16, 1927, in ibid., 170; and BV to Alfonsina Brini, March 23, 1927, in ibid., 177.

109. BV to LV, June 17, 1925, in ibid., 125.

110. BV to Irene Benton, June 20, 1925, in *Letters*, 155; BV to Roger Baldwin, November 14, 1925, Lilly; and BV to ASB, June 18, 1925, Lilly.

CHAPTER 13: BATTLES IN AND OUT OF COURT

1. *Transcript*, 4:3549–50; see 4:3549–53 for McAnarney affidavit.

2. Simmons, "Jurors Unshaken"; and "Foreman of Jury in Murder Trial Dead," *BG*, October 11, 1921.

3. *Transcript*, 4:3580; see 4:3579–80 for Daly affidavit.

4. Ibid., 4:3505; see 4:3502–05 for Gould affidavit; and ibid., 5:5577; see 5:5564–77 for Pelser statement.

5. Ibid., 4:3733–41; see 4:3733–3891 for Goodridge documents.

6. Ibid., 4:3896; see 4:3896–99 for Andrews affidavit.

7. Ibid., 4:3608; see 4:3608–35 for Hamilton affidavit.

8. Ibid., 4:3641; see 4:3638–41, 3648–50 for Gill affidavits.

9. Ibid., 4:3642–43; see 4:3641–43 for Proctor affidavit.

10. Ibid., 5:5054–55.

11. Ibid., 4:3642, 3681.

12. HBE, *Case That Will Not Die*, 149.

13. CUOHROC: AF, 61–62; MD, "No Tears for My Youth" (unpublished autobiography), Lilly; and BV to ASB, November 13, 1925, in *Letters*, 181.

14. CUOHROC: AF, 117.

15. Lamson, *Roger Baldwin*, 170; and FM to Selma Maximon, September 3, 1923, BPL, Series 4, Box 36, Folder 8.

16. CUOHROC: GJ, 232, 255; and CUOHROC: AF, 108.

17. CUOHROC: AF, 108–109, 89, 103, 117.

18. Special Agent R. B. Spencer to William Burns, April 26, 1922, in F.B.I. FOIA File 61–126, Sacco/Vanzetti Case: CD-ROM, vanzetti6b.pdf, 105–106.

19. FM to Matilda Robbins, May 6, 1924, BPL, Series 4, Box 37, Folder 2; and FM to EGF, May 25, 1922, BPL, Series 4, Box 34, Folder 17.

20. FM to AF, July 24, 1922, BPL, Series 4, Box 34, Folder 25; and Emilio Coda to FM, August 11, 1922, BPL, Series 4, Box 34, Folder 27.

21. FM to Eugene Lyons, July 7, 1923, BPL, Series 4, Box 36, Folder 2.

22. FM to Salvatore A. Cotillo, September 10, 1923, BPL, Series 4, Box 36, Folder 8; and FM to Carlo Tresca, September 25, 1923, BPL, Series 4, Box 36, Folder 10.

23. CUOHROC: GJ, 245.

24. FM to WGT, June 29, 1923, BPL, Series 4, Box 35, Folder 26.

25. FM to EGF, October 18, 1923, BPL, Series 4, Box 36, Folder 11.

26. BV to WGT, October 4, 1923, in *Letters*, 102–103; and NS to CCJ, November 3, 1923, in ibid., 9.

27. Russell, *Tragedy in Dedham*, 252.

28. Lyons, *Assignment in Utopia*, 35.

29. FM to Felice Guadagni, April 2, 1924, BPL, Series 4, Box 36, Folder 29.

30. Felice Guadagni to FM, April 5, 1924, BPL, Series 4, Box 36, Folder 29.

31. CUOHROC: AF, 106–107.

32. NS to FM, August 18, 1924, in *Letters*, 22–24.

33. MD, "No Tears," Lilly.

34. Ibid.

35. *Transcript*, 4:3602–04

36. Ibid., 4:3514 and 2:2251.

37. Ibid., 5:5596–97.

38. Ibid., 4:3888–91.

39. Ibid., 4:3951–59.

40. Ibid., 4:3721.

41. Ibid., 4:3701–02.

42. MD, "No Tears," Lilly.

43. EGF, *Rebel Girl*, 324; and BV to LV, October 5, 1924, in *Il Caso*, 117–118.

44. *Transcript*, 5:5065–69.

45. EGE to Friends of Sacco-Vanzetti New Trial League, September 12, 1924, BPL, Series 3, Box 30.

46. WGT to Upton Sinclair, June 23, 1928, HLSL, Box 14, Folder 16; and EGF, *Rebel Girl*, 330.

47. Lyons, *Assignment in Utopia*, 13, 32.

48. CUOHROC: GJ, 235; and MD, "No Tears," Lilly.

49. *Transcript*, 5:4399.

50. Ibid., 5:4497.

51. Herbert Ehrmann, *The Untried Case: The Sacco-Vanzetti Case and the Morelli Gang*, 2nd ed. (New York: Vanguard Press, 1960), 30–33.

52. *Transcript*, 5:4398, 4479; and HBE, *Case That Will Not Die*, 405.

53. *Transcript*, 5:4667; and see ibid., 5:4416–18 for affidavit of Madeiros.

54. Frankfurter, *Case of Sacco and Vanzetti*, 89.

55. EGE, "When the Downtrodden Ask Justice," *Bulletin*, December 1925, 2.

56. *Transcript*, 4:4037, 4008, 4141.

57. CUOHROC: AF, 128; BV to LV, January 11, 1926, in *Il Caso*, 135; and ASB to BV, January 29, 1926, Lilly.

58. RS to CCJ, [January 20, 1926?], LoC; BV to Maude Pettyjohn, February 13, 1926, in *Letters*, 189; RS to CCJ, March 24, 1926, LoC; and BV to ASB, March 24, 1926, in *Letters*, 190.

59. *Transcript*, 4:4359; see ibid., 4:4269–4359 for the decision.

60. Lyons, *Life and Death*, 113.

61. BV to VMM, May 15, 1926, in *Letters*, 195.

62. HBE, *Untried Case*, 19.

63. Ibid., 72–84; and *Transcript*, 5:4426.

64. *Transcript*, 5:4448–50, 4487, and HBE, *Untried Case*, 45, 50–51.

65. *Transcript*, 5:4407, 4438–42, 4448, 4367.

66. Ibid., 5:4419–22.

67. Witnesses identifying Morelli's photograph as Sacco's were Lewis Wade (ibid., 5:4469–70); Mary Splaine (ibid., 5:4470–72); Frank Burke (ibid., 5:4484–85); and Dominic DiBona, Emielio Falcone, Pedro Iscorla, Nicolo Gatti, and Fortinato Antonello (ibid., 5:4465–66).

68. Ibid., 5:4663, 4477.

69. Witnesses validating the Madeiros confession were James Weeks (ibid., 5:4400–03), Barney Monterio (ibid., 5:4472–75), and May Monterio (ibid., 5:4475–78). The jail officer was Oliver Curtis (ibid., 5:4573–74).

70. Ibid., 5:4526 (Dow); ibid., 5:4509 (Kennedy); and ibid., 5:4513 (Kelly).

71. *Boston Post*, [January 16, 1921?], quoted in Shields, *Are They Doomed?*, 8.

72. *Transcript*, 5:4568.

73. Ibid., 5:4502–04.

74. Ibid., 5:4506.

75. Ibid., 5:4610.

76. Frank P. Sibley, *BG*, September 15, 1926, repr. in "Complete Report of the Last Hearing," *Bulletin*, September 1926, 7.

77. Ibid.

78. *Transcript*, 5:4377–80.

79. Ibid., 5:4379, 4384.

80. Sibley, *BG*, September 16, 1926, repr. in "Complete Report," *Bulletin*, September 1926, 8.

81. Sara Ehrmann in Feuerlicht, *Justice Crucified*, 318n; and HBE, *Case That Will Not Die*, 389.

82. Sibley, *BG*, September 17, 1926, repr. in "Complete Report," *Bulletin*, September 1926, 8; and *Transcript*, 5:4371.

83. HBE, *Untried Case*, 166.

84. BV to MD, October 24, 1926, Lilly.

85. *Transcript*, 5:4726.

86. Madeiros said he was positive he confessed before seeing the financial report (*Transcript*, 5:4662), while Officer Oliver Curtis said Madeiros confessed after seeing the report (ibid., 5:4574).

87. Ibid., 5:4745–46.

88. Ibid., 5:4748.

89. Ibid., 5:4748–59; 5:4377–80.

90. Ibid., 5:4748–50.

91. Ibid., 5:4762–63.

92. Ibid., 5:4767–68; Ibid., 5:4724, 4748, 4749, 4772, 4777; and Frankfurter, *Case of Sacco and Vanzetti*, 106.

93. *Transcript*, 5:4776; and Montgomery, *Murder and the Myth*, 283.

94. F. Lauriston Bullard, "We Submit," *BH*, October 26, 1926, in Topp, *Brief History with Documents*, 158–160.

95. Schuyler Patterson, "Why I Believe in Capital Punishment: An Interview with Alvan T. Fuller," *Success Magazine*, December 1926, 14–16, 94.

96. BV to John J. Leary, Jr., November 18, 1926, in *Letters*, 213.

97. NS to Jessica Henderson, November 21, 1926, in ibid., 37.

98. NS to CCJ, December 27, 1926, in ibid., 39; and RS to CCJ, January 6, 1927, LoC.

99. NS to [EGE?], December 1926, BPL, Series 1, Box 1, Folder 12.

100. BV to Maude Pettyjohn, December 11, 1926, in *Letters*, 221; BV to Leonard Abbott, November 25, 1926, in ibid., 216; and BV to ASB, January 10, 1927, in ibid., 230.

101. NS and BV, "A Message from Behind the Bars, January 1, 1927," *Bulletin*, December 1926, 4.

CHAPTER 14: CLINGING TO RAZOR BLADES

1. BV to MD, October 3, 1926, Lilly; NS to International Protelariat, May 1, 1927, BPL, Series 1, Box 1, Folder 16; BV to MD, October 3, 1926, Lilly; and BV to ASB, January 10, 1927, in *Letters*, 234.

2. *Transcript*, 5:4810, 4814, 4816, 4853, 4858.

3. Ibid., 5:4867, 4870.

4. CUOHROC: GJ, 183, 193; and MD, "No Tears," Lilly.

5. CUOHROC: GJ, 236.

6. Harlan B. Phillips, *Felix Frankfurter Reminisces* (New York: Reynal & Company, 1960), 213.

7. Frankfurter, *Case of Sacco and Vanzetti*, Prefatory Note, 67–68, 88, 104.

8. Robert Grant, *Fourscore: An Autobiography* (Boston: Houghton Mifflin, 1934), 368.

9. Charles A. Fecher, ed., *The Diary of H. L. Mencken* (New York: Alfred A. Knopf, 1989), 44; William Taft to Robert Grant, November 4, 1927, in Grant, *Fourscore*, 373; Oliver Wendell Holmes to Harold Laski, April 25, 1927, in *Holmes-Laski Letters: The Correspondence of Mr. Justice Holmes and Harold J. Laski, 1916–1935*, vol. 2, ed. Mark DeWolfe Howe (Cambridge, MA: Harvard University Press, 1953), 938; and Oliver Wendell Holmes to Lewis Einstein, May 19, 1927, in *The Holmes-Einstein Letters, Correspondence of Mr. Justice Holmes and Lewis Einstein, 1903–1935*, ed. James Bishop Peabody (London: Macmillan, 1964), 268.

10. Philippa Strum, *Louis D. Brandeis: Justice for the People* (Cambridge, MA: Harvard University Press, 1984), 372.

11. Leonard Baker, *Brandeis and Frankfurter: A Dual Biography* (New York: Harper & Row, 1984), 241–242.

12. Louis Brandeis to Felix Frankfurter, November 19, 1916, in *Letters of Louis D. Brandeis*, vol. 4, ed. Melvin I. Urofsky and David W. Levy (Albany: State University of New York Press, 1978), 266.

13. Louis Brandeis to Felix Frankfurter, June 2, 1927, in ibid., vol. 5, 290; Strum, *Louis D. Brandeis*, 375 (Brandeis to Julian Mack), and Baker, *Brandeis and Frankfurter*, 243.

14. Louis Brandeis to Felix Frankfurter, November 25, 1916, in Urofsky and Levy, *Letters of Louis D. Brandeis*, vol. 4, 267.

15. Louis Brandeis to Felix Frankfurter, September 24, 1925, in ibid., vol. 5, 187.

16. Strum, *Louis D. Brandeis*, 375.

17. Louis Brandeis to Felix Frankfurter, April 26, 1927, May 2, 1927, and May 25, 1927, in Urofsky and Levy, *Letters of Louis D. Brandeis*, vol. 5, 280–281, 284, 287.

18. Louis Brandeis to Felix Frankfurter, June 2, 1927, in ibid., 290.

19. Strum, *Louis D. Brandeis*, 374.

20. NS to EGE, July 7, 1925, and August 23, 1925, BPL, Series 1, Box 1, Folder 9, and June 10, 1927, in ibid., Folder 17; and BV to EGE, June 22, 1927, Lilly.

21. NS to EGE, March 16, 1927, in *Letters*, 48.

22. NS to Jessica Henderson, February 9, 1927, in *Letters*, 45; NS to CCJ, March 25, 1927, in ibid., 49; and BV to Gertrude Winslow, April 3, 1927, in ibid., 241.

23. *Transcript*, 5:4880, 4884.

24. Ibid., 5:4881, 4883.

25. Lyons, *Life and Death*, 131.

26. MD, "No Tears," Lilly.

27. "Judges Guarded after Sacco-Vanzetti Denial," *BG*, April 6, 1927.

28. Ibid.; and BV to LV, April 6, 1927, in *Il Caso*, 178.

29. BV to Gertrude Winslow, April 6, 1927, in *Letters*, 243. The same day, he also wrote to ASB, EGE, and LV; the next day, to MD, CCJ, and Katherine Codman.

30. BV to CCJ, April 7, 1927, Lilly.

31. Myerson, April 7, 1927, HLSL, Box 13, Folder 16. Dr. Myerson's report is the source of Sacco's remarks that follow.

32. BV to LV, April 6, 1927, in *Il Caso*, 178.

33. MD, "No Tears," Lilly.

34. *Transcript,* 5:4896.

35. Ibid., 5:4896–97.

36. Ibid., 5:4898.

37. Ibid., 5:4900, 4902.

38. Ibid., 5:4904.

39. Thomas Carens, "History of Case Which Started World-Wide Controversy," *BH,* August 4, 1927; and HBE, *Untried Case,* 181–182.

40. *Transcript,* 5:4904.

41. MD, "No Tears," Lilly.

42. *Transcript,* 5:4905.

43. Appendix 2, *Letters,* 379.

44. WGT and HBE to Gov. Fuller, May 4, 1927, in *Transcript,* 5:4907; Hill, "Impasse," *Bulletin,* August 1930, 5; and Appendix 2, *Letters,* 380.

45. *Reel 3,* 257.

46. NS to BV, December 28, 1924, in *Letters,* 25; BV to CCJ, October 21, 1924, LoC; and BV to MD, May 22, 1927, in *Letters,* 266.

47. BV to MD, April 27, 1927, in *Letters,* 253; BV to VMM, April 25, 1927, in ibid., 250; and BV to Gertrude Winslow, April 19, 1927, in ibid., 248.

48. NS to EGE, June 10, 1927, BPL, Series 1, Box 1, Folder 17.

49. Ibid.; BV to Gertrude Winslow, June 10, 1927, in *Letters,* 280–281; CUOHROC: GJ, 206; and Martin Barrett in HBE, *Untried Case,* 92.

50. NS to EGE, June 10, 1927, BPL, Series 1, Box 1, Folder 17.

51. BV to VMM, April 25, 1927, in *Letters,* 249.

52. BV to Gertrude Winslow, May 7, 1927, in ibid., 256; BV to LV, April 11, 1927, in *Il Caso,* 180; and BV to International Anarchist Defense Committee, 7.

53. HBE, *Untried Case,* 90, and *Case That Will Not Die,* 530; and Sara Ehrmann in Avrich, *Anarchist Voices,* 123.

54. NS to EGE, May 8, 1927, in *Letters,* 53.

55. *Transcript,* 5:4908.

56. Ibid., 5:4910.

57. Ibid., 5:4920–22.

58. Obituary of Alvan Fuller, *BG,* May 1, 1958.

59. Ibid., and *ANB,* s.v. "Fuller, Alvan Tufts."

60. Lyons, *Life and Death,* 143; and Phillips, *Frankfurter Reminisces,* 206.

61. CUOHROC: GJ, 200; and Musmanno, *After Twelve Years,* 337.

62. CUOHROC: AF, 138.

63. Morison, *Ropemakers,* 90n; Solomon, *Ancestors and Immigrants,* 123; and Henry Aaron Yeomans, *Abbott Lawrence Lowell, 1856–1943* (Cambridge, MA: Harvard University Press, 1948; repr., New York: Arno Press, 1977), 488.

64. Grant, *Fourscore,* 367; and A. Scott Berg, *Max Perkins, Editor of Genius* (New York: E. P. Dutton, 1978), 96.

65. A. E. Kennelly, *Biographical Memoir of Samuel Wesley Stratton, 1861–1931* (Washington, DC: National Academy of Sciences, 1936), 257–258; and *ANB,* s.v. "Stratton, Samuel Wesley."

66. CUOHROC: AF, 137; and Phillips, *Frankfurter Reminisces,* 203.

67. NS to Gertrude Winslow, June 30, 1927, in *Letters,* 61.

68. BV to International Anarchist Defense Committee, 3, 9.

69. *Transcript*, 5:4948; see ibid., 5:4949–5378 for the incomplete record of committee hearings.

70. Ibid., 5:4968–74 (Crocker); ibid., 5:5064–69 (Richardson); ibid., 5:5018–22 (Benchley); ibid., 5:4954–63 (Sibley); ibid., 5:4963–68 (Bernkopf); ibid., 5:4929–31 (Beffel); and ibid., 5:5023–27 (Rantoul).

71. Ibid., 5:5335, 5347.

72. Ibid., 5:5040, 5084.

73. Ibid., 5:5235–36.

74. Ibid., 5:5555, 4765, 5295, 5170, 5182–83.

75. HBE, *Case That Will Not Die*, 20.

76. WGT and HBE to Gov. Fuller, June 15, 1927, in *Transcript*, 6:341.

77. Ibid., 5:5305, 5328–30.

78. CUOHROC: AF, 141, 143; CUOHROC: GJ, 222; and HBE, *Case That Will Not Die*, 536–537.

79. HBE, *Case That Will Not Die*, 386; see also *Transcript*, 5:5256a–g.

80. BV to International Anarchist Defense Committee, 12.

81. CUOHROC: AF, 146; and BV to Harry Dragan, July 22, 1927, in *Letters*, 307.

82. BV to ASB, July 27, 1927, in *Letters*, 311.

83. Cynthia Anthonsen Foster Papers; Carl Anthonsen diary; entries for June 7 and 21, July 21, and August 6, 1927; MC653, Schlesinger.

84. "Vanzetti and Sacco Refuse All Solid Food," unidentified newspaper clipping, July 18, 1927 (loose-leaf vol., HLSL).

85. NS to EGE, July 5, 1927, in *Letters*, 64–65.

86. BV to LV, July 18, 1927, in *Il Caso*, 201.

87. MD, "No Tears," Lilly.

88. NS to Ines Sacco, July 19, 1927, in *Letters*, 67–69.

89. "Thompson Note Goes to Fuller," *BH*, June 21, 1927.

90. "Sacco-Vanzetti and the Red Peril," speech by Frank A. Goodwin to the Lawrence Kiwanis Club, June 30, 1927.

91. "Fuller Visits Scene of Murder to Check Sacco Case Evidence," *BH*, July 26, 1927.

92. *Springfield Republican*, August 2, 1927, quoted in M. Dickey Drysdale, "World-Famous Sacco-Vanzetti Case's 40th Anniversary Occurs Tuesday," *Springfield Republican*, August 20, 1967.

93. HBE, *Case That Will Not Die*, 533.

94. CUOHROC: GJ, 212–13.

95. Lyons, *Life and Death*, 153; and Musmanno, *After Twelve Years*, 281–283.

96. *Transcript*, 5:5378h.

97. HBE, *Case That Will Not Die*, 539; and MD, "Reminiscences," *Bulletin*, [August 1928?], 8.

98. *Transcript*, 5:5378c–h.

99. "Judge Thayer Makes 18 Holes in 84 at the Cliff Country Club," unidentified newspaper clipping, August 3, 1927 (loose-leaf vol., HLSL).

100. Louis Brandeis to Felix Frankfurter, August 5, 1927, in Urofsky and Levy, *Letters of Louis D. Brandeis*, vol. 5, 299; and *NYT*, August 5, 1927, in Lyons, *Life and Death*, 154–155.

101. "Receive Decision without Emotion," *BH*, August 4, 1927.

102. AF, "Sacco-Vanzetti: A Memoir," *The Nation*, August 14, 1967, 108–109; and CUOHROC: AF, 148.

103. BV to EGE, August 4, 1927, in *Letters*, 315; and BV to "My Dearest Ones," August 4, 1927, in *Il Caso*, 204–205.

104. Norman Hapgood to HBE, August 31, 1928, HLSL, Box 12, Folder 16: and Ellery Sedgwick to H. L. Mencken, February 19, 1932, in Fecher, *Diary of H. L. Mencken*, 44.

105. *Transcript*, 5:5378j–l.

106. State Sen. David Locke quoted in Israel Shenker, "Sacco-Vanzetti Case Evoking Passions 50 Years after Deaths," *NYT*, August 23, 1977.

107. *Transcript*, 5:5378n.

108. Ibid., 5:5378o–q, 5378t.

109. Ibid., 5:5378m, 5378v.

110. Ibid., 5:5378y–z.

111. Laski to Holmes, August 9, 1927, in Howe, *Holmes-Laski Letters*, vol. 2, 968; and John Moors to Felix Frankfurter, in Phillips, *Felix Frankfurter Reminisces*, 202.

112. John Dewey, "Psychology and Justice," *Bulletin*, February 1928, 6.

113. Taft to Grant, November 4, 1927, in Grant, *Fourscore*, 373; and Taft to Lowell, October 30, 1927, in Yeomans, *Abbott Lawrence Lowell*, 494.

CHAPTER 15: GROUNDSWELL

1. "Stop Sacco Rallies, Four Arrests Made," *BG*, August 8, 1927.

2. MD, "No Tears" Lilly; and CUOHROC: GJ, 214.

3. CUOHROC: AF, 154–155.

4. BV to ASB, May 31, 1926, Lilly; and BV to Friends of the Committee, November 2, 1926, BPL, Series 1, Box 2, Folder 21.

5. NS to International Proletariat, May 1, 1927, BPL, Series 1, Box 1, Folder 16; and "Sacco Letter Tells of Despair at Fate," unidentified newspaper clipping, July 30, 1927 (loose-leaf vol., HLSL).

6. Avrich, "Sacco and Vanzetti's Revenge," 166; and Lamson, *Roger Baldwin*, 170.

7. "An Open Letter to Pres. Lowell and Gov. Fuller," *Bulletin*, September 1927, 4.

8. *Transcript*, 5:5428, 5424.

9. Musmanno, *After Twelve Years*, 294; and *Transcript*, 5:5425.

10. *Transcript*, 5:5428; and "Judge Thayer Eludes Guards, Takes Stroll with Pet Bull Dog," *Providence Journal*, August 10, 1927.

11. Jeannette Marks, *Thirteen Days* (New York: Albert & Charles Boni, 1929), 1–2.

12. BV to LV, May 7, 1927, in *Il Caso*, 186; BV to Maude Pettyjohn, May 26, 1927, Lilly; and BV to MD, April 27, 1927, in *Letters*, 252.

13. CUOHROC: GJ, 230; Katherine Anne Porter, *The Never-Ending Wrong* (Boston: Little, Brown, 1977), 23; and Grant, *Fourscore*, 369.

14. Sacco-Vanzetti Conference of Chicago to Sacco-Vanzetti Defense Committee, August 1927, Lilly.

15. CUOHROC: GJ, 236; and Lyons, *Life and Death*, 134.

16. Confidential report of operative, August 29, 1927, MA/SP, Box 2, 16291, 1, Vol. 4, Folder 2; Max Shachtman, *Sacco and Vanzetti: Labor's Martyrs* (New York: International Labor Defense, 1927), 40, 58; and CUOHROC: GJ, 215.

17. "Henry Ford Opposes Sacco-Vanzetti Deaths," *Providence Journal*, August 10, 1927.

18. Laski to Holmes, August 9, 1927, in Howe, *Holmes-Laski Letters*, vol. 2, 968.

19. "Borah Urges Publicity of All Sacco Records; Attacks Secrecy of Federal Proceedings," *NYT*, August 11, 1927; William Borah to Defense Committee, August 9, 1927, BPL, Series 2, Box 9, Folder 15; and "Borah Criticizes 'Protests,'" *NYT*, August 19, 1927.

20. Laski to Holmes, August 19, 1927 in Howe, *Holmes-Laski Letters*, vol. 2, 972; and Laski to Holmes, September 2, 1927, in ibid., vol. 2, 976–977.

21. "Asks Premier to Intervene to Save the Life of the Condemned Man," *NYT*, August 10, 1097.

22. Philip Cannistraro, "Mussolini, Sacco-Vanzetti, and the Anarchists: The Transatlantic Context," *Journal of Modern History* 68, no. 1 (March 1996): 35, 49, 56–57.

23. "Portuguese President Pleads for Madeiros," *NYT*, August 19, 1927.

24. "Evil of Delayed Justice," *WP*, August 24, 1927.

25. CUOHROC: GJ, 282.

26. "As Others See Us: Governor Fuller in Berlin," *Living Age* 339, no. 4370 (November 1930): 320.

27. Holmes to Laski, August 18, 1927, in Howe, *Holmes-Laski Letters*, vol. 2, 971; and *Transcript*, 5:5532.

28. *Transcript*, 5:5533.

29. "Borah Urges Publicity," *NYT*, August 11, 1927.

30. "Police Guard Alert for Any Emergency," *NYT*, August 11, 1927; and "Family of Sacco Sure He's Innocent," *NYT*, August 11, 1927.

31. "Disperse Sacco Gathering; 2 Arrests," *Boston Daily Advertiser*, August 15, 1927 (photograph); and Musmanno, *After Twelve Years*, 307.

32. BV to MD, August 6, 1927, Lilly; BV to MD, July 22, 1925, in *Letters*, 165; and BV to MD, n.d., Lilly.

33. Robert G. Elliott, *Agent of Death: The Memoirs of an Executioner*, with Albert R. Beatty (New York: E. P. Dutton, 1940), 180; Musmanno, *After Twelve Years*, 299; and MD, "No Tears," Lilly.

34. Elliott, *Agent of Death*, 180–181.

35. Ibid.

36. MD, "No Tears," Lilly; and Marks, *Thirteen Days*, 11–13.

37. MD, "No Tears," Lilly.

38. Marks, *Thirteen Days*, 15.

39. Russell, *Tragedy in Dedham*, 425.

40. "Fuller Asks Council for Added Delay," *Providence Journal*, August 11, 1927.

41. *ANB*, s.v. "Fuller, Alvan Tufts."

42. Russell, *Tragedy in Dedham*, 434; and "Cardinal O'Connell Speaks," *Bulletin*, May 15, 1927, 3.

43. Rt. Rev. Paul Marella to O'Connell, August 10, 1927, in Rosario Joseph Tosiello, "'Requests I Cannot Ignore'": A New Perspective on the Role of Cardinal O'Connell in the Sacco-Vanzetti Case," *Catholic Historical Review* 68, no. 1 (January 1982): 50.

44. O'Connell to Marella, August 10, 1927, in Tosiello, "Requests I Cannot Ignore," 50.

45. O'Connell to Fuller, August 10, 1927, in Tosiello, "Requests I Cannot Ignore," 51–52.

46. *L'Osservatore Romano*, August 13, 1927, 1, in Tosiello, "Requests I Cannot Ignore," 52.

47. O'Connell to Hayes, August 15, 1927, in Tosiello, "Requests I Cannot Ignore," 53.

48. MD, "No Tears," Lilly.

49. *The Final Fight* (broadside), August 11, 1927, Lilly.

CHAPTER 16: BRINK

1. Elliott, *Agent of Death*, 20.

2. Richard Moran, *Executioner's Current: Thomas Edison, George Westinghouse, and the Invention of the Electric Chair* (New York: Alfred A. Knopf, 2002), 79, 85–86.

3. Ibid., 3, 15–16. Kemmler's electrocution may have taken as long as eight minutes.

4. Elliott, *Agent of Death*, 38.

5. Ibid., 72–76.

6. Pettigrove, *Prisons of Massachusetts*, 22; and Elliott, *Agent of Death*, 101.

7. *Transcript*, 5:5451.

8. Ibid., 5:5470, 5492.

9. "Sacco Backers to Defy Police Today," *Boston Post*, August 14, 1927; and CUOHROC: GJ, 216–217.

10. "Sacco Backers to Defy Police," *Boston Post*, August 14, 1927.

11. Ibid.; Musmanno, *After Twelve Years*, 308; and NS to Dante Sacco, August 18, 1927, in *Letters*, 71.

12. Unidentified newspaper clipping [Boston Daily Advertiser?], August 15, 1927, Lilly; and NS to Dante Sacco, August 18, 1927, in *Letters*, 72–74.

13. Musmanno, *After Twelve Years*, 311–312; and *Transcript*, 5:5500–01.

14. Musmanno, *After Twelve Years*, 313; and "Court Dooms Sacco, Vanzetti; Slayers Back in Death House," *Baltimore News*, August 19, 1927.

15. BV to LV, April 4, 1922, in *Il Caso*, 78–79; BV to LV, October 10, 1926, in ibid., 152; and BV to LV, September 4, 1921, in ibid., 75.

16. BV to LV, September 4, 1921, in *Il Caso*, 75; and BV to LV, June 26, 1926, in ibid., 145.

17. AF, "Sacco-Vanzetti: A Memoir," 110.

18. Ibid.; Porter, *Never-Ending Wrong*, 39; and Colp, "Bitter Christmas," 499.

19. CUOHROC: AF: 151; Feuerlicht, *Justice Crucified*, 397; and BV to Jessica Henderson, August 21, 1927, in *Letters*, 319.

20. BV to Dear Friends, Dearest Sister, ca. August 21, 1927, in *Il Caso*, 205.

21. Unidentified newspaper clipping [Boston Daily Advertiser?], August 15, 1927, Lilly.

22. CUOHROC: GJ, 250–251, and MD, "No Tears," Lilly. Jackson said the plan was Felicani's idea.

23. *Transcript*, 5:5534.

24. Ibid., 5:5516; and "Stone Also Declines a Stay in Sacco Case," *BET*, August 22, 1927.

25. Musmanno, *After Twelve Years*, 357.

26. "20,000 on Common, See Four Outbreaks" and "Baseball and Music Fans Ignore Affairs on Common," *BG*, August 22, 1927.

27. BV to Henry Ford, August 21, 1927, BPL, Series 1, Box 3, Folder 6; and BV to Dante Sacco, August 21, 1927, in *Letters*, 321–323.

28. NS and BV to Friends and Comrades, August 21, 1927, in *Letters*, 320–21.

29. "Round-the-World Briefs on Sacco-Vanzetti Case," *BG*, August 23, 1927; and additional briefs in *BG* and *BET*, August 22, 1927.

30. "Paris Police on Guard against Sacco Outbreaks," *BH*, ca. August 22, 1927.

31. "Strike Called in Chicago," *BG*, August 22,1927; "Weapons Given Guards Watching over Capitol," in ibid.; "Call for Strike in New York," *BET*, August 22, 1927; and "State Trooper Is Killed in Sacco, Vanzetti Riot," *BET*, August 22, 1927.

32. MD, "No Tears," Lilly; "20,000 on Common," *BG*, August 22, 1927; and CUOHROC: GJ, 285–287.

33. Eric Foner, "Sacco and Vanzetti," 140; and "Letters to the Editor," *BET*, August 22, 1927.

34. "Relatives of Men Are Given Ovation," *BG*, August 22, 1927.

35. CUOHROC: AF, 152; and *BH*, August 21, 1927, quoted in Tosiello, "Requests I Cannot Ignore," 47.

36. Musmanno, *After Twelve Years*, 382–385.

37. Ibid., 383–386.

38. "The Last Hour," *Bulletin*, [1928?], 1; and Musmanno, *After Twelve Years*, 386.

39. Musmanno, *After Twelve Years*, 388.

40. Ibid., 363.

41. Clarke A. Chambers, *Paul U. Kellogg and the Survey: Voices for Social Welfare and Social Justice* (Minneapolis: University of Minnesota Press, 1971), 223.

42. Arthur Garfield Hays, "Conference with Governor Fuller," *The Nation*, September 21, 1927, 285–286.

43. Musmanno, *After Twelve Years*, 364, 366; and HBE, *Case That Will Not Die*, 540.

44. "Three Men Refuse Rites of the Church," *BG*, August 22, 1927.

45. Ibid.

46. Elliott, *Agent of Death*, 138–139.

47. Ibid., 181.

48. WGT, "Vanzetti's Last Statement: A Record by W. G. Thompson," *The Atlantic Monthly*, February 1928, repr. in *Bulletin*, February 1928, 5.

49. Ibid.

50. Ibid.

51. HBE, *Case That Will Not Die*, 544; and WGT, "Vanzetti's Last Statement," in *Bulletin*, 5–6.

52. HBE, *Case That Will Not Die*, 544.

53. "Men Eat Little as Last Meal Is Served," *BG*, August 22, 1927.

54. Unidentified newspaper clipping, Lilly; and "Sacco and Vanzetti Die Calmly Denying Guilt," *Boston Post*, August 23, 1927.

55. Joe Morelli, *Introduceing* [sic] *the Most Famous Case of the World, The Sacco-Vanzetti Case and the Morelli Gang*, 68, 89, Harvard Law School Library, Small Manuscript Collection, Historical & Special Collections.

56. BV to H. W. L. Dana, August 22, 1927, in *Letters*, 325–326.

57. CUOHROC: AF, 153.

58. AF, "Sacco-Vanzetti: A Memoir," 112.

59. "Leave-Taking Pathetic One," unidentified newspaper clipping, Lilly; and "WBET Will Broadcast News," *BET*, August 22, 1927.

60. "Vanzetti Forgives, Sacco Says Goodby," *BG*, August 23, 1927.

61. Ibid.

62. Ibid.

63. *Boston Traveler*, August 23, 1927, in Musmanno, *After Twelve Years*, 393.

64. "Vanzetti Forgives," *BG*, August 23, 1927; and "Sacco and Vanzetti Die Calmly Denying Guilt," *Boston Post*, August 23, 1927.

65. "A Letter of Import," *Lantern*, August 1929, 25. Stong used irregular spelling in an attempt to reproduce Vanzetti's accent.

66. Elliott, *Agent of Death*, 141.

67. Ibid., 181–182.

68. "Vanzetti Forgives," *BG*, August 23, 1927.

69. Lyons, *Life and Death*, 202.

70. "Sacco and Vanzetti Die Calmly Denying Guilt," *Boston Post*, August 23, 1927.

71. Lyons, *Life and Death*, 203; and Elliott, *Agent of Death*, 182.

72. "Vanzetti Forgives," *BG*, August 23, 1927.

73. Elliott, *Agent of Death*, 182.

74. "Vanzetti Forgives," *BG*, August 23, 1927.

75. Elliott, *Agent of Death*, 183.

76. "Vanzetti Forgives," *BG*, August 23, 1927.

77. Ibid.; and Elliott, *Agent of Death*, 183.

78. "Vanzetti Forgives," *BG*, August 23, 1927.

79. Elliott, *Agent of Death*, 184.

80. Attilio Bortolotti in Avrich, *Anarchist Voices*, 183.

81. Valerio Isca in ibid., 149.

82. Thomas Longo to Paul Buhle, May 22, 1984, R.I. Labor History Project, R.I Historical Society Library.

83. Betty Jack Wirth to author, October 19, 2000; and Powers Hapgood to his parents, August 23, 1927, Lilly.

84. CUOHROC: GJ, 240–241; and obituary of Felix Frankfurter, *NYT*, February 23, 1965.

85. MD, "Reminiscences," *Bulletin*, [August 1928?], 8; MD, "No Tears," Lilly; and "Frenzy of Grief at News," unidentified newspaper clipping, Lilly.

86. "Heaviest Rainfall in Years in Many Places," *BG*, August 24, 1927.

CHAPTER 17: AFTERLIVES

1. Atty. Gen. Arthur Reading to Gen. Alfred Foote, Commissioner of Public Safety, August 1, 1927; and Reading to Foote, August 8, 1927, MA/SP, Box 2, Vol. 4, Folder 1 (both).

2. August 24, 1927, MA/SP, Box 2, 16291, 1, Vol. 4, Folder 2; and "Madeiros' Body Viewed by 10,000 Persons," *BG*, August 25, 1927.

3. "Many Seeking 'Thrill' Join Sympathizers," *Boston Advertiser*, August 28, 1927; "About 2000 Passed By Sacco's Body This Morning," *BG*, August 27, 1927; and "The Funeral," *Bulletin*, [August 1928?], 3.

4. "The Funeral," *Bulletin*, [August 1928?], 3; and "Sacco-Vanzetti Ashes in Safe," *BG*, August 29, 1927.

5. "The Funeral," *Bulletin*, [August 1928?], 3.

6. "Funeral Procession Passes Peacefully Until Then — Two Arrested," *BG*, August 29, 1927.

7. Low crowd estimates by police; see Lt. Joseph Ferrari to Gen. Foote, also Lt. Albert Dasey to Capt. Charles Beaupre, August 29, 1927, MA/SP, Box 2, 16291, 1, Vol. 4, Folder 2 (both). High crowd estimate from press; see "50,000 March in Sacco Funeral," *Boston Advertiser*, August 29, 1927.

8. "Funeral Procession Passes," *BG*, August 29, 1927.

9. Marks, *Thirteen Days*, 58; "Address at Crematory," August 28, 1927, Lilly (for Jackson's authorship, see CUOHROC: AF, 160); Patrolman Frank Sanborn to Gen. Foote, August 30, 1927, MA/SP, Box 2, 16291, 1, Vol. 4, Folder 2; and MD, "No Tears," Lilly.

10. CUOHROC: AF, 160.

11. Joughin and Morgan, *Legacy of Sacco & Vanzetti*, 315.

12. "Drop Resolve on Sacco Case," *BG*, August 30, 1927; Joughin and Morgan, *Legacy of Sacco & Vanzetti*, 315; and GJ, "Sacco and Vanzetti Ghosts, 1928–1929," *Lantern*, August 1929.

13. Obituary of Webster Thayer, *BG*, April 19, 1933.

14. A. C. Palmer to Thayer, October 23, 1932, MA/SP, Box 4, 107368, Vol. 3, Folder 5; and obituary of Webster Thayer, *BG*, April 19, 1933.

15. Boston Chief of Detectives Thomas Bligh to Des Moines Chief of Police H. A. Alber, November 4, 1932, MA/SP, Box 4, 107368, Vol. 3, Folder 5; and Officer [J. C. Crescio?], State Police Detective Bureau Case Review, August 18, 1949, MA/SP, Box 4, 107368, Vol. 3, Folder 5.

16. Obituary of Webster Thayer, *BG*, April 19, 1933; and *Transcript*, 5:5273.

17. Gallagher, *All the Right Enemies*, 80, 85; and Russell, *Tragedy in Dedham*, 256.

18. *Transcript*, 5:4467 (New York); and "An Open Letter to Pres. Lowell and Gov. Fuller," *Bulletin*, September 1927, 3 (Colorado).

19. Michael Musmanno to AF, April 6, 1962, BPL, Series 6, Box 54, Folder 56.

20. "Mooney in Boycott on Olympiad," *Los Angeles Times*, October 12, 1931; and T. H. Bell, "In Memoriam, Fred Moore," *Freedom*, September 1933, 4.

21. Hawley and Potts, *Counsel for the Damned*, 320.

22. HBE, *Untried Case*, 240; and obituary of WGT, *BET*, September 12, 1935.

23. WGT to Gertrude Winslow, April 23, 1934, Schlesinger, Reel 8, No. 137; obituary of WGT, *BET*, September 12, 1935; and EGE to Dante Sacco, September 13, 1935, Schlesinger, Reel 8, No. 121.

24. Obituary of WGT, *BH*, September 12, 1935; and Joseph Moro in Avrich, *Anarchist Voices*, 115.

25. Obituary of F. G. Katzmann, *BG*, October 16, 1953.

26. Michael Dray in Russell, *Tragedy in Dedham*, 24–25.

27. Musmanno, *After Twelve Years*, 288, and Rev. Roland Sawyer, *Public Hearing*, 85.

28. CUOHROC: GJ, 293–94; "Fuller Not Going to Paris," *NYT*, March 22, 1929; *ANB*, s.v. "Fuller, Alvan Tufts"; and "Fuller Candidate for Vice-President At '32 Convention," *BG*, May 1, 1958.

29. Obituary of Alvan Fuller, *BG*, May 1, 1958.

30. "As Others See Us: Governor Fuller in Berlin," *Living Age* 339, no. 4370 (November 1930): 320; and Norman Thomas di Giovanni, "Aldino Felicani: The Man and His Collection," in *Sacco-Vanzetti: Developments and Reconsiderations*, 30.

31. Yeomans, *Abbott Lawrence Lowell*, 483; and Charles Angoff and others, *Walled in This Tomb: Questions Left Unanswered by the Lowell Committee in the Sacco-Vanzetti Case* (Boston: Excelsior Press, [1936?]), 4.

32. Kennelly, *Samuel Wesley Stratton*, 258.

33. Grant, *Fourscore*, 371, 373, 369.

34. Oliver Wendell Holmes to Harold Laski, November 23, 1927, in Howe, *Holmes-Laski Letters*, vol. 2, 999.

35. Philip J. McNiff, Introduction, *Sacco-Vanzetti: Developments and Reconsiderations*, ix; and Oreste Fabrizi in Avrich, *Anarchist Voices*, 140.

36. CUOHROC: GJ, 115, 255, 203; GJ to AF, June 9, 1958, BPL, Series 6, Box 54, Folder 16; and obituary of Gardner Jackson, *NYT*, April 18, 1965.

37. EGF, *Rebel Girl*, 334; Gallagher, *All the Right Enemies*, 96–97; and Pernicone, *Carlo Tresca*, 244.

38. Pernicone, *Carlo Tresca*, 198–199, 232–235 (Communists); ibid., 127–131, 218–219, 255–261 (Fascist supporters); and ibid., 116–121, 160, 199–201, 236 (anarchists); also EGF to FM, August 16, 1923, BPL, Series 4, Box 36, Folder 6, and Valerio Isca in Avrich, *Anarchist Voices*, 147.

39. Pernicone, *Carlo Tresca*, 269.

40. Introduction to Galleani, *End of Anarchism?*

41. Avrich, *Sacco and Vanzetti*, 210, 211; Michele Presutto, "The Man Who Made Wall Street Explode: The History of Mario Buda" ("L'uomo che fece esplodere Wall Street: La storia di Mario Buda"), *Altreitalia*, January-June 2010 (trans. Patrizia Danese and Patrizia Panettieri, 9–10 of translation); Creagh, *Sacco et Vanzetti*, 166; and Charles Poggi in Avrich, *Anarchist Voices*, 132.

42. *ANB*, s.v. "Giovannitti, Arturo Massimo."

43. Jennie Paglia and Concetta Silvestri in Avrich, *Anarchist Voices*, 97, 108, and Avrich, *Sacco and Vanzetti*, 215.

44. Unidentified newspaper clipping, February 27, 1936, Schlesinger; and obituary of EGE, *BG*, December 12, 1937.

45. RS to CCJ, April 5, 1932, LoC; Conny Cross (granddaughter of Cerise Jack), note to and telephone conversation with author, ca. February 15, 2011; and Betty Jack Wirth to author, October 19, 2000.

46. Jim MacMechan (nephew of Virginia MacMechan), e-mail to author, May 1, 2000.

47. Powers Hapgood to his parents, September 4, 1927, Lilly.

48. Gertrude Winslow to Powers Hapgood, November 1, 1929, Lilly; Powers Hapgood to his parents, July 30, 1929, Lilly; and Barta Hapgood Monro to author, in-person interview, June 21, 2001, in Indianapolis, IN.

49. Powers Hapgood memorial booklet, Lilly; and obituary of Mary Donovan Hapgood, *BG*, June 28, 1973.

50. "Sig. Vanzetti Near Death," *Labor's News*, March 14, 1929, 8; and Feuerlicht, *Justice Crucified*, 342.

51. MD, "No Tears," Lilly; and Vincenzina Vanzetti in Feuerlicht, *Justice Crucified*, 429.

52. Lyons, *Assignment in Utopia*, 36.

53. EGE to Editor, *Springfield Republican*, January 12, 1932, Schlesinger, Series 3; and "Milestones," *Time*, January 18, 1932.

54. Spencer Sacco to author, October 25, 1998; Claire Finn Kirwan to author, February 7, 2000; and Spencer Sacco to author, March 21, 1999, in-person interview in Providence, RI.

55. Claire Finn Kirwan to author, February 3, 2000 (letter) and February 7, 2000; and Gertrude Winslow to AF, December 26, 1935, BPL, Series 6, Box 50, Folder 60.

56. EGE to Alice Brandeis, October 3, 1932, Schlesinger, Reel 2; Rudolph J. Vecoli, "The Making and Un-Making of the Italian American Working Class," in *Lost World*, 74n55; and Dominick Sallitto and Lino Molin in Avrich, *Anarchist Voices*, 166, 168.

57. Spencer Sacco to author, October 25, 1998. Unless otherwise noted, the source of this and other family information in the following paragraphs is Spencer Sacco in telephone interviews with author on October 25, 1998, and April 20, 1999, and in-person interviews on March 21, 1999, and December 19, 2004, in Providence, RI.

58. Spencer Sacco in Avrich, *Anarchist Voices*, 94.

59. AF to Michael Musmanno, May 27, 1960, BPL, Series 6, Box 54, Folder 37.

60. Upton Sinclair, "The Fishpeddler and the Shoemaker," *Institute of Social Studies Bulletin* 2, no. 2 (Summer 1953): 24; and Francis Russell, *Sacco & Vanzetti: The Case Resolved* (New York: Harper & Row, 1986), 191.

61. Robert and Michael Meeropol, *We Are Your Sons: The Legacy of Ethel and Julius Rosenberg* (Boston: Houghton Mifflin Company, 1975), 241, 250, 260–261, 275; and Robert Meeropol, *An Execution in the Family: One Son's Journey* (New York: St. Martin's Press, 2003), 3, 132.

62. Jeannette Parmenter Murphy (daughter of Fred Parmenter) to author, telephone interview, February 10, 2004.

63. *The Observer*, May 1920, quoted in Rick Collins, "Famous Braintree Murders, Sacco-Vanzetti Case Still Poses Mystery, Who Were the Two Men They Were Convicted of Killing?" *Patriot Ledger*, May 4, 2005, www.southofboston.net/specialreports/saccovanzetti/pages/050405.shtml (accessed August 10, 2011); and Jeannette Parmenter Murphy to author, February 10, 2004.

64. Rick Collins, "Forgotten Victims: Descendants Say Both Were Hard-Working Family Men," *Patriot Ledger*, July 27, 2005, www.southofboston.net/specialreports/saccovanzetti/pages/072705.shtml (accessed August 10, 2011); and Jeannette Parmenter Murphy to author, February 10, 2004.

65. *Patriot Ledger*, April 16, 1920, quoted in Collins, "Who Were the Two Men?," *Patriot Ledger*, May 4, 2005.

66. Copy of Marriage Record, July 1, 1912, BPL, Series 4b, Box 41, Folder 6; and Dina Chieffo (great-granddaughter of Alessandro Berardelli) to author, telephone interview, September 24, 2008.

67. SB to FK, February 12, 1921, 7, 10, MA/SP, Box 1, No. 7; and manifest of the *Alesia*, arriving NY October 21, 1890.

68. 1920 federal census for Quincy, MA; SB to FK, February 12, 1921, 5, 15, MA/SP, Box 1, No. 7; and Mrs. Joseph Florence to FM and others, December 1, 1921 (2 reports), BPL, Series 4b, [Box 41?].

69. Albert Nelson [to Thomas Doyle?], December 8, 1921; SB to Thomas Doyle, March 29, 1923; Rebecca Sachs to Thomas Doyle, December 7, 1921; and Frederick Webster to R. Reid, March 28, 1921, BPL (all), Series 4b, Box 41.

70. Dina Chieffo to author, September 24, 1908; *Transcript*, 1:806; SB to Thomas Doyle, March 29, 1923, BPL, Series 4b, Box 41; and Rebecca Sachs to Thomas Doyle, December 7, 1921, BPL, Series 4b, Box 41.

71. Dina Chieffo to author, September 24, 1908, and Marriage License, March 14, 1923, CT Bureau of Vital Statistics; "Widow Sends Plea on Sacco and Vanzetti," *Los Angeles Times*, July 29, 1927; and "No Plea by Victim's Widow," *NYT*, August 5, 1927.

72. Tom Gorman, staff photo, www.wickedlocal.com/holbrook/photos/x749208343/Sacco-and-Vanzetti-victims-remembered?photo=7.

73. Elliott, *Agent of Death*, 112, 76.

74. Ibid., 114–121.

75. Ibid., 302–304, 286.

76. James O. Welch, "The Last to Die," *BH*, December 23, 1982, and Marvin Pave, "Last Execution in Mass. Brought Little Reaction," *BG*, December 23, 1982.

77. "Governor Signs Bill Scrapping Prisoners' Cage," *BG*, August 20, 1963.

78. Malcolm X, *The Autobiography of Malcolm X*, with Alex Haley (New York: Ballantine Books, 1965), 152.

79. Diane Smith (Library Director, Bunker Hill Community College), e-mail to author, July 10, 2005, and Harold E. Shively, *Bunker Hill Community College: The First Twenty Years* (1993), 14.

80. Kathleen Stanley, "Captive Audience," *Builder Magazine*, August 1, 2006, (accessed January 17, 2007).

81. "$210M in Sales at Wall Street's First Luxury Condo," *Real Estate Weekly*, October 6, 2004, and Justin Davidson, "Paradise on Wall Street," *Newsday*, November 10, 2004.

82. George Nutter, President, MA Bar Assoc., December 1928, in Joughin and Morgan, *Legacy of Sacco and Vanzetti*, 316.

83. Pub. Doc. No. 144, November 1927, in Edwin M. Borchard, *Convicting the Innocent: Errors of Criminal Justice* (New Haven, CT: Yale University Press, 1932; repr. New York: DaCapo Press, 1970), xxii.

84. Mass. G.L. c. 278, § 33E, in Supreme Judicial Court, *The Case of Sacco and Vanzetti: Justice on Trial*, Virtual Tour, Screen 29, www.mass.gov/courts/sjc/sacco-vanzetti-29.html (accessed July 19, 2010).

85. Ibid.

CHAPTER 18: TWO MYSTERIES

1. *BH*, April 3, 1959; and Antone Silva in *Public Hearing*, 29.

2. Gov. Michael Dukakis, "Proclamation," July 19, 1977, in Topp, *Brief History with Documents*, 184; Daniel Taylor, "Report to the Governor," July 13, 1977, in Brian Jackson, *The Black Flag: A Look Back at the Strange Case of Nicola Sacco and Bartolomeo Vanzetti* (Boston: Routledge & Kegan Paul, 1981), 170–196; and Israel Shenker, "Sacco-Vanzetti Case Evoking Passions," *NYT*, August 23, 1977.

3. Alejandro Anreus (curator) to author, telephone interview, February 27, 2001; and Merrill H. Diamond, in Stanley, "Captive Audience," *Builder Magazine*, August 1, 2006.

4. *BH*, in Lyons, *Life and Death*, 205; Louis Brandeis to Felix Frankfurter, August 24, 1927, Urofsky and Levy, *Letters of Louis D. Brandeis*, vol. 5, 300; and Oliver Wendell Holmes to Harold Laski, August 24, 1927, in Howe, *Holmes-Laski Letters*, vol. 2, 974.

5. Fraenkel, *Sacco-Vanzetti Case*, 330.

6. *Transcript*, 4:3514.

7. Young and Kaiser, *Postmortem*, 64–66.

8. *Transcript*, 2:1753, 1948–54; BV statement, 9, MA/SP, Box 1, Folder 5; and NS statement, 7–9, MA/SP, Box 1, Folder 5.

9. Young and Kaiser, *Postmortem*, 67.

10. *Transcript*, 5:5042.

11. Ibid., 2:1724, 1841.

12. Ibid., 1:752–53 (Dedham); ibid., 6:144–149 (Plymouth); Young and Kaiser, *Postmortem*, 69 (grand jury); and Michael Connelly [*sic*] statement, May 19, 1921, MA/SP, Box 4, Vol. 3, No. 3 (to Stewart).

13. "List of Property Held by Captain William H. Proctor in the Sacco and Vanzetti Case," n.d., MA/SP, Box 1, Folder 5.

14. *Transcript*, 2:2183–84

15. Ibid., 5:5235–36.

16. Ibid., 5:5234–36.

17. SB to Michael Stewart, January 31, 1921, 1, 3, MA/SP, Box 1, No. 7; and SB to FK, February 12, 1921, 1, MA/SP, Box 1, No. 7.

18. Memorandum by M. E. Stewart, February 18, 1921, MA/SP, Box 1, No. 7.

19. Young and Kaiser, *Postmortem*, 89, 174n14.

20. Starrs, " Once More Unto the Breech: Part 1," 636, 651n55.

21. Ibid., 640; and *Transcript*, 2:2223–28.

22. Starrs, "Once More Unto the Breech: Part 1," 635.

23. *Transcript*, 4:3643, 3633.

24. Ibid., 6:358.

25. Ibid., 5:5373, 5320–21, 5314.

26. James Grossman, "The Sacco-Vanzetti Case Reconsidered," *Commentary* 33, no. 1 (January 1962): 37.

27. *Transcript*, 5:5320, 5378m.

28. Ibid., 1:76–77, 281, 288; and Fraenkel, *Sacco-Vanzetti Case*, 342.

29. Young and Kaiser, *Postmortem*, 96, 104, 113.

30. The experts were Calvin Goddard in 1927: Grossman, "Case Reconsidered," 37, and Young and Kaiser, *Postmortem*, 94; unknown experts in 1944: Starrs, "Once More Unto the Breech: Part 2," 1052; Frank Jury and Jac Weller in 1961: Starrs, "Once More Unto the Breech: Part 2," 1052–53, 1065–66, and Young and Kaiser, *Postmortem*, 95; Regis Pelloux in 1982: Young and Kaiser, *Postmortem*, 119; and Henry Lee, Anthony Paul, Marshall Robinson, and George Wilson in 1983: Starrs, "Once More Unto the Breech: Part 1," 631, 644, and Young and Kaiser, *Postmortem*, 95–96.

31. Starrs, "Once More Unto the Breech: Part 2," 1069.

32. Jack Thomas, "A Story of Trickery Told Much Too Late," *BG*, January 7, 1988.

33. *Transcript*, 4:3732aa–3732tt.

34. Dudley Ranney to Alfred Foote, February 11, 1927, 4, MA/SP, Box 1, 16291, Vol. 3, Folder 2.

35. FM to WGT, June 29, 1923, BPL, Series 4, Box 35, Folder 26; and Sinclair, "Fishpeddler and the Shoemaker," 24.

36. Sinclair, "Fishpeddler and the Shoemaker," 24; and WGT to Upton Sinclair, June 23, 1928, HLSL, Box 14, Folder 16.

37. Nunzio Pernicone, "Carlo Tresca and the Sacco-Vanzetti Case," *Journal of American*

History 66 (December 1979): 537, 543–545; Max Eastman, "Is This the Truth about Sacco and Vanzetti?," *National Review*, October 21, 1961, 264; and Feuerlicht, *Justice Crucified*, 423.

38. Pernicone, *Carlo Tresca*, 116–121, 160, 199–201, 236; and Pernicone, "Carlo Tresca and the Sacco-Vanzetti Case," 546–547. Other sources of hearsay are contradictory. Hugo Rolland and Charles Poggi told Paul Avrich that they heard that Sacco was guilty, and Ideale Gambera told Francis Russell the same thing: Avrich, *Anarchist Voices*, 132–133, 160, and Russell, *Case Resolved*, 12. On the other hand, Harry Richal, Febo Pomilia, and Galileo Tobia told Avrich that Sacco and Vanzetti were not guilty: Avrich, *Anarchist Voices*, 129, 135, 137.

39. Grossman, "Case Reconsidered," 42.

40. NS, quoted in William West to J. Edgar Hoover, August 15, 1927, in FBI FOIA File 61–126, Sacco/Vanzetti Case: CD-ROM, vanzetti12a.pdf, 14; and NS to BV, December 28, 1924, in *Letters*, 24–25.

41. NS, quoted in William West to J. Edgar Hoover, August 15, 1927, in FBI FOIA File 61–126, Sacco/Vanzetti Case: CD-ROM, vanzetti12a.pdf, 13.

42. Sibley, "Both Found Guilty," *BG*, July 15, 1921; and *Transcript*, 2:2266.

43. *Reel 3*, 273 (Dr. Edward Lane).

44. Pernicone, "Carlo Tresca and the Sacco-Vanzetti Case," 543.

45. Colp, "Sacco's Struggle for Sanity," 67–68.

46. *Transcript*, 5:4896.

47. Sara Ehrmann in Avrich, *Anarchist Voices*, 123.

48. Isidore Zimmerman, described in Michael L. Radelet, Hugo Adam Bedau, and Constance E. Putnam, *In Spite of Innocence: Erroneous Convictions in Capital Cases* (Boston: Northeastern University Press, 1992), 51.

49. BV to LV, March 15, 1923, in *Il Caso*, 92.

50. BV to Dante Sacco, August 21, 1927, in *Letters*, 321–323; and WGT, "Vanzetti's Last Statement," in *Bulletin*, 5.

51. Galleani, *End of Anarchism?*, 58.

52. Porter, *Never-Ending Wrong*, 6.

53. Sinclair, "Fishpeddler and the Shoemaker," 24; and Avrich, *Anarchist Voices*, 118, 129, 131, 152, 159.

54. Vorse, *Footnote to Folly*, 333.

55. Myerson, HLSL, Box 13, Folder 16.

56. BV to EGE, July 22, 1921, in *Letters*, 81.

57. W. G. Gavin, *Boston Traveler*, August 22, 1927, quoted in HBE, *Case That Will Not Die*, 61.

58. Grossman, "Case Reconsidered," 40.

59. *Transcript*, 5:5186.

60. Ellsworth Jacobs, in Van Amburgh, "Hidden Drama," Part 3, June 1935, 35; and Joseph Macone, in Sacco bio by Officer John H. Scott, January 21, 1921, MA/SP, Box 1, Folder 5.

61. William O. Douglas, "The Sacco-Vanzetti Case: Some Forty Years Later," *Transcript*, 1: xvii; and Michael Kelley in GJ, "Sacco and Vanzetti," *The Nation*, August 22, 1928, 173.

62. Kadane and Schum, *Probabilistic Analysis*, 197, 283.

63. HBE, *Case That Will Not Die*, 148; *Transcript*, 5:4504, 4506; and HBE in *Public Hearing*, 20.

64. Morelli, *Most Famous Case*, 14; Ben H. Bagdikian, "New Light on Sacco and

Vanzetti," *The New Republic*, July 13, 1963, 14; "Morelli-Sacco-Vanzetti Story Retold," *Providence Evening Bulletin*, April 3, 1959; *Transcript*, 5:4420; and HBE, *Untried Case*, 76.

65. Van Amburgh, "Hidden Drama," Part 5, August 1935, 100; HBE, *Untried Case*, 75; Vincent Teresa, *My Life in the Mafia*, with Thomas C. Renner (Garden City, NY: Doubleday & Company, 1973), 44; *Transcript*, 5:4421; HBE, *Case That Will Not Die*, 425n31; and Brian Andrews (former Providence police officer) to author, telephone interview, January 26, 2006.

66. "Story Retold," *Providence Evening Bulletin*, April 3, 1959.

67. Bagdikian, "New Light," 14; HBE, *Untried Case*, 50, 52, 79; and *Transcript*, 5:4418.

68. *Transcript*, 5:4407–09, and HBE, *Untried Case*, 53, 207–208.

69. *Transcript*, 5:4367.

70. Ibid., 5:4420.

71. Ibid., 5:4421.

72. HBE, *Untried Case*, 44–45; and *Transcript*, 5:4417–18.

73. HBE, *Untried Case*, 67–84.

74. Ibid., 82, 118, 116.

75. Obituary of Vincent Teresa, *NYT*, February 26, 1990.

76. Teresa, *My Life in the Mafia*, 44–46.

77. Morris L. Ernst, *The Best Is Yet . . .* (New York: Harper & Brothers, 1945), 247; and Ernst in *Public Hearing*, 94–96.

78. Ernst, *Best Is Yet*, 248–49, and Ernst in *Public Hearing*, 94–95, 102–103, 110.

79. Ernst in *Public Hearing*, 98–99.

80. Russell, *Tragedy in Dedham*, 311; and Bagdikian, "New Light," 14–15.

81. Russell, *Tragedy in Dedham*, 313–314.

82. Coacci description by Officer John H. Scott, January 22, 1921, MA/SP, Box 1, Folder 5; and *Transcript*, 1:726.

83. Morelli, *Most Famous Case*, Harvard Law School Library, Small Manuscript Collection, Historical & Special Collections. This manuscript is shorter than the one that Morelli described to Ernst, and less incriminating than the one that Russell described, but David Kaiser, who was instrumental in obtaining it, believes it is authentic because of its provenance and perspective.

84. Bagdikian, "New Light," 13, 16.

85. Morelli, *Most Famous Case*, 20, 81, 94; and *Transcript*, 2:1606, 1612, 1617–18.

86. Manifest of the *Alesia*.

87. [Names redacted] to author, e-mail, April 21, 2011; manifest of the *Chandernagor*, arriving U.S. April 27, 1888; [name redacted] to author, telephone interview, June 8, 2008; manifest of the *Entella*, arriving U.S. July 5, 1893; manifest of the *Karamania*, arriving NY May 17, 1899; and 1900 federal census for Providence, RI.

88. *Providence Directory, 1897–1898*, 605; and *Providence Directory, 1904–1905*, 597.

89. "Providence Neighborhood Profiles: Federal Hill," www.providenceri.com/neighborhoods/fedhill.html (accessed March 18, 2009); and [names redacted] to author, telephone interviews, June 8, 2008, and August 5, 2008.

90. "Italians Celebrate Garibaldi Centenary," unidentified newspaper clipping, Giuseppe Zambarano scrapbook, RI Historical Society Library.

91. "Defense Interviews," BPL, Ms. 2030; SB to Thomas Doyle, March 29, 1923, BPL, Series 4b, Box 41; and SB to FK, February 12, 1921, 7, 9, MA/SP, Box 1, No. 7.

92. Albert Nelson [to Thomas Doyle?], December 8, 1921, BPL, Series 4b, Box 41; and W. J. Watts, November 4, 1921, BPL, Series 4b, Box 41, Folder 6.

93. Frederick Webster to R. Reid, March 28, 1921, BPL, Series 4b, Box 43, Folder 23.

94. SB to FK, February 12, 1921, 13, MA/SP, Box 1, No. 7; and SB to Michael Stewart, January 31, 1921, 3, MA/SP, Box 1, No. 7.

95. SB to Michael Stewart, January 31, 1921, 1, MA/SP, Box 1, No. 7.

96. SB to Michael Stewart, January 31, 1921, 2, MA/SP, Box 1, No. 7; and SB to FK, February 12, 1921, 2, MA/SP, Box 1, No. 7.

97. SB to Michael Stewart, January 31, 1921, 2, MA/SP, Box 1, No. 7; and SB to FK, February 12, 1921, 5, MA/SP, Box 1, No. 7. .

98. SB to Michael Stewart, January 31, 1921, 2, MA/SP, Box 1, No. 7.

99. Van Amburgh, "Hidden Drama," Part 1, April 1935, 80.

100. Mrs. Joseph Florence to FM and others, December 1, 1921 (2 reports), BPL, Series 4b, [Box 41?].

101. SB to FK, February 12, 1921, 4, MA/SP, Box 1, No. 7.

102. SB to Michael Stewart, January 31, 1921, 3, MA/SP, Box 1, No. 7.

103. Mrs. Joseph Florence to FM and others, December 1, 1921 (2 reports), BPL, Series 4b, [Box 41?].

104. *Transcript*, 6:408.

105. SB to FK, February 12, 1921, 7–8, MA/SP, Box 1, No. 7.

106. *Transcript*, 1:171, 6:411, and Callanan and Sullivan, "Sacco-Vanzetti Live On," *BG*, April 10, 1960.

107. *Transcript*, 5:4634; ibid., 6:444, 411; Michael Stewart, Memorandum, n.d., MA/SP, Box 1; Leo Farrel to [John Nicholas Beffel?], n.d., BPL, Ms. 2030; and *Transcript*, 2:1687, 1689.

108. *Transcript*, 6:444; Ibid., 1:196 and Ibid., 6:397.

109. Ibid., 5:4416–17, 4638.

110. CUOHROC: GJ, 294–95; Joughin and Morgan, *Legacy of Sacco & Vanzetti*, 318, 548n27; and *Transcript*, 1: Prefatory Note.

111. Woody Guthrie, "You Souls of Boston" (New York: Folkways Records, 1960).

112. Bower Aly and Lucile Folse Aly, eds., *American Short Speeches, An Anthology* (New York: Macmillan, 1968), 89–90; and Henry Steele Commager, ed., *Documents of American History*, 7th ed. (New York: Appleton-Century-Crofts, 1963), 2:218–219.

113. *Transcript*, 2:2176 and 5:4772.

114. Bernard Flexner and Charles C. Burlingham to Thomas McAnarney, March 11, 1938, HLSL, Box 9, Folder 6. This part of Thomas McAnarney's testimony to the Advisory Committee was omitted from the transcript, but Dudley Ranney, William Thompson, and Herbert Ehrmann all remembered it: HBE, *Case That Will Not Die*, 476n34.

115. Supreme Judicial Court, *The Case of Sacco and Vanzetti: Justice on Trial*, Virtual Tour, Screen 2, www.mass.gov/courts/sjc/sacco-vanzetti-2.html (accessed July 19, 2010).

116. *Transcript*, 4:3549–53, 3579–80; and Hastie, Penrod, and Pennington, *Inside the Jury*, 4.

117. *Miranda v. Arizona*, 384 U.S. 436 (1966).

118. *Transcript*, 2:2244; and *Commonwealth v. Pinckney*, 644 N.E. 2d 973 (Mass. 1995), in John Cavicchi, "Today, Would the Supreme Judicial Court of Massachusetts Have Granted Sacco and Vanzetti a New Trial Based on Current, Retroactively Applied Case Law?," *The Digest: The Law Journal of the National Italian-American Bar Association*, 1999, 36–37.

119. Douglas, "Forty Years Later," *Transcript*, 1:xxi–xliv.

120. U.S. Census Bureau, *Statistical History*, 105; the exact number was 782,870.

121. See Borchard, *Convicting the Innocent*, and Brandon L. Garrett, "A World Without: DNA Evidence," *WP*, May 15, 2011.

122. Edmund Wilson to John Peale Bishop, October 22, 1928, in Edmund Wilson, *The Twenties, from Notebooks and Diaries of the Period*, ed. Leon Edel (New York: Farrar, Straus and Giroux, 1975), 389.

123. BV to John J. Leary, Jr., November 18, 1926, in *Letters*, 213.

Selected Bibliography

A complete record of sources cited in this book, including interviews, electronic sources,
newspapers, statutes of the United States, oral histories, and unpublished sources from
research archives—as well as books, articles, and pamphlets not listed below due to space
considerations—may be found in the Notes.

Adamic, Louis. *Dynamite: A Century of Class Violence in America, 1830–1930*. London: Rebel
Press, 1984.

Alexander, Yonah, and Kenneth A. Myers, eds. *Terrorism in Europe*. New York: St. Martin's
Press, 1982.

Angoff, Charles, and others. *Walled in This Tomb: Questions Left Unanswered by the Lowell
Committee in the Sacco-Vanzetti Case*. Boston: Excelsior Press, [1936?].

"As Others See Us: Governor Fuller in Berlin." *Living Age* 339, no. 4370 (November 1930):
320.

Avrich, Paul. *Anarchist Portraits*. Princeton, NJ: Princeton University Press, 1988.

———. *Anarchist Voices: An Oral History of Anarchism in America*. Princeton, NJ: Princeton
University Press, 1995.

———. *Sacco and Vanzetti: The Anarchist Background*. Princeton, NJ: Princeton University
Press, 1991.

Bagdikian, Ben. "New Light on Sacco and Vanzetti." *New Republic*, July 13, 1963, 13–17.

Baker, Leonard. *Brandeis and Frankfurter: A Dual Biography*. New York: Harper & Row,
1984.

Beffel, John Nicholas. "Eels and the Electric Chair." *New Republic*, December 29, 1920,
127–129.

Bell, T. H. "In Memoriam, Fred Moore." *Freedom: A Monthly Journal of Anarchist News and
Opinion*, September 1933, 4.

Bing, Alexander M. *War-Time Strikes and Their Adjustment*. New York: E. P. Dutton, 1921.
Reprint, New York: Arno Press, 1971.

Borchard, Edwin M. *Convicting the Innocent: Errors of Criminal Justice*. New Haven, CT: Yale
University Press, 1932. Reprint, New York: DaCapo Press, 1970.

Boston Police Strike: Two Reports. New York: Arno Press, 1971.

Brissenden, Paul Frederick. *The I.W.W.: A Study of American Syndicalism*. New York:
Columbia University, 1920.

Brown, R. G., and others. *To the American People: Report upon the Illegal Practices of the
United States Department of Justice*. Washington, DC: National Popular Government
League, 1920.

Buhle, Mari Jo, Paul Buhle, and Harvey J. Kaye, eds. *The American Radical*. New York:
Routledge, 1994.

Buhle, Paul, and Dan Georgakas, eds. *The Immigrant Left in the United States*. Albany: State University of New York Press, 1996.

Cannistraro, Philip V. "Mussolini, Sacco-Vanzetti, and the Anarchists: The Transatlantic Context." *Journal of Modern History* 68, no. 1 (March 1996): 31–62.

Cannistraro, Philip V., and Gerald Meyer, eds. *The Lost World of Italian-American Radicalism: Politics, Labor, and Culture*. Westport, CT: Praeger, 2003.

Capozzola, Christopher. *Uncle Sam Wants You: World War I and the Making of the Modern American Citizen*. New York: Oxford University Press, 2008.

Chaffee, John, ed. *Beyond Plymouth Rock: America's Hometown in the 20th Century*. Vol. 1, *Ties That Bind*. Plymouth. MA: Plymouth Public Library Corp., 2002.

Chambers, John Whiteclay II, ed. *The Eagle and the Dove: The American Peace Movement and United States Foreign Policy, 1900–1922*. 2nd ed. Syracuse, NY: Syracuse University Press, 1992.

Claghorn, Kate Holladay. *The Immigrant's Day in Court*. New York: Harper & Brothers, 1923. Reprint, New York: Arno Press, 1969.

Coben, Stanley. *A. Mitchell Palmer: Politician*. New York: Columbia University Press, 1963.

Colp, Ralph, Jr. "Bitter Christmas: A Biographical Inquiry into the Life of Bartolomeo Vanzetti." *Nation*, December 27, 1958, 485–500.

———. "Sacco's Struggle for Sanity." *Nation*, August 16, 1958, 65–70.

Conlin, Joseph R., ed. *At the Point of Production: The Local History of the I.W.W.* Westport, CT: Greenwood Press, 1981.

Cook, Fred J. "Sacco and Vanzetti: The Missing Fingerprints." *Nation*, December 22, 1962, 442–451.

Creel, George. *How We Advertised America: The First Telling of the Amazing Story of the Committee on Public Information That Carried the Gospel of Americanization to Every Corner of the Globe*. New York: Harper & Brothers, 1920.

Delamater, Jerome, and MaryAnne Trasciatti, eds. *Representing Sacco and Vanzetti*. New York: Palgrave Macmillan, 2005.

Dorgan, Maurice B. *History of Lawrence Massachusetts*. Published by the author, 1924.

Dos Passos, John. *Facing the Chair: The Story of the Americanization of Two Foreignborn Workmen*. Boston: Sacco-Vanzetti Defense Committee, 1927. Reprint, New York: DaCapo Press, 1970.

Dubofsky, Melvyn. *We Shall Be All: A History of the Industrial Workers of the World*. 2nd ed. Urbana: University of Illinois Press, 1988.

Eastman, Max. "Is This the Truth about Sacco and Vanzetti?" *National Review*, October 21, 1961, 261–264.

———. "Profiles: Troublemaker." *The New Yorker*, September 15, 1934, 31–36 (part 1), and September 22, 1934, 26–29 (part 2).

Ebert, Justus. *Trial of a New Society*. Cleveland: I.W.W. Publishing Bureau, 1913.

Ehrmann, Herbert. *The Case That Will Not Die: Commonwealth vs. Sacco and Vanzetti*. Boston: Little, Brown, 1969.

———. *The Untried Case: The Sacco-Vanzetti Case and the Morelli Gang*. 2nd ed. New York: Vanguard Press, 1960.

Elliott, Robert G., with Albert R. Beatty. *Agent of Death: The Memoirs of an Executioner*. New York: E. P. Dutton & Co., 1940.

Ernst, Morris L. *The Best Is Yet . . .* New York: Harper & Brothers, 1945.

Evans, Elizabeth Glendower. *Outstanding Features of the Sacco-Vanzetti Case, Together with Letters from the Defendants*. Boston: New England Civil Liberties Committee, 1924.

Feuerlicht, Roberta Strauss. *Justice Crucified: The Story of Sacco and Vanzetti*. New York: McGraw-Hill, 1977.

Flynn, Elizabeth Gurley. *Rebel Girl: An Autobiography, My First Life (1906–1926)*. New York: International Publishers, 1973.

Foner, Philip S. *History of the Labor Movement in the United States*. Vol. 4, *Industrial Workers of the World, 1905–1917*. New York: International Publishers, 1965.

Fraenkel, Osmond K. *The Sacco-Vanzetti Case*. New York: Alfred A. Knopf, 1931.

Frankfurter, Felix. *The Case of Sacco and Vanzetti: A Critical Analysis for Lawyers and Laymen*. New York: Grosset & Dunlap, 1962.

Frankfurter, Marion D., and Gardner Jackson, eds. *The Letters of Sacco and Vanzetti*. New York: Viking Press, 1928. Reprint, New York: E. P. Dutton, 1960.

Gage, Beverly. *The Day Wall Street Exploded: A Story of America in Its First Age of Terror*. New York: Oxford University Press, 2009.

Gallagher, Dorothy. *All the Right Enemies: The Life and Murder of Carlo Tresca*. New Brunswick, NJ: Rutgers University Press, 1988.

Galleani, Luigi. *The End of Anarchism? (La Fine dell'anarchismo?)*. Translated by Max Sartin and Robert D'Attilio. Orkney, Scotland: Cienfuegos Press, 1982.

Garaty, John A., and Mark C. Carnes, general eds. *American National Biography*. New York: Oxford University Press, 1999.

Grant, Madison. *Passing of the Great Race*. New York: Charles Scribner's Sons, 1916.

Grant, Robert. *Fourscore: An Autobiography*. Boston: Houghton Mifflin, 1934.

Grossman, James. "Sacco-Vanzetti Case Reconsidered." *Commentary* 33, no. 1 (January 1962): 31–44.

Higham, John. *Strangers in the Land: Patterns of American Nativism, 1860–1925*. 2nd ed. New Brunswick, NJ: Rutgers University Press, 1988.

Howe, Mark DeWolfe, ed. *Holmes-Laski Letters, Correspondence of Mr. Justice Holmes and Harold J. Laski, 1916–1935*. Vols. 1 and 2. Cambridge, MA: Harvard University Press, 1953.

Joint Committee on the Judiciary of the Massachusetts Legislature. *Record of Public Hearing on the Resolution of Rep. Alexander J. Cella Recommending a Posthumous Pardon for Nicola Sacco and Bartolomeo Vanzetti, April 2, 1959*. Boston: Committee for the Vindication of Sacco and Vanzetti, 1959.

Joughin, Louis, and Edmund M. Morgan. *The Legacy of Sacco & Vanzetti*. Princeton, NJ: Princeton University Press, 1948.

Kadane, Joseph B., and David A. Schum. *A Probabilistic Analysis of the Sacco and Vanzetti Evidence*. New York: John Wiley & Sons, 1996.

Kellogg, Walter Guest. *The Conscientious Objector*. New York: Boni & Liveright, 1919. Reprint, New York: Garland Publishing, 1972.

Kennedy, David M. *Over Here: The First World War and American Society*. Oxford: Oxford University Press, 1980.

Kennelly, A. E. *Biographical Memoir of Samuel Wesley Stratton*. Washington, DC: National Academy of Sciences, 1936.

Koppes, Clayton R. " Kansas Trial of the IWW, 1917–1919." *Labor History* 16, no. 3 (Summer 1975): 338–358.

Kraut, Alan M. *The Huddled Masses: The Immigrant in American Society, 1880–1921.* Arlington Heights, IL: Harlan Davidson, 1982.

Lamson, Peggy. *Roger Baldwin, Founder of the American Civil Liberties Union.* Boston: Houghton Mifflin, 1976.

Lantern, a Monthly Countercurrent Publication. "Those Two Men!" (special Sacco-Vanzetti memorial issue), August 1929.

Leighton, Isabel, ed. *Aspirin Age, 1919–1941.* New York: Simon & Schuster, 1949.

Lyons, Eugene. *Assignment in Utopia.* New York: Harcourt, Brace and Company, 1937. Reprint, New Brunswick, NJ: Transaction Publishers, 1991.

———. *The Life and Death of Sacco and Vanzetti.* New York: International Publishers Co., 1927. Reprint, New York: DaCapo Press, 1970.

———. "Torremaggiore: A Glimpse of Sacco's Birthplace." *The World Tomorrow*, September 1921, 273.

Marks, Jeannette. *Thirteen Days.* New York: Albert & Charles Boni, 1929.

McCormick, Charles H. *Hopeless Cases: The Hunt for the Red Scare Terrorist Bombers.* Lanham, MD: University Press of America, 2005.

Mommsen, Wolfgang J., and Gerhard Hirschfeld, eds. *Social Protest, Violence and Terror in Nineteenth- and Twentieth-Century Europe.* New York: St. Martin's Press, 1982.

Mondello, Salvatore. *The Italian Immigrant in Urban America, 1880–1920, as Reported in the Contemporary Periodical Press.* New York: Arno Press, 1980.

Montgomery, Robert H. *Sacco-Vanzetti: The Murder and The Myth.* New York: Devin-Adair, 1960.

Morison, Samuel Eliot. *Ropemakers of Plymouth: A History of the Plymouth Cordage Company 1824–1949.* Cambridge, MA: Riverside Press, 1950.

Murray, Robert K. *Red Scare: A Study in National Hysteria, 1919–1920.* Westport, CT: Greenwood Press, 1955.

Musmanno, Michael A. *After Twelve Years.* New York: Alfred A. Knopf, 1939.

Official Bulletin of the Sacco-Vanzetti Defense Committee. Boston: Defense Committee, August, September, December 1926; January, February, May, August, September 1927; February, August 1928; August 1930.

Patterson, Schuyler. "Why I Believe in Capital Punishment, An Interview with Alvan T. Fuller, Governor of Massachusetts." *Success Magazine* 10, no. 12 (December 1926): 14–16, 94.

Pernicone, Nunzio. "Carlo Tresca and the Sacco-Vanzetti Case." *Journal of American History* 66, no. 3 (December 1979): 535–547.

———. *Carlo Tresca: Portrait of a Rebel.* New York: Palgrave Macmillan, 2005.

Phillips, Dr. Harlan B. *Felix Frankfurter Reminisces.* New York: Reynal & Company, 1960.

Pillon, Cesare, and Vincenzina Vanzetti, eds. *Il caso Sacco e Vanzetti: Lettere ai familiari* (formerly titled *Non piangete la mia morte*). 3rd ed. Rome: Editori Riuniti, 1972.

Post, Louis F. *Deportations Delirium of Nineteen-Twenty.* Chicago: Charles H. Kerr, 1923.

Preston, William, Jr. *Aliens and Dissenters: Federal Suppression of Radicals, 1903–1933.* New York: Harper & Row, 1963.

Presutto, Michele. "The Man Who Made Wall Street Explode: The History of Mario Buda"

("L'uomo che fece esplodere Wall Street: La storia di Mario Buda"). Translated by
Patrizia Danese and Patrizia Panettieri. *Altreitalia*, January-June 2010, 83–108.

Renshaw, Patrick. *The Wobblies: The Story of Syndicalism in the United States*. Garden City,
NY: Doubleday, 1967.

Richards, Vernon, ed. *Errico Malatesta: His Life and Ideas*. London: Freedom Press, 1965.

Roberts, Kenneth L. *Why Europe Leaves Home*. Bobbs-Merrill, 1922. Reprint, New York:
Arno Press, 1977.

Ross, Edward Allsworth. "Italians in America." *Century* (July 1914): 439–445.

Russell, Francis. *Sacco & Vanzetti: The Case Resolved*. New York: Harper & Row, 1986.

———. *Tragedy in Dedham: The Story of the Sacco-Vanzetti Case*. New York: McGraw-Hill,
1962.

*Sacco-Vanzetti Case, Transcript of the Record of the Trial of Nicola Sacco and Bartolomeo
Vanzetti in the Courts of Massachusetts and Subsequent Proceedings, 1920–1927*, Vols. 1–5,
and *Supplemental Volume*, Vol. 6. Mamaroneck, NY: Paul P. Appel, 1969.

*Sacco-Vanzetti Case Papers (American Legal Manuscripts from the Harvard Law School
Library)*. Microfilm, 23 reels. Frederick, MD: University Publications of America, 1985.

Sacco-Vanzetti: Developments and Reconsiderations — 1979, Conference Proceedings. Boston:
Trustees of the Public Library of the City of Boston, 1982.

Sartorio, Enrico Charles. *Social and Religious Life of Italians in America*. Boston: Christopher
Publishing House, 1918. Reprint, Clifton, NJ: Augustus M. Kelley Publishers, 1974.

Shields, Art. *Are They Doomed? The Sacco-Vanzetti Case and the Grim Forces Behind It*. New
York: Workers Defense Union, 1921.

———. *On the Battle Lines, 1919–1939*. New York: International Publishers, 1987.

Sinclair, Upton. "The Fishpeddler and the Shoemaker." *Institute of Social Studies Bulletin* 2,
no. 2 (Summer 1953): 13, 23–24.

Slater, Joseph. "Public Workers: Labor and the Boston Police Strike of 1919." *Labor History*
38, no. 1 (Winter 1996–1997): 7–27.

Solomon, Barbara Miller. *Ancestors and Immigrants: A Changing New England Tradition*.
Cambridge, MA: Harvard University Press, 1956.

Songs of the Workers to Fan the Flames of Discontent. 32nd edition. Chicago: Industrial
Workers of the World, 1968.

Starrs, James E. "Once More unto the Breech: Firearms Evidence in the Sacco and Vanzetti
Case Revisited." *Journal of Forensic Sciences* 31, no. 2 (April 1986): 630–654, and no. 3
(July 1986): 1050–1078.

St. John, Vincent. *The I.W.W.: Its History, Structure and Methods*. Cleveland: I.W.W.
Publishing Bureau, 1913.

Stella, Antonio. *Some Aspects of Italian Immigration to the United States*. New York: G. P.
Putnam's Sons, 1924.

Strum, Philippa. *Louis D. Brandeis: Justice for the People*. Cambridge, MA: Harvard
University Press, 1984.

Taft, Philip. " Federal Trials of the IWW." *Labor History* 3, no. 1 (Winter 1962): 57–91.

Teresa, Vincent, with Thomas C. Renner. *My Life in the Mafia*. Garden City, NY: Doubleday,
1973.

Tomasi, Lydio F., ed.. *The Italian in America: The Progressive View, 1891–1914*. New York:
Center for Migration Studies, 1972.

Topp, Michael M. *The Sacco and Vanzetti Case: A Brief History with Documents*. New York: Palgrave Macmillan, 2005.

Tosiello, Rosario Joseph. "'Requests I Cannot Ignore': A New Perspective on the Role of Cardinal O'Connell in the Sacco-Vanzetti Case." *Catholic Historical Review* 68, no. 1 (January 1982): 46–53.

Townsend, John Clendenin. *Running the Gauntlet: Cultural Sources of Violence Against the I.W.W.* New York: Garland Publishing, 1986.

Trask, David F. *World War I at Home: Readings on American Life, 1914–1920*. New York: John Wiley & Sons, 1970.

Urofsky, Melvin I., and David W. Levy. *Letters of Louis D. Brandeis*. Vols. 4 and 5. Albany: State University of New York Press, 1978.

U.S. Bureau of the Census. *Statistical History of the United States from Colonial Times to the Present*. New York: Basic Books, 1976.

Van Amburgh, Charles, as told to Fred H. Thompson. "Hidden Drama of Sacco and Vanzetti." *True Detective Mysteries*, Parts 1–6, April–September 1935.

Vanzetti, Bartolomeo. *Background of the Plymouth Trial*. Chelsea, MA: Road to Freedom Group, n.d.

———. *The Story of a Proletarian Life*. Boston: Sacco-Vanzetti New Trial League, 1924.

———. "To the International Anarchist Defense Committee, July 10, 1927" (published as *In the Presence of Vanzetti*). Boston: Sacco-Vanzetti Defense Committee, 1927.

Vecoli, Rudolph J., ed. *Italian American Radicalism: Old World Origins and New World Developments — Proceedings of the Fifth Annual Conference of the American Italian Historical Association*. Staten Island, NY: AIHA, 1972.

Vellon, Peter. "Black, White, or In Between?" *Ambassador Magazine*, Fall 2000, 10–13.

Vorse, Mary Heaton. *Footnote to Folly: Reminiscences of Mary Heaton Vorse*. New York: Farrar & Rinehart, 1935.

Yeomans, Henry Aaron. *Abbot Lawrence Lowell, 1856–1943*. Cambridge, MA: Harvard University Press, 1948. Reprint, New York: Arno Press, 1977.

Young, William, and David E. Kaiser. *Postmortem: New Evidence in the Case of Sacco and Vanzetti*. Amherst: University of Massachusetts Press, 1985.

INDEX

Throughout index, "Vanzetti" refers to Bartolomeo Vanzetti, and "Sacco" refers to Nicola Sacco.

condition of, 181, 286; demolition, 286; power failure, 258–59

Chase, Elmer, 137

Chase, George, 58

child labor, 44, *44*, 45

Christophori, Esther Esteno, 80, 329n24

Cleveland, Grover, 18

Coacci, Feruccio, 24–25, 59, 60, 304

Codman, Katherine, 350n29

Coes, Loring, 169–70

Colbert, Maurice, 6, 7

Coldwell, Joseph, 51–52

Cole, Austin, 81, 140, 156

Colp, Ralph, Jr., 186, 194

Committee on Public Information (CPI), 69

Commonwealth vs. Bartolomeo Vanzetti.
    See Vanzetti trial (Plymouth)

Commonwealth vs. Sacco and Vanzetti. See Sacco-
    Vanzetti trial (Dedham)

communism and communists, 113–15, 248–49

Communist Labor Party, 113, 115

Communist Party, 113, 115–16

Connolly, Michael, 27–28, 82, 152–53, 156, 165, 290–91

conscientious objectors, 64, 70–72

consciousness of guilt: in closing arguments, 165; evidence against Sacco, 155–60, 289–91; evidence against Vanzetti, 152–55, 289–91; in Thayer's instructions to jury, 172, 174, 206; in Vanzetti trial, 81

conscription. *See* draft, military

Constantino, Dominic, 134

Coolidge, Calvin, 56, 121, 241, 249, 260

Corl, Melvin, 143

Cox, Alfred, 22, 77, 78, 81

CPI (Committee on Public Information), 69

Creel, George, 66, 69–70, 73

Crocker, George, 170, 234

Cronaca sovversiva (Subversive chronicle), 51, 55, 65–67, 105–6, 119

cross-examination techniques, 164

Curtis, Oliver, 184, 348n69, 349n86

Czolgosz, Leon, 19, 99–100

Daly, William, 200, 243

Damato, Nicola, 137

Dana, Henry Wadsworth Longfellow, 266–67

De Amezaga, Gualtiero, 180

DeBerardinis, Louis, 135

Debs, Eugene, 158, 182, 193

Dedham Jail: capacity, 177; condition of, 177, 286; redevelopment, 286–88; work by prisoners, 183

DeFalco, Angelina, 92–95, 131

Dempsey, Jack, 71, 74

Dentamore, Antonio, 142

Department of Justice. *See* Justice Department

deportation, 29, 114–16

Desmond, Walter, 138

Dever, John, 173

Devlin, Frances, 136, 167

Dewey, John, 244

DiBona, Dominic, 138, 348n67

DiBona, Donato, 138

DiBona, Tobia, 138

DiCarli, John, 79, 83, 329n24

Dillingham, William, 19–20

Dolbeare, Harry, 3, 139

Donato, Narciso, 26

Donovan, Mary, *188*; background, 205–6; banned from jail, 229; on denial of motions for new trial, 208, 217, 224, 241; execution and, 254, 259, 262; invisible ink, 346n92; later life, 279–80; public opinion campaign, 221, 245; Sacco and, 229, 239; Sacco and Vanzetti's funeral, 272–73; Sacco-Vanzetti Defense Committee, 205–6; on sentencing, 227; Vanzetti and, 206, 229, 247, 251–52, 350n29

Dorr, Wilson, 138

Dos Passos, John, 68, 102, 247

Douglas, William O., 299, 310

Downey, John, 262

draft, military (1917): evasion, 60, 66–68, 70–72, 74, 154, 157, 171; exemptions, 71–72; registration, 64–66; in Sacco-Vanzetti trial, 74, 119, 154, 157, 171; Selective Service Act (1917), 64, 71. *See also* conscientious objectors

Draper, Eben, 52

Draper Company, 51–53, 60

Dubofsky, Melvyn, 54

Dukakis, Michael, 288

dynamite, anarchist use of, 102–5, 108. *See also* terrorism

Eastman, Max, 49, 295

Ebert, Justus, 49

Ehrmann, Herbert: Advisory Committee and, 235, 237, 293, 365n114; appeals, 217, 220, 241, 246, 264; on evidence tampering, 293; investigation notes and, 236; on Moore, 92, 129–30; on Morelli gang and South Braintree, 212–13, 300–302; Ranney and, 216; Sacco and, 92, 102;

Montgomery, Robert, 85, 218, 337n29

Moore, Fred, 87; on anarchists' expropriation, 297; background, 86–88; Everett Massacre defense, 88; expenses, 88; Felicani and, 202–3; hired by Sacco-Vanzetti Defense Committee, 50, 86, 90; as IWW counsel, 87–90; later life, 274–75, 295; Lawrence strike defense, 49–50, 87–88; motions for new trial, 200–202, 207; personal instability, 89, 130; politicization of cases, 88, 94–95, 152; public relations, 91, 308; resignation from Sacco-Vanzetti Defense Committee, 208–9, 248; Sacco and, 92, 108, 183–85, 205; on Sacco and Vanzetti's guilt, 294–95; Sacco-Vanzetti Defense Committee finances, 202–5; severance motions, 160–61; Spokane free-speech fight, 87; Thayer's antipathy toward, 87, 129–31, 155, 207, 235, 337n29; Thompson and, 204; Tulsa defense, 89–90; Vanzetti and, 192; on Wall Street bombing article, 122; Wichita defense, 90; witness intimidation, 207

Moore, Fred, and Sacco-Vanzetti trial (Dedham): ballistics evidence, 147; closing arguments, 162–63; defense team, 125, 129–30; examination of Sacco, 155–57, 160; eyewitnesses, 200; jury, 128; physical evidence, 145, 168; politicization, 152; pre-trial courthouse corruption, 93–95

Moore, Lola, 295

Moors, John, 244

Morelli, Frank (Butsey), 212–13, 300–302

Morelli, Fred, 212, 300–301

Morelli, Helen, 304

Morelli, Joe, 212–13, 266, 300–304, 308, 348n67, 364n83

Morelli, Mike, 212–13, 300, 302

Morelli, Pasquale, 212–13, 300–01

Morelli gang, 212–13

Morgan, J. P., 110

Morison, Samuel Eliot, 39, 53, 54

Moro, Joseph, 68, 275

Morton, James, 259

Most, Johann, 103

motions for new trial, 183, 204, 213–17; Andrews motion, 201, 207, 209; Goodridge motion, 200–01, 207, 209; Gould-Pelser motion, 200, 206–7, 209, 243; Hamilton-Proctor motion, 201–2, 204, 207–9, 243; Madeiros motion, 213, 215–17, 220–21, 224–43; Ripley-Daly motion, 200, 206, 209, 243

Moustache Pete (fictional character), 17

Murphy, Francis, 81

Murphy, Jeannette Parmenter, 283

Murphy, John, 82

Murphy, Michael, 267–68

Murray, H. J., 23

Musmanno, Michael, 246, 252, 259–60, 263–64, 268

Mussolini, Benito, 249–50

Myerson, Abraham, 197, 225–26, 298

nativism, 14–15, 17–18

Neal, Shelley, 3, 4, 236, 316n26 (chap. 1)

Nelles, Walter, 152–53

New Orleans, LA: lynchings, 17

New Trial League. See Sacco-Vanzetti New Trial League

New York, NY: bombings, 96–98, 97, 103, 110, 119–22; Italian American successes, 16–17

Nichols, Annie, 6, 7, 135, 307

Nobel, Alfred, 102–3

Norton, Clement, 240

Novelli, Jennie, 135

O'Connell, William Cardinal, 253–54, 262

Orciani, Ricardo: alibi, 62; anarchist literature disposal, 26–27, 156; arrest, 30; Buda's car, 153; eyewitness identification of, 59–60; gun, 150, 169; initial charges, 58; Sacco-Vanzetti trial (Dedham), 169; search of his home, 59; as South Braintree crime confederate, 304

Overland (car), 24, 25, 26–27

Palmer, A. Mitchell, 98, 111–19, 121

Palmer raids, 114–17

Parker, Dorothy, 247

Parmenter, Frederick, 283; autopsy, 145; bullet wound, 145; family, 5, 283; grave, 284; gun, 7, 149, 292; murder, 4–6; payroll delivery, 4, 307

Parmenter, Hattie, 283

Parmenter, Jeannette, 283

Parmenter, Richard, 283

Parsons, Albert, 103

Paterson, NJ: Italian anarchists, 117–18

patriotism, 63, 69, 171

Paul, Anthony, 362n30

Peabody, Endicott, 286

Pelletier, Joseph, 94

Pelloux, Regis, 362n30

Pelser, Louis, 134, 163, 167, 200, 207

Pernicone, Nunzio, 86, 99, 295

Picchione, Pasquale, 305

Pieraccini, Raphael, 301
Pinkerton detective agency, 22–23, 77
Pius XI, Pope, 254
Playfair, William, 268
Plymouth, MA: immigrants, 39–40, 75; industry, 38–39; Patriots' Day parade, 63; tercentenary celebration, 162
Plymouth Cordage Company, 39–40, 53–54, 60
Plymouth Rock, 38, 57, 83
Poggi, Charles, 120, 363n38
Pomilia, Febo, 363n38
Porter, Katherine Anne, 247, 258, 297
Post, Louis, 113, 115–19
Pound, Roscoe, 232
Pratt, Ernest, 139
Proctor, William: affidavit, 222; Sacco-Vanzetti ballistics evidence, 147–48, 168, 201–2, 207–8, 291–92; Sacco-Vanzetti investigation, 58; on South Braintree assailants, 300; Vanzetti trial (Plymouth), 82

Quintiliano, Luigi (Louis), 25, 152–53, 296

Ranney, Dudley, 158, 214, 216, 220–21, 235, 365n114
Rantoul, Lois, 235
Ravarini, Eugenio, 117
Reading, Arthur, 94, 256, 274
Red Sox, 3, 55
Reed, Austin, 139–40
Rehnquist, William, 107
Remi, John, 48–49
Reynolds, James, 4
Ricci, Angelo, 138
Ricci, Dominick, 141–42
Richal, Harry, 363n38
Richardson, James, 208, 234–35
Ripley, Walter, 173–74, 200, 243
Roberts, Kenneth, 15–16
Robinson, Marshall, 362n30
Rockefeller, John D., 103, 110
Rockefeller, John D., Jr., 308
Rolland, Hugo, 363n38
Roosevelt, Theodore, 70
Rosen, Joseph, 143, 164
Rosenberg, Ethel, 282–83
Rosenberg, Julius, 282–83
Ross, Edward Alsworth, 16
Ross, Joseph (Joe Rossi), 94, 160
runners (lawyers' agents), 61–62, 94
Russell, Francis, 282, 304, 308, 363n38

Ruth, Babe, 3, 55
Ruzzamenti, John, 179–80

Sacco, Alba, 55
Sacco, Angelina, 12, 27
Sacco, Dante: birth, 53; father and, 56, 191, 257; Italy trip preparations, 27, 141; Jack family and, 190, 219; later life, 275, 281–82; Sacco-Vanzetti case, 125, 282; in Stoughton, 56; Vanzetti and, 260, 297
Sacco, Ines, 92, 125, 179, 191, 219, 239, 281
Sacco, Michele, 12–13, 101, 249–50
Sacco, Nicola, 226; Advisory Committee interviews, 237–38; alibi, 62, 140–42, 237, 289; anarchism, 51, 100–102; anarchist literature, 26–27, 30, 156, 158, 168–69; appearance, 31–32, 34–35, 35, 127; arrests, 28, 55; atheism, 100–101; Berardelli and, 33; Brandeis and, 223; Buda's car, 153; charges against, 29; childhood, 12–13, 101, 183, 220; citizenship, 327n20; class consciousness, 157–58, 227; consciousness of guilt, 155–60, 289–91; courtship and marriage, 46, 48, 324n70; Cronaca sovversiva subscription, 51, 66–67, 119; daughter Alba and, 55; daughter Ines and, 125, 191, 239; declarations of innocence, 227, 296–97; Dedham Jail incarceration, 91, 92, 177–81, 183–85, 188–89, 191, 229–30; denial of clemency for, 242; denial of motion for new trial, 219, 224–26; Donovan and, 229; draft evasion, 60, 66–68, 74, 157; English-language tutor, 188, 192; Evans and, 183, 186–87, 191–92, 223, 230, 238; execution, 234, 251, 253, 266–67, 269–70; on expropriation, 225, 298; eyewitness identification of, 59–60, 289; eyewitness misidentification of, 213–14, 348n67; family, 12, 92, 125, 141, 179, 224; Felicani and, 61, 203; funeral, 272, 273; gardening, 56–57, 299; gun and ammunition, 28, 56, 132, 146–48, 201, 207, 292–94, 299–300; hand size, 136, 214; hunger strikes, 183–85, 238, 251, 256–57; idealism, 52; immigration, 13, 34; immortalized, 209, 308–9; interrogation of, 29, 32–33; Italy trip preparations, 27, 33, 140–42, 141, 290, 327n20; jail visitors, 30–31, 83, 101, 182, 188–89, 191–92, 256–57, 260; labor activism, 46–47, 50–52, 54–55, 60; love of country, 157–58; lying to investigators, 29, 33, 146, 159, 163, 168–69; Madeiros's confession, 209; mental state, 179–80, 183–88, 191–92, 229–30; Moore and, 92, 108, 183, 205; mug shots, 30, 32; as

night watchman, 56; petition to governor, 230–31; posthumous pardon legislation, 288; radicalization of, 44, 51, 100–101; religion, 100–101, 178, 267–68; request for attorney during interrogation, 32; resemblance to Joe Morelli, 213, 348n67; Sacco-Vanzetti New Trial League and, 205; sanity hearing, 184–85; sentencing, 226–28; severance motions, 160; shoe industry work, 35–36, 46, 143; son Dante and, 53, 56, 191, 257; South Braintree bandit identification, 203; South Braintree involvement, hearsay, 294–97, 304, 363n38; as South Braintree suspect, 29, 62; in Stoughton, 56–57; Thompson and, 204, 266; trial verdict, 174; urging public demonstration, 245–46; Vanzetti and, 67, 229–30, 296–97; on violence, 107–9; work history, 34, 36, 56, 68; World War I employment, 68, 74, 328n58; in Youngstown, Ohio, 109. *See also* Sacco-Vanzetti case (pre-trial); Sacco-Vanzetti case (trial aftermath); Sacco-Vanzetti trial (Dedham)

Sacco, Rosina (Zambelli): burning of radical literature, 60, 163; children, 52–53, 55, 92; courtship and marriage, 46, 48, 324n70; Felicani and, 203; health, 219, 223–24, 230; Italy trip preparations, 27, 141; C. Jack and, 190–91, 279; later life, 280–81; Moore and, 92, 130; remarriage, 280–81; Sacco's appeals for new trial, 212, 241, 242; Sacco's arrest, 30; Sacco's execution and, 252–53, 260, 262–65, 267, 271; Sacco's mental state, 185; Sacco-Vanzetti trial (Dedham), 125, 138, 141, 145–46, 174, 282; in Stoughton, 56; support for, 190–91; L. Vanzetti and, 258; visiting Sacco, 182, 186, 191, 256, 260, 264–65, 267

Sacco, Sabino, 13, 34, 35, 52, 101

Sacco-Vanzetti case (pre-trial): alibis, 62; arrests, 27–28; Braintree shootings, 29; courthouse corruption, 92–95; eyewitnesses at police station, 59–60; fingerprint evidence, 58–59; informers, 179–80; initial charges, 29, 58; interrogations, 28–29, 32–33; jail visitors, 30–31; legal defense fund, 60–61; lineups, 59; lying to investigators, 28, 29; politicization of, 91

Sacco-Vanzetti case (trial aftermath): Advisory Committee and, 233–38; bills of exceptions, 256–57; new eyewitnesses, 289; public support, 218–19, 221, 229, 245, 247; Vanzetti's advice to Moore, 192. *See also* motions for new trial

Sacco-Vanzetti Defense Committee: Communists and, 248–49; execution day protests, 254; finances, 202–5, 208, 217; formation, 60–61; friction with Moore, 202–5; headquarters, 252; internal discord, 205; legal counsel, 208–9; public opinion campaign, 221, 245, 247; Sacco's sanity hearing, 184–85; Sacco-Vanzetti New Trial League and, 205

Sacco-Vanzetti New Trial League, 205

Sacco-Vanzetti trial (Dedham): accusations against Sacco, 132; accusations against Vanzetti, 132; alibi of Sacco, 140–42, 237, 289; alibi of Vanzetti, 142–43, 167–68, 289; anarchism in, 119, 214–15; audience, 125–26, 154, 162; ballistics evidence against Sacco, 146–48, 165, 168, 202, 207–8, 292–94; ballistics evidence against Vanzetti, 148–51, 164–65, 168, 200, 235–36, 291–92; ballistics evidence chain of custody, 82, 145–46, 163; caged defendants, 127, 138; character witnesses, 143–44; closing arguments, 162–69, 309; consciousness of guilt, 165, 172, 174, 206, 289–91; consciousness of guilt evidence against Sacco, 155–60, 289–91; consciousness of guilt evidence against Vanzetti, 152–55, 289–91; defense attorneys, 125, 129–30; defense errors, 165, 201–2; draft evasion in, 74, 119, 154, 157, 171; duration, 132; evidence, amount of, 173; eyewitnesses identifying Sacco, 133–38, 200–201, 289; eyewitnesses identifying Vanzetti, 139–40, 289; getaway car testimony, 134, 136–40, 166; judicial prejudice, 95, 169–70, 174, 234–35, 246; jury, 126, 127–29, 152, 169, 172, 172–74, 200, 206, 342n55; jury instructions, 135, 168, 170–72, 206, 309; lasting impact, 288; location, 125; opening arguments, 132; patriotism in, 128, 171; physical evidence against Sacco, 132, 144–48, 160, 236, 243, 291; physical evidence against Vanzetti, 148–51; politicization, 151–52; prosecution team, 125; security, 126; severance motions, 160–61; testimony by Sacco, 145, 155–60; testimony by Vanzetti, 151, 152–55; Vanzetti trial (Plymouth) influence on, 85; verdict, 173–74; witnesses, number of, 132, 173, 337n3

Salsedo, Andrea, 25–26, 118–20, 152–53

Salute è in voi, La (*Health is within you*), 102–3

Sartorio, Enrico, 16

Sassi, Matthew, 83

Sawyer, Roland, 51

Schilling, Joseph, 144

trial attorney, 129–30, 242, 248, 250; on
Thayer, 274, 337n29; Vanzetti and, 270, 297;
Vanzetti trial (Plymouth), 265–66
Three K (company), 56
Tobia, Galileo, 363n38
Tosiello, Rosario Joseph, 253, 254
Townsend, John Clendenin, 43
Tracy, Tom, 88
Tracy, William, 3, 133–34
Trading with the Enemy Act (1917), 106
Treacy, Thomas, 316n26 (chap. 1)
Tresca, Beatrice, 295
Tresca, Carlo: background, 49; bank accounts,
59; V. Brini and, 101; Elia-Salsedo situation,
25, 153; feuds with anarchists, 86, 278, 295–96;
E. Flynn and, 50, 278; Haywood and, 55;
IWW and, 55; labor activism, 49–50, 54–55;
later life, 278, 295–96; Moore and, 50, 203–4;
Sacco-Vanzetti case, 86, 90–91, 294–95;
suspicions about Ravarini, 117; Wall Street
bombing and, 120
Tufts, Nathan, 94
Tulsa, OK: IWW trial, 89–90

Umberto I, King (Italy), 99–100, 102
Union of Russian Workers, 114
U.S. Immigration Commission, 17, 19

Vahey, James, 61
Vahey, John, 61–62, 75, 82–83, 85–86, 275
Valdinoci, Carlo, 104–5, 117
Valentino, Rudolph, 17
Van Amburgh, Charles, 148, 165, 168
Vanderveer, George, 88–89, 275
Vanzetti, Bartolomeo, 226; admiration for Debs,
193; adolescence, 10–11; Advisory Committee
interviews, 237–38; alibi, 62, 142–43, 237,
289; anarchism, 100–102; anarchist literature
disposal, 26–27, 153–54, 156, 168–69; appearance, 31–32, 39, 77–78, 127, 181; arrest, 28;
atheism, 100–101; autobiography, 74, 192,
205; Brandeis and, 223; as Bridgewater case
defendant (See Vanzetti trial [Plymouth]);
as Bridgewater case suspect, 62; Brini
family and, 40–41, 192; Buda's car, 153;
charges against, 29; Charlestown State
Prison incarceration, 85, 91, 177, 181–82, 192,
196–97; childhood, 9; citizenship, 327n19;
class-consciousness, 38, 40; consciousness
of guilt, 152–55, 289–91; Cronaca sovversiva
subscription, 51, 66, 100, 119; declarations of

innocence, 227, 296, 297; denial of clemency
for, 242; denial of new trial motions, 217,
219, 224–26, 350n29; Donovan and, 206,
229, 251–52; draft evasion, 60, 66–68, 74,
154; Elia-Salsedo situation, 25, 152–53;
English-language tutor, 190, 195; execution,
234, 251–53, 265–67, 270; on expropriation,
298; eyewitness identification of, 60, 289;
family, 9, 10, 40, 239, 252; father and, 10–12,
40, 91–92, 151, 193; Felicani and, 60–61, 203; as
fish peddler, 57, 78–80, 142–43; funeral, 272,
273; gun and ammunition, 28, 82–85, 148–49,
153–54, 164–65, 168, 201, 235–36, 291; hunger
strike, 238; illness during Sacco-Vanzetti
trial, 161; immigration, 12, 37; immortalized,
308–9; interrogation of, 28–29, 32–33, 153–54;
invisible ink, 346n92; on Italian immigrants,
16–17; Cerise Jack and, 224–25; jailhouse
work, 181, 192; jail visitors, 30–31, 101, 258,
260; labor activism, 50–51, 53–54, 60; lying to
investigators, 28, 33, 81, 152, 154–55, 168–69;
MacMechan and, 195–96, 224–25, 230; on
Malatesta, 99; Massachusetts Supreme
Court appeal, 212; on May Day raids, 25–26;
mental state, 196–99, 257; Moore and, 192;
mother and, 11–12, 40, 193–94; mug shots, 30,
32; mustache, 39, 77–78; optimism, 37, 208;
pessimism, 209, 219–20; petition to governor,
108, 230–33; in Plymouth, 38, 40–41, 57; on
Plymouth trial, 80, 82–83, 85–86; political
beliefs, 82–83, 227–28, 231; posthumous
pardon legislation, 288; radicalization
of, 44, 51; reading habits, 30, 40, 100, 182;
religion, 12, 100–101, 267–68; romantic life,
194–96, 224–25; Sacco and, 67, 160, 184,
187, 228–30, 256, 297; R. Sacco and, 224; on
Sacco-Vanzetti Defense Committee donations, 202; sentencing, 226–28; severance
motions, 160–61, 184; singing voice, 75, 230;
sister Luigia and, 12, 40, 239, 257–58; South
Braintree bandit identification, 203; South
Braintree involvement, hearsay, 294–95, 304;
as South Braintree suspect, 62; supporters,
50, 247; Thompson and, 204, 265–66, 270;
trial testimony, 151, 152–54; trial verdict, 174;
urging public demonstration, 245–46; on
violence, 107–9; work history, 10, 37–38, 40,
57, 69; World War I, 68–69; writings of, 74,
192, 195; in Youngstown, Ohio, 109. See also
Sacco-Vanzetti case; Sacco-Vanzetti trial
(Dedham); Vanzetti trial (Plymouth)

PERMISSIONS ACKNOWLEDGMENTS

Excerpts from the papers of Mary Donovan Hapgood and of Powers
Hapgood are used with the permission of Liza Newman and of Lilly
Library, Indiana University, Bloomington, Indiana.

Excerpts from the oral histories of Aldino Felicani (1954) and
Gardner Jackson (1955), in the Columbia University Oral History
Research Office Collection, are used with the permission of the
Columbia University Oral History Research Office.

Excerpts from the Herbert Ehrmann Papers and from the Small
Manuscript Collection, Historical & Special Collections are used
with the permission of the Harvard Law School Library.

Excerpts from the Elizabeth Glendower Evans Papers are used
with the permission of Schlesinger Library, Radcliffe Institute for
Advanced Study, Harvard University.

Excerpts from the Aldino Felicani Collection are used with the
permission of the Boston Public Library.

The following materials are used with the permission of the
Massachusetts Archives: Massachusetts Archives, AG1/Series 2062X
Attorney General's Office, Sacco and Vanzetti Case File, 1919–1976;
Massachusetts Archives, HS9.01/Series 305 Mass. State prison,
Inmate case files, 1910–1941; and Massachusetts Archives, PS11/
Series 2084X, State Police, Sacco and Vanzetti Case File, 1920–1977.